Open Source Innovation –
The Phenomenon, Participant's
Behavior, Business Implications

T0291384

Open Source Innovation (OSI) has gained consid[...] last years. Academic and management practice i[...] grows as more and more end-users consider and even participate in Open Source product development like Linux, Android, or Wikipedia.

Open Source Innovation: Phenomenon, Participant Business Implications Behavior, brings together rigorous academic research and business importance in scrutinizing OCI from three perspectives: the Phenomenon, Participant's Behavior, Business Implications. The first section introduces OCI artifacts, including who is participating and why, and provides a systematic overview of the literature. The second section stresses the behavior of participants, highlighting participation progression, community selection, user entrepreneurship and fair behavior, and answering key questions like how to manage governance rules, openness and community design aspects. The third section explores the impact and implications of OSI for firms and economies by evaluating business models, uncovering opportunities for firms to interact with communities, and presenting value capture mechanisms.

Open Source Innovation provides a full picture of the movement to help readers understand and engage with OSI from the micro perspective of individuals, to the community, to the macro perspective of firms and economies.

Cornelius Herstatt is full professor and director of the Institute of Technology and Innovation Management. His research focuses on lead user and open innovation in global contexts. His recent work involves combining elements of this research with the investigation of community driven innovation projects. He holds a guest professorship with Tohoku-University in Sendai and is co-founder of the European Institute for Technology and Innovation Management (EITIM). Professor Herstatt is a research alumni/fellow of the East-West Centre (Honolulu), JSPS (Japanese Society for promoting Science) and Templeton College in Oxford (UK).

Daniel Ehls is Senior Research Fellow and lecturer at the Institute of Technology and Innovation Management (TIM) at Hamburg University of Technology (TUHH). His research concentrates on Open and User Innovation and in particular on user behavior and collaborating with distributed volunteers. He studied Technology Management and worked as a management consultant. After gaining his PhD he was invited scholar at Tokyo Tech University (Japan) and now leads the research unit 'Open Foresight' at the TIM institute of Professor Herstatt.

Routledge Studies in Innovation, Organization and Technology

For a full list of titles in this series, please visit www.routledge.com

Open Source Innovation – The Phenomenon, Participant's Behavior, Business Implications

Edited by Cornelius Herstatt and Daniel Ehls

LONDON AND NEW YORK

First published 2015 by Routledge

2 Park Square, Milton Park, Abingdon, Oxfordshire OX14 4RN
52 Vanderbilt Avenue, New York, NY 10017

Routledge is an imprint of the Taylor & Francis Group, an informa business

First issued in paperback 2018

Copyright © 2015 Taylor & Francis

The right of the editor to be identified as the author of the editorial material, and
of the authors for their individual chapters, has been asserted in accordance with
sections 77 and 78 of the Copyright, Designs and Patents Act 1988.

All rights reserved. No part of this book may be reprinted or reproduced or
utilised in any form or by any electronic, mechanical, or other means, now
known or hereafter invented, including photocopying and recording, or in any
information storage or retrieval system, without permission in writing from
the publishers.

Notice:
Product or corporate names may be trademarks or registered trademarks, and
are used only for identification and explanation without intent to infringe.

Library of Congress Cataloging-in-Publication Data
Herstatt, Cornelius.
   Open source innovation : phenomenon, participant behaviour, impact /
by Cornelius Herstatt, Daniel Ehls. — 1st Edition.
      pages cm. — (Routledge studies in innovation, organization and technology ; 37)
   Includes bibliographical references and index.
 1. Open source software.   2. Technological innovations.   3. New products.
I. Ehls, Daniel.   II. Title.
   QA76.76.S46H47   2015
   005.3—dc23
   2014040611

ISBN: 978-1-138-80202-5 (hbk)
ISBN: 978-1-138-62404-7 (pbk)

Typeset in Sabon
by Apex CoVantage, LLC

Contents

SECTION 2
Participant's Behavior

SECTION 3
Business Implications

Figures and Tables

FIGURES

TABLES

Acknowledgements

This collection was made possible only by many helping hands we would like to remember.

First of all, we would like to give a big thank to Prof. Dr. Christina Raasch for her excellent research guidance and wonderful work during her time as the head of the Open Source Innovation research unit at our institute. Without her effort, much of the research presented in this book would not have become reality. Thank you, Christina!

We would also like to thank Prof. Eric von Hippel for his inspiring work and guidance he gave to all of us. You are truly the "father" of the OUI-Community, Eric! We look forward to more collaborative work to come.

In preparing this collection many invisible hands supported our efforts, particularly Christina Pieper and Sara Bermudez Tamayo for supporting our manuscript preparation. Our thanks also go to you both.

This research was also made possible by two grants. The DFG (German Research Foundation) and BMBF (Federal Ministry of Education and Research) funded research with the grants "Reziprozität und Value Capture in Open Source Innovation" respective "Open Source Innovation" (Identification Nr. 16I1573). We also owe tribute to the journals 'Research Policy' and 'Creativity and Innovation Management' for their friendly and uncomplicated permission for reusing two articles. We also thank Routledge for their fruitful collaboration and publishing this book, including three anonymously reviewers putting huge confidence in us.

Finally, the biggest thank you belongs to the many authors who contributed to this collection with their brilliant chapters. For us, this book is not only an inspiring collection of papers, but also a token of collaboration, friendship and research with you and we owe a big thank you.

Foreword

Beginning from the time that I was a 12-year-old boy, I was allowed to wander around MIT hallways (my father was a MIT professor, and would take me to the campus from time to time), politely peeking into laboratory doors. If lucky enough to be invited in, I would watch what the scientists and students were doing, and ask questions. During these visits, I noticed that, often, the scientists and students were developing new scientific instruments, or modifying commercial ones, to better serve their own research needs.

Years later when studying economics and innovation at university, I was confronted with the conventional Schumpetarian wisdom that product innovations are developed by firms and not by users—the individuals or firms who will use them. I remembered what I had observed in my younger days, and doubted the universal truth of that theory. I therefore was motivated to investigate the phenomenon of innovation by users. In the specific case of scientific instruments, it turned out that users, not producers, were the actual developers of about 80% of the most important innovations later commercialized by scientific instrument producers. Theoretical and empirical research by many has since clarified the importance of innovation by users.

From that early experience, I grew to deeply appreciate the importance of careful empirical investigations to research progress in the field of innovation. Innovation theory is still in a pre-paradigmatic state, and deep understanding of how the world works is still required for productive theorizing. I am happy to say that the senior editor of this book, Professor Dr. Cornelius Herstatt, is very much of the same opinion, and that he runs his Institute of Technology and Innovation Management at Hamburg University of Technology with that research strategy in mind.

In this book, Professor Herstatt and his graduate students report upon many studies they have made into what they term Open Source Innovation. All of these studies include thoughtful empirical work. Their book is very timely because, today, open and user innovation is no longer considered an anomaly, but is an accepted, impactful phenomenon of great interest to many.

The book is divided into three sections, each with four independent chapters to guide the reader into the Open Source Innovation phenomenon step-by-step. For those with a managerial interest in the innovation process, an entire section is dedicated to describing business implications. In effect, the book extends from the micro-perspective of individuals on Open Source Innovation, to the community perspective, and then up to the perspective of firms and the larger economy. I expect it will be a very interesting and useful collection of work and findings for both researchers and practitioners, and congratulate my colleagues on what I know has been a great creative effort.

Eric von Hippel
MIT-Sloan School of Management

Preface

Open Source Innovation (OSI) has gained considerable momentum within the last years. Academic and management practice interest grows as well as more and more end-users consider and even participate in Open Source product development. Iconic examples include Linux operating system, Mozilla Firefox browser, or Wikipedia encyclopedia, and further cases are regarded as globally leading projects like OpenOffice, the strongest rival to Microsoft for office suites; WordPress, one of the world's most popular blogging platforms; VLC, one of the most downloaded media players; Apache, the most widely installed web server platform; or Android, which powers millions of smartphones. Open Source Innovation (OSI) is no longer a niche phenomenon, but a serious business.

OBJECTIVE AND SCOPE OF THIS COLLECTION

In this collection at hand we have collected inspiring key facets of Open Source Innovation and connect the reader to ongoing discussions and latest research. Thereby, the scope of this book is Business Management with its sub-streams Open and User Innovation, Distributed or Collaborative Innovation, and Open Source. We do not try to promote coding skills or hacking practices, but analyze OSI from a product development and innovation management perspective. This book is not a step-by-step guide but a collection of exceptional insights into the phenomenon. It is meant to provide food for thought enabling the reader to tap into unknown areas on their own and equip them for future developments. We have prepared the book in order that no specific prior knowledge is necessary and the book is understandable with basic management knowledge and curiosity. It offers multiple insights and unites academic research with managerial hot topics for postgraduate researchers, cutting-edge consultants, community entrepreneurs, and business decision makers.

CONTENTS AND STRUCTURE OF THIS COLLECTION

This book comprises of 12 insightful chapters based on several years of research at the Institute of Technology and Innovation Management at Hamburg University of Technology. The starting point to this was our research on Open Source Innovation, which started in 2007 supported by both, the Ministry for Education and Research (BMBF) and the German Research Foundation (DFG). The chapters cover the spectrum from the base of OSI research to latest findings and patterns of the main subjects and ends with valuable business implications. The independent chapters concentrating on specific aspects enable the reader to focus on particular points of interest, but also to tap into upcoming new challenges, we might be not even aware of today. A particular focus of this collection are the individuals ("distributed volunteers"), because without these participants OSI collapses. We therefore highlight their 'user behavior' as we believe understanding member actions represents a key for collaborating with participants and stimulate further innovation. Thereby we combine the individual, the community, and firm level perspective, highlighting the bigger picture about user behavior, community spirit, and firm value capture mechanisms. We present mechanisms stimulating OSI and latest insights how innovation influences companies strategy and economic development. Thus we shed light on the underpinning innovation management aspects from three perspectives: the Phenomenon, Participants' Behavior, and Business Implications.

The first section, called "The Phenomenon", sheds light on the phenomenon and answers the basic questions: What is open source innovation? And why do volunteers contribute and freely reveal their knowledge? Moreover OSI types are presented (software, content, hardware), differences highlighted, openness scrutinized, and a systematic academic literature analyzes provided. Thus, this section clarifies the phenomenon in terms of understanding and artifacts, and lays the framework for further chapters.

The second section, "Participant's Behavior", concentrates on individual behavior. The first chapter of the section introduces a participation lifecycle framework that shows user progression steps into, and social interaction within a community. The next chapter aims to analyze participation trade-off decisions, analyze why users choose one community over another and provide a contingency model of individual user traits to joining preferences. The next chapter covers governance rules and delivers recommendations how to avoid conflict, stimulate individual contributions and stresses the fair behavior of participants. The final chapter in this section highlights user entrepreneurship and shows how entire firms are run open source and which roles are essential.

The third section, "Business Implications", discusses opportunities for firms to benefit from open source up to the impact for entire economies.

The first chapter in this section dives into physical open source products and shows that open design companies can successfully implement strategies of partial openness to safeguard value capture without alienating their developer community. The next chapter explores a dedicated option for community interaction: firm employees working within the community, or so-called Men on the Inside. The third chapter in this section shows via a formal model that purposeful and skilled harnessing of participation motives can greatly amplify the total amount of paid and unpaid R&D and innovation carried out. The final chapter in this section discusses major challenges with this new innovation approach, but also offers a solution, namely a dual innovation logic for the transformation towards a truly integrated new innovation paradigm.

This collection enables new as well as "OSI-experienced" readers to follow latest discussions from a managerial sciences perspective. Of particularly importance in each section are the managerial implications. We deliver recommendations and link insights to business practices to go beyond academic analysis. Moreover, this book opens avenues for interacting with OSI and fostering innovations—a key topic within theory and praxis for nurturing welfare.

Cornelius Herstatt and Daniel Ehls
Hamburg, December 2014

Section 1
The Phenomenon

1 What Is Open Source Innovation?

An Economic, Social, Artifact, and Innovation-Incentive Perspective with Implications for Firms

Daniel Ehls and Cornelius Herstatt

The open source phenomenon has gained tremendous traction within praxis and theory. Thereby various concept now dilute the phenomenon and mix different perspectives. This contribution aims to provide an introduction and overview to the concept open source innovation. An open source taxonomy is offered viewing the phenomenon from an economic perspective, concentrating on openness and free revealing, a social perspective, highlighting collaboration and movements, artifacts, differentiating terminology and classifications, and finally a theoretical view delivering an innovation-incentive perspective. Based on this understanding, participation drawbacks and benefits for firms and individual contributors are shown and strategies for managing open source innovation provided.

Keywords: open source, review, taxonomy

1 WHAT IS OPEN SOURCE INNOVATION?

1.1 Introduction: The Momentum of Open Source Innovation

Recent examples of collaborative product creation have evidenced a new phenomenon: open source innovation. Innovative goods are produced by volunteers, who "program to solve their own as well as shared technical problems, and freely reveal their innovations without appropriating private returns from selling the software" (Hippel and Krogh 2003, p. 209). Open Source is a product which allows the developers to access all information to create, modify and distribute it under the same license as the original product (Open Source Initiative). Examples of this phenomenon include software development (e.g. Linux, Apache, Debian or Mozilla) and content creation projects (e.g. Wikipedia, LibriVox, Open Directory Project or Open Street Map) that involve numerous people, question the boundaries of the firm, and impact market share.

The large number of open source projects and people involved is illustrated by the open source directory SourceForge. SourceForge lists more than 324,000 projects with a total of over 3.4 million developers on the supply side, and on the demand side more than 4 million downloads a day connecting 46 million consumers as of September 2013.[1] Further projects not listed on SourceForge like the Open Directory Project or Wikipedia consist of more than 10,000 contributors (Cedergren 2003; Glott et al. 2010). The Linux Kernel project and Debian have more than 1,000 contributors each.

Regarding the locus of innovation, distributed volunteers work together in self-governing communities rather than under contract for firms. The locus of knowledge creation shifts outside the boundaries of the firm and there is no contractual member commitment.

Additionally, market analysis provides astonishing figures for openly developed products. As of August 2013, Apache has a market share for web server software of 52.19%, followed by Microsoft with 19.65%.[2] Microsoft Internet Explorer (proprietary but available for free), Google Chrome (based mainly on open source project Chromium, but proprietary and for free), and the open source browser Firefox represent the top three browsers worldwide with market shares of 22.35%, 37.54%, and 18.66% respectively as of June 2013.[3] Total factory revenues in the worldwide server market of $11.9 billion breaks down to 16.9% for Linux, 21.8% for Unix, and 48.5% for Windows in the first quarter of 2011.[4] However, initial software deployment on sold servers does not represent actual market share, but the high share of open source products in commercial distribution. An actual market share is obtained by measuring internet traffic. These analyses reveal a market share of 32.6% for Linux (special Unix distribution), 31.2% for other Unix distributions, and 36.1% for Windows.[5]

Following this discussion, open collaboratively developed products are accepted in the market. They have even driven incumbent firms out of the market, or at least significantly reduced their market share. To develop the products, a large number of volunteers provide their input outside the boundaries of the firm. It is for these reasons that the open source phenomenon attracts the interests of scholars, governments and businesses, and substantiates the relevance for management and science.

However, with the raise of open source innovation, the application of the term increased and was transferred to further areas, thereby sometimes misleading or vaguely applied. We pursue to address this inconsistency and elucidate open source innovation. We describe open source innovation in more detail and provide an overview of current understanding from different points of views. We do not aim to provide a comprehensive literature review about the open source innovation, research directions or present key findings,[6] but to take stock of the understanding of the phenomenon. In order to focus our understanding and create coherence we provide a multi-perspective view of open source taxonomy and highlight key characteristics of open source innovation.

1.2 Open Source Taxonomy

The term 'open source' describes a phenomenon where volunteers[7] create a product, make it publicly available and relinquish most of their intellectual property rights (IPR), but do not receive a direct compensation (Hars and Ou 2002). Open source implies that the instructions for creating the product are human readable and fully and freely revealed to the public. Central to both aspects is the understanding of openness. However, openness and the phenomenon of open source are "spectacularly stratified" (Healy and Schussman 2003) and attract attention from (social) science academics and practitioners. In order to reflect the highly stratified nature, we introduce four perspectives: economic, social, artifact and innovation-incentive. The economic perspective concentrates on free revealing and openness in terms of the boundaries of the firm and the product. The social perspective includes open source communal aspects, stresses the debate about the meaning of open and free as well as the collaborative mode of working. The artifact perspective provides definitions and classifies open source projects. Finally, the innovation incentive view provides a theoretical modeling explaining why people innovate and freely reveal their contributions.

1.2.1 An Economic Perspective: Openness and Free Revealing

The classic approach to product development represents a 'producer' model, where "most important designs for innovations would originate from producers and be supplied to consumers via goods and services that were for sale" (Baldwin and Hippel 2011, p. 1). The open source phenomenon challenges this model. Many open source users are at the same time consumers using the product as well as producers creating the product (Baldwin and Hippel 2011; Roberts et al. 2006). These users conduct tasks ranging from producing core elements and suggesting new features (Lakhani and Wolf 2005; Hertel et al. 2003; Jeppesen and Frederiksen 2006), to testing and giving feedback (Hars and Ou 2002; Bagozzi and Dholakia 2006) and to providing user assistance and mundane tasks (Lakhani and Wolf 2005). In contrast to the classic approach, the development process is changed both at the supply side, because users represent additional sources of innovation, and at the demand side, because users are enabled to integrate their requirements directly into the product, thus extending the traditional choice of building or buying (Fitzgerald 2006). Essential within the integration in the open development process are access to information and the use of IPR. The creator grants "access to his proprietary information to all interested agents without imposition of any direct payment", defined as 'free revealing' (Harhoff et al. 2003, p. 1754). The product is considered open "when all information related to the innovation is a public good—non-rivalrous and non-excludable" (Baldwin and Hippel 2011, p. 1401). However, this does not mean that the full product needs to be open, but maybe only certain product modules. Besides, openness is described more specifically. Openness is broken down into the two factors 'access control' and 'usage regulations'. This subdivided concept of openness repudiates the one-dimensional view of revealing 'all' or no proprietary information (Harhoff et al. 2003, p. 1753). The dichotomy of being fully open or fully closed is overcome. Openness is described more specifically and the dichotomous concept is transferred into a multidimensional concept[8] (Henkel 2006; West and O'Mahony 2008; Balka et al. 2009; Dahlander and Gann 2010).

Viewed from a strict economic-legal perspective, the term 'open source' is defined by the type of license applied to the product (Hippel and Krogh 2003; Krogh et al. 2012). The license waives the principal rights assigned to the product creator by copyright law and grants users the right to access, modify and redistribute the creation instructions (Fosfuri et al. 2008). In this creator- or product-centered concept, open source products are a public good, created by private investments (Crowston et al. 2012; O'Mahony 2003).

Open source is furthermore discussed from an organizational studies description related to 'Open Innovation'[9] while concentrating on the revenue generating practices of firms (Vanhaverbeke et al. 2008). Open source represents an external source of innovation and opportunity for commercialization (Bogers and West 2012). Firms maximize innovation effectiveness by co-operating across firms' boundaries. They source external innovations in order to inbound knowledge or outbound knowledge they cannot utilize. Openness "emphasizes the permeability of firms' boundaries where ideas, resources and individuals flow in and out of organizations" (Dahlander and Gann 2010, p. 699). This organizational or process view differs from the above view concentrating on the creator and product. The organizational-process view focuses on organizational permeability and commercialization supported by IPR, whereas the creator-centered view focuses on the free revealing of information and developing practices (Baldwin and Hippel 2011). In other words, openness within the organizational view refers to openness of the firms' boundaries as well as knowledge inflows and outflows. In contrast, openness in the creator- or product-centered view refers to the openness of the product creation, including the development process. Additionally, organizational utilization of openness and open innovation research is directed (so far) at producer benefits, whereas user innovations focus on the motivations of why users innovate and how they can be supported (Bogers and West 2012).

Nevertheless, open source innovation is able to combine both perspectives (Bogers and West 2012) and stresses the cooperation between different actors to pool product development (West and Gallagher 2006a, 2006b). Furthermore, open source innovation represents an "extreme version of Open Innovation" (Gassmann 2006, p. 227) with low control of the development process (Demil and Lecocq 2006) and resources being made available for others to exploit (Dahlander and Gann 2010), or even fully giving up the exclusive exploitation opportunities (Harhoff et al. 2003). Both perspectives interact with each other—not antagonistically, but represent two sides of the same coin. Moreover, open source may provide a practical answer to the question raised by Hayek of how to use the dispersed knowledge in society. Open source depends on distributed independent "single minds" collaborating for "rapid adaptation" and promptly using knowledge of the "particular circumstances of time and place" (Hayek 1945).

1.2.2 A Social Perspective: Collaboration and Movements

Besides the economic perspective, open source is also described from a social perspective. The social perspective stresses the personal commitment beyond the product or monetary profit. It discusses the communal model of development and points to an open source ideology that is even seen as a social movement.

The ideology of open source dates back to the early times of software development. During the 1960s and earlier, software development was mainly driven by academics, small groups, or employees who complementarily shared code amongst each other for review and recognition according to scientific-like behavior[10] (Bonaccorsi and Rossi 2003; Hertel et al. 2003). As software development evolved and commercial investments grew, complementary software distribution discontinued. Software was no longer available for inspection or modification by others (Hertel et al. 2003). A prominent example is AT&T's decision in 1979 to enforce restrictive Unix licenses. In response to this tendency, in 1983 Richard Stallman started the GNU project to provide a 'free' alternative for proprietary software. In 1983, the GNU project led to the founding of the 'Free Software Foundation' aiming to "promote computer user freedom and to defend the rights of all free software users" (Free Software Foundation, p. 'about'). A product is considered free if it respects four essential freedoms for users: to use, study, change and distribute it (Hippel 2001). Following this definition, a free product not only grants access to its source code or instructions, but also challenges IPR. In 1997, Eric Raymond published the paper 'The Cathedral and the Bazaar' shedding light on the hacker culture and describing their working practices based on the idea of distributed peer review. Following his principle that "given enough eyeballs, all bugs are shallow" (Raymond 1999, p. 32), Netscape asked Raymond to support them in releasing their browser code as free software. However, to break with the "moralizing and confrontational attitude that had been associated with 'free software'" and to focus on the "same pragmatic, business-case grounds that had motivated Netscape",[11] Raymond's team decided to create the label 'open source.' Thereafter and later represented by the 'Open Source Initiative', open source became a product which allows the developers to access the source code and modify and distribute it under the same license as the original product (Lerner and Tirole 2001).[12] Even though the definition is very similar to free, the meaning for open source is intended to focus on the fact that "You can look at the source code", and comprises free and proprietary products (Stallman 2009).

Following these social practices, open source and free software are both described as 'social movements'[13] (Hertel et al. 2003; Hippel and Krogh 2003; Ljungberg 2000; Stallman 2009). Loosely coupled development projects are bound together by strong common values (Ljungberg 2000) and guided by strong ideologies (Stewart and Gosain 2006) to create a public good that shapes society (Krogh and Spaeth 2007). Nonetheless, the free and the open source movement are distinguished:

> The fundamental difference between the two movements is in their values, their ways of looking at the world. For the Open Source movement, the issue of whether software should be open source is a practical question, not an ethical one. As one person put it, "Open source is a development methodology; free software is a social movement". For the Open Source movement, non-free software is a suboptimal solution. For the Free Software movement, non-free software is a social problem and free software is the solution.
>
> (Stallman 2009, p. 31)

In order to avoid discussions about ideologies and social movements, the weakening of terms, and also to focus on the largely similar development processes, further authors (Dalle and David 2003; Ghosh et al. 2002; Crowston et al. 2012) coined a neutral combined term: 'Free/Libre/Open Source Software' (FLOSS). FLOSS describes a product which is distributed via an open license and allows access to its design, including the human readable instructions, in order to inspect, use, modify and redistribute the source principles of the product.[14]

Concerning the social aspect and the communal model of development, the description lacks the explicit mentioning of collaboration. For authors such as Lerner and Tirole (2001), Hippel and Krogh (2003), and Lakhani and Wolf (2005), a major aspect of the open source phenomenon represents the collaborative nature of development. A product is collaboratively created by a large number of distributed volunteers united in a community. Within this community, members support each other and share knowledge openly and freely with each other (Raasch et al. 2008). However, the communal mode is only a potential option in the production process. The mode highlights the broad opportunities that open access provides but they do not necessarily take place. Accessibility determines the degree to which external contributors could influence the production (West and O'Mahony 2008). This aspect is even more important, as most projects only have a single creator and do not evolve into a community (Lakhani and Hippel 2003; Crowston et al. 2012; Colazo and Fang 2009). However, these single-person projects do not differ from communal projects in terms of the key aspects of open source. Following Baldwin and Hippel, many, but not all, open source projects have these collaborative and communal characteristics. In order to highlight the communal model, this specialized form is termed "Open Collaborative Innovation" (Baldwin and Hippel 2011). An open collaborative innovation project involves contributors who share the work of generating a design and reveal the outputs from their individual and collective design efforts openly for anyone to use. Open Collaborative Innovation is hence described according to four key principles: "Participants create goods and services of economic value, they exchange and reuse each other's work, they labor purposefully with just loose coordination, and they permit anyone to contribute and consume" (Levine and Prietula 2014).

1.2.3 An Artifact Perspective: Terminology and Classification

The principles of open source spread well beyond software (Shah 2006) and lead to the not only digital production related expression 'open collaborative innovation' (Baldwin and Hippel 2011, Levine and Prietula 2014). Examples of open source projects include open encyclopedias like Wikipedia, open learning materials like open courseware (MIT), audiobook creation (LibriVox), structured data (freebase), computer motherboards (BeagleBoard), 3D printers (RepRap), or even cars (OScar). Open source represents not only an ideology or innovation model, but also embodies several product types. A first distinction between open source product types is the concreteness of the created product; whether it is of a tangible or intangible nature (Raasch 2011). Tangible objects are objects of a physical nature (e.g. open source hardware) whereas intangible objects represent objects of a digital nature (e.g. open source software, open source content). Other classifications are proposed by Stallman (2009), Cheliotis (2009) and Okoli (2010). Their classifications are more granular and refer to aspects of functionality and aesthetics. Even though developed independently, they overlap in certain categories and sometimes only differ marginally. We briefly introduce Okoli's model, being the latest and finest granulated approach. Okoli distinguishes open source objects according to the two dimensions 'truth' and 'value assessment.' Truth represents how truth is judged, based on the duality of value-laden. Value assessment is value evaluation from the view of an assessor. Both dimensions offer two categories, thus in total presenting a four-field matrix as illustrated in Figure 1.1 by Okoli (2010). Truth perception is divided into universal and relative. Relativism holds that truths are not absolute and depend on individual factors. It is a relativistic assessment of work and how worthy of appreciation it is. Universalism holds that truths are absolute, irrespective of the subject or context. It represents an assessment of how work conforms to some universally held standard. Value assessment can be objective or subjective. Subjectively evaluated works are artistic works which people judge based on their personal preferences, e.g. beautiful or ugly. Objective judgment represents a purposeful evaluation of quantifiable criteria based on a comparison against an outside standard of accuracy—for example, how well a certain aim is achieved.

Dimension	Value Perspective		
	Category	Objective	Subjective
Truth Perspective	Relativist	Utilitarian (e.g. Software, Engineering Designs, Taxonomies)	Aesthetic (e.g. Fine Art, Music, Poetry, Games)
	Universalist	Factual (Textbooks, Dictionaries, Encyclopedias, Maps)	Opinioned (Essays, Editorials, Commentaries, Reviews)

Figure 1.1   Truth and value category assessment for digital open source projects
Source: Okoli (2010).

Okoli's concept benefits from a more differentiated view in contrast to the criterion of the nature of the object. However, the framework concentrates on intangible objects and suffers from a strict application of criteria. As Okoli (2010) notes, the dimensions are not seen as dichotomous but as a spectrum, and the positioning of works may differ according to individual evaluation. As we aim to apply the criteria on a broader base and with a clear differentiation, we propose the criterion of the nature of the object. Open source products are differentiated based on whether they are intangible or tangible.

1.2.3.1   Open Source Tangible Goods

Tangible products, so-called 'open design' (Vallance et al. 2001; Raasch et al. 2009), or 'open hardware,' are touchable physical objects, in contrast to intangible digital products. To be a tangible product, the object needs to be physically created. In order to produce the object, higher production and development costs occur compared to digital projects (Lee and Cole 2003), even if much of the development process can be done digitally. Digital product development includes requirement management, computer aided design (CAD), and test simulations. Nevertheless, the product only exists virtually and not physically. Someone needs to manufacture the product, apply tools, and transport it to the intended location (Hippel and Krogh 2003). In these terms, Demil and Lecoq argue that economies of scale are hard to achieve due to distributed production capacities, but distributed production capacities lie at the heart of open source (Demil and Lecocq 2006). Seen from a financial perspective, some upfront investment is required to buy the physical raw goods and cover the material costs. Hence, providing resources and 'getting hands dirty' with production are two essential aspects that go substantially beyond providing labor resources. A second differentiation beyond physical production is the source code implication. While the source code in digital products is innate, the instructions, specifications and drawings in open design objects are essential to producing the physical object (Smith 2008). Consequently, free revealing of the physical end product and granting access to the tangible information (e.g. size, surface) does not enable the copying of the design and reassembling of the object. Notwithstanding these difficulties, open design "enter[s] the world of atoms" (Balka et al. 2009) with several examples. These examples range from Nokia tablet PC creation (Stuermer et al. 2009) to open source cars (Müller-Seitz and Reger 2010) and even entire open design project catalogues (Raasch et al. 2009). These examples demonstrate the applicability of open source principles in open design projects.

1.2.3.2 Open Source Intangible Goods

Open source commenced in the digital world, more precisely with open source software. Open source software is defined as "software where users can inspect the source code, modify it, and redistribute modified or unmodified versions for others to use" (Krogh et al. 2012). These characteristics—seeing software as digital goods—can and have been applied to further digital products, such as medical textbooks (OpenAnesthesia) or geographical maps (open street maps). The application of open source principles to non-software digital products is termed 'open content' (Pfaffenberger 2001). In fact, David Wiley in 1998 applied a General Public License (GPL) to educational material:

> OpenContent.org is now online. OpenContent is an attempt to take Content where GNU/FSF has taken Software. A preliminary version of the OpenContent Principles/License (OP/L) is available for comment and immediate use. Contributors to the cause include none other than rms and Eric S. Raymond. If Slashdot readers have "educational" content they'd like to make freely available for others to use in its entirety (like HOW-TO docs, etc.) while still maintaining ownership and some assurance of proper recognition, they should check it out.
>
> (Wiley 1998, Slashdot message)

Wiley primarily aimed at applying open source software principles to educational material. However, the license provided does not solely refer to educational material but to content in general. The license is appropriate for further content areas like texts, music, design blueprints, etc. Differentiating intangible open source goods leads to a further classification of the digital product. Digital open source products can be classified according to the type of product into open source software and open source content. The criterion for determining whether it is software or content depends on if the digital open source product is executable, meaning procedural, or not (Raymond

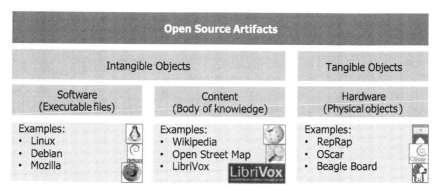

Figure 1.2 Open source software, content, and hardware differentiation

2002; Cedergren 2003; Rosenzweig 2006; Nov and Kuk 2008). An executable program file is understood as software. Content represents anything not executable, including text, image, sound, video, and combinations of them (Clarke 2004, section 'Open Content'). Thus, Oreg and Nov describe this distinction as follows: "Whereas the product in open source software initiatives is software, open source content projects involve the creation of a body of knowledge" (Oreg and Nov 2008, p. 2056). Figure 1.2 shows the open source artifacts in relation to each other.

1.2.4 *An Innovation-Incentive Perspective*

Open source innovation projects have puzzled researchers with their distinctive features of voluntary contribution and free revealing and created a theoretical tension (Krogh and Spaeth 2007). Recalling the private-investment model (Demsetz 1967, Arrow 1962), inventions are stimulated by exclusive rights enabling private rewards. Contributors voluntarily take the risk of investing in innovation but for that they secure exclusive utilization of the knowledge. In contrast, the collective model of innovation (Olson 1965) assumes that innovations are freely released. However, as free riding is possible and private incentives are rare, a subsidy or social rewards are required. Comparing the private model of innovation with the collective model of innovation, it becomes clear that the tension between creating private rewards by exclusive knowledge and a public good by free revealing is at the core of innovation models.

The phenomenon of open source deviates sharply from both concepts (Krogh and Spaeth 2007). Open source projects attract voluntary contributors who freely reveal the innovative outcome for a public good (Hippel and Krogh 2003). In open source projects the innovative outcome is a public good and contributors voluntarily contribute without direct compensation. Contributors solve their own need and community problems without appropriating private returns from selling the software. Hence, open source combines the 'best of both worlds' and leads to a compound model: the 'Private-Collective Model of Innovation' (Hippel and Krogh 2003). The Private-Collective Model of Innovation describes the usage of private investments to create a public good. Contributors gain private returns related to their participation, and the free revealing of proprietary innovations increases private returns even further. Private returns from participation include an increase in one's own knowledge and reputation through learning and community feedback as well as developing a perfectly fitted solution for one's own requirements. Free riders cannot obtain these rewards as returns are directly related to participation in the community and making contributions. The benefits of contributing are stronger than for free riding. Furthermore, free riding is welcome as it increases market share, helps to spread the project importance, and thus further boosts private benefits.

The Private-Collective Model of Innovation deviates in several key aspects from the private model and the collective model. In contrast to the private model, firstly, the typical innovators are users rather than manufacturers. Secondly, the proprietary information is freely revealed with an increased profit for the innovator rather than protected by IPR. In contrast to the collective model, the assumption of equal rewards for contributors and free riders is eliminated, as private rewards for contributors are stronger than those for free riders within the private-collective model. Hippel and Krogh (2006) summarize the key differences, illustrated in Table 1.1.

The Private-Collective Model of Innovation was developed based on observation of open source software projects. However, in applying the model, two distinctive characteristics of the open source world need to be taken into account: product character and market character. Regarding the product character, open source software is a non-rivalrous good, meaning consumption does not reduce the availability of it. In contrast to physical goods, less hardware investment (raw materials, production facilities) is required for production, costs of product revealing are lower due to digital platforms (like SourceForge), and product diffusion (download compared to shipment) is faster. Regarding the market character, the competition and the availability of similar products is low. Taking these observations into account, the opportunity costs of free revealing are low and rivalry minimal. Following this reasoning, Stürmer et al. point out two challenges in applying the model: Firstly, it may be difficult to attract volunteers in areas requiring costly apprenticeships and with prevalent, tacit knowledge. Secondly, private investments may be more attractive in industries of non-virtual goods or where product development constitutes a minor share of the fixed costs of production (Stuermer et al. 2009). Additionally, open collaborative innovation (as well as user innovation) is not viable if the sum of the design and communication costs is too high (Baldwin and Hippel 2011). Following this reasoning, the Private-Collective Model of Innovation occupies the intermediate ground between the private investment model and the collective action model, not replacing but offering a third

Table 1.1 Comparison of models of innovation

Criteria	Private Investment Model	Collective action model	Private-collective Model
Applies to provision of	Private goods	Public goods	Public goods
Key assumptions	Higher benefit for contributors than free riders if innovation is not freely revealed as public good.	Contributors and free riders equally profit from innovation revealed as public good.	Higher benefit for contributors than free riders from public goods due to private benefits from innovation creation.
Impact on social welfare	Monopoly control granted to innovators represents a loss to society relative to free use of all knowledge created.	Free revealing avoids social loss problem, but public subsidy may be required to reward contributors.	'Best of both worlds': Public goods produced at private expense with no public subsidy.
Examples	Patented inventions (medicine)	Public Research (CERN, ITER)	Open Source Products (Linux, Wikipedia)

Source: Hippel and Krogh (2006), extended.

model of innovation (Hippel and Krogh 2006). It offers a combined view of established models and explains participation behavior in innovation actions by way of individual benefits only receivable through individual participation.

1.3 Implications for Firms

1.3.1 *Open Source Innovation—A Major Mind Change*
The participation of firms in open source is based on its strategy to actively drive open innovation and capture value[15] (West and Gallagher 2006b; Garud et al. 2002). Some business models explicitly rely on active community involvement for value capture (Chesbrough and Rosenbloom 2002). However, the nature of open source, targeted at openness and distributed development, contests the traditional mode of organization.

Firms relinquish the exclusive right to commercialize inventions and share the outcome of private investments for free (Harhoff et al. 2003) or even give it up as a public good (Henkel 2006; Hippel and Krogh 2003). Firms "perform a part of their product development open to the public—an unthinkable idea for traditionally minded managers" (Henkel 2006,

p. 953). Open source interactions raise a fundamental tension to manage several trade-offs rooted in openness. On the one hand, there is the paradigm of competitive advantages due to the bundling and protection of valuable resources (Wernerfelt 1984; Penrose 1959) and private rents (Granstrand 1999). Firms do not freely reveal their developments, but also do not benefit from distributed knowledge and volunteer support through open production. On the other hand, the utilization of complementary assets and significant community support represents a benefit (Teece 1986; Dahlander and Wallin 2006). Firms share the good publicly, but at the cost of taking on coordination (transaction) costs and higher risks (Williamson 1973; West and O'Mahony 2008), and relinquishing control and ownership. Participation intentions of firms contradict the participation rationales of communities (Dahlander and Magnusson (2005). The tension is rooted in firms aiming for profits and exploiting products commercially, having workforces with contractual agreements, and usually excluding competitors from utilizing their developments. In contrast, the open source approach aims at publicly available source code supported by independent contributors outside hierarchical control. Firms participating in open source innovation thus need to consider several incentives, drawbacks and threats, also not to scare off contributors.

1.3.2 Benefits, Drawbacks and Threats for Firms and Users in Open Source Innovation

1.3.2.1 Participation Benefits for Firms

Firms already actively participate in open source communities with individual employees (Dahlander and Wallin 2006; Dahlander and Magnusson 2005; Bonaccorsi and Rossi 2003), develop business models around the open source phenomenon (Rolandsson et al. 2011; Bonaccorsi et al. 2006; West and Gallagher 2006b), create open source products (Fosfuri et al. 2008), or even form their own open source communities (Jeppesen and Frederiksen 2006), referred to as a sponsored community (West 2003; Stewart et al. 2006; West and O'Mahony 2005, 2008). Several benefits exist for firms to engage in open source development. These rationales are classified as direct benefits, for example innovative input and suggestions, and indirect benefits such as marketing effects and adoption benefits (West and O'Mahony 2008). Another approach is to look at the structuring of benefits according to the affected domain, that is as, technical, social and economic benefits (Bonaccorsi and Rossi 2003; Dahlander and Magnusson 2005). Technological benefits comprise effects related to support for development, faster development speed, receiving feedback and welcoming lead users, signaling technical excellence, promoting standards, as well as compatibility (West 2003). Social benefits are the sharing of code and greater corporate citizenship by accepting free code. The economic dimension embodies benefits of increased speed of the development process, greater innovative capacity, cost reduction of marketing effects, and the selling of complementary services (Henkel 2006; Bonaccorsi et al. 2006; Dahlander and Magnusson 2005).

1.3.2.2 *Participation Drawbacks for Firms*

Certain downsides exist for commercial actors participating in open source innovation. These drawbacks are relevant for the sponsoring organization and especially for competing organizations also participating in the open project. The participation hurdles for commercial for-profit involvement mainly reside in the economic realm. Due to the nature of openness and free revealing, organizations need to rethink their opportunities for value capture. The potential to sell the 'open' product, which is publicly available for free, is obliterated. Competitive advantages due to superior products are eliminated and new business models required (Henkel 2006; West 2003). Free riding by competitors is possible and represents an obstacle to competitive advantages due to a loss of monopolistic rents. Moreover, a loss of control of the development might affect the organization as the direction of the future product trajectory as well as governing decisions within the community can get out of the organization's control (Henkel 2006; Dahlander and Wallin 2006; Stuermer et al. 2009). Increased transaction costs due to external product development, legal requirements due to license obligations, and the need to integrate the community output into the commercial organization are further drawbacks of open source participation for for-profit organizations (Lakhani and Tushman 2012; Rolandsson et al. 2011).

1.3.2.3 *Participation Benefits for Contributors in Projects with Firm Involvement*

Taking a contributors' view, commercial organizational sponsorship carries benefits for the user. Benefits for the participant exist within social, technical and economic dimensions. Within the technological dimension, development support represents a benefit as commercial institutions frequently contribute code and personal resources to the community (Dahlander and Magnusson 2005; Shah 2006; Henkel 2006; West and O'Mahony 2005). Firms can take over routine tasks, maintain the code base, and, as a consequence, the product quality can be higher. Additionally, users report higher excitement levels and revolutionary approaches in projects controlled by commercial organizations. Within the social dimension, for-profit participation may benefit users in terms of recognition (Jeppesen and Frederiksen 2006). Also feeling proud, signaling skills to the organization and having greater visibility are concrete user benefits (Shah 2006; Roberts et al. 2006). Economic benefits for participants exist in the form of incentives for contribution (Dahlander and Magnusson 2005). Firms can stimulate activity by awarding honors, arranging competitions, or even remunerating participants for contributions. Furthermore, organizations drive development by providing guidance and organization in the form of effective leadership (Garud et al. 2002).

1.3.2.4 Perceived Threats for Contributors in Projects with Firm Involvement

Besides the potential positive influences resulting from commercial institutional involvement in open source communities, the affiliation can also be "controversial and tetchy" (Harhoff and Mayrhofer 2010, p. 142). Some examples are the collapse of a community (Harhoff and Mayrhofer 2010; Dahlander and Magnusson 2005), or the forking of a project due to concerns with the sponsor[16] (Kogut and Metiu 2001). Some rationales for the tension are rooted in the drawbacks frequently associated with firm involvement.

From a community participant's point of view, two dimensions are critical: social and economic influences. Within the social dimension, the fear of disrespecting the community values is vital. Disrespect includes eroding community structures, values, as well as community authorities, crowding-out contributors, and making participants feel constrained or even manipulated (Agerfalk and Fitzgerald 2008; O'Mahony and Ferraro 2007; Dahlander and Magnusson 2005). Within the economic dimension, the primary threat contributors feel is the appropriation of their contributions. This threat directly points to the 'adoption versus appropriation' trade-off within open source; the interest of for-profit organizations to generate returns from their investment versus the interest of communities protecting their intellectual property and 'being hijacked' (Lerner and Tirole 2002; O'Mahony 2003; West and O'Mahony 2008; West 2003). A second threat is the perceived loss of control within the community. Community participants feel the influence of the organization, dominating ways of working, changing rules, or eroding community authority (Agerfalk and Fitzgerald 2008; O'Mahony and Ferraro 2007; Dahlander and Magnusson 2005). This aspect directly nurtures the 'control versus growth' tension in governance structures as well as in production. Even though appropriation and control mechanism may be steered by different means—and are independent from each other and from organizations' involvement—both mechanisms are perceived as closely connected to organizational involvement.

1.3.3 Strategies for Managing Open Source Innovation

To mitigate the tensions rooted in openness, firms can selectively reveal their knowledge (Henkel 2006; Bonaccorsi et al. 2006) and strategically utilize openness (Fosfuri et al. 2008). They should expose their knowledge carefully and decide about their degree of openness. One application of the selective revealing strategy[17] is the disclosure of single (peripheral) modules while keeping further (core) modules closed (Fosfuri et al. 2008; Casadesus-Masanell and Llanes 2011; Henkel 2006). West (2003) describes this approach as "opening parts", revealing (commodity) layers but retaining control of other (distinctive) layers. These distinctive layers provide unique aspects for differentiation while at the same time they enable gaining traction for the entire project. Another strategy is to "partly open" the project: disclosing knowledge differently for different stakeholders (West 2003). This means granting valuable rights for customers while imposing restrictions for competitors to deter utilization. A practice employed for partly open technologies is 'dual licensing.' Dual licensing involves granting different licenses for for-profit and non-profit use (Fitzgerald 2006; West and Gallagher 2006a; Dahlander and Magnusson 2005). The tension between appropriability and adoption is essential in this discussion about 'melding proprietary and open source platform strategies.' There exists a trade-off between appropriating economic benefits from innovation and providing benefits to the project users to get the project adopted (West 2003).

The appropriation versus adoption challenge depends on the ownership and derived usage regulations. The usage regulations can be set out by the intellectual property regime applied to the product, namely its license (West 2003; West and O'Mahony 2008; Dahlander and Magnusson 2005). The license[18] contains information about usage regulations, ownership rights, and restrictions to product application. Thus, the license embodies essential elements of the open source phenomenon as well as regulations for the use, production, modification and distribution of the product. License agreements form the basis for collaboration between firms, communities, individual users, and competitors (Dahlander and Magnusson 2005).

The degree of control of production represents a further basis for collaboration between firms and their stakeholders (West and O'Mahony 2008; Dahlander and Wallin 2006). While usage regulations govern the process of utilizing and owning the product, the degree of control describes the level of the participants' influence on production. West and O'Mahony (2008) discover three types[19] of control mechanisms: proprietary control, transparency and accessibility.

Proprietary control means closed products and production; it limits the control of external contributors as well as their influence on production. Transparency allows internal or external contributors to follow and understand production, grasp why something is happening, and use the product according to the usage regulations. The product is publicly available and discussions occur on open communication platforms. Thus, transparency supports reading of code, but not the writing back to the code repository. Accessibility goes beyond visibility of the production and describes the allowed degree of external impact on production. Specifically, accessibility determines the degree to which participants are able to influence the product directly. Accessibility allows reading, writing and changing the code within the code repository. Therefore, accessibility allows users to meet their specific needs, but requires the community owner, for example, a sponsoring firm, to relinquish control. Thus, the control versus growth tension is fundamental in this discussion (West and O'Mahony 2008). In order to leverage the community in its interest, the community owner needs to control the community and product development. In turn, such behavior scares off contributors and limits the opportunities of communities to grow (West and O'Mahony 2008).

Firms can solve above mentioned tensions with the multidimensional concept of openness. Firms are capable of applying hybrid strategies for melding proprietary and open source platform strategies (West 2003). They can steer and align their strategy according to several dimensions of openness in order to design the community to capture value and attract users. West and O'Mahony refer to this as 'participation architecture,' defined as "the socio-technical framework that extends opportunities to external participants and integrates their contributions" (West and O'Mahony 2008, p. 6). The participation architecture guides interactions between the firm and an online community, encompassing social, legal and technical capabilities. With regard to access control, it guides code development in production. Regarding usage regulations, it governs the allocation of rights to use the community's output. The participation architecture thus impacts participation, free riding, code contribution and joining (Baldwin and Clark 2006). It is dependent on the strategy of the firm and the decision how to capture value with open source innovation.

1.4 Conclusion

Open Source Innovation and its specific communal approach open collaborative innovation have puzzled researchers and practitioners due to their distinguish features. We elucidate the phenomenon from different angles. While free revealing of knowledge is essential for economic understanding, the applied license is central from a legal perspective, and the communal character from a social perspective. The innovation-incentive view even provides a new theoretical model.

From an innovation-incentive point of view, the Private-Collective Model of Innovation solves the contradictions of private innovation and collective innovation in open collaborative innovation. The theory has been developed based on the phenomenon of open source, offers a complementary view on innovation, and aims to explain participation behavior. Participants contribute in open source innovation because contribution provides benefits only obtainable for active engagement, e.g. reputation, learning, or fun aspects. This view enriches innovation management theory and offers a complementary view in addition to the private model and the collective model of innovation.

The social perspective highlights the users' "increasing discomfort about the cost, complexity, and constraints of many commercial products" (Fuggetta 2003, p. 78), which led to the inception of the free [software] foundation. A more practical and business related approach is presented by the open source [software] foundation. In order to avoid the ideology discussion between 'open source' and 'free' a third term is 'Free/Libre/Open Source Software' (FLOSS). A central element within all approaches is collaboration on one common valuable good. However, collaboration is no decisive factor. Instead, it highlights the opportunities that are provided by open source innovation but not necessarily realized. Most open source projects are single user activities that probably could evolve to a flourish community. This specialized communal form of open source innovation is called 'open collaborative innovation.'

The economic perspective discusses the role of participants, the creation of open source products, as well as the meaning of openness in regard to the free revealing of information and to the boundaries of the firm. Openness is described as a multidimensional view broken down in different levels of access control and usage regulation. Open source innovation can be viewed from an open innovation point of view, as well as from an user point of view, representing two sides of the same coin.

Finally, we provide an artifact perspective. While open source is frequently described from a methodological perspective, the term is also applicable as an umbrella term subsuming intangible and tangible products. Open source software and content represent intangible goods, whereby open source hardware shows the existence of physical tangible products.

The resulting implication for firms are multifold. Firms need to rethink their value capture model and how to response to open source innovation. They face new competitors, but also new mechanism for product development. Thereby, firms can play an active role and benefit from open and distributed development. Nevertheless, the interaction with their open product followers becomes crucial. Users and participants feel threatened by firms. However, if firms manage to attract contributors, open source innovation could represent a new paradigm in technology and innovation management.

NOTES

This contribution is based on the dissertation by Daniel Ehls, but further developed and refined.

1. See http://sourceforge.net/about, retrieved 4 September 2013.
2. See http://news.netcraft.com/, retrieved 7 August 2013.
3. Average calculation based on figures from: http://www.getclicky.com/market share/global/web-browsers/; http://stats.wikimedia.org/wikimedia/squids/Squid ReportClients.htm; http://www.w3counter.com/globalstats.php?year=2013& month=6; http://gs.statcounter.com/?PHPSESSID=9m281rk3g8534t8rtvmtq7nkt2, retrieved 4 September 2013.
4. See http://www.idc.com/getdoc.jsp?containerId=prUS22841411, retrieved 30 September 2012.
5. Data sourced from http://w3techs.com/technologies/overview/operating_system/ all; https://secure1.securityspace.com/s_survey/data/200907/index.html; http://www.gartner.com/it/page.jsp?id=1654914, retrieved 30 September 2012.

6. For a more comprehensive review of the emergence of the research field, see for example von Krogh and von Hippel (2006); Okoli (2010); Dahlander and Gann (2010); Raasch et al. 2013; Crowston et al. (2012).
7. Volunteering exhibits "any activity in which time is given freely to benefit another person, group, or organization" (Wilson 2000, p. 215). Volunteers are neither contractually obliged to participate in communities, nor are they directed by formal hierarchical control (Setia et al. 2012); however, volunteers are not precluded from benefiting from their work (Wilson 2000).
8. Instead of referring to openness as a 'gradual concept' on one continuum, we regard openness as a multidimensional construct through the separation of access control and usage regulations with each aspect containing individual degrees of application.
9. "Open Innovation is the use of purposive inflows and outflows of knowledge to accelerate internal innovation, and expand the markets for external use of innovation, respectively. Open Innovation is a paradigm that assumes firms can and should use external ideas as well as internal ideas, and internal and external paths to market, as they look to advance their technology" (Chesbrough et al. 2006, p. 1).
10. Scientific-like behavior is described as knowledge exchange by free revealing and paying each other with recognition (e.g. Cole and Cole 1967).
11. However, key rationales for free revealing were at the root of Netscape's economic weakness and lost competitive context in both altruism and recognition.
12. Originally, the term 'software' instead of 'product' is used. However, for the underlying principles, this thesis regards software as a category of product.
13. A social movement represents a collective challenge by people with common purposes and solidarities in sustained interaction with others outside the movement (Tarrow 1994. p. 4).
14. A specification about open source licenses is provided by the open source initiative (http://www.opensource.org/), which also provides several open source licenses.
15. Strategies for value capture include embedding complementary products, services and support (Dahlander and Magnusson 2005; Bonaccorsi et al. 2006; Dahlander 2005; West and Gallagher (2006a).
16. OpenOffice was also forked into LibreOffice after disputes with the OpenOffice commercial sponsor.
17. Strategies for 'guarding the commons,' including legal and normative tactics, reveals O'Mahony (2003).
18. For a detailed description of open source licenses see, for example, the open source initiative, a non-profit organization for maintaining the open source definitions: www.opensource.org.
19. Balka et al. (2010) add the criteria 'replicability' for open design products.

REFERENCES

Agerfalk, P.J., and Fitzgerald, B. (2008): "Outsourcing to an unknown workforce: exploring opensourcing as a global sourcing strategy", *MIS Quarterly* 32(2), pp. 385–409.

Arrow, K. (1962): "Economic welfare and the allocation of resources for invention", in *The rate and direction of inventive activity: economic and social factors*, H. M. Groves (ed.), National Bureau of Economic Research, pp. 609–626.

Bagozzi, R.P., and Dholakia, U.M. (2006): "Open source software user communities: a study of participation in linux user groups", *Management Science* 52(7), pp. 1099–1115.

Baldwin, C. Y., and Clark, K. B. (2006): "The architecture of participation: does code architecture mitigate free riding in the open source development model?" *Management Science* 52(7), pp. 1116–1127.

Baldwin, C. Y., and Hippel, E. von (2011): "Modeling a paradigm shift: from producer innovation to user and open collaborative innovation", *Organization Science* 22(6), pp. 1399–1417.

Balka, K., Raasch, C., and Herstatt, C. (2009): "Open source enters the world of atoms: a statistical analysis of open design", *First Monday* 14(11).

Balka, K., Raasch, A.-C., and Herstatt, C. (2010): "How open is open source? software and beyond", *Creativity and Innovation Management* 19(3), pp. 248–256.

Bogers, M., and West, J. (2012): "Managing distributed innovation: strategic utilization of open and user innovation", *Creativity and Innovation Management* 21(1), pp. 61–75.

Bonaccorsi, A., Giannangeli, S., and Rossi, C. (2006): "Entry strategies under competing standards: hybrid business models in the open source software industry", *Management Science* 52(7), pp. 1085–1098.

Bonaccorsi, A., and Rossi, C. (2003): "Why open source software can succeed: open source software development", *Research Policy* 32(7), pp. 1243–1258.

Casadesus-Masanell, R., and Llanes. G. (2011): "Mixed source", *Management Science* 57(7), pp. 1212–1230

Cedergren, M. (2003): "Open content and value creation", *First Monday* 8(8). http://firstmonday.org/ojs/index.php/fm/article/view/1071/991.

Cheliotis, G. (2009): "From open source to open content: organization, licensing and decision processes in open cultural production", *Decision Support Systems* 47(3), pp. 229–244.

Chesbrough, H. W., and Rosenbloom, R. (2002): "The role of the business model in capturing value from innovation: evidence from Xerox corporation's technology spin-off companies", *Industrial & Corporate Change* 11(3), pp. 529–555.

Chesbrough, H. W., Vanhaverbeke, W., and West, J. (eds.) (2006): *Open innovation: researching a new paradigm*, Oxford University Press, New York.

Clarke, R. (2004): "Open source software and open content as models for ebusiness". 17th Bled eCommerce Conference, eGlobal. Bled, Slovenia. http://www.rogerclarke.com/EC/Bled04.html. Accessed 3 December 2014.

Colazo, J., and Fang, Y. (2009): "Impact of license choice on open source software development activity", *Journal of the American Society for Information Science and Technology* 60(5), pp. 997–1011.

Cole, S., and Cole, J. (1967): "Scientific output and recognition: a study in the operation of the reward system in science", *American Sociological Review* 32(3), pp. 377–390.

Crowston, K., Wei, K., Howison, J., and Wiggins, A. (2012): "Free/Libre opensource software development: what we know and what we do not know", *ACM Computing Surveys* 44(2), pp. 7:1–7:35.

Dahlander, L. (2005): "Appropriation and appropriability in open source software", *International Journal of Innovation Management* 9(3), pp. 259–285.

Dahlander, L., and Gann, D. M. (2010): "How open is innovation?" *Research Policy* 39(6), pp. 699–710.

Dahlander, L., and Magnusson, M. (2005): "Relationships between open source software companies and communities: observations from nordic firms", *Research Policy* 34(4), pp. 481–493.

Dahlander, L., and Wallin, M. W. (2006): "A man on the inside: unlocking communities as complementary assets", *Research Policy* 35(8), pp. 1243–1259.

Dalle, J.-M., and David, P. M. (2003): "The allocation of software development resources in 'open source' production mode", SIEPR Discussion Paper 02-27, Stanford Institute of Economic Policy Research, Stanford, CA.

Demil, B., and Lecocq, X. (2006): "Neither market nor hierarchy nor network: the emergence of bazaar governance", *Organization Studies* 27(10), pp. 1447–1466.

Demsetz, H. (1967): "Toward a theory of property rights", *American Economic Review* 57(2), pp. 347–359.

Fitzgerald, B. (2006): "The transformation of open source software", *MIS Quarterly* 30(3), pp. 587–598.

Fosfuri, A., Giarratana, M., and Luzzi, A. (2008): "The penguin has entered the building: the commercialization of open source software products", *Organization Science* 19(2), pp. 292–305.

Fuggetta, A. (2003): "Open source software—an evaluation", *Journal of Systems and Software* 66(1), pp. 77–90.

Garud, R., Jain, S., and Kumaraswamy, A. (2002): "Institutional entrepreneurship in the sponsorship of common technological standards: the case of Sun Microsystems and Java", *Academy of Management Journal* 45, pp. 196–214.

Gassmann, O. (2006): "Opening up the innovation process: towards an agenda", *R&D Management* 36(3), pp. 223–228.

Ghosh, R., Glott, R., Kreiger, B., and Robles-Martinez, G. (2002): "The Free/ Libre/ Open Source Software Developers Survey". http://www.flossproject.org/report/Final4.htm. Accessed 3 December 2014.

Glott, R., Schmidt, P., and Ghosh, R. A. (2010): *Wikipedia Survey—Overview of Results.* http://www.wikipediasurvey.org/docs/Wikipedia_Overview_15March 2010-FINAL.pdf. Accessed 30 October 2012.

Granstrand, O. (1999): *The economics and management of intellectual property*, Edward Elgar Publishing, Cheltenham, U.K.

Hayek, F. A. (1945): "The use of knowledge in society", *American Economic Review* 35(4), pp. 519–530.

Harhoff, D., Henkel, J., and Hippel, E. von (2003): "Profiting from voluntary information spillovers: how users benefit by freely revealing their innovations". *Research Policy* 32(10), pp. 1753–1769.

Harhoff, D., and Mayrhofer, P. (2010): "Managing user communities and hybrid innovation processes: concepts and design implications", *Organizational Dynamics* 39(2), pp. 137–144.

Hars, A., and Ou, S. (2002): "Working for free? motivations for participating in opensource projects", *International Journal of Electronic Commerce* 6(3), pp. 25–39.

Healy, K., and Schussman, A. (2003): "The ecology of open-source software development", Department of Sociology, University of Arizona, Tucson.

Henkel, J. (2006): "Selective revealing in open innovation processes: the case of embedded Linux", *Research Policy* 35(7), pp. 953–969.

Hertel, G., Niedner, S., and Herrmann, S. (2003): "Motivation of software developers in Open Source projects: an Internet-based survey of contributors to the Linux kernel", *Research Policy* 32(7), pp. 1159–1177.

Hippel, E. A. von (2001): Perspective: User toolkits for innovation. *Journal of Product Innovation Management* 18(4), pp. 247–257.

Hippel, E. A. von, and Krogh, G. von (2003): "Open source software and the 'private-collective' innovation model: issues for organization science", *Organization Science* 14(2), pp. 209–223.

Hippel, E. A. von, and Krogh, G. von (2006): "Free revealing and the private-collective model for innovation incentives", *R&D Management* 36(3), pp. 295–306.

Jeppesen, L. B., and Frederiksen, L. (2006): "Why do users contribute to firm-hosted user communities? the case of computer-controlled music instruments", *Organization Science* 17(1), pp. 45–63.

Kogut, B., and Metiu, A. (2001): "Open-source software development and distributed innovation", *Oxford Review of Economic Policy* 17(2), pp. 248–264.

Krogh, G. von, Haefliger, S., Späth, S., and Wallin, M. W. (2012): "Carrots and rainbows: motivation and social practice in open source software development", *MIS Quarterly* 36(2), pp. 649–676.

Krogh, G. von, and Hippel, E. A. von (2006): "The promise of research on open source software", *Management Science* 52(7), pp. 975–983.

Krogh, G. von, and Späth, S. (2007): "The open source software phenomenon: Characteristics that promote research", *The Journal of Strategic Information Systems* 16(3), pp. 236–253.

Lakhani, K. R., and Hippel, E. A. von (2003): "How open source software works: 'free' user-to-user assistance", *Research Policy* 32(6), pp. 923–943.

Lakhani, K. R., and Tushman, M. (2012): "Open Innovation and Organizational Boundaries: The Impact of Task Decomposition and Knowledge Distribution on the Locus of Innovation", *HBS Working Papers* 12–57, Harvard Business School, Cambridge.

Lakhani, K. R., and Wolf, R. (2005): "Why Hackers Do What They Do: Understanding Motivation and Effort in Free/Open Source Software Projects", in *Perspectives on Free and Open Source Software*, J. Feller, B. Fitzgerald, S. Hissam, and K. Lakhani (eds.), MIT Press, Boston, pp. 3–22.

Lee, G. K., and Cole, R. E. (2003): "From a firm-based to a community-based model of knowledge creation: the case of the Linux Kernel development", *Organization Science* 14(6), pp. 633–649.

Lerner, J., and Tirole, J. (2001): "The open source movement: key research questions", *European Economic Review* 45(4–6), pp. 819–826.

Lerner, J., and Tirole, J. (2002): "Some simple economics of open source", *The Journal of Industrial Economics* 50(2), pp. 197–234.

Levine, S., and Prietula, M. (2014): "Open collaboration for innovation: principles and performance". *Organization Science* 25(5), pp. 1414–1433.

Ljungberg, J. (2000): "Open source movements as a model for organizing", *European Journal of Information Systems* 9(4), pp. 501–508.

Müller-Seitz, G., and Reger, G. (2010): "Networking beyond the software code? an explorative examination of the development of an open source car project", *Technovation* 30(11/12), pp. 627–634.

Nov, O., and Kuk, G. (2008): "Open source content contributors' response to free-riding: the effect of personality and context", *Computers in Human Behavior* 24(6), pp. 2848–2861.

Okoli, C. (2010): "Beyond open source software: an introduction to researching open content", *Sprouts: Working Papers on Information Systems* 9(64).

Olson, M. (1965): *The Logic of Collective Action: Public Goods and the Theory of Groups* (Rev. ed.). Harvard University Press, Cambridge, MA.

O'Mahony, S. (2003): "Guarding the commons: how community managed software projects protect their work", *Research Policy* 32(7), pp. 1179–1198.

O'Mahony, S., and Ferraro, F. (2007): "The emergence of governance in an open source community", *Academy of Management Journal* 50(5), pp. 1079–1106.

Oreg, S., and Nov, O. (2008): "Exploring motivations for contributing to open source initiatives: the roles of contribution context and personal values", *Computers in Human Behavior* 24(5), pp. 2055–2073.

Penrose, E. T. (1959): *The Theory of the Growth of the Firm*, Oxford University Press, New York.

Pfaffenberger, B. (2001): "Why open content matters", *Knowledge, Technology & Policy* 14(1), pp. 93–102.

Raasch, A.-C. (2011): "Product development in open design communities: a process perspective", *International Journal of Innovation and Technology Management* 8(4), pp. 557–576.

Raasch, A.-C., Herstatt, C., and Balka, K. (2009): "On the open design of tangible goods", *R&D Management* 39(4), pp. 382–393.

Raasch, C., Herstatt, C., and Lock, P. (2008): "The dynamics of user innovation: drivers and impediments of innovation activities", *International Journal of Innovation Management* 12(3), pp. 377–398.

Raasch, C., Lee, V., Spaeth, S., and Herstatt, C. (2013): "The rise and fall of interdisciplinary research: the case of open source innovation", *Research Policy* 42(5), pp. 1138–1151.

Raymond, E. S. (1999): "Articles—The Cathedral and the Bazaar", *Knowledge, Technology and Policy* 12(3), pp. 23–49.

Raymond, E. (2002): Afterword: "Beyond Software?" http://catb.org/~esr/writings/homesteading/afterword/. Accessed August 2011.

Roberts, J. A., Hann, I.-H., and Slaughter, S. A. (2006): "Understanding the motivations, participation, and performance of open source software developers: a longitudinal study of the Apache Projects", *Management Science* 52(7), pp. 984–999.

Rolandsson, B., Bergquist, M., and Ljungberg, J. (2011): "Open source in the firm: opening up professional practices of software development", *Research Policy* 40(4), pp. 576–587.

Rosenzweig, R. (2006): "Can history be open source? Wikipedia and the future of the past", *The Journal of American History* 93(1), pp. 117–146.

Setia, P., Rajagopalan, B., Sambamurthy, V., and Calantone, R. (2012): "How peripheral developers contribute to open-source software development", *Information Systems Research* 23(1), pp. 144–163.

Shah, S. K. (2006): "Motivation, governance, and the viability of hybrid forms in open source software development", *Management Science* 52(7), pp. 1000–1014.

Smith, Z. (2008): "Objects as software: the coming revolution", 25th Chaos Communication Congress.

Stallman, R. M. (2009): "Viewpoint: Why 'open source' misses the point of free software", *Communications of the ACM* 52(6), pp. 31–33. doi:10.1145/1516046.1516058

Stewart, K. J., Ammeter, A. P., and Maruping, L. M. (2006): "Impacts of license choice and organizational sponsorship on user interest and development activity in open source software projects", *Information Systems Research* 17(2), pp. 126–144.

Stewart, K., and Gosain, S. (2006): "The impact of ideology on effectiveness in open source software development teams". *MIS Quarterly* 30(2), pp. 291–314.

Stuermer, M., Krogh, G. von, Spaeth, S., and Hertel, G. (2009): "Results of maemo and openmoko community survey". http://public.smi.ethz.ch/files/MaemoOpenmoko/PublicDescriptiveStatistics.html. Accessed 6 October 2009.

Stuermer, M., Späth, S., and Krogh, G. von (2009): "Extending private-collective innovation: a case study", *R&D Management* 39(2), pp. 170–191.

Tarrow, S. (1994): *Power in movement: social movements, collective action and mass politics in the modern*, Cambridge University Press, New York.

Teece, D. J. (1986): "Profiting from technological innovation: implications for integration, collaboration, licensing and public policy", *Research Policy* 15(6), pp. 285–305.

Vallance, R., Kiani, S., and Nayfeh, S. (2001): "Open design of manufacturing equipment". Proceedings of the CHIRP 1st International Conference on Agile, Reconfigurable.

Vanhaverbeke, W., Van De Vrande, V., and Chesbrough, H. W. (2008): "Understanding the advantages of open innovation practices in corporate venturing in term of real options", *Creativity and Innovation Management* 17, pp. 251–258.

Wernerfelt, B. (1984): "A resource-based view of the firm", *Strategic Management Journal* 5(2), pp. 171–180.

West, J. (2003): "How open is open enough? melding proprietary and open source platform strategies: open source software development", *Research Policy* 32(7), pp. 1259–1285.

West, J., and Gallagher, S. (2006a): "Challenges of open innovation: the paradox of firm investment in open source software", *R&D Management* 36(3), pp. 315–328.

West, J., and Gallagher, S. (2006b): "Patterns of open innovation in open source software", in *Open innovation: researching a new paradigm*, H. W. Chesbrough, W. Vanhaverbeke, and J. West (eds.), New York: Oxford University Press.

West, J., and O'Mahony, S. (2005): "What makes a project open source? migrating from organic to synthetic communities", Academy of Management Conference, Technology and Innovation Management Division, Honolulu.

West, J., and O'Mahony, S. (2008): "The role of participation architecture in growing sponsored open source communities", *Industry and Innovation* 15(2), pp. 145–168.

Wiley, D. (1998): *OpenContent*. http://slashdot.org/articles/older/9806260926218. shtml. Accessed 30 September 2012.

Williamson, O. (1973): "Markets and hierarchies: some elementary considerations", *American Economic Review* 63(2), pp. 316–325.

Wilson, J. (2000): "Volunteering", *Annual Review of Sociology* 26, pp. 215–240.

2 Motivations to Contribute for Free in Online Communities

Lars Janzik

Online communities (OCs), especially those related to particular products or brands, have evolved into an important source for identifying user needs and solution ideas, thereby supporting companies to innovate. Despite its practical relevance, user innovation activities within consumer OCs still are comparatively underexplored. Members' motivations to innovate and contribute to OCs for free, in particular, belong to a young line of research requiring further investigation. This study contributes to this line of research by providing an in-depth netnographic analysis of innovative, privately operated OCs dedicated to tangible consumer products. Most fundamentally, I differentiate (1) motives to sign up to OCs, (2) motives to innovate, and (3) motives to publish personal innovations in OCs. This study categorizes the motives of innovative OC members depending on membership lifecycle and situational factors. My results support companies in understanding members' motives in privately operated OCs relating to the company's brand or products. Thus it provides a foundation how to use the innovative potential of OCs and gives implication for potential manufacturer's strategies.

Keywords: user innovation, online communities, motivation, netnography.

2 MOTIVATIONS TO CONTRIBUTE FOR FREE IN ONLINE COMMUNITIES

2.1 Introduction

In 2013, approximately more than 2 billion people worldwide were active in online communities (OCs) and social networks (according to the official member statistics from e.g. www.facebook.com, www.qq.com, www.linkedin.com and www.twitter.com). The active usage and understanding of OCs have gained great importance for companies of nearly all lines of business. For participants, OCs have been established as knowledge and communication platforms and have become important sources for the exchange of information and experience. Beside general interest social networks such as Facebook, there exists a huge number of specialized OCs for almost every niche, topic, brand or product. Some are operated by companies themselves, e.g. for customer support, to increase brand awareness and reach or as instrument for market research. Due to low technical barriers and costs as well as an increasing segmentation of thematic online groups, the majority of OCs are privately operated by hobbyists, fans or extreme users of a related brand or product. OCs have proven their impact to identify the requirements of users, source ideas, and even provide solutions to companies' problems (Jeppesen and Molin 2003). For example, successful community-based interaction between users and manufacturers has created highly innovative products in the consumer goods sector (Luethje 2000; Luethje 2004).

As illustrated in Figure 2.1 product-related innovative OCs can be differentiated in three dimensions: Dimension one defines if the OC is operated by a company or a user; Dimension two describes the artifact developed by the OC that can be a tangible (physical) product such as extreme sports equipment (Franke and Shah 2003; Luethje 2004; Luethje et al. 2005) or intangible (non-physical) such as software (Dahlander and Magnusson 2005; Jeppesen and Frederiksen 2006). The third dimension is related to the primarily used medium for the exchange and collaboration inside the OC, which is predominantly online or offline.

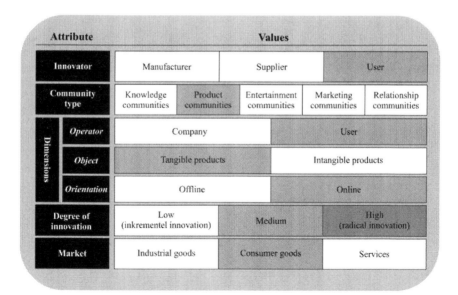

Figure 2.1 Attributes of OCs and their value for this research

Despite its practical relevance, the field of user innovation in OCs for consumer goods is still comparatively underexplored, especially in the case of tangible products. Füller et al. (2007), Antorini (2008), and Jawecki (2008) paved the ground for this line of research in recent years. The communication and collaboration in innovative OCs related to tangible products is an online process while the physical realization of an innovation needs to be executed offline. In spite of these barriers, the number of such innovative product communities related to tangible consumer product is huge and still growing.

This research will take a closer look at the motivation of members in innovative product communities to participate and contribute for free. Members' motivation is the most critical success factor of an OC as it has a direct impact on the quality and quantity of community content (Ardichvili et al. 2003). Following study investigates four main research questions analyzing a privately operated innovative OC related to tangible consumer products.

(1) What drives users' motivation to join such OCs?

(2) What motivates members to innovate and to create or to modify products?

(3) What are the key motives of innovators to share knowledge and creations with others?

A categorization for different motives of OC members will deliver deeper insights into the creation processes of innovative product communities. The aim of this research is to enable firms to better interact with OC members and to provide a framework for specific incentives to stimulate OC participants' contributions.

Several studies on consumer OCs describe user innovation as a phenomenon of emerging markets (e.g. Jeppesen and Molin 2003; Shah 2005) and trendy products (e.g. Jeppesen and Frederiksen 2006; Jawecki 2008). By way of contrast, this research will investigate user innovation in consumer OCs in a mature market. The fourth research question therefore is:

(4) Do consumer OCs in mature markets show potential for radical user innovations?

In the following two sections of this chapter, prior research on user innovation and innovative OCs will be reviewed (section 2.2) as well as the theory of user motivation (section 2.3). Section 2.4 includes an overview of the selected research field and methodology, and section 2.5 delivers principal findings of this study on members' motivations and on types of user innovation in OCs. Finally the chapter closes with the discussion of the findings (section 2.6) and a summary of the implication for research and companies (section 2.7).

2.2   User Innovation in Online Communities and Community Member Types

2.2.1   *User Innovation—Selected Results from Prior Research*

The role of lead users in the new product development (NPD) process of companies has been analyzed on a wide scale, especially for industrial goods markets (Urban and Hippel 1988; Herstatt and Hippel 1992; Morrison et al. 2000). Lead users have individual needs that mirror potential requirements of the future market, and they benefit greatly from new solutions according to their needs (Hippel 1986). It has been verified that innovations, especially radical innovations, often result from ideas of these lead users (Hippel 1978; Hippel 1988). User innovations are mostly based on voluntary and collaborative activities of users (Shah 2005). The integration of innovative users, especially into early stages of NPD, creates an important additional, external source for new ideas and problem solutions and supports to reduce a company's flop rate (Hippel and Katz 2002; Gassmann and Wecht 2006).

In the market of industrial goods, companies often only have few clients or several major potential customers. Therefore they know the characteristics of each user quite well and have established contact with important lead users (Hippel 1986). In the consumer goods market, the numbers of users are much larger. To acquire information about changing user needs is more complex and costly here, as well as to identify and integrate innovative users into NPD (Spann et al. 2009). The online world offers companies the opportunity to identify, integrate and monitor innovative users easily at low costs especially for the consumer goods market (Dahan and Hauser 2002; Jeppesen and Frederiksen 2006).

2.2.2   *Innovative Online Communities in the Social Web*

The buzzword "Web 2.0", recently described as "Social Web" (Porter 2008; Kim et al. 2010), represents the evolutionary development of the Web into an interactive user-centric network of websites since 2004 (Janzik and Herstatt 2008; Buyya et al. 2008; Iriberri and Leroy 2009).

These changes in the web can be divided into a social, a technical and a commercial dimension. The social dimension is represented by the changed role of online users from pure consumers to producers and active co-designers, while the technical dimension can be subdivided into technologies for communication and exchange, technologies for easy access and usage, and technologies for viral distribution (O'Reilly 2007; Vossen and Hagemann 2007; Janzik and Herstatt 2008). The interaction of social and technical dimensions enables new online business models and marketing instruments that represent the commercial dimension (Wirtz et al. 2010).

While offline communities are based on real-world meetings and synchronous face-to-face communication (Shumar and Renninger 2002), the communication and exchange in OCs are often asynchronous (e.g. via posts and personal messaging); still, most OC platforms offer additional synchronous communication channels (e.g. chats) as they are essential for building up closer social ties among community members (Fuchs 2008). Within this research, I concentrate on OCs that are geographically dispersed (Hiltz 1984). Members participate due to their shared interest in a specific topic, irrespective of their location (Blanchard and Horan 2000). OCs do not preclude face-to-face meetings among members, but are mainly characterized as online interactions. Accordingly, I use the term "meet" in reference to OCs in this figurative sense, knowing that members are not necessarily online at the same time and may not physically meet ever.

I define an OC as an association of individuals who share a common interest or goal and regularly "meet" and communicate virtually via a technical platform on the Internet (Preece 2000; Kim 2000; Tietz and Herstatt 2007). OCs related to particular topics, i.e. special interest and product-related OCs, also known in literature as "Communities of Consumption", are virtual meeting points for hobbyist experts and extreme users (Kozinets 1999). These micro-communities are particularly well suited for integration into NPD as they frequently include members with lead user characteristics and reveal innovative potentials (Luethje 2000; Shani et al. 2003). I will call this type of OC an "innovation community".

A special type of OC is dedicated to particular brands. Following Muniz and O'Guinn (2001), a brand community is a specialized OC, based on a structured social network among enthusiasts of a specific brand or brand product. Brand communities are often product-related and in some cases also innovation communities (Füller et al. 2008).

Community-based innovation (CBI) picks up the advantages of virtual customer integration via the Internet, using the available innovative potential of OCs for the NPD process (Füller et al. 2004).

2.2.3 Member Types in Online Communities

Members of OCs are not a homogenous group and differ in their abilities and motivations to participate in innovation projects (Nambisan 2002; Luethje 2004; Hippel 2005). To contribute successfully to an innovation project, a member must have several abilities and competences in the specific domain of the OC. Only a small percentage of members own such competence which can be described as object knowledge (Luethje 2000) and solution information (Luethje et al. 2005; Piller and Walcher 2006).

According to their abilities and activities, I will distinguish between five groups of innovation community members: (1) innovators, (2) activists, (3) fellow-travelers, (4) tourists and (5) free-riders (c.f. Kozinets 1999; Preece 2000; Curien et al. 2006). In privately operated OCs, the owner often is also a moderator and mediator as well as an opinion leader within the community (Preece 2000). The two groups of innovators and activists lead discussions and form opinions, and are fundamental drivers of the OC for its survival and advancement (Cothrel and Williams 1999; Kim 2000). In opposite to pure activists, innovators release their ideas, designs and developments frequently within the OC. Tourists have a passing interest in the main topic of the OC. Fellow-travelers have individual interests differing from the main topic of the OC and participate in discussions for other reasons, e.g. closer social ties (Kozinets 1999; Kim 2000). Free-riders (Olson 1965) participate without contributing within the OC (Nonnecke and Preece 2000). They can be differentiated in lurkers, that only read inside the OC and opportunists that additional post questions to get solution information, but do not provide expertise and knowledge about the topic in return (Sarner 2008; Antorini 2008). Both break the norm of reciprocity because they consume content and knowledge in the OC without providing an equivalent or any kind of active participation (Kollock and Smith 1996; Blanchard and Horan 2000). Contributions are revealed freely among members for the purpose of collaborative exchange and co-development (Harhoff et al. 2003). The provided information and knowledge of the OC becomes a public good, accessible and also utilizable by lurkers and opportunists for free (Wang and Fesenmaier 2003; Lakhani and Wolf 2005). Beside free-riders, most OCs include a completely inactive group of registered people who have not yet deleted their data. They are either former active members who have lost interest in the OC or fake registrations based on false data. This group can be described as "sleeping members". Most research of OC participation does not differ between lurkers and sleeping members. This may be due to the fact that such a distinction requires internal login information that may not be accessible to scholars. It should be emphasized that sleeping members could "wake up" and (re-)activate their accounts. Therefore, I argue that they should be considered as part of the community unless the permanency of deactivation is ascertained. Figure 2.2 illustrates the five different types

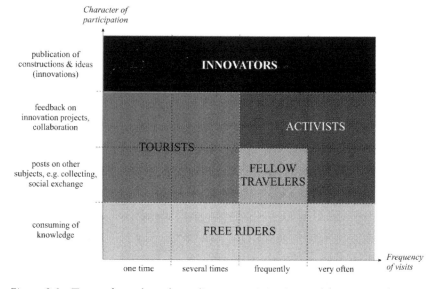

Figure 2.2 Types of members depending on participation and frequency of visits

of members in relation to the character of participation (ordinate) and the frequency of visits (abscissa).

The roles of OC members can change during the lifecycle of their membership (Wenger 1998): They start as visitors of the OC, become newcomers after joining and can evolve from regular participants into innovators and activists (Kim 2000). Through a series of different roles, users improve skills, collect experience during their membership lifecycle, and also assume reputation and status (Wenger 1998; Kim 2000; Iriberri and Leroy 2009).

2.3   Motivation for Participation in Innovation Communities

2.3.1   *The Sources of Motivation—Theoretical Background*
The question of motivation is the search for the cause and drive of human behavior (Reeve 2005). Motivation of members to participate and contribute in innovation communities is most critical as a factor for the emergence of innovative user ideas and products (Shah 2006).

Motives represent a willingness to act but are purely hypothetical. They are individual tendencies, relatively stable and the basis for achieving several positive goals or to avoid negative consequences (Atkinson 1982; McClelland et al. 1989). Motivation arises from the interaction between motives (individual factors) and incentives (situational factors) (Atkinson 1958; Heckhausen and Heckhausen 2008). Psychologists characterize motivation as the process that refers to releasing, controlling and maintaining physical and mental activities (Pintrich and Schunk 2007). According to Expectancy Theory, the motivation of individuals depends on the expectation of the outcome, on the perception of a clear relation between the result of an effort and its consequences as well as on the fact that an outcome has a specific positive value (Vroom 1964). Thus, it is possible to influence individuals' actions by designing incentives appealing to pre-existing motives (Brown 1961; McClelland et al. 1989).

Self-Determination Theory (SDT) tells us that there is a basic qualitative distinction between extrinsic and intrinsic motivation (Deci and Ryan 1985). Typically, factors of intrinsic and extrinsic motivation are both active within a complex interaction and jointly constitute individual motivation.

Extrinsic motivation is based on external incentives linked to the differentiable outcome of an action (Pintrich and Schunk 2007). Extrinsic incentives can be classified as either material, such as payment and financial rewards, or immaterial, such as awards and career opportunities (Frey 2002). Intrinsic motivation, by contrast, arises from a drive, motivated from within an individual, for a state of inherent satisfaction, and therefore does not focus on the outcome of an activity (Malone and Lepper 1987; Ryan and Deci 2000). Enjoyment and altruism are examples of intrinsic motives (Lin 2007). For this research, the influence of contextual factors on intrinsic motivation is of particular interest. Cognitive Evaluation Theory, a sub-theory of SDT, focuses on that question. It tells us that the basic psychological needs of an individual (innate needs for autonomy, competency and relatedness) have to be satisfied to support intrinsic motivation (Deci and Ryan 1985; Ryan and Deci 2000).

A special form of intrinsic motivation is released by the "flow experience". Flow is defined as a "holistic experience" whereby somebody is totally involved in a task (Csikszentmihalyi 2000), as a mental state of people who are completely absorbed in a fluently running, enjoyable activity (Csikszentmihalyi 1990).

2.3.2   *Selected Research Results on User Motivation in Online Communities*

Table 2.1 presents the most important findings concerning members' motivation from 22 selected researches on different types of communities. The displayed "-", "0", "+", "++" and "+++" describe the strength of the different motives in the findings. Because the researchers used different samples, methods and scales, Table 2.1 shows only tendencies and has ordinal character. I reviewed researches from open source software (OSS) OCs, consumer goods OCs, consumer goods offline communities and content OCs.

In most of these empirical studies on user innovation in OCs, the motivations to innovate are differentiated by qualitative characteristics such as intrinsic or extrinsic, but not evaluated according to situational groups (Lakhani and Wolf 2005; Jeppesen and Frederiksen 2006; Füller et al. 2007; Nov 2007; Antorini 2008). Only 2 authors of the 22 listed researches investigate motivation also for different member activities. Jawecki subdivides innovation-related motivation into three different dimensions: (1) motivations to innovate, (2) motivations to contribute to joint innovation activities within the OC, and (3) motivations to collaborate with companies (Jawecki 2008). All other researchers mix different characters of activity motivation and rather analyze those as general motivation for participation without considering situational factors. The motivation to join OCs was not analyzed separately so far. But this type is of considerable interest as joining to OCs is likely to be related to the innovative activities of the users later on in the lifecycle (Ghosh 2005; David et al. 2003).

In research on user motivation in OSS online communities, two specific external rewards are often found to be key for participation: the improvement of individual skills and personal need (Hars and Ou 2002; David et al. 2003; Lakhani and Wolf 2005; Ghosh 2005). The latter was also identified as the strongest determinant of participation in innovative offline hobby communities for emerging markets (Franke and Shah 2003; Luethje 2004; Luethje et al. 2005). According to these studies, material incentives such as direct financial rewards either do not exist or tend to play a minor role for the extrinsic motivation of users.

Extrinsic motivation by itself is not sufficient to explain innovative activities, voluntary participation and engagement of members in innovation communities (Jeppesen and Molin 2003; Lakhani and Wolf 2005). In

Table 2.1 Research results on members' motivation in communities

Research	Community operator	Object/ product	Intrinsic motivation						Extrinsic motivation			
			Fun, enjoyment	Community identification	Self-determination	Altruism	Improve skills	Personal need	Reputation (Status)	Reciprocity	Material compensation	Situative factors
OPEN SOURCE SOFTWARE ONLINE COMMUNITIES												
Hars and Ou (2002)	User	Intangible		++	+++	+	+++	++	++		+	No
Lakhani and Hippel (2003)	User	Intangible	++	++		++			++	+++		No
Hertel et al. (2003)	User	Intangible	+++	+++			++	++	++			No
David et al. (2003)	User	Intangible		+++	+++	++	++	++		+++		No
Oreg and Nov (2008)	User / foundation	Intangible			++	++	++		++			No
Ghosh (2005)	User	Intangible		++	++	+++	+++	++	+	++	0	Partly
Lakhani and Wolf (2005)	User	Intangible	+++	++	++		+++	+++	+	++	0	No
Shah (2006)	User / sponsor	Intangible	+++	++				+++		++	0	No

(*Continued*)

Table 2.1 (Continued)

Research	Community operator	Object/product	Intrinsic motivation						Extrinsic motivation			Situative factors
			Fun, enjoyment	Community identification	Self-determination	Altruism	Improve skills	Personal need	Reputation (Status)	Reciprocity	Material compensation	
CONSUMER GOODS ONLINE COMMUNITIES												
Jeppesen and Frederiksen (2006)	Company	Intangible						++	+++	++		No
Füller (2006)	Company	Tangible	+++		+++	++	+++	+++	++	+	+	No
Füller et al. (2007)	User / company	Tangible	+++				++	+	++			No
Walcher (2007)	Company	Tangible	++	+++		+	+	+++	++		++	No
Jawecki (2008)	User	Tangible	+++	+					+++	++		Partly
Antorini (2008)	User	Tangible	+++	+	++			+++			0	No
CONSUMER GOODS OFFLINE COMMUNITIES												
Franke and Shah (2003)	User	Tangible	+++	+++				++	+	++		No
Lüthje (2004)	User	Tangible	+					+++			0	No

CONTENT ONLINE COMMUNITIES

Study												
Wasko and Faraj (2000)	User	Intangible	+	0	▨	++	+++	+++	▨	+++	▨	No
Wang and Fesenmeier (2003)	Company	Intangible	+	++	▨	++	+++	+++	+++	+++	▨	No
Wasko and Faraj (2005)	Company	Intangible	+	+	▨	+	+++	++	–	▨	▨	No
Nov (2007)	Foundation	Intangible	+++	+++	++	▨	▨	▨	▨	▨	▨	No
Schroer and Hertel (2009)	Foundation	Intangible	+++	++	▨	+	+++	▨	▨	▨	0	No
Nov et al. (2010)	Company	Intangible	0	++	▨	▨	–	▨	0	▨	▨	No

Effect = +++ = very strong positive, ++ = strong positive, + = positive, 0 = neutral, - = negative most studies on motivation in OCs, intrinsic motives have been identified as key drivers of participation and contribution. The most important internal motives found are fun and enjoyment (Lakhani and Hippel 2003; Hertel et al. 2003; Lakhani and Wolf 2005; Shah 2006; Füller et al. 2007; Nov 2007; Antorini 2008; Jawecki 2008; Schroer and Hertel 2009), self-determination (Hars and Ou 2002; Schroer and Hertel 2009) and community identification (Hars and Ou 2002; Lakhani and Hippel 2003; Hertel et al. 2003; Schroer and Hertel 2009).

Reputation and reciprocity are relevant extrinsic motives in researches of all types of communities, but have a particular strong effect in OCs for consumer goods.

2.4   Research Design

2.4.1   *Netnography as Method for Data Collection*
Netnography is a method to observe OCs and to collect data about online consumer groups (c.f. Kozinets 1997; Kozinets 1998). As a qualitative research approach it offers a way of exploring online user behavior, activities and cultures in OCs or weblogs without any direct exercise of influence by the researcher (Kozinets 2006). The netnographic approach follows traditional offline ethnography (Arnould and Wallendorf 1994; Thompson 1997) and adapts it for market research in OCs as a simpler, faster and cheaper variation (Kozinets 2002).

A great advantage of the method is the anonymous direct access to unfiltered information and user experience in the natural OC environment without direct participation or an exercise of influence by the researcher (Langer and Beckmann 2005). Such information that is publicly available on the Internet can generate a special understanding on certain research questions, a "grounded knowledge" rooted in Grounded Theory (Glaser and Strauss 1967; Glaser 1978). Furthermore, netnography allows the researcher to study attitudes, opinions and feelings that are harder to uncover with quantitative methods (Sandlin 2007). In empirical studies of OCs it was used successfully as a method to investigate the members' behavior, attitudes and perceptions (Valck 2005; Jeppesen and Frederiksen 2006; Füller et al. 2007; Antorini 2008; Jawecki 2008; Broillet and Dubosson 2008; Mathwick et al. 2008).

In order to derive answers to my four research questions it is necessary to study OC members' behaviors, thoughts and feelings. I choose to employ netnography as this is the only suitable method for data collection within my research frame.

There is a spectrum of researchers' participation intensities in investigated OCs, starting from a purely observational through a participant-observational to an auto-netnographic approach (Kozinets 2006). As I posted messages in the OCs as a regular member and attended offline conventions, I used participant-observational netnography. Participative elements of netnography can internalize emic meanings as a form of close ethnography (Thompson and Arsel 2004; Kozintes 2006).

2.4.2 Description of the Research Field: The Selected Online Communities

A research field suitable for the investigation of my research questions has to meet the following five criteria:

1. The OCs spawn user innovations,
2. the OCs are dedicated to physical consumer products,
3. the products belong to a mature or shrinking market,
4. the OCs are privately operated and independent of manufacturers and
5. members are hobbyists and participate voluntarily.

This empirical research focuses on selected OCs dedicated to specific physical toys: Playmobil products (Playmobil products are physical toys for children based on the elements of action figures, buildings and vehicles. They are available for specific game worlds or themes such as pirates, knights, railways, the Wild West, or space). Playmobil OCs are chosen as they meet all of my four criteria.

First, in the OCs, I found various Playmobil products that have been modified, enhanced or newly created and are presented online by users. Second, Playmobil toys are physical products from the consumer goods sector, where so far comparatively little research on user innovation exists and member motivation is still underexplored. Third, physical traditional toys belong to a shrinking market in a late stage of their life cycle (DePamphilis 2002). The competition in the toy market has changed greatly with the emergence of computers, game consoles and the Internet since the mid-1990s. Fourth, the Playmobil OCs are all operated by private persons and do not depend in any direct or indirect way on the manufacturer Geobra. Fifth and finally, members participate and contribute to the OC as a hobby and voluntarily.

As I did not want to investigate OCs as a local phenomenon, I looked for an international sample. Playmobil OCs are very international and have members from many different countries. In addition, all OCs are interlinked and jointly create an international network of Playmobil fans.

2.4.3 The Playmobil Online Communities

During my research I identified four different principal types of user websites dedicated to Playmobil: personal homepages, weblogs, photo albums and stand-alone OCs that use "social software" in the form of bulletin board forum technology. Most of these websites are interconnected by numerous links. For my research I only took websites into account that show ideas, designs, developments of users or any other kind of user innovations related to Playmobil.

Within the network of privately operated Playmobil websites, user creations are termed "customizations". In some cases, customizations include simple modifications or variations of existing original Playmobil products and themes, i.e. the level of innovation can be very low, even inside the Playmobil world. In a large number of cases, however, the developments include new ideas, themes or products that have not been offered by the manufacturer yet. These include painting and massive modification of Playmobil figures (e.g. hair types, body shapes), creation of new accessories with several shaping materials (e.g. clothes, furniture, objects of daily use), creation of new vehicles and buildings, or electrification of certain functions. Highly innovative user creations are exemplified by the user-created ancient Egyptian theme world, which was developed and presented on the OC "Playmoboard" in 2003, but launched by Playmobil manufacturer Geobra as a new theme only in 2008.

In addition to pictures of the creation outcome, innovative Playmobil users often document the various steps of the development and production process with images, drawings, and descriptions of material, equipment and procedures ("making-of"). These types of documentation are concentrated in Playmobil OCs because bulletin boards in general enable support, discussion and feedback processes as well as collaborations on specific themes (Harman and Koohang 2005). Finished customizations, drafts and construction techniques are presented, reviewed and discussed.

I reviewed seven OCs to identify the most suited for an in-depth analysis and chose "Customize it!" (CI) and "Playmoboard" (PB), as presented in Table 2.2.

Table 2.2   Selected Playmobil OCs

Community	Members	Posts	Language	Operator (since)	Structure, user innovations/ customizations
Playmoboard	3,736	239,143	English	Private (2001)	Start page, forum, photo gallery Forum with six main categories Customizations in sub-categories and in a photo gallery Customization instructions in sub-category
Customize it!	395	17,294	German	Private (2005)	Forum only Forum with nine main categories Customizations in main-category Customization instructions in main category

Regarding the total number of registered members, CI is a comparatively small community. I selected CI because user creation and individual development of Playmobil products are the main topic and core content of this OC. I found many customization-related categories and suspected high innovative activities. PB was chosen because it is the oldest Playmobil OC with the most registered members. PB is nearly 10 times larger than CI. Moreover, I found huge categories related to customizations with a high number of posts in PB.

2.4.4 Research Process

My research process was structured as follows: First, I analyzed the observed structure of members and their activities for the OCs (CI) and (PB). This enabled an overview of member types and characteristics as well as levels of activities in these OCs.

Next, the posts by the members of CI and PB were analyzed using the netnographic approach for data collection. In total, more than 40,000 posts (14,000 for CI, 26,000 for BP) in about 4,300 threads (1,300 for CI, 3,000 for BP) were read and scanned for motivational sources in August and September 2008. Relevant text posts were downloaded and saved as a text file. I used existing classifications of member motives in OCs (e.g. Hars and Ou 2002; Lakhani and Wolf 2005; Janzik and Herstatt 2008) to start my identification and categorization process. Based on the motivational statements, I found modified previous classifications to better incorporate motives manifested in the selected OCs. I proceeded to code and categorize the text file into 13 identified different types of motives falling into three situational groups. An OSS program for qualitative text analysis was used for this purpose (Weft QDA). The 13 motives were named after the most used keywords in the analyzed statements.

Next, I researched, analyzed and ranked the published creations of OC members for different types of customizations, ranging from simple improvements to highly innovative developments. For this classification, I took three different criteria into consideration: newness of the creation to the Playmobil world, number of non-Playmobil components used, and modification of the entire play concept compared to the manufacturer's catalogue of Playmobil products (Hennel 2006). The customizations can be either limited or advanced improvements of existing products, innovative developments inside the existing play concept or the creation of new use cases outside the traditional play concept. The innovativeness in my classification is always evaluated in relation to the Playmobil play world only.

To check the quality of my assessments, I performed "member checks" as proposed by Kozinets (2002 2006). The findings were reviewed and validated with ten selected active members who develop and present their own designs in the OCs.

2.5   Empirical Findings

2.5.1   *Levels of Members' Activity*

I identified a total of at least 665 different customizations in CI, carried out by users and documented by photos (images that show a number of individual designs and creations are counted as only one customization). In PB, I discovered about 1,200 documented user customizations.

In Table 2.3, I present an overview of the various levels of member activity in the OCs CI and PB. Instead of using the total number of contributions

Table 2.3   Levels of member activities in the OCs "Customize it!" and "Playmoboard"

Posts per day	Members		Age/gender		Characteristics and member type	
	CI	PB	CI	PB	CI	PB
> 0.5	9%	2%	∅: 36.5 years ♂: 79% ♀: 21%	∅: 34.6 years ♂: 76% ♀: 24%	mostly **innovators** 35 of 36 members have published customizations distinctive object knowledge and solution information	mostly **activists** occasional, but rare customizations partly object knowledge and solution information
					post and contribute frequently high status and reputation in the OC cultivate social contacts to other members	
> 0.1 < 0.5	19%	4%			many **innovators** some **tourists** and **fellow-travelers** more than 80% have published customizations	some **innovators** many **tourists** and **fellow-travelers** occasional, but rare customizations
					post and contribute occasionally interested in social exchange often active in different Playmobil OCs	
> 0 < 0.1	72%	94%	–		**free-riders** never or rarely contribute, few or no posts, consume information observe without active participation no social ties within the OC	
					sleeping members have an inactive account	

per member, the average contribution per day appears a more appropriate measure of the activity level: new members with high activity are identified correctly, and members with a long-term, but passing interest in the OC are likewise classified correctly as tourists rather than activists.

For the classification I use the five groups of members I introduced in section 2.3. The groups of innovators and activists cover 9% of the members of CI and are the essential carrier and mediator of expert knowledge. With only one exception, all members of this group have already published customizations in the OC. Very active members who only rarely published customizations mostly belong to a sub-group of activists who focus on collecting Playmobil. In PB, the groups of innovators and activists cover only 2%. In the cases of CI and PB, the private operator is also a moderator and mediator as well as an opinion leader within the OC.

For the groups of innovators, activists, tourists and fellow-travelers, I was able to analyze age and gender from profile information of the OCs: The majority of these members are male adults over 30 years.

As in other research contributions on OCs, free-riders and sleeping members represent the largest group of members in both Playmobil OCs (c.f. Jones and Raffaeli 2000; Nonnecke and Preece 2000; Nonnecke et al. 2004; Füller et al. 2007). 8.6% of the members of CI submitted more than 200 posts in total, and 62% of members did not have any or a maximum of 10 posts. In PB only 4% of the members added more than 200 posts in total, and 82% had 0 to 10 posts. CI shows better rates in this regard as it is a smaller and more specialized OC with comparatively fewer sleeping members and lurkers, and also almost 20% occasional posters.

In research on considerably larger OCs, the identified rate of active members is even lower than in PB. As found by a study on an innovative, large-scale iPod OC (91,000 members), for instance, only 1.3% of the members added more than 100 posts and 88.3% wrote fewer than 10 posts (Jawecki 2008). This suggests that the group of active members grows disproportionally more slowly than the number of total members.

2.5.2 Categorization of Member Motives and Empirical Findings

In this section, the posts of members in the OCs CI and PB are analyzed and categorized into 13 different types of motives as described in the research process (section 2.4). As started by Jawecki's research, I differentiate motivation according to situational factors. In the case of the Playmobil OCs no direct cooperation with the manufacturer is apparent. For this reason, I did not find any statements in the OCs relating to a collaboration process with companies. Only a few statements indicate that members are interested in sharing their customizations and ideas with the manufacturer. Therefore I did not find sufficient sources to analyze the motivation to collaborate with companies as a separate type within my study. However, I identified, distinguished and investigated another fundamental type of motivation in Playmobil OCs: the motivation to join the OC.

Unlike Jawecki I will use the term "groups of motives" instead of "dimensions of motivation". I prefer to focus on motives instead of motivations as the interaction between motives and situational factors causes motivation (Atkinson 1958; Heckhausen and Heckhausen 2008). My "groups of motives" are defined as aggregations of motives that are activated due to different situational factors in the stages of membership. Motives from variable situational groups are connected closely and influence each other, depending on which incentives are active (c.f. Klein and Krech 1951; Markus et al. 2000; Gollwitzer and Oettingen 2001). Thus, I distinguish three groups of member motives, each related to different situations:

1. Motives to sign up to OCs,
2. motives to develop individual products and
3. motives to publish personal innovations in OCs.

More than 85% of all contributions in CI show a reference to user creations, as this is the core topic of that innovation community. Posts in both OCs often predominantly include pictures of the customizations and the design process, which are connected only by short text. For this reason the source of motivation does not always become entirely clear. For CI, a total of 648 statements relating to motivation were identified and coded for 13 different motives in three groups. For the much larger OC PB, 1,325 statements with motivation-related content were found and coded for the same categorization. Table 2.4 presents a quantitative categorization of all coded text passages, assigning them to my three groups of user motives.

I classified each motive according to its predominant characteristics as either intrinsic or extrinsic, also making comparisons to categorizations of intrinsic and extrinsic motives prevalent in OCs from prior research (e.g. Hars and Ou 2002; Lakhani and Wolf 2005; Janzik and Herstatt 2008): 168 of the statements from CI and 607 from PB are coded for the *group of motives to sign up to OCs* (1). In this group I distinguish four different motives: join to get help, suggestions and to learn something (1.1), join to show personal ideas and creations (self-marketing (1.2), join driven by passion for the product (1.3), and join the community because it is fun to see creations of other members (1.4).

Intrinsic motives slightly prevail over extrinsic motives in both OCs in this group. At CI three motives are similarly important for signing up (motives 1.1, 1.3 and 1.4; see Table 2.4, part 1), while at PB the passion for the product and the desire to share this with others is most frequently identified as a motive for joining. The users explain their reasons for registration in the category "introduce yourself":

> *"Until now I felt I was crazy with the hobby [Playmobil] I had, but now that I'm not alone, that I know this community, I feel really great".*

Table 2.4 Motives of OCs' members

1. Motives to sign up to OCs	Customize it! 168	Playmoboard 607	Classification
(1.1) Help, suggestions, learning	49 (29%)	176 (29%)	extrinsic
(1.2) Self-marketing	22 (13%)	31 (5%)	extrinsic
(1.3) Passion for the product (desire to share the passion)	47 (28%)	377 (62%)	intrinsic
(1.4) Fun (to see customizations of others)	50 (30%)	23 (4%)	intrinsic

2. Motives to develop individual products	Customize it! 200	Playmoboard 286	Classification
(2.1) Personal need (not available on the market)	58 (29%)	122 (42.7%)	extrinsic
(2.2) Improvement of personal skills	3 (1.5%)	1 (0.3%)	extrinsic
(2.3) Community identification	47 (23.5%)	30 (10.5%)	intrinsic
(2.4) Material compensation	3 (1.5%)	10 (3.5%)	extrinsic
(2.5) Fun	89 (44.5%)	123 (43%)	intrinsic

3. Motives to publish personal innovations in OCs	Customize it! 280	Playmoboard 432	Classification
(3.1) Feedback and learning	103 (37%)	269 (62%)	extrinsic
(3.2) Social exchange	2 (1%)	3 (1%)	extrinsic
(3.3) Inspiring the manufacturer	6 (2%)	8 (2%)	extrinsic
(3.4) Give something to the community	169 (60%)	152 (35%)	
Fun to share	*53*	*55*	intrinsic
Reciprocity	*9*	*0*	extrinsic
Community identification	*107*	*97*	intrinsic

Many members regard the connection Playmobil to childhood memories a primary source of their passion for the product. Some new members explain that their passion was reactivated when their own children started playing with Playmobil.

> *"Playmobil is something I can share with my child. Playmobil is the good side of my own childhood. Playmobil is making fun".*

In the *group of motives to develop individual products (2)*, I identified five principal types of motives. Fun prevails as the one most frequently found in CI with 44.5% (similarly, PB: 43%). The users' descriptions of the customizations undertaken include many of the characteristics of flow experience, such as being totally absorbed by a smoothly running, enjoyable activity (Csikszentmihalyi 1990).

> *"It was fun to create him [the toy figure], I enjoyed the challenge".*

It also becomes evident how several of the very active members improve their skills with each customization by permanent learning effects: Encouraged by experience, positive feedback and input from other OC members, the quality of their customizations improves and they seek new and greater challenges. Following the flow-model, the experience itself and growing abilities are the main reasons of innovators to return to the activity (Nakamura and Csikszentmihalyi 2002).

In comparison to CI, the extrinsic motive "personal need" (2.1) is considerably more distinctive in PB and is found almost as frequently as fun (2.5) (PB: 42.7% vs. 43%).

> *"There was nothing on the market :(so we decided to build our own".*

This predominantly is not such a type of solution to an urgent problem caused by personal needs as confirmed in researches on OSS OCs (David et al. 2003; Lakhani and Wolf 2005; Shah 2006). An imperative to improve a certain condition is missing here. Far more, it can be assumed that personal need is related to fun and enjoyment of the customization activity itself (this assumption cannot be covered within this study and needs to be verified in further quantitative research).

Overall, there is rare evidence for direct, material motives to innovate and develop individual Playmobil products (motive 2.4). In the few discussions on this topic it turns out that money is not the driving motive, even if the creations are sold:

> *"We sold a few of these figures for fun on eBay last year, packaged in the labeled boxes. :)"*

On eBay, several user creations are offered and sold as unique items (see Figure 2.3). These auctions are linked to and promoted in posts within the OCs.

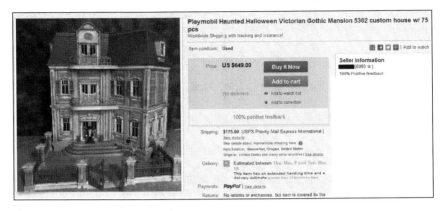

Figure 2.3   eBay auction of a Playmobil user creation (eBay 2014)

In the *group of motives to publish personal innovations in OCs* (3) I again distinguish four different types of motives.

The most frequently coded motive for CI was the desire to contribute something to the community (3.4, 60%). To create a broader understanding, I split this motive in three sub-motives. Key driver here was identification with the community, but also fun to share the creations with others. The third sub-motive reciprocity was only identified in a few cases. For PB, the motive to give something to the community was less often coded (35%). Still, visual descriptions of the creation process and explanations of building techniques are very common in both OCs and are publicly shared with any member.

> *"Since I don't feel the necessity to keep any of these techniques as a secret you may of course copy any of them if you like to".*

The motive to contribute to get feedback and to learn is the most distinctive one for PB in this last group (Section 3.1 in Table 2.4: 62%), but less often identified for CI (37%). As every published image of a customization always receives feedback from other OC members, the publication of such a picture is automatically connected to an expectation of a response, even without asking for it. Therefore, I presume the motive "to receive feedback" is in fact even more important in both OCs.

2.5.3   *Typification of User Innovation in the Selected Online Communities*

In this section, I examine the degree of innovativeness achieved within the Playmobil OCs and also show some examples for radical user innovations, thereby addressing the fourth research question. I investigate innovativeness of customizations from the perspective of Playmobil users, as seen from within

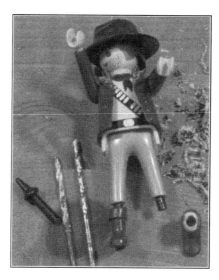

Figure 2.4 Extension of legs for a Playmobil figure by *"Kaalman"* seen in Playmoboard, 2009

Figure 2.5 M1 Abrams Tank for Playmobil by *"Oni"* (Customize it!, 2009)

my narrow field of study. Figures 2.4, 2.5, and 2.6 depict user innovations by OC members with varying degrees of novelty inside the Playmobil world. Figure 2.4 shows an example of a very simple creation. An OC member has sawed the legs of two different Playmobil figures up and created a new extra large figure. Such large figures are not available as original product.

Figure 2.6 Playmobil chess game by "MacGayver" (Customize it!, 2007)

Figure 2.5 illustrates the construction of a Playmobil tank in an extract of four pictures from a total of 45 shots that document and explain the entire creation process. A pair of tracks and the chassis of an original Playmobil digger were used as a basis. The tank was completed using several parts from other toys as well as self-manufactured components and was repainted.

The realization of a chess game with individually customized Playmobil figures is illustrated in Figure 2.6. Until now, such a chess game had never been launched by manufacturer Geobra. This creation is an example of a user innovation outside of the original play concept, a first-of-type innovation for Playmobil products (Hippel 1988).

In sum, I can identify innovations that can be categorized into four different levels:

1. Limited improvement of existing products,
2. advancement based on existing products with noticeable improvements,
3. innovative new development inside the original play concept and
4. innovative new development outside the original play concept.

Although I did not conduct a quantitative analysis of the degree of innovativeness (c.f. Garcia and Calantone 2002) of user customizations, my findings indicate that consumer OCs, even from mature markets, are not limited to producing incremental innovations, as sometimes suggested in the literature (e.g. Carr 2007). On the contrary, the OCs in this study regularly spawned new designs that can be described as radically new from the viewpoint of a Playmobil user. Further research in consumer OCs from other mature markets will be required to support this finding.

2.6   Discussion

This section aims to highlight and further explore principal findings of my study. I want to discuss in particular, first, the motives I identified as most important and compare my results to findings from previous research (2.6.1); and second, I discuss the relations between motives originating from different situational groups (2.6.2).

2.6.1   *Essential Motives in Comparison to Results from Prior Research*

2.6.1.1   *Personal Need and Fun*
In a number of prior studies on user motivation to innovate, personal need and fun have also turned out to be the two most essential motives (Hemetsberger 2003; Lakhani and Wolf 2005; Shah 2006; Füller et al. 2007; Jawecki 2008). Overall, fun is a more important motive than personal need in both Playmobil OCs. Personal need is related to a specific problem solution in less than half of all relevant posts. This result differs from the results for hobbyist communities in very young or emerging product segments and OSS communities where innovations frequently arise due to problems and dissatisfaction with existing solutions as well as personal need (e.g. Franke and Shah 2003; Luethje 2004).

2.6.1.2   *Brand Passion*
Brands can be used as relationship partners and convey a sense of identity and independence (Fournier 1998). As found in research, users in strong and passionate brand relationships often characterize brands as irreplaceable (Keller et al. 2008). I gather from my findings and from similar results in previous research (Pichler and Hemetsberger 2007; Antorini 2008) that in the presence of strong brand identification and loyalty among community members, fun and passion are particularly potent as members' motives to invest time in development. In their posts, the community members of PB and CI very often associate the brand Playmobil with the term "passion", emphasizing strong ties to the brand. In fact, these OCs are also Playmobil brand communities, even though they are not operated by the brand manufacturer. The members virtually feel part of the brand (Upshaw and Taylor 2000).

It may be amazing that adult men and women are so passionate about Playmobil that they build communities and develop innovative products around what is ultimately a toy. A potent driver of this behavior is the fascination of collecting. Collecting is a social phenomenon, and especially miniatures and toys are popular collectibles (Belk 1995). Miniatures such as model railways (Grasskamp 1983) provide a sense of physical control over objects that may create an illusion of generalized control in other domains (Belk 1995). Lego (Antorini 2008), Carrera racetrack (Smits-Bode 2002),

Maerklin model railways (Posey 2004) and Mattel's Hot Wheels cars (Zarnock 2009) provide other examples of branded miniatures and toys that are collected by adults.

2.6.1.3   *Social Motives*
A social reward can also cause high motivation to create individual customizations (Hemetsberger 2002; Butler et al. 2002). Social motives play an important role in all my three groups of motives. The comparison of voluntary participation in CI and PB suggests that the social ties and thus motivation in small expert groups is stronger than in larger groups. The larger the group, the less the members are willing to make contributions, thus tending to act as free-riders (Olson 1965). In CI, a relatively small OC, I found that most customization posts received prompt and detailed feedback from a group of experts. In contrast, PB as the much larger OC shows more sporadic and temporally outspread feedback on customizations from different member groups. It is noteworthy that there is less feedback per customization in PB than in CI, even though PB has nearly 10 times more members. I assume that social ties among a small group of OC members support collaborative activities.

2.6.2   *Interdependencies Among Motives from Different Situational Groups*
My findings suggest that there are interdependencies among the motives across the three situational groups that I will describe exemplary in the following section.

The motive to receive help and suggestions and to learn (1.1) from group (1) motives to sign up to OCs is related to group and (2) motives to develop individual products: Users explain in posts that they join the OC to learn how to customize individual products or how to improve their already existing customizations. So, after joining, these newcomers expect additional information, support and ideas that have positive effects on their developments.

Also from group 3, motives to publish personal innovations in OCs, I suggest an affection regarding the motivation of members to innovate (group 2). The members publish ideas in order to learn from feedback and to improve customizations (motive 3.1). The expected outcome of this activity can change the motivation to develop individual products: The innovator learns of new ideas or receives input for major improvements and is more motivated to start further developments (e.g. for fun, motive 2.5).

The results show also that some motives are relevant in all three groups such as "fun" that is a driver to join (1.4), to innovate (2.5) and to share the developed products (3.4).

In addition, users join OCs to present their already existing creations (self-marketing, 1.2), which connects the groups of motives (1) and (3). In collaborative OCs there is a strong relationship between joining and contributing to show knowledge and skills (Krogh et al. 2003).

I suggest that the desire to give something to the community (motive 3.4), especially the fun to share, also works as an incentive stimulating the motives to develop customizations. This exemplifies the influence of motives from group (3) on those from group (2).

2.7   Conclusion and Implications

2.7.1   *Summary*
It was the aim of this study to investigate members' motivation in innovation communities in relation to situational factors. Two OCs dedicated to Playmobil products were selected as research field. After an analysis of previous research, I pursued a netnographic approach for data collection, coded and classified relevant posts into 13 different types of motives, and validated and reviewed the results with members. My research shows that user motives in innovative OCs differ not only by qualitative characteristics, but also by activating situations related to different phases of membership. I identified and categorized motives for three different situational groups: (1) Motives to sign up to OCs, (2) motives to develop individual products, and (3) motives to share personal customizations and ideas within OCs. Moreover, my study provides insights into the innovative activities of brand communities dedicated to physical consumer products and shows how OCs in a mature consumer market develop radical user innovations for the specific segment. In the remainder of this paper I discuss the limitations of my findings and the implications for research and industry practice.

2.7.2   *Limitations in the Interpretation of the Results*
Netnography can lead to insights into members' motivation and participation behavior within an innovation community. The method has its limitations as it is primarily based on the observation of textual elements and lacks other contextual clues.

Moreover, since I cannot generalize from a single case of innovation communities, I am limited to interpretations within this case. The field of this study exemplifies a physical product in the consumer goods market. My results need to be tested in a wider range of innovative OCs for different market segments and products. In order to generalize the findings outside of my online research sample, multiple methods should be employed for triangulation (Kozinets 2002). For instance, quantitative analysis will be required to explore the relations and dependencies between various members' motives in innovation communities in detail.

Further research should deepen insights into different groups of motives, e.g. exploring additional situational factors. Another promising question to investigate is whether motivation changes when there is direct cooperation between OCs and manufacturers.

2.7.3 Implications for Research

In most empirical studies on user innovation in OCs, motives related to innovative activity are only differentiated by qualitative characteristics, particularly extrinsic versus intrinsic sources of motivation. In such a case motivation is analyzed predominantly as a general driver of participation. My study provides three major findings for research.

First, this study investigates different influencing situational factors and provides a foundation for a better understanding of the complex connections and interactions between situational groups of motives. Motivation can be grouped for different kind of activities to enable a separated analysis.

Second, I explore the impact of different phases of OC membership on motivation. To my knowledge, this study is the first to group motives for specific activities related to stages of OC membership and assigning them to different situational factors.

Third, my findings are also relevant to the research on user innovation and open source innovation as I provide an example of how tangible products are improved or newly developed with the help of a virtual community. Despite the fact that communication and collaboration in OCs related to physical products takes place online while the act of production is an offline process, members develop and publish the designs of innovative prototypes and benefit not only from innovating, but also from freely revealing their information.

2.7.4 Managerial Implications

All of the identified five major Playmobil OCs include innovators who have improved existing products significantly or developed new first-of-type Playmobil products. In addition, these innovative members published and shared their creations within the OC to receive feedback and to collaborate on projects. Some members express openly their willingness and desire to share their ideas with the manufacturer as well. In fact, they are even disappointed that their ideas mostly seem to be disregarded.

My research has yielded five major findings that can support companies in collaborating with OCs.

First, my results can help companies to understand and distinguish better the motivations of members in privately operated OCs related to their brand or products. The differentiation of situational groups of motives is important for companies wanting to stimulate and support specific user activities, e.g. by providing toolkits (Piller and Walcher 2006) or incentives such as awards (Frey 2007). A situational grouping of motives helps companies to design structures and incentives to foster (1) new registrations for OCs or (2) innovative activities of members or (3) collaboration and contribution within OCs, depending on the companies' predefined goals. Table 2.5 puts motives identified as most relevant in relation to three potential goals of a manufacturer working with an innovative OC.

Table 2.5   Implications for potential manufacturer strategies

Goal of company	Related motives
Increase number of OC members	Fun to see others' innovations Help, suggestions, learning Passion for the product and brand
Stimulate innovative user activities of OC members	Fun to innovate Personal need Community identification
Foster collaboration and contribution within the OC	Get feedback Community identification Fun to share

Second, findings point out the importance of brand passion for user motivation in OCs. Enthusiasm and passion of an existing user base can drive their involvement in OCs and foster the emergence of new ideas and prototypes. Companies can use their brand power to build up their own OCs, especially if they own established brands with a strong base of fans or extreme users and are therefore likely to gather a sufficiently large group of potential OC members. Moreover, I have shown that companies can find passionate extreme users of their products in already existing privately operated OCs related to their brands.

Third, my findings exemplify that OCs in mature consumer goods markets can be a source of new, even radical ideas, and support the development of new innovative products within a specific segment. Innovative OCs are not only a phenomenon limited to emerging markets and trendy products.

Fourth, one important insight for firms is that a non-core target group of a product, in this case adults for toys, can be a prolific source of innovative product ideas. It is even more astonishing that this unexpected user group even assumes organizational tasks within OCs and devotes considerable resources to the generation of new designs. Companies should look out for existing online user groups beside the main target group as they could inspire in-house developers, support the NPD process (Nambisan 2002) and help expand the market for their products.

At the same time, companies need to be aware that serving the so-called long tail of users with exceptional needs may not be profitable. Therefore they need to analyze the concepts of OC members thoroughly in order to distinguish between 'needs preceding a larger market', in accordance with lead user theory, and small niches that cannot be profitably targeted. For that purpose, they need to combine their classical market research instruments with new online tools and cooperate with OCs to get an accurate estimation of market potential.

And finally fifth, my case shows that some companies are still hesitant in using OCs as an innovative instrument, even though OC members are open to cooperation and freely reveal their ideas and knowledge. My research did not explore the barriers that keep companies from integrating ideas from privately operated OCs. While I therefore cannot offer insights into the optimality of this behavior, the fact that users can be an important source for new ideas and designs as well as an early indicator for changes affecting the industry (Birkinshaw et al. 2007) suggests that companies should at least carefully weigh the potential OCs hold for them. Further research needs to address the questions of the conditions for integrating OCs into NPD as well as the methods and the extent of optimal cooperation.

REFERENCES

Antorini, Y. M. (2008): *Brand community innovation: an intrinsic case study of the adult fans of LEGO community*, Copenhagen Business School, Frederiksberg.

Ardichvili, A., Page, V., and Wentling, T. (2003): "Motivation and barriers to participation in virtual knowledge-sharing communities of practise", *Journal of Knowledge Management* 7(1), pp. 64–77.

Arnould, E. J., and Wallendorf, M. (1994): „Market-oriented ethnography: interpretation building and marketing strategy formulation", *Journal of Marketing Research* 31, pp. 484–504.

Atkinson, J. W. (1958): *Motives in fantasy, action and society: a method of assessment and study*, Van Nostrand, Princeton, NY.

Atkinson, J. W. (1982): "Old and new conceptions of how expected consequences influence actions", in *Expectations and actions: expectancy value models in psychology*, N. T. Feller (ed.), pp. 17–52, Lawrence Erlbaum Associates, Hillsdale, NJ.

Belk, R. W. (1995): *Collecting in a consumer society*, Routledge, New York.

Birkinshaw, J., Bessant, J., and Delbridge, R. (2007): "Finding, forming and performing: creating networks for discontinuous innovation", *California Management Review* 49(3), pp. 67–83.

Blanchard, A., and Horan, T. (2000): "Virtual communities and social capital", in *Social dimensions of information technology: issues for the new millennium*, G. David Garson (ed.), pp. 5–20, Idea Group Publishing, Hershey.

Broillet, A., and Dubosson, M. (2008): Analyzing Web 2.0 Internet users in order to drive innovation in distribution strategy of luxury watches: a netnography analysis, Cahier de recherche, Haute Ecole de Gestion de Genève.

Brown, J. S. (1961): *The motivation of behaviour*, McGraw-Hill, New York.

Butler, B. S., Sproull, L., Kiesler, S., and Kraut, R. (2002): "Community effort in online groups: who does the work and why", in *Leadership at a distance: research in technologically supported work*, S. Weisband and L. Atwater (eds.), pp. 171–194, Lawrence Erlbaum, Hillsdale, NJ.

Buyya, R., Yeo, C. S., and Venugopal, S. (2008): "Market-oriented cloud computing: Vision, hype, and reality for delivering IT services as computing utilities", in *Proceedings of the 10th IEEE International Conference on High Performance Computing and Communications* (HPCC-08, IEEE CS Press, Los Alamitos, CA, USA), 25–27 September 2008, Dalian, China.

Carr, N. G. (2007): "The ignorance of crowds", *Business & Strategy* 47, pp. 1–5.

Cothrel, J., and Williams, R. L. (1999): "On-line communities: helping them form and grow", *Journal of Knowledge Management* 3(1), pp. 54–60.

Csikszentmihalyi, M. (1990): *Flow—the psychology of optimal experience*, Harper-Collins, New York.

Csikszentmihalyi, M. (2000): *Beyond boredom and anxiety: experiencing flow in work and play*, 25th anniversary edition, Jossey-Bass, San Francisco.

Curien, N., Fauchart, E., Laffond, G., and Moreau, F. (2006): "Online consumers communities: escaping the tragedy of the digital commons", in *Internet and digital economics*, E. Brousseau and N. Curien (eds.), pp. 201–220, Cambridge University Press, Paris.

Dahan, E., and Hauser, J. R. (2002): "The virtual customer", *Journal of Product Innovation Management* 19(5), pp. 332–353.

Dahlander, L., and Magnusson, M. G. (2005): "Relationships between Open Source software companies and communities: observations from Nordic firms", *Research Policy* 34(4), pp. 481–493.

David, P. A., Waterman, A., and Arora, S. (2003): FLOSS-US, the free/Libre/Open Source software survey for 2003, Stanford Project on the Economics of Open Source Software, September 2003.

Deci, E. L., and Ryan, R. M. (1985): *Intrinsic motivation and self-determination in human behavior*, Plenum Press, New York.

Depamphilis, D. (2002): *Mergers, acquisitions, and other restructuring activities: an integrated approach to process, tools, cases, and solutions*, 2nd ed., Elsevier Academic Press, Burlington.

Fournier, S. (1998): "Consumers and their brands: developing relationship theory in consumer research", *Journal of Consumer Research* 24(4), pp. 343–373.

Franke, N., and Shah, S. (2003): "How communities support innovative activities: an exploration of assistance and sharing among end-users", *Research Policy* 32(1), pp. 157–178.

Frey, B. (2002): "How does pay influence motivation?" in *Successful management by motivation: balancing intrinsic and extrinsic incentives*, B. Frey and M. Oster-loh (eds.), pp. 55–87, Springer, Berlin.

Frey, B. (2007): "Awards as compensation", *European Management Review* 4(1), pp. 6–14.

Fuchs, C. (2008): *Internet and society: social theory in the information age*, Routledge, New York.

Füller, J., Bartl, M., Ernst, H., and Mühlbacher, H. (2004): "Community based innovation: a method to utilize the innovative potential of online communities", in *Proceedings of the 37th HICSS Conference*, Hawaii.

Füller, J., Jawecki, G., and Mühlbacher, H. (2007): "Innovation creation by online basketball communities", *Journal of Business Research* 60(1), pp. 60–71.

Füller, J., Matzler, K., and Hoppe, M. (2008): "Brand community members as a source of innovation", *Journal of Product Innovation Management* 25(6), pp. 608–619.

Garcia, R., and Calatone, R. (2002): "A critical look at technological innovation typology and innovativeness terminology: a literature review", *Journal of Product Innovation Management* 2(19), pp. 110–132.

Gassmann, O., and Wecht, C. H. (2006): "Early customer integration into the innovation process", in *Proceedings of the 12th International Product Development Management Conference*, Kopenhagen.

Ghosh, R. A. (2005): "Understanding free software developers: findings from the FLOSS study", in *Perspectives on free and open source software*, J. Feller, B. Fitzgerald, S. Hissam, and K. R. Lakhani (eds.), pp. 23–46, MIT Press, Cambridge, MA.

Glaser, B. G., and Strauss, A. (1967): *The discovery of grounded theory*, Aldine Publishing, New York.

Glaser, B. G (1978): *Theoretical sensitivity: Advances in the methodology of grounded theory*, Sociology Press, Mail Valley, CA.

Gollwitzer, P. M., and Oettingen, G. (2001): "Psychology of motivation and action", in *International encyclopedia of the social and behavioral sciences*, vol. 15, Co 10105–10109, M. Smelser (ed.), Elsevier, Amsterdam.

Graskamp, W. (1983): "Les artistes et les autres collectionneurs" [Artists and other collectors], in *Museums by artists*, A. A. Bronson and P. Gale (eds.), pp. 129–148, Art Metropole, Toronto.

Harhoff, D., Henkel, J., and Hippel, E. von (2003): "Profiting from voluntary information spillovers: how users benefit by freely revealing their innovations", *Research Policy* 32(1), pp. 1753–1769.

Harman, K., and Koohang, A. (2005): "Discussion board: a learning object", *Interdisciplinary Journal of Knowledge and Learning Objects* 1, pp. 67–77.

Hars, A., and Ou, S. (2002): "Working for free?—motivations of participating in Open Source projects", *International Journal of Electronic Commerce* 6(3), pp. 25–39.

Heckhausen, J., and Heckhausen, H. (2008): *Motivation and action*, Cambridge University Press, Cambridge.

Hemetsberger, A. (2002): "Fostering cooperation on the Internet: social exchange processes in innovative virtual consumer communities", *Advances in Consumer Research* 29, pp. 354–356.

Hemetsberger, A. (2003): "When consumers produce on the Internet, revised version of: 'When consumers produce on the Internet: An inquiry into motivational sources of contribution to joint-innovation', with R. Pieters", in *Proceedings of the Fourth International Research Seminar on Marketing Communications and Consumer Behavior, 2001*, Ch. Derbaix et al. (eds.), pp. 274–291, La Londe.

Hennel, A. (2006): *Playmobil collector 1974–2006*, international version, 2nd ed., Fantasia Verlag, Dreieich.

Herstatt, C., and Hippel, E. von (1992): "From experience: developing new product concepts via the lead user method: a case study in a 'low tech' field", *Journal of Product Innovation Management* 9(3), pp. 213–221.

Hertel, G., Niedner, S., and Hermann, S. (2003): "Motivation of software developers in the F/OSS projects: an Internet-based survey of contributors to the Linux kernel", *Research Policy* 32(7), pp. 1159–1177.

Hiltz, S. R. (1984): *Online communities: A case study of the office of the future*, Ablex Publishing, Norwood.

Hippel, E. von (1978): "Successful industrial products from customer ideas", *Journal of Marketing* 42(1), pp. 39–49.

Hippel, E. von (1986): "Lead users: a source of novel product concepts", *Management Science* 32(7), pp. 791–805.

Hippel, E. von (1988): *The sources of innovation*, Oxford University Press, New York.

Hippel, E. von (2005): *Democratizing innovation*, MIT Press, Cambridge.

Hippel, E. von, and Katz, R. (2002): "Shifting innovation to users via toolkits", *Management Science* 48(7), pp. 821–833.

Iriberri, A., and Leroy, G. (2009): "A life cycle perspective on online community success", *ACM Computing Surveys* 41(2), pp. 1–29.

Janzik, L., and Herstatt, C. (2008): "Innovation communities: motivation and incentives for community members to contribute", in *Proceedings of the 4th IEEE International Conference on Management of Innovation & Technology*, pp. 350–355, Bangkok.

Jawecki, G. (2008): "Differences in motives to innovate, to engage in innovation activities, and to collaborate with producers—the chase of iLounge and iPod hacks", 15th International Product Development Management Conference, Hamburg.

Jeppesen, L. B., and Frederiksen, L. (2006): "Why do users contribute to firm-hosted user communities? the case of computer-controlled music instruments", *Organization Science* 17(1), pp. 45–63.

Jeppesen, L. B., and Molin, M. J. (2003): "Consumers as co-developers: learning and innovation outside the firm", *Technology Analysis & Strategic Management* 15(3), pp. 363–384.

Jones, Q., and Rafaeli, S. (2000): "Time to split, virtually: 'discourse architecture' and 'community building' create vibrant virtual publics", *Electronic Markets* 10(4), pp. 214–223.

Keller, K. L., Apéria, T., and Georgson, M. (2008): *Strategic brand management: a European perspective*, Pearson, Harlow.

Kim, A. J. (2000): *Community building on the Web: secret strategies for successful online communities*, Addison-Wesley Longman, Berkeley.

Kim, W., Jeong, O. R., and Lee, S. W. (2010): "On social Web", *Information Systems* 26(2), pp. 215–236.

Klein, D., and Krech, G. S. (1951): "The problem of personality and its theory", *Journal of Personality* 20, pp. 2–23.

Kollock, P., and Smith, M. (1996): "Managing the virtual commons: cooperation and conflict in computer communities", in *Computer-mediated communication: linguistic, social, and cross-cultural perspectives*, S. Herring (ed.), pp. 109–128, Amsterdam, John Benjamins.

Kozinets, R. V. (1997): "I want to believe: a netnography of the X-Philes subculture of consumption", *Advances in Consumer Research* 24(1), pp. 470–475.

Kozinets, R. V. (1998): "On netnography: initial reflections on consumer research investigations of cyberculture", *Advances in Consumer Research* 25(1), pp. 366–371.

Kozinets, R. V. (1999): "E-tribalized marketing?: the strategic implications of virtual communities of consumption", *European Management Journal* 17(3), pp. 252–264.

Kozinets, R. V. (2002): "The field behind the screen: using netnography for marketing research in online communities", *JMR, Journal of Marketing Research* 39(1), pp. 61–72.

Kozinets, R. V. (2006): "Netnography 2.0", in *Handbook of qualitative research in marketing*, R. W. Belk (ed.), pp. 129–142, Edward Elgar Publishing, Cheltenham.

Krogh, G. von, Spaeth, S., and Lakhani, K. R. (2003): "Community, joining, and specialization in Open Source software innovation: a case study", *Research Policy* 32(7), pp. 1217–1241.

Lakhani, K. C., and Hippel, E. von (2003): "How open source software works: 'free' user-to-user assistance", *Research Policy* 32(9), pp. 923–943.

Lakhani, K. C., and Wolf, R. G. (2005): "Why hackers do what they do: understanding motivation and effort in free/Open Source software projects", in Perspectives on free and open source software, J. Feller, B. Fitzgerald, S. Hissam, and K. R. Lakhani (eds.), pp. 3–21, MIT Press, Cambridge, MA.

Langer, R., and Beckmann, S. C. (2005): "Sensitive research topics: netnography revisited", *Qualitative Market Research—An International Journal* 8(2), pp. 189–203.

Lin, H. F. (2007): "Effects of extrinsic and intrinsic motivation on employee knowledge sharing intentions", *Journal of Information Science* 33(2), pp. 135–149.

Luethje, C. (2000): *Kundenorientierung im Innovationsprozess: Eine Untersuchung der Kunden-Hersteller-Interaktion in Konsumgütermärkten*, Gabler, Wiesbaden.

Luethje, C. (2004): "Characteristics of innovating users in a consumer goods field: an empirical study of sport-related product consumers", *Technovation* 24(9), pp. 683–695.

Luethje, C., Herstatt, C., and Hippel, E. von (2005): "The dominant role of 'local' information: the case of mountain biking", *Research Policy* 34(6), pp. 951–965.

Malone, T. W., and Lepper, M. R. (1987): "Making learning fun: a taxonomy of intrinsic motivations for learning", in Aptitude, learning and instruction:

III. Cognitive and affective process analyses, R.E. Snow and M.J. Farr (eds.), pp. 223–253, Lawrence Erlbaum, Hillsdale, NJ.

Markus, M.L., Manville, B., and Agnes, C. (2000): "What makes a virtual organization work?" *MIT Sloan Management Review* 42(1), pp. 13–26.

Mathwick, C., Wiertz, C., and Ruyter, K. de (2008): "Social capital production in a virtual P3 community", *Journal of Consumer Research* 34(6), pp. 832–849.

McClelland, D.C., Koestner, R., and Weinberg, J. (1989): "How do self-attributed and implicit motives differ?" *Psychological Review* 96(4), pp. 690–702.

Morrison, P. D., Roberts, J.H., and Hippel, E. von (2000): "Determinants of user innovation and innovation sharing in a local market", *Management Science* 46(12), pp. 1513–1527.

Muniz, A.M., Jr., and O'Guinn, T.C. (2001): "Brand community", *Journal of Consumer Research* 27(4), pp. 412–432.

Nakamura, J., and Csikszentmihalyi, M. (2002): "The concept of flow", in Handbook of positive psychology, C.R. Snyder and S.J. Lopez (eds.), pp. 89–107. Oxford University Press, Oxford.

Nambisan, S. (2002): "Designing virtual customer environments for new product development: toward a theory", *Academy of Management Review* 27(3), pp. 392–413.

Nonnecke, B., and Preece, J. (2000): "Lurker demographics: counting the silent", in *Proceedings of CHI 2000, Conference on Human Factors in Computing Systems*, pp. 73–80, DenHaag.

Nonnecke, B., Preece, J., and Andrews, D. (2004): "What lurkers and posters think of each other", in *System Sciences, 2004*, Proceedings of the 37th Annual Hawaii International Conference.

Nov, O. (2007): "What motivates Wikipedians", *Communications of the ACM* 50(11), pp. 60–64.

Nov, O., Naaman, M., and Ye, C. (2010): "Analysis of participation in an online photo sharing community: a multi-dimension perspective", *Journal of the American Society for Information Science and Technology* 63(3), pp. 555–566.

Olson, M.L., Jr. (1965): *The logic of collective action: public goods and the theory of groups*, Harvard University Press, Cambridge.

Oreg, S., and Nov, O. (2008): "Exploring motivations for contributing to open source initiatives: the roles of contribution context and personal values", *Computers in Human Behavior* 24(5), pp. 2055–2073.

O'Reilly, T. (2007): "What is Web 2.0 design patterns and business models for the next generation of software", *Communication & Strategies* 65, pp. 17–37.

Pichler, E.A., and Hemetsberger, A. (2007): "'Hopelessly devoted to you': toward an extended conceptualization of consumer devotion", *Advances in Consumer Research* 34, pp. 194–199.

Piller, F.T., and Walcher, D. (2006): "Toolkits for idea competitions: a novel method to integrate users in new product development", *R&D Management* 36(3), pp. 307–318.

Pintrich, P.R., and Schunk, D.H. (2007): *Motivation in education: theory, research and applications*, 3rd ed., Prentice Hall, Englewood Cliffs, NJ.

Porter, J. (2008): *Designing for the social Web*, New Riders, Berkeley, CA.

Posey, S. (2004): *Playing with trains: a passion beyond scale*, Random House, New York.

Preece, J. (2000): *Online communities: designing usability, supporting sociability*, Wiley, Chichester.

Reeve, J. (2005): *Understanding motivation and emotion*, 4th ed., Wiley, New Jersey.

Ryan, R.M., and Deci, E.L. (2000): "Intrinsic and extrinsic motivations: classic definitions and new directions", *Contemporary Educational Psychology* 25(1), 54–67.

Sandlin, J. A. (2007): "Netnography as a consumer education research tool", *International Journal of Consumer Studies* 31(3), pp. 288–294.

Sarner, A. (2008): "How to determine levels of engagement for generation virtual", in Gartner Industry Research (ID number: G00158087), 2 June.

Schroer, J., and Hertel, G. (2009): "Voluntary engagement in an open Web-based encyclopedia: Wikipedians, and why they do it", *Media Psychology* 12(1), pp. 96–120.

Shah, S. (2005): "Open beyond software", in *Open sources 2.0: the continuing evolution*, D. Cooper, C. DiBona, and M. Stone (eds.), pp. 339–360. O'Reilly Media, Sebastopol.

Shah, S. (2006): "Motivation, governance, and the viability of hybrid forms in Open Source software development", *Management Science* 52(7), pp. 1000–1014.

Shani, A. B., Sena, J. A., and Olin, T. (2003): "Knowledge management and new product development: a study of two companies", *European Journal of Innovation Management* 6(3), pp. 137–149.

Shumar, W., and Renninger, K. A. (2002): "Introduction on conceptualizing community", in *Building virtual communities*, K. A. Renninger and W. Shumar (eds.), pp. 1–17, Cambridge University Press, Cambridge.

Smits-Bode, H. (2002): *Carrera 160–132 Universal—124—Jet*. MekCar, Bissendorf.

Spann, M., Ernst, H., Skiera, B., and Soll, J. H. (2009): "Identification of lead users for consumer products via virtual stock markets", *Journal of Product Innovation Management* 26(3), pp. 322–335.

Thompson, C. J. (1997): "Interpreting consumers: a hermeneutical framework for deriving marketing insights from the texts of consumers' consumption stories", *Journal of Marketing Research* 34, pp. 438–455.

Thompson, C. J., and Arsel, Z. (2004): "The Starbucks brandscape and consumers' (anticorporate) experience of globalization", *Journal of Consumers Research* 31(3), pp. 631–642.

Tietz, R., and Herstatt, C. (2007): "How to build a virtual community—a process model", in Proceedings of European Academy of Management Conference (EURAM 2007), Paris.

Upshaw, L. B., and Tailor, E. L. (2000): *The masterbrand mandate—the management strategy that unifies companies and multiplies value*, Wiley, New York.

Urban, G. L., and Hippel, E. von (1988): "Lead user analyses for the development of new industrial products", *Management Science* 34(5), pp. 569–582.

Valck, K. de (2005): *Virtual communities of consumption: networks of consumer knowledge and companionship*, ERIM Electronic Series Portal, Rotterdam.

Vossen, G., and Hagemann, S. (2007): *Unleashing Web 2.0—from concepts to creativity*, Academic Press, Burlington.

Vroom, V. H. (1964): *Work and motivation*, Wiley, New York.

Walcher, D. (2007): *Der Ideenwettbewerb als Methode der aktive Kundenintegration, Theorie, empirische Analyse und Implikationen für den Innovationsprozess*, DUV, Wiesbaden.

Wang, Y., and Fesenmeier, D. R. (2003): "Understanding the motivation of contribution in online communities: an empirical investigation of an online travel community", *Electronic Markets* 13(1), pp. 33–45.

Wasko, M. M., and Faraj, S. (2000): "'It is what one does': why people participate and help others in electronic communities of practice", *Journal of Strategic Information Systems* 9(2–3), pp. 155–173.

Wasko, M. M., and Faraj, S. (2005): "Why should I share? examining social capital and knowledge contribution in electronic networks of practice", *MIS Quarterly* 29(1), pp. 35–57.

Wenger, E. (1998): "Communities of practice—learning as a social system", *Systems Thinker* 9(5), pp. 3–7.

Wirtz, B.W., Schilke, O., and Ullrich, S. (2010): "Strategic development of business models: implications of the Web 2.0 for creating value on the Internet", *Long Range Planning* 32(2–3), pp. 172–194.

Zarnock, M. (2009): *Hot Wheels: Warman's companion*, Krause, Cincinnati.

3 Diversity of Participants in Open Source Projects

Comparing Individual Demographics and Participation Rationales in Software, Content, Fun, and Business Communities

Daniel Ehls

Open source innovation gained its momentum with software development but nowadays spread well beyond this project type and has attracted numerous participants. So far, literature ignores widely these further project examples and assumes that project types are equal in terms of their participants. We challenge this assumption and postulate member diversity between project types. We stretch beyond repeatedly analyzed cases of iconic software initiatives by including content communities as well as we introduce fun and business project types to have a appropriate resemblance of digital production communities. Our analysis reveals significant differences within and between projects in both, participants' demographic and contribution rationales. Thus the contributions of this study are multifold and target (1) phenomenon enrichment, e.g. a detailed comparison of the open source landscape with as yet unconsidered community types, (2) research validation, e.g. replication of earlier studies aligned to latest developments and with yet lacking samples, and (3) theoretical advancement as we respond to the call to contextualize research and spark off the discussion of diversity in open source innovation.

Keywords: diversity, contextualization, open source

3 DIVERSITY OF PARTICIPANTS IN OPEN SOURCE PROJECTS

3.1 Introduction

Open source innovation started with software development some years ago. Meanwhile, the open source approach has well spread beyond software development and gained traction, e.g. in content (e.g. Wikipedia or OpenStreetMap), and hardware creation (e.g. RepRap or OSCar). These projects follow the same open source approach: Innovative goods are produced by volunteers, who develop "to solve their own as well as shared technical problems, and freely reveal their innovations without appropriating private returns from selling" (Hippel and Krogh 2003, p. 209). 'Open source' describes a phenomenon where volunteers create a product, make it publicly available and relinquish most of their IPR, but do not receive a direct compensation (Hars and Ou 2001).

Yet, the phenomenon of open source is "spectacularly stratified" (Healy and Schussman 2003) and special care in comparative analysis and research objective selection is required (Boudreau 2010; Eisenmann et al. 2008). Most studies regard single case projects as representative for the entire phenomenon. Thereby, they most often concentrate on iconic and very successful initiatives like Linux, Apache or Wikipedia. However, it is unclear whether their contributor base is comparable. Raymond proposed that "given enough eyeballs, all bugs are shallow" (Raymond 1999, p. 32), but who are these eyeballs also in non-iconic projects? Finally, the open source landscape provides a rich ground for different project types. Besides software and content projects, an additional informative differentiation is whether the communities' common objective is to create an entertaining product or a business service. Recently, research identified a shift from fun and ideology driven participants to communities as business opportunity and calls for a reinterpretation of earlier findings (Rolandsson et al. 2011; Fitzgerald 2006; West 2003; Bonaccorsi and Rossi 2003). However, the influence whether the community context is fun or professional services orientated is lacking in this conversation.

We target these questions and analyzes member diversity contingent on the community context. In particular, we pursue to describe member heterogeneity in terms of participation rationales, demography and participation activity. The contributions of this study target a broader description of the phenomenon, replicate earlier findings and analyze contextual influences. We enlarge the open collaborative community landscape with as yet unconsidered groups and the discovering of similarities and differences between the project types. We point to a potential link of participants' diversity to project types and provide detailed insights into project heterogeneity by studying 12 different communities beyond one-dimensional samples and iconic projects.

3.2 Research Background

3.2.1 Open Source Project Types

The phenomenon of open source commenced with software, but soon the principles of open source software that "users can inspect the source code, modify it, and redistribute modified or unmodified versions for others to use" (Krogh et al. 2012) are adapted for digital content goods; e.g. open encyclopedias (Wikipedia) or audiobook creation (LibriVox). These intangible open source products are classified into 'open content' (Wiley 1998; Pfaffenberger 2001) and 'software'. Software products are understood as executable, meaning procedural, program files, and content as any not executable file (Raymond 2002; Cedergren 2003; Rosenzweig 2006; Nov and Kuk 2008). Thus, "whereas the product in open source software initiatives is software, open source content projects involve the creation of a body of knowledge" (Oreg and Nov 2008, p. 2056). Open content represents "digital open source works other than software, including text, image, sound, video, and combinations of them" (Clarke 2004, section 'Open Content').

3.2.2   *Individual Participants' Demography*

"I don't know who these crazy people are who want to write, read and even revise all that code without being paid anything for it at all", writes Glass (1999, p. 104). In 1999, open source was predominantly associated with software development. Open source community members were described as "hackers", including a positive connotation and badge of honor (Raymond 1999; Lakhani and Wolf 2005), participants in a "gift" culture (Bergquist and Ljungberg 2001), or as "geeks" (Pavlicek 2000). Open source conventions were a "meeting place between the informality of geek culture and the buttoned-down business world" (Deckmyn 2002).

Several studies have enriched the picture of a technically skilled contributor working with peers and creating a subculture. Three principal types of contributors have been identified: individual contributors, non-profit organizations and for-profit firms.

Individual contributors are participants without affiliations, for example, students, academics and hobbyists. In software communities, students account for 14% and hobbyists for 25% (Hars and Ou 2001). According to Lakhani and Wolf (2005), students represent 20% and academic researchers 7% of the population. In content communities, Schroer and Hertel (2009) calculated a student share of 32%.

Professional participants are a further participant type (Bonaccorsi et al. 2006; Henkel 2006; Rolandsson et al. 2011). The private firm Netscape offered its browser Mozilla under an open source license, but continued to support the project. Linux Kernel 3.2 is written by 1,316 developers, including 226 known companies. The top 10 firms participating in the Linux Kernel project account for over 60% of the total contributions; paid developers even account for 75% of all kernel developments (Linux Foundation 2012). Hars and Ou (2001) disclose that 16% of their study respondents are paid directly for their contribution and account for 38% of total contribution efforts. Lakhani and Wolf (2005) report that 53% of survey respondents contribute during paid working time, whereby 70% of those 53% are supported by their supervisors. Hence, approximately 37% of total respondents indicate tolerated firm contributions. With respect to content, the literature is silent for firm participation. Yet, some indications of firm support are present. The non-profit Wikipedia foundation is the organizational sponsor of Wikipedia. The Open Directory Project is owned by Netscape, and the Freebase project is owned by Google. These "men on the inside" examples

(Dahlander and Wallin 2006; Lee, chapter 10, this volume) reveal the strategic influence of firms in open source software communities including its significant amount of contribution and sponsorship.

In terms of demographic diversity, open source participants vary in a wide range of aspects including age, gender, and additional educational background. The age of software contributors ranges from 14 to 73 years (Ghosh et al. 2002), with a mean age of 27 (Ghosh et al. 2002) to 32 years (Oreg and Nov 2008). Gender diversity is strongly biased toward male participation as female programmers are rare (Rolandsson et al. 2011). The share of male participation ranges from 91% (Hertel et al. 2003) to 98% (Oreg and Nov 2008). The age of open source content participants varies from 16 to 70 years, with a population mean age of 33 years (Schroer and Hertel 2009). Even more extremely distributed are the worldwide Wikipedia study findings. They reveal an age range from 10 to 85 years, with a mean age of 25 years (Glott et al. 2010). Male participants in open content represent 75% (Glott et al. 2010) up to 91% of participants (Oreg and Nov 2008).

Regarding educational background, participants are often knowledgeable people (Bryant et al. 2005) with 26 months experience in contributing to wikis in general, reading 3.4 different wikis daily, and contributing to 1.5 wikis (Majchrzak et al. 2006). The distribution of Wikipedia contributors in terms of education is 33% with secondary education, 26% undergraduates, and 23% masters and doctors (of Philosophy) (Glott et al. 2010). In software samples, 51% of contributors had university-level training, 9% had on-the-job training, and 40% were self-taught. Most participants had an undergraduate degree, followed by people with a master's degree (Hars and Ou 2001; Ghosh et al. 2002).

3.2.3 Individual Participants' Participation Rationales

Lerner and Tirole (2002, p. 198) are among the first to ask the question: "Why should thousands of top-notch programmers contribute freely to the provision of a public good?" Their question has triggered a plethora of participation behavior research and encourages studies to clarify online field support or mundane tasks (Lakhani and Hippel 2003), progression of users to leaders (Dahlander and O'Mahony 2011), and organizational involvement (Henkel 2006) in terms of why volunteers participate.

Lerner and Tirole (2002) reveal in their qualitative study that benefits for the contributors are essential for participation. Contributors are motivated by opportunity to solve information technology problems and gain reputational benefits. Many contributors later become employees of commercial partnering organizations. Hars and Ou (2001) conducted one of the first quantitative studies explaining participation in open source projects. Their survey reveals intrinsic motivation and altruism, as well as the role of external rewards, such as expected future returns and personal needs. Lakhani and Hippel (2003) extended the scope of participation from direct code contribution to user-to-user assistance. Their survey of field support within the Apache community found reciprocity, helpfulness, reputation, career prospects and intrinsic motives as reasons. They indicate that participation could be due to it being part of the job. Following the above seminal publications, further studies support the reported motives for contribution. These publications apply further methods, for example, netnography (Janzik et al., chapter 1, this volume), or target different participation stages, for instance, enduring participation (Wu et al. 2007). Table 3.1 provides an overview of key participation rationales ranging from getting paid, reputation, learning, and own need, to ideology and altruism.[1]

Participation behavior research in open content is still nascent. Research is rare or the studies concentrate on one research object, Wikipedia.[2]

One of the first studies of open content user motivation was conducted by Cedergren in 2003. He analyzes the driving forces behind three open content projects by interviewing representatives of Wikipedia, Prelinger's movies and Open Directory Project. In his qualitative research, "learning new stuff", "stimulating task to work together", "ego gratification" (feedback and acknowledgment), intrinsic motivation, altruism (even if used commercially), possibilities for publicity, and indirect revenues are the main influence factors. He concludes that the most important driving forces behind open content contribution are benefits for the end user. A quantitative study about open content participation was conducted by Glott et al. in 2010. Their Wikipedia survey includes 176,192 cases, containing replies from 22 different language versions of Wikipedia, and spanning 57 home countries of respondents. They reveal that participation motivations include professional reasons (earn money, progress career), intrinsic motives (fun, ideology), fixing and improving articles, learning, and reputation (also in view of career). They further note that two motivations stand out: the wish to share knowledge and the desire to fix errors. Professional reasons motivate only "a very small share of respondents". Table 3.2 provides an overview of motivations to contribute to open content.

3.2.4   *Participation Diversity*

"Why does a user participate in open collaborative innovation?" was one of the first questions raised in open source research. Research has applied a wide variety of theoretical frameworks including Self-determination theory (SDT) (Deci and Ryan 1985), a joint framework from the IS field (Feller and Fitzgerald 2000), or combined approaches of a social movement teamwork model (Hertel et al. 2003). However, the applied frameworks are "closely related" (Krogh et al. 2012) or "compatible" (Schroer and Hertel 2009). Actually identified motivations do not differ much. Building on this consistency of identified participation rationales in open source software and content, users in both project types have similar motives for contribution—at least from a qualitative point of view. Detailed research about motivations to contribute reveals two remarkable aspects: A shift in participation rationales, and project type diversity.

Table 3.1 Overview participation rationales in open source software communities

Criterion	Altruism	Ideology	Fun	Own need	Reciprocity	Learning	Reputation	Career advancement	Commercial reasons	Community feeling
Hars and Ou (2001)	x		x	x		x	x		x	x
Lakhani and Hippel (2003)		x	x		x		x	x	x	
McLure et al. (2005)	x				x		x			x
Shah (2006)			x	x	x			x		
Roberts et al. (2006)			x	x			x	x		
Jeppesen and Frederiksen (2006)					x		x	x	x	
Wu et al. (2007)			x	x	x	x				

Table 3.2 Overview participation rationales in open content communities

Criterion	Altruism	Ideology	Fun	Own need	Fix Error	Share knowledge	Learning	Reputation	Career advancement	Commercial reasons	Community feeling
Cedergren (2003)	x		x				x	x			x
Glott et al. (2010)	x	x	x	x	x	x	x	x	x	x	x
Bryant et al. (2005)	x	x			x	x		x			x
Majchrzak et al. (2006)	x			x		x		x			
CERI (2007)	x					x		x		x	x
Müller-Seitz and Reger (2010)	x		x				x	x	x		x
Oreg and Nov (2008)	x						x	x			
Schroer and Hertel (2009)	x		x			x	x				x

First, a shift in motivations for participation is discovered. A transformation of the member base is observed from participants who are less profit-driven to seekers of stronger commercial benefits, as well as from open source being an ideological movement to it being a serious business opportunity (Rolandsson et al. 2011; Fitzgerald 2006; West 2003; Bonaccorsi and Rossi 2003). The reasons for this transformation are explained by increased firm participation, changing user bases, and the implementation of commercial licenses. Considering these aspects of user motivation transformation, the identified motivations need to be reinterpreted in a commercial context (Rolandsson et al. 2011).

Second, there are differences between software and content communities. Software contributions provide strong personal benefits in terms of own use value. Participants code with a view to using the software afterwards for themselves, to gain a reputation, or to get paid. In contrast, these motivations are ranked much lower in content communities (Schroer and Hertel 2009). Oreg and Nov (2008) report that self-development and reputation building are more strongly present in software than content communities. Majchrzak et al. (2006) discovered that in organizational wikis, reputation enhancement is low. In contrast, intrinsic motivations are more important in content communities (Schroer and Hertel 2009; Oreg and Nov 2008). Finally, by comparing two similar large-scale surveys by the United Nations University (Ghosh et al. 2002; Glott et al. 2010), their findings reveal striking differences in the dimensions 'like form of cooperation', 'like sharing knowledge', 'learn new skills', 'fix an error', 'proprietary solution does not solve problem', 'demonstrate skills', and 'friends doing it'. Based on above reasoning, we postulate that user motivation is different contingent on the project type.

H1: Software and content communities attract different contributors in terms of their motivation for participation.

Moreover, different knowledge sets and computer literacy skills are frequently stated barriers to participation. To contribute to software communities, a detailed knowledge of programming and being able to 'speak' the coding language is necessary. Conversely, in content communities, contributors use an easy-to-use and friendly user interface. For example, wiki technology requires little skill, lowering the technical participation barriers and enabling users to contribute immediately upon arrival (Okoli and Oh 2007; Oreg and Nov 2008). Investigations into the background and motivations of users further support this argument. The majority of open source contributors are skilled programmers with a professional background in coding (Henkel 2006; Lakhani and Wolf 2005) and 83% work within the IT sector (Ghosh et al. 2002). In contrast, open content contributors are mostly knowledgeable amateurs (Oreg and Nov 2008; Rettberg 2005; Bryant et al. 2005) who enjoy contributing to the community (Benkler 2002). We thus formulate:

H2: *Software and content communities attract different contributors in terms of demographics.*

Demographics are examined in terms of sex, age, work experience, degree of education and expertise.

3.3   Research Approach

3.3.1   Participation Diversity
Due to the distinctive traits of open source projects, it is challenging to transfer findings from proprietary circumstances into the open source world (Fang and Neufeld 2009). Moreover, as open regimes differ widely in their contextual setting, care in comparative analysis is required (Boudreau 2010). In order to achieve a high sampling variance, particularly on community heterogeneity, and also to avoid sampling bias, we echo the call for the "highly stratified nature" of open source and different project ecologies. We include software and content communities, but also business and fun communities for greater sample variance, avoiding local research bias, and advancing theory with a broader case base. Iconic projects[3] are excluded to avoid skewed sampling and multi-sampling on known cases.[4] Second, we only include well-established and active communities. This criterion is rooted in the criticism of random database sampling as, for instance, 80% of projects at SourceForge.net are abandoned (Comino et al. 2007). Data was collected from May 2011 to end of July 2011, and a second wave[5] from November 2011 to December 2011. Upfront permission to contact members was given by community administrators. To avoid self-selection bias in online surveys (Wright 2005; Stanton 2006,) we invited randomly sampled members out of each community per private message. However, each member must have been active in the last 90 days before data collection in order to avoid 'dead' users. The collected and cleaned replies resulted in a pooled total sample of 184 participants with a response rate of 19.77%.[6] Table 3.3 shows respondents per community and the 12 considered communities.

The collected sample is furthermore compared against earlier studies (Hertel et al. 2003; Oreg and Nov 2008; Glott et al. 2010) in terms of sex, age, and work background and similar data spans found.

3.3.2   Psychometric Construct Evaluation
The selection of participation rationales is based on the top five stated rationales (Crowston et al. 2012), and motivations repeatedly found insignificant for contribution effort[7] are discarded. In order to enable comparison to earlier research and to endorse external validity, we employ multi-item constructs from anchored open source literature targeting participation rationales (Roberts et al. 2006; Wu et al. 2007; Hars and Ou 2001;Wasko and Faraj 2005; Lakhani and

Table 3.3 Overview of sampled community members

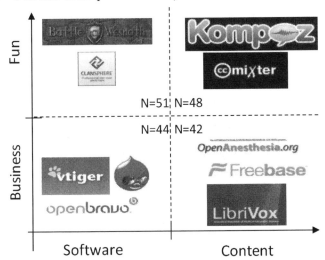

Hippel 2003). In order to determine the level of knowledge of participants, we apply the novice-to-expert scale (Dreyfus et al. 1987; Benner 1984).

As to ensure construct reliability and validity, the utilized multi-item constructs of participation rationales are scrutinized in terms of internal consistency and construct structure. Internal consistency is tested with coefficient alpha (Cronbach) and item-to-total correlation. Both analyses recommend dropping 'one' item due to low measures.[8] The corrected latent constructs now internally correlate well above the recommendation of 0.6 (Bearden et al. 2011; Robinson et al. 1991) for a smaller number of item constructs, as well as above the general recommendation of 0.7 (Churchill Jr 1979; Nunnally 1978), and support reliability and scale unidimensionality. Additionally, mean inter-item correlation scores of above 0.4 for narrow constructs (Clark and Watson 1995), and, besides use, above the general recommendation of 0.5 (Bearden et al. 1989) provide a second criterion for scale homogeneity, as seen in Table 3.4.

In order to validate the construct structure, we conduct a confirmative factor analysis using a varimax rotation. All five constructs suggest validity convergence for the conceptual components and quintuple dimensionality due to directed loadings of items, as shown in Table 3.5.[9]

For further statistical analysis, the average of each construct is calculated and corresponding variables created (AFN=Fun, AON=Own Need, AL=Learning, AR=Reputation, APY=Payment). In addition to statistical construct assessment, overall survey evaluation by respondents by means of an open question provided positive support statements like 'survey was clear, concise and easy to follow', 'looks good to me :)' and 'good work!'

Table 3.4   Scores of internal consistency checks of psychometric constructs

Construct	Cronbach's alpha	Inter-item correlation	Number of Items
Fun	0.798	0.576	3
Use	0.648	0.480	2
Learning	0.839	0.723	2
Reputation	0.759	0.622	2
Payment	0.697	0.576	2

Table 3.5   Scores of construct structure checks of psychometric constructs

	Conceptual Component 1	Conceptual Component 2	Conceptual Component 3	Conceptual Component 4	Conceptual Component 5
Use2					0.833
Use3		0.315			0.760
Fun1	0.655	0.301	0.321		
Fun2	0.838				
Fun3	0.834				
Learn1		0.888			
Learn2		0.808	0.359		
Reput1			0.875		
Reput2			0.799		
Pjob				0.823	
Pmny				0.907	

Note: Loadings below 0.3 are hidden.

3.4   Inferential Statistic Results

3.4.1   *Determining of Test Approach*

In order to determine an appropriate test approach we use Kolmogorov-Smirnov testing and evaluation of skewness and kurtosis. The former test reveals asymptotically significant results for all variables. The latter shows off-limits of skewness or kurtosis[10] for the measures sex (sex), tenure in community (tenure), hours moderating (Hmod), fun participation rationale (AFN), learning participation rationale (AL), and payment participation rationale (APY). Following both tests, we reject the assumption of a normal distribution. We proceed for sample comparison and in line with further open source research (e.g. McLure Wasko and Faraj 2005; Mockus et al. 2002) with non-parametric statistics, specifically, Mann-Whitney-U tests.

3.4.1 Demographic Differences

Mann-Whitney-U tests[11] are conducted for all variables with a focus on the heterogeneity between software and content and the heterogeneity between fun and business communities. The results (compare Table 3.6) support a systematic mean difference between software and content projects on a two-tailed 95% confidence level for the age of participants (Age), work situation (Work), highest degree (Degree). Also test results for the population difference between fun and business communities provide significant insights. A systematic difference between the mean values is significantly supported (p value ≤ 0.005) at the 95% confident level for the age of participants (Age), work situation (Work), highest degree (Degree) and hours moderating (Hmod).

3.4.2 Participation Rationales Differences

Conducting Mann-Whitney-U tests for mean comparison between community types reveals significant differences as shown in Table 3.7. Significant difference between software and content communities exists only in regards to fun motivation (AFN).[12] In contrast, between fun and business communities exist significant differences in regards to own need (AON), reputation (AR) and payment (APY).

We furthermore compare participation motives within each project type to determine relative differences. Table 3.8 shows the results: the upper-left value represents software communities, the upper right content, lower right business, and the lower left fun communities differences for a given participation motive crossing each other.

3.4.3 Hypotheses Evaluation

The research hypotheses 1 and 2 are answered with the above evaluations. Heterogeneity is revealed in socio-demographic and community participation, aspects at a 95% confidence level.[13] Based on these statistics, hypothesis 1,

Table 3.6 Test results of demographic group differences

	Criterion	Software Content Differentiation			Fun Business Differentiation		
	Construct	Mean Rank Software	Mean Rank Content	Sign. (*p* value)	Mean Rank Fun	Mean Rank Business	Sign. (*p* value)
Demographics	Sex	93.10	82.35	ns (0.962)	87.39	88.67	ns (0.772)
	Age	62.23	120.63	*** (0.003)	80.10	104.22	*** (0.002)
	Work	75.02	99.99	*** (<.001)	75.40	98.73	*** (<.001)
	Degree	73.06	98.20	*** (<.001)	68.14	107.29	*** (<.001)
	Expertise	86.66	93.53	ns (0.358)	84.97	95.68	ns (0.153)

Table 3.7   Test results of participation motives group differences

	Criterion	Software Content Differentiation			Fun Business Differentiation		
	Construct	Mean Rank Software	Mean Rank Content	Sign. (*p* value)	Mean Rank Fun 1	Mean Rank Business	Sign. (*p* value)
Demographics	Sex	93.10	82.35	ns (0.962)	87.39	88.67	ns (0.772)
	Age	62.23	120.63	*** (0.003)	80.10	104.22	*** (0.002)
	Work	75.02	99.99	*** (<.001)	75.40	98.73	*** (<.001)
	Degree	73.06	98.20	*** (<.001)	68.14	107.29	*** (<.001)
	Expertise	86.66	93.53	ns (0.358)	84.97	95.68	ns (0.153)
Community Participation	Fun	84.36	101.00	** (0.027)	97.59	86.70	ns (0.149)
	Own Need	90.31	82.01	ns (0.270)	70.93	103.59	*** (<.001)
	Learning	86.69	97.61	ns (0.142)	90.29	93.92	ns (0.626)
	Reputation	88.98	94.19	ns (0.499)	83.01	101.4	** (0.017)
	Payment	97.38	87.29	ns (0.158)	70.19	118.49	*** (<.001)
	H Reading	97.46	83.87	ns (0.074)	94.15	87.28	ns (0.368)
	H Writing	80.08	93.71	ns (0.061)	88.90	83.68	ns (0.473)
	H Moderating	80.48	79.42	ns (0.841)	73.55	87.99	*** (0.006)
	Tenure	89.07	93.04	ns (0.601)	96.34	84.83	ns (0.130)

Table 3.8   Inferential statistics of participation rationales differentiation tests

		AFN		AON		AL		AR		APY	
AFN	OSS/OSC	**	***	***	***	*	***	***	***	***	
	OSF/OSB	ns	***	**	***	ns	***	***	***	***	
AON	***	***	OSS/OSC	ns	***	***	*	ns	***	***	
	***	***	OSF/OSB	***	***	*	ns	***	***	***	
AL	***	**	**	***	OSS/OSC	ns	***	***	***	***	
	***	ns	***	ns	OSF/OSB	ns	***	***	***	***	
AR	***	***	**	ns	***	***	OSS/OSC	ns	***	***	
	***	***	ns	**	***	**	OSF/OSB	**	***	***	
APY	***	***	***	***	***	***	***	***	OSS/OSC	ns	
	***	***	***	***	***	***	***	***	OSF/OSB	***	

'Software and content communities attract different contributors in terms of their motivation for participation', is (partly) supported. Comparing software and content communities, significant evidence is found supporting motivation heterogeneity in terms of fun, but not for own need, learning, reputation or payment. Hypotheses 2, 'Software and content communities attract different contributors in terms of demographics', is supported by significant evidence for heterogeneity in terms of age, work and degree.

3.5   Discussion

3.5.1   *Implications*

Up to now, most open source studies concentrate on iconic open source software projects. Research finds a high share of paid contributors in these projects—in contrast, our study shows only minor participation of paid members. Thus, there are strong differences between projects and it is questionable whether these iconic projects are representative of the entire open source domain, or if they represent the tip of the iceberg. Open content research concentrates on Wikipedia. We stretch beyond this classical example and sample several other content projects.

We strengthen research rigorousness in that we replicate earlier studies and corroborate their findings for participation motives. We go further and overcome sampling bias of earlier studies concentrating on single cases, lighthouse projects or only one project type. Going beyond these constraints allows higher levels of validity and objectivity. In reaching out to further projects, this study details the open source landscape and enables comparison of findings for consistency in open source research. We tackle the lack of comparative studies as the literature is silent about an evaluation of the differences between software and content, and especially business and fun communities.

As earlier research has considered digital open source innovation types to be almost identical, we provide contrasting empirical findings. We identify highly heterogeneous communities with significant differences between project types. These findings open a theoretical discussion and provide a third contribution besides phenomenological amplification (introducing business and fun communities) and methodological benefits (replicating studies without sampling bias by avoiding iconic projects). In particular, we contribute to the research area of contingency evaluation and diversity by discovering and quantifying member heterogeneity and link them to contextual factors. Krogh et al. (2012) highlight the need to link motivations to institutional settings. Motivations should not be analyzed independently, but with respect to contextual settings. They address this research gap commenting that "most of this work is recent and difficult to categorize" (p. 645), but at the same time, social practices are strongly related to contributors' motivations. We relate individual aspects like participation motives and demographics to project types and show that the different community types attract different members. Thus, we reject the assumption of participant homogeneity and highlight the need to consider the context participants are embedded. Due to the diversity one must carefully consider the underpinning research object when generalizing findings and scrutinizing particular socio-demographic or psychometric aspects. Analyzing only successful and iconic projects carries a potential research bias and does not represent the entire open source ecology. Our study maps for the first time member diversity and highlights who is participating in different community types.

3.5.2   Limitations

With this study, we approach a new topic in open source innovation, namely diversity and contingency to contextual factors. However, this study has certain limitations. We concentrate on digital production communities and neglect further types like open source hardware also the differentiation between funded business needs to be shaped. We need to limit our findings to our analyzed types, but acknowledge further community types. Also, we analyze the individual volunteer and derive implications for community types. Thus, we conduct multi-level analysis and change the analysis view from the individual level to aggregations of communities. However, it is unclear whether the differences are actually caused by different structural characteristics of the considered project types. Nevertheless, these indications provide a fruitful field for future research.

3.5.3   Directions for Future Research

Future research should extend our research with more community types and larger samples. Moreover, research is lacking with respect to knowledge-intense areas with highly expert information exchange.[14] Our study also supports the assumption of participants' diversity. This also means researchers should think twice about their research object and be careful in drawing the research samples. Subsequent research should distinguish more clearly between members and refrain from averaging participants. Furthermore, our contribution opens a fundamentally new avenue for diversity research: Why do these differences exist? Are open source projects really so similar? What causes different member attractions?

NOTES

This contribution is based on the dissertation by Daniel Ehls, but further developed and refined.

1. For a recent and extended review of motives for participation see e.g. Crowston et al. 2012 or Krogh et al. (2012).
2. Due to the multi-year collaboration, popularity and success of Wikipedia, Wikipedia is considered a robust setting for research (Ransbotham and Kane 2011; Majchrzak et al. 2006; Raasch et al. 2008).
3. Very highly reputable, well-known and successful projects like Linux, Apache and Wikipedia.
4. Two-thirds of studies concentrate on Linux or Apache (Crowston et al. 2012).
5. The second wave was necessary to have at least two communities for each area. Unfortunately, some communities provided no replies in the first round, or only from administrators; these were discarded to avoid bias. In particular, medical communities were less responsive.

6. Interestingly, community members of Battle of Wesnoth forwarded the link in the private message to each other and posted the link.
7. Social motivations like altruism and ideology are usually present, but only explain little or no participation effort in open source. Hars and Ou (2001) as well as Bagozzi and Dholakia (2006) proved this relationship in open source software; Nov and Kuk (2008) as well as Schroer and Hertel (2009) highlighted this connection in open content.
8. Detailed inspection confirms a slightly different meaning for the 'use' items. Own use items two and three are adopted from Roberts et al. (2006), whereas own use item one originates from Hars and Ou (2001). Use1 indicates a wider product usage without necessarily contributing, but items two and three asked for active contribution, thus use 1 is dropped by arguments and statistics.
9. Loadings below 0.3 are hidden.
10. Skewness and kurtosis values between minus one and plus one represent a sufficient indicator for assuming a normal distribution (Osborne 2008, p. 199)
11. Comparison is also done with a t-test based on the Levene test, and reveals no differences except with relation to the variable AFN in software/content evaluation.
12. Assuming a normal distribution and conducting t-test and Levene tests reveals no significant difference in regards to for fun participation.
13. Due to fewer degrees of freedom, the 90% significance level is ignored and considered insignificant.
14. This thesis includes a medical community as example, but received little support from other medical communities.

REFERENCES

Bagozzi, R. P., and Dholakia, U. M. (2006): "Open source software user communities: a study of participation in Linux user groups", *Management Science* 52(7), pp. 1099–1115.

Bearden, W. O., Netemeyer, R. G., and Haws, K. L. (2011): *Handbook of marketing scales: multi-item measures for marketing and consumer behavior research*, SAGE: Los Angeles.

Bearden, W. O., Netemeyer, R. G., and Teel, J. (1989): "Measurement of consumer susceptibility to interpersonal influence", *Journal of Consumer Research* 15(4), pp. 473–481.

Benkler, Y. (2002): "Coase's penguin, or, Linux and 'the nature of the firm'", *The Yale Law Journal* 112(3), pp. 369–446.

Benner, P. (1984): *From novice to expert: excellence and power in clinical nursing practice*, Addison-Wesley, Menlo Park.

Bergquist, M., and Ljungberg, J. (2001): "The power of gifts: organizing social relationships in open source communities", *Information Systems Journal* 11(4), pp. 305–320.

Bonaccorsi, A., Giannangeli, S., and Rossi, C. (2006): "Entry strategies under competing standards: hybrid business models in the Open Source software industry", *Management Science* 52(7), pp. 1085–1098.

Bonaccorsi, A., and Rossi, C. (2003): "Why Open Source software can succeed: Open Source software development", *Research Policy* 32(7), pp. 1243–1258.

Boudreau, K. (2010): "Open platform strategies and innovation: granting access vs. devolving control", *Management Science* 56(10), pp. 1849–1872.

Bryant, S. L., Forte, A., and Bruckman, A. (2005): "Becoming Wikipedian: transformation of participation in a collaborative online encyclopedia", in *Proceedings of the 2005 international ACM SIGGROUP Conference on Supporting Group Work*, pp. 1–10, ACM, Sanibel Island, FL.

Cedergren, M. (2003): "Open content and value creation", *First Monday* 8(8).

Churchill, G., Jr. (1979). "A paradigm for developing better measures of marketing constructs", *Journal of Marketing Research* 16, pp. 64–73.

Clark, L., and Watson, D. (1995): "Constructing validity: basic issues in objective scale development", *Psychological Assessment* 7(3), pp. 309–319.

Clarke, R. (2004): Open Source software and open content as models for ebusiness. http://www.rogerclarke.com/EC/Bled04.html. Accessed 22 November 2012.

Comino, S., Manenti, F.M., and Parisi, M.L. (2007): "From planning to mature: on the success of open source projects", *Research Policy* 36(10), pp. 1575–1586.

Crowston, K., Wei, K., Howison, J., and Wiggins, A. (2012): "Free/Libre open-source software development: what we know and what we do not know", *ACM Computing Surveys* 44(2), pp. 7:1–7:35.

Dahlander, L., and O'Mahony, S. (2011): "Progressing to the center: coordinating project work", *Organization Science* 22(4), pp. 961–979.

Dahlander, L., and Wallin, M.W. (2006): "A man on the inside unlocking communities as complementary assets", *Research Policy* 35(8), pp. 1243–1259.

Deci, E.L., and Ryan, R.M. (1985): *Intrinsic motivation and self-determination in human behavior*, Plenum Press, New York.

Deckmyn, D. (2002): Suits, geeks seek Open Source entente. http://www.computerworld.com.au/article/65320/suits_geeks_seek_open_source_entente/. Accessed 1 October 2012.

Dreyfus, H., Dreyfus, S., and Zadeh, L. (1987): "Mind over machine: the power of human intuition and expertise in the era of the computer", *IEEE Expert* 2(2), pp. 110–111.

Eisenmann, T., Parker, G., and van Alstyne, M. (2008): "Opening platforms: how, when and why?" *HBS Working Papers 09–030*, Harvard Business School, Cambridge.

Fang, Y., and Neufeld, D. (2009): "Understanding sustained participation in Open Source software projects", *Journal of Management Information Systems* 25(4), pp. 9–50.

Feller, J., and Fitzgerald, B. (2000): "A framework analysis of the open source software development paradigm", in *Proceedings of the Twenty-First International Conference on Information Systems* (ICIS '00), pp. 58–69, Association for Information Systems, Atlanta, GA.

Fitzgerald, B. (2006): "The transformation of Open Source software", *MIS Quarterly* 30(3), pp. 587–598.

Ghosh, R.A., Glott, R., Krieger, B., and Robles, G. (2002): Free/Libre and Open Source software: survey and study, part IV: survey of developers. http://www.flossproject.org/report/Final4.htm. Accessed 30 September 2012.

Glass, R.L. (1999): "The loyal opposition of open source, Linux . . . and hype: software, IEEE", *Software, IEEE* 16(1), pp. 126–127.

Glott, R., Schmidt, P., and Ghosh, R.A. (2010): Wikipedia survey—overview of results. http://www.wikipediasurvey.org/docs/Wikipedia_Overview_15March2010-FINAL.pdf. Accessed 30 October 2012.

Hars, A., and Ou, S. (2001): "Working for free? motivations for participating in Open-Source projects", in *Proceedings of the 34th Annual Hawaii International Conference on System Sciences* (HICSS-34), pp. 25–39, IEEE Computer Society, Washington, DC.

Healy, K., and Schussman, A. (2003): "The ecology of open-source software development", Department of Sociology, University of Arizona, Tucson.

Henkel, J. (2006): "Selective revealing in open innovation processes: the case of embedded Linux", *Research Policy* 35(7), pp. 953–969.

Hertel, G., Niedner, S., and Herrmann, S. (2003): "Motivation of software developers in Open Source projects: an Internet-based survey of contributors to the Linux kernel", *Research Policy* 32(7), pp. 1159–1177.

Hippel, E. A. von, and Krogh, G. von (2003): "Open Source software and the 'private-collective' innovation model: issues for organization science", *Organization Science* 14(2), pp. 209–223.

Jeppesen, L. B., and Frederiksen, L. (2006): "Why do users contribute to firm-hosted user communities? the case of computer-controlled music instruments", *Organization Science* 17(1), pp. 45–63.

Krogh, G. von, Haefliger, S., Späth, S., and Wallin, M. W. (2012): "Carrots and rainbows: motivation and social practice in open source software development", *MIS Quarterly* 36(2), pp. 649–676.

Lakhani, K. R., and Hippel, E. A. von (2003): "How open source software works: 'free' user-to-user assistance", *Research Policy* 32(6), pp. 923–943.

Lakhani, K. R., and Wolf, R. (2005): "Why hackers do what they do: understanding motivation and effort in free/Open Source software projects", in *Perspectives on free and Open Source software*, J. Feller, B. Fitzgerald, S. Hissam, and K. Lakhani (eds.), pp. 3–22, Boston: MIT Press.

Lerner, J., and Tirole, J. (2002): "Some simple economics of open source", *The Journal of Industrial Economics* 50(2), pp. 197–234.

Linux Foundation. (2012): *The Linux Foundation releases annual Linux development report*, http://www.linuxfoundation.org/news-media/announcements/2012/04/linux-foundation-releases-annual-linux-development-report. Accessed 1 October 2012.

Majchrzak, A., Wagner, C., and Yates, D. (2006): "Corporate wiki users: results of a survey", in *Proceedings of the 2006 international symposium on Wikis*, pp. 99–104, ACM, New York.

McLure Wasko, M., and Faraj, S. (2005): "Why should I share? examining social capital and knowledge contribution in electronic networks of practice", *MIS Quarterly* 29(1), pp. 35–58.

Mockus, A., Fielding, R., and Herbsleb, J. (2002): "Two case studies of open source software development: Apache and Mozilla", *ACM Transactions on Software Engineering and Methodology (TOSEM)* 11(3), pp. 309–346.

Müller-Seitz, G., and Reger, G. (2010): "Networking beyond the software code? an explorative examination of the development of an open source car project", *Technovation* 30(11–12), pp. 627–634.

Nov, O., and Kuk, G. (2008): "Open source content contributors' response to free-riding: the effect of personality and context", *Computers in Human Behavior* 24(6), pp. 2848–2861.

Nunnally, J. C. (1978): *Psychometric theory*, McGraw-Hill, New York.

Okoli, C., and Oh, W. (2007): "Investigating recognition-based performance in an open content community: a social capital perspective", *Information & Management* 44(3), pp. 240–252.

Oreg, S., and Nov, O. (2008): "Exploring motivations for contributing to open source initiatives: the roles of contribution context and personal values", *Computers in Human Behavior* 24(5), pp. 2055–2073.

Osborne, J. W. (2008): "Best practices in data transformation: the overlooked effect of minimum values", in *Best Practices in Quantitative Methods*, J. W. Osborne (ed.), Los Angeles: Sage.

Pavlicek, R. (2000): *Embracing insanity: Open Source software development*, Sams, Indianapolis.

Pfaffenberger, B. (2001): "Why open content matters", *Knowledge, Technology & Policy* 14(1), pp. 93–102.

Raasch, A.-C., Herstatt, C., and Abdelkafi, N. (2008): "Open source innovation: characteristics and applicability outside the software industry", *Working Paper* 53, Hamburg University of Technology, Hamburg.

Ransbotham, S., and Kane, G. (2011): "Membership turnover and collaboration success in online communities: explaining rises and falls from grace in Wikipedia", *MIS Quarterly* 35(3), pp. 613–627.

Raymond, E. S. (1999): "Articles—The cathedral and the bazaar", *Knowledge, Technology and Policy* 12(3), pp. 23–49.

Raymond, E. S. (2002): Afterword: beyond software? http://catb.org/~esr/writings/homesteading/afterword/. Accessed 30 September 2012.

Rettberg, S. (2005): "All together now: collective knowledge, collective narratives, and architectures of participation", Digital Arts and Culture Conference, The Richard Stockton College of New Jersey Arts and Humanities, http://catb.org/~esr/writings/homesteading/afterword/. Accessed 30 September 2012.

Roberts, J. A., Hann, I.-H., and Slaughter, S. A. (2006): "Understanding the motivations, participation, and performance of Open Source software developers: a longitudinal study of the Apache Projects", *Management Science* 52(7), pp. 984–999.

Robinson, J. P., Shaver, P., and Wrightsman, L. (1991): "Criteria for scale selection and evaluation", in *Measures of personality and social psychological attitudes*, J. P. Robinson (ed.), pp. 1–16, Academic Press, San Diego.

Rolandsson, B., Bergquist, M., and Ljungberg, J. (2011): "Open source in the firm: opening up professional practices of software development", *Research Policy* 40(4), pp. 576–587.

Rosenzweig, R. (2006): "Can history be Open Source? Wikipedia and the future of the past", *The Journal of American History* 93(1), pp. 117–146.

Schroer, J., and Hertel, G. (2009): "Voluntary engagement in an open web-based encyclopedia: Wikipedians and why they do it", *Media Psychology* 12(1), pp. 96–120.

Shah, S. K. (2006): "Motivation, governance, and the viability of hybrid forms in open source software development", *Management Science* 52(7), pp. 1000–1014.

Stanton, J. (2006): "An empirical assessment of data collection using the Internet", *Personnel Psychology* 51(3), pp. 709–725.

West, J. (2003): "How open is open enough?: melding proprietary and open source platform strategies: Open Source software development", *Research Policy* 32(7), pp. 1259–1285.

Wiley, D. (1998): OpenContent. http://slashdot.org/articles/older/9806260926218.shtml. Accessed 30 September 2012.

Wright, K. (2005): "Researching Internet-based populations: advantages and disadvantages of online survey research, online questionnaire authoring software packages, and web survey services", *Journal of Computer-Mediated Communication* 10(3). http://onlinelibrary.wiley.com/doi/10.1111/j.1083-6101.2005.tb00259.x/full

Wu, C.-G., Gerlach, J. H., and Young, C. E. (2007): "An empirical analysis of open source software developers' motivations and continuance intentions", *Information & Management* 44(3), pp. 253–262.

4 The Rise and Fall of Interdisciplinary Research

The Case of Open Source Innovation

Christina Raasch, Viktor Lee,
Sebastian Spaeth, and Cornelius Herstatt

Reprint: *Research Policy*, Volume 42, Issue 5, June 2013, Pages 1138–1115.

A large and purportedly increasing number of research fields in modern science require scholars from more than one discipline to understand their puzzling phenomena. In response, many scholars argue that scientific work needs to become more interdisciplinary, and is indeed becoming so. This paper contributes to our understanding of the evolution of interdisciplinary research in new fields. We explore interdisciplinary co-authorship, co-citation and publication patterns in the recently emergent research field of open source innovation during the first 10 years of its existence. Utilizing a database containing 306 core publications and over 10,000 associated reference documents, we find that inquiry shifts from interdisciplinary to multidisciplinary research, and from joint puzzle solving to parallel problem solving, within a very few years after the inception of the field. "High-involvement" forms of interdisciplinary exchange decline faster than "low-involvement" forms. The patterns we find in open source research, we argue, may be quite general. We propose that they are driven by changes in task uncertainty and the ability to modularize research, among other factors. Our findings have important implications for individual scholars, research organizations and research policy.

Keywords: interdisciplinary research, evolution of research fields, open source, bibliometric analysis, co-author analysis, co-citation analysis, phenomenon-based research

4 THE RISE AND FALL OF INTERDISCIPLINARY RESEARCH

4.1 Introduction and Overview

Many fields in modern science require scholars from more than one discipline to effectively address principal research questions (Becher and Trowler 2001; Hessels and van Lente 2008). Interdisciplinary fields are also more likely to provide findings of high novelty (Dogan and Pahre 1990; Bartunek

2007). Many scholars have argued that scientific work needs to become more interdisciplinary, and is indeed becoming so (Chubin 1976; Nissani 1997; Metzger and Zare 1999; Forman and Markus 2005).

At the same time, interactions across disciplines can be more costly than within-discipline interactions (Klein and Porter 1990). Whether or not the benefits outweigh the costs of interdisciplinary research is contingent on the nature of the scientific problem at hand as well as the availability and distribution of prior related knowledge (Birnbaum 1981; Kötter and Balsiger 1999). Changes in these factors can therefore be assumed to affect the effectiveness and efficiency of interdisciplinary research.

However, there are very few studies to date that measure how interdisciplinary collaboration among researchers evolves over time and theorize the contingencies. We believe that this is an important gap to address. It has wide-ranging implications for individual researchers, research organizations and research policies that seek to adopt or promote the most efficacious research strategies. Scholars as well as research practitioners and managers will wish to know when interdisciplinary work is most appropriate.

This paper contributes to filling this gap by investigating three principal questions:

1. *Do scholars from different disciplinary backgrounds jointly solve the puzzles of the new research field, or do they mostly co-evolve their understandings without tight integration?*
2. *How does this change, as the field matures?*
3. *What factors can explain such changes?*

To address these questions, we use a comprehensive set of comparative-static bibliometric analyses to conduct a longitudinal study of one research field, open source innovation, a fast-growing and supposedly interdisciplinary field. Our analyses rest on several databases of researchers' attributes and co-authoring, publishing and citation behaviors. We analyze 306 core publications on open source innovation and over 10,000 reference documents cited therein.

We find a close and continual relatedness of content, i.e. strong substantive coherence of OS research as a field. However, we find that the substitute preference of interdisciplinary work decreases as the field matures. Researchers from different disciplines still study the same topics years into the creation of the field, but do so increasingly from their own disciplinary lenses (co-authoring within their discipline, citing within their discipline, publishing within and for their discipline). Interestingly, we find that "high-involvement" forms of interdisciplinary exchange such as coauthoring and cross-disciplinary publishing drop sharply only a few years after the inception of the research field. "Low-involvement forms" such as cross-disciplinary citations are slower to decline.

We propose, based on extant studies of other fields, that the pattern we have found in open source research may in fact be quite general: inquiry into a new field often shifts from interdisciplinary to multidisciplinary research, and from joint puzzle solving to parallel problem solving. This pattern may be particularly prevalent among phenomenon-based research fields.

Finally, we explore the contingency factors underlying these patterns. We explain initial high levels of interdisciplinary work as being driven by researchers' need to draw upon theories or methods established in disciplines other than their own to achieve their research goals (functional dependence). Interdisciplinary functional dependence declines over time, as the understanding of the field increases. Increased understanding enables modularization of further problem solving, often within disciplinary boundaries. Moreover, we argue that task uncertainty declines over time, and that expanding research fields enable researchers to deploy lower-cost strategies of accessing knowledge from other disciplines.

Our paper contributes to the literature in several ways. First, we propose a set of bibliometric tools that allows a comprehensive assessment of the cohesion of research fields. For any field, cohesion among disciplines, but also among geographies or schools of thought, can be studied from multiple angles by applying this set of tools.

We advocate using more than one publication database (e.g. Google Scholar, Ebsco, and the Institute for Science Information [ISI] database) and show that the common practice of using just one source may come at the cost of a substantial loss of relevant data.

Next, we apply this tool-set in one case, which future work on interdisciplinary research can use as a reference case. Our bibliometric findings relating to our specific case, the thriving field of open source research, are relevant to scholars interested in that field as well as to scholars interested in the emergence of successful new research fields.

Further and more generally, we theorize how changes in three underlying variables affect the disciplinary nature of research undertaken in afield at any point in time. We advance testable propositions that can guide future research. Our findings have important implications for individual researchers, research organizations, and research funding policies that seek to design and promote optimal research strategies, and to science media that assess and publish scholarly work.

The remainder of the paper is structured as follows: Section 4.2 describes prior related research and outlines important gaps. Our research methodology and data collection are explained in Section 4.3. In Section 4.4, the main findings section, we analyze the coherence of the OS field, and its change over time, along multiple dimensions. In Section 4.5, we consider the generality of our bibliometric findings and advance propositions to explain them. Finally, Section 4.6 discusses the contribution of this paper in relation to prior research and derives implications for future research, practice and policy.

4.2   Prior Research and Research Gap

4.2.1   *Background and Definitions*

A scientific discipline is "a specialized field of knowledge" (Chubin et al. 1986a). Disciplines "represent historical, evolutionary aggregates of shared scholarly interest", which typically gain legitimacy in a university as departments (Chubin et al. 1986a, p. 4). Throughout this paper, when referring to disciplines, we mean aggregations as represented in university departments, e.g. management studies, psychology, or law. Following Qin et al. (1997, p. 894), we define interdisciplinary research as "the integration of disciplines within a research environment". This integration consists of interactions among scientists (possibly mediated by their research outputs) and is motivated by a common problem-solving purpose.

A research field, or specialty, is an area of science that is defined by its intellectual coherence as well as its social coherence (Chubin 1976, p. 451). Research fields cluster around 'central problems'; they address specific and recognizable sets of questions (Darden and Maull 1977).

Building on groundwork laid by Kuhn (1962), Merton (1973), and Chubin (1976), among others, many scholars study the emergence and evolution of new research fields (Bonaccorsi and Vargas 2010). They find that new research fields often (but not always) form around a puzzling phenomenon that deviates from what theory tells us to expect (Davis 1971; Christensen 2006). The goal is to distinguish, describe and theorize the puzzling phenomenon (Krogh et al. 2012b).

Chubin (1976) suggests that new research fields tend to fall between research disciplines and that core researchers advance their field by drawing inspiration and insight from its margins (cf. Dogan and Pahre 1990). As a consequence, researchers in new fields, and in phenomenon-based ones in particular, often have shared interests but different educational backgrounds (Chubin 1976; Birnbaum 1981; Gibbons et al. 1994). With sometimes very little common ground among them, they need to create a shared set of concepts, goals, and norms—a liability that phenomenon-based fields have often struggled with (Merton 1973).

Some new research fields attract so much immigration and make findings that are so distinct from researchers' home disciplines, that a new discipline begins to emerge. (Such was the case for material science, for instance, that did not disintegrate back into metallurgy and ceramics.) In most cases, however, cross-disciplinary research fields remain narrower, more or less formalized, and sometimes long-lasting, "hybrids" (Dogan and Pahre 1990). Our paper focuses on such hybrids and their evolution, arguing that they may be inherently unstable.

4.2.2   *Overview of Related Literature*

Many scholars argue that, in order to extend our understanding of the evolution of emergent new research fields, it is important to study how scholars jointly create and recombine knowledge within and across disciplines

(Birnbaum 1981; McCain 1998; Hessels and van Lente 2008; Tsai and Wu 2010). Our contribution builds on three streams of literature:

(1) A number of studies conduct comparative-static analyses of particular research fields, e.g. for the field of strategic management. Ramos-Rodríguez and Ruíz-Navarro (2004) and Nerur et al. (2008) find that different time periods exhibit different co-citation patterns. While the initial stage was more cohesive, subsequent stages showed a greater number of clusters (Nerur et al. 2008). However, these studies do not systematically investigate the disciplinary anchoring of the authors and their works, nor intend to generalize from such findings (one exception being, e.g., Ponzi 2002).

(2) Another and mostly distinct literature rooted in information science and library science investigates interdisciplinarity, its measurement, prominence, costs and benefits, and organizational practices (see http://transdisciplinarity.ch/e/ for an extensive bibliography). These studies mostly remain at the macro/meso levels, focusing on disciplines, subject categories and journals, rather than researchers and research teams. For example, van Leeuwen and Tijssen (2000) analyze macro-level data on the prevalence of boundary-crossing co-citations in many disciplines of modern science; they compare their findings for 1985 and 1995, but in most cases find little change at the aggregate discipline level.

Perhaps more important to our research, Morillo et al. (2003) show that research fields that have been added to the ISI list of subject categories more recently are more multidisciplinary than established fields in the following sense: they feature a higher percentage of journals assigned to more than one subject category. In addition, such multi-assignments link them to a greater number and diversity of other subject categories. McCain (1998) conducts a journal-level investigation of the interdisciplinary roots and evolution of neural networks research, using co-citation analysis. In much of this literature, management studies are neglected; and they are usually not regarded as being among the vanguard of interdisciplinary scholarship (Knights and Willmott 1997; van Leeuwen and Tijssen 2000).

(3) A third stream of literature focuses on individual researchers' motivations, incentives and research strategies (Aksulu and Wade 2010; Krogh et al. 2012a). Fundamentally, researchers are known to have a preference for intra-disciplinary work (Whitley 2000). Individual expertise and communication skills, career incentives and rewards, the orientation of publication outlets, and the organizational structures of research institutions all tend to favor disciplinary research (Klein and Porter 1990).

This general preference notwithstanding, scholars sometimes encounter conditions that call for interdisciplinary inquiry. Birnbaum (1981) finds that interdisciplinary research tends to yield superior results when the problem is little understood and when many interrelationships engender high complexity. Novel research fields are usually believed to host more interdisciplinary research than mature fields (Dogan and Pahre 1990).

4.2.3   Research Gap and Objectives

As shown in the previous section, interdisciplinary collaboration has been studied from various vantage points. However, prior literature mostly lacks a longitudinal, micro-level approach that is central to measuring and understanding the evolution of interdisciplinary research (McCain 1998; Pieters and Baumgartner 2002; Moody 2004; Fagerberg and Verspagen 2009).

Our study therefore examines scholars' micro-level choices relating to interdisciplinary research, their changes over time, and the reasons that may explain these changes. We believe that a micro-level analysis of scholars' research-related choices is crucial for understanding the extent to which scholars actually collaborate, and integrate their findings, across epistemic divides (Smeltzer 1994; Forman and Markus 2005 and references cited therein). This point is also argued by Smeltzer (1994, p. 158), who emphasizes that macro-level multidisciplinarity should not be mistaken for micro-level interdisciplinary.

It is particularly important to better understand researchers' choices of disciplinary or interdisciplinary approaches in emergent new research fields. The early development of research fields is shaped by a relatively small number of researchers who affect the future of the field to a large extent. The diversity of knowledge they import, its subsequent integration, and its recombination shape the development of the field.

4.3   Methodology

4.3.1   Research Design and Choice of Research Field

Our research design is exploratory in nature. Our findings rest on a detailed and comprehensive analysis of very extensive data on one research field. We have no conclusive proof that this field is representative of many others. However, there is evidence to corroborate our findings, as we will show in the discussion section (Section 4.6).

We devote great care to measuring interdisciplinarity in this field along multiple dimensions, and to establishing what kinds of interdisciplinary research behavior scholars do or do not engage in at any point in time. We use extensive bibliometric and other secondary data, which has the advantage of being comprehensive and objective (De Glas 1986; Gmür 2003). We then advance causal propositions that seek to explain the observed patterns. The propositions are derived from the interpretation of our bibliometric data as well as conceptual arguments that leverage prior literature as available.

For our study, we selected the research field of open source innovation. "Open source" refers to the source code of software, revealed for anyone to access, inspect, utilize, modify and re-distribute in changed or unchanged form (Raymond 1999). Open source innovation refers to the creation of products and services incorporating the principles of free access to the design source as mainly found in, but not limited to, the software industry (Baldwin and Hippel 2011). We follow this expansive use of the term.

Open source innovation is not a new phenomenon. In the 1970s, practically all software was free (Stallman 1999). Hacker communities shared the source code of operating systems and applications without hesitation or restriction (Levy 1984). Still, OS development (also called free software) was not on the agenda of most researchers until 1998/1999, when Netscape first released the source code of its widely used Mozilla web browser suite, Oracle announced its support of Linux, and Eric Raymond, a practitioner, published his catalyzing book, *The Cathedral and the Bazaar* (Raymond 1999). Today, open source software is ubiquitous in software-creating as well as software-consuming organizations, with companies expending billions of dollars on its creation (Ghosh 2006).

The empirical context of OS is particularly well suited to our research for several reasons. First, it is a recently emergent and successful field (at the time of this writing, Thomson Reuters Web of Science lists approximately 10,500 publications pertaining to "open source") that attracted researchers from many disciplines. Second, the term open source is used by researchers throughout the field. It refers to a specific and narrow phenomenon that is distinct, comprehensive and self-contained. This facilitates exhaustive data extraction. Third, several studies review the literature on open source innovation in substance and methods (Rossi 2006; Krogh and Hippel 2006; Dalle et al. 2008; Crowston et al. 2012; Aksulu and Wade 2010; Krogh et al. 2012a), and thereby provide valuable qualitative input for interpreting and theorizing our findings. In this respect, our own familiarity with the field is an additional asset.

4.3.2 Research Method

Bibliometry analyses ties among researchers, specifically in co-authorship and co-citation networks, taking them as indicators of knowledge exchange (Small 1978; Lievrouw 1990; Hoffman and Holbrook 1993). Co-authorship is an indicator for collaboration; interdisciplinary co-authorship can be seen as a sign that researchers depend on methods and knowledge from other disciplines to solve their research puzzles (Moody 2004). Document co-citation analysis seeks to identify relationships between publications that are considered to be important by authors in the research field, suggesting a relatedness of content (Small and Griffith 1974; Gmür 2003). Whether these indicators are valid and reliable has been subject to extensive scholarly debate (Small 1973). Some limitations notwithstanding, bibliometric analysis is mostly considered a legitimate method for analyzing the cognitive and social structures of research fields (Merton 1973; White and Griffith 1981; Ramos-Rodríguez and Ruíz-Navarro 2004; Eom 2008).

We compiled three principal databases (Figure 4.1): (A) an extensive database of OS publications, which we use to analyze the bibliometric structure of the research field; (B) a database of researchers "knowledge

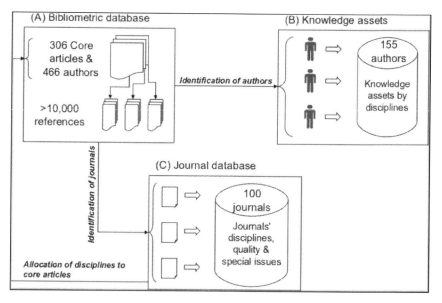

Figure 4.1   Data sources and their purpose in this study

assets", used for the analysis of their disciplines; (C) a database of journals publishing OS articles, including information on discipline, quality, and special issues.

4.3.3   Bibliometric Data (Database A)

Our bibliometric database was created in four steps: (1) identification and selection of data sources, (2) search of OS-related literature, (3) qualitative filtering of documents, and (4) creation of the bibliometric database.

(1) In order to reduce the risk of missing publications, four separate sources were mined: ISI Web of Science, GoogleScholar, EbscoHost and ProQuest. A redundancy rate[1] of only 27% suggests that a multi-source approach improves the composition of the database. At the same time, it casts doubt on the comprehensiveness of findings drawing on just one of these sources (an approach which has been dominant in bibliometric research to date).

(2) Next, we extract from each of the four sources all the publications that include the term "open source" or "open-source" in the title, abstract, or keywords. Due to our focus on the OS phenomenon, we can run a search-term based analysis (cf. Ponzi 2002; Charvet et al. 2008). This approach has the advantage of being the most comprehensive but comes at the cost of a very large number of entries that require extensive screening. Our search yielded more than 60,000 documents (as of May 2009).

(3) The majority of these documents were then excluded from further analysis by means of three filtering procedures:

First, we only consider (i) journal publications that (ii) belong to the management discipline or are interdisciplinary and relate to management studies and that (iii) do more than mention OS in passing. Publication in a scholarly journal is commonly regarded as an indicator of 'certified knowledge' (Callon et al. 1995). The last criterion excludes many papers that do not investigate OS development but simply use OS software for their analyses. To increase reliability, two authors independently rated all papers (inter-rater reliability: 95.7%). Differential opinions were aligned by means of a more in-depth study of the paper in question, followed by a discussion between both raters as well as a third author. By applying these criteria, we reduced the preliminary database to 701 non-redundant items.

Second, we asked leading scholars of OS innovation to verify our preliminary set of papers. Based on their total number of citations in the preliminary database, 15 out of the leading 30 scholars were randomly chosen and contacted. Seven of these scholars verified our preliminary database and occasionally pointed out missing or inapposite papers.

As a third qualitative filter, we applied JCR Social Science 2005 (ISI), Jourqual2, and six other journal rankings to cut down the number of papers to those published in 'A', 'B', or 'C' journals (or equivalent in other metrics).[2]

This three-step filtering process gives us a database of 306 'core articles', of which 83% are included based on Journal Citation Reports (JCR) Social Science 2005 and/or Jourqual2.[3]

(4) We then filled in the references cited in each of the 306 core articles. For each reference of each paper, we collected the names of all the authors, title, year of publication, and publication outlet. Since none of our four data sources offered the extraction of all of this information, considerable manual input effort was required. For example, none of the sources allows the retrieval of information on all authors of a reference; the ISI convention just provides first authors, for instance (Eom 2008). More than 10,000 references were thus included in our bibliometric database.

As a final step, we corrected errors and inconsistencies, spelling mistakes, and non-uniform abbreviation formats. From the resulting database, co-citation and co-authorship tables were calculated.

4.3.4   *Data on Scholars' Disciplines (Database B)*

Using ISI Web of Science, we tracked the publication history of 94 out of 466 OSS scholars.[4] We recorded each author's number of overall publications, year of first publication, number of "open source" publications and first year of OS publication, as well as the number and disciplines of publications prior to the first OS publication ("knowledge assets"). For all pre-OS publications we registered the subject areas as indicated on ISI, as selected by the authors. If more than one category was assigned, the article was allotted to all of these categories. A knowledge asset can thus belong to one or more disciplines. Based on the aggregate of their knowledge assets, all researchers could be assigned one or multiple disciplines.

Disciplinary co-author analysis required discipline information of an additional 61 authors for whom no knowledge asset data was available (typically due to the lack of ISI knowledge assets predating their first OS publication). We determined the disciplinary affiliation of those scholars based on information from their websites and their research institutes. At least two of the authors of this paper independently researched the disciplines of each of these scholars; in 82% of all cases, the ratings agreed. Where there were discordant findings, further research was undertaken by three of the authors of this paper until consensus was reached.

Our findings are summarized in a database showing the disciplinary background of 155 OS scholars. We distinguish ten disciplinary categories: business and management, economics, computer science, information science and library science, engineering, natural sciences, psychology, social sciences, law and "other disciplines". The first nine disciplines account for 90% of the knowledge assets in our database. None of the remaining "other" disciplines exceeds a share of 1% of knowledge assets.

4.3.5   Data on Journals and Journal Disciplines (Database C)

We also identified the disciplines of all journals in which at least one of the 306 core OS articles was published. We included the ISI impact factor for each year of our study (1999–2009), according to availability. For all journals covered by ISI, we added journal disciplines as derived from ISI subject areas (on the advantages of using the ISI classification, cf. Morillo et al. 2003). Where these were not available, three of the authors jointly determined the discipline of each journal, based on their prior knowledge of the journal and additional investigation.

4.4   Coalescence and Fragmentation of Open Source Research

In this section we study the coherence of the OS research field over time, focusing on integration between disciplines. We begin by giving a short overview of the field and our set of core papers (Section 4.1). Next, we show that open source is one research field—although several different themes are being researched, there is strong substantive coherence (inter-relatedness of content) among them (Section 4.2). The next three sub-sections investigate to what extent different disciplinary bodies of knowledge are integrated in a joint puzzle solving process. We analyze four different measures of interdisciplinary integration: interdisciplinary co-authorships (Section 4.3), publications in journals outside the authors' home disciplines and publications that are relevant for scholars from several disciplines (Section 4.4), and cross-disciplinary co-citations (Section 4.5). While the former two can be considered to be "high-involvement" (involving substantial engagement in and commitment to interdisciplinary work), the latter two may be seen as requiring lower involvement. In brief summary, we find that the OS field is fragmenting along disciplinary faultlines. Scholars make increasingly intra-disciplinary contributions, co-authoring within their discipline, publishing within and for their discipline, and citing within their discipline.

4.4.1 Overview of the OS Research Field

The disciplinary composition and temporal distribution of our set of 306 core papers are shown in Figure 4.2: It indicates the expansion of the OS field and shows the preponderance of management, economics, computer science, and information and library science papers in our dataset.

Within the management discipline, both general management journals, such as Management Science and Long Range Planning, and more specialized journals, mostly in innovation management and organization studies, are the most prolific publishers of OS research (Table 4.1).

Our database contains 468 unique authors. Two scholars, Eric von Hippel and Georg von Krogh, stand out by their high number of OS publications (our database contains 12 open source publications by each). They are experienced scholars with a strong research record in other, related fields. Other leading scholars include Lerner and Tirole (6 publications each), and Dahlander, Henkel, O'Mahony and Spaeth (5 publications each).

Table 4.1 Leading journals by number of open source publications in our database

	Journal name	No. of publications	% of publications
1.	*IEEE Software*	35	11.1%
2.	*Research Policy*	26	8.3%
3.	*Communications of the ACM*	18	5.7%
4.	*Management Science*	16	5.1%
5.	*Information Economics and Policy*	12	3.8%
6.	*IEEE Transactions on Software Engineering*	11	3.5%
7.	*Journal of Management and Governance*	9	2.9%
8.	*MIT Sloan Management Review*	8	2.5%
9.	*R&D Management*	7	2.2%
10.	*Organization Science*	7	2.2%
11.	*Journal of Database Management*	7	2.2%
12.	*Harvard Business Review*	7	2.2%
13.	*Long Range Planning*	5	1.6%
14.	*Journal of the American Society for Information Science & Technology*	5	1.6%
15.	*Information & Management*	5	1.6%
16.	*Industrial and Corporate Change*	5	1.6%
17.	*Oxford Review of Economic Policy*	4	1.3%
18.	*MIS Quarterly*	4	1.3%
19.	*Journal of Management Information Systems*	4	1.3%
20.	*Journal of Industrial Economics*	4	1.3%

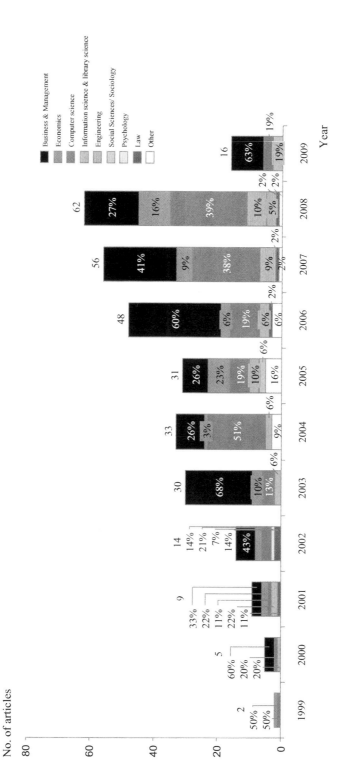

No. of articles

Business & Management
Economics
Computer science
Information science & library science
Engineering
Social Sciences/ Sociology
Psychology
Law
Other

Figure 4.2   Number of OS articles by year (as of May 2009)

Seminal OS publications, by their number of citations, are listed in Table 4.2. Three interesting observations stand out: first, citation concentration is not very high. On average, an OS paper cites only 2.4 of the 20 most cited papers in the field (this contrasts with studies of more mature fields, e.g. by Fagerberg and Verspagen 2009). Second, almost all of the 20 most-cited

Table 4.2 Most-cited publications, sorted by citations

	Title of publication	First author	Citations
1.	*The Cathedral and the Bazaar* (1999)	E. S. Raymond	92
2.	*Some Simple Economics of Open Source* (2002)	J. Lerner	80
3.	*Motivation of Software Developers in Open Source Projects . . .* (2003)	G. Hertel	63
4.	*Open Source Software and the "Private-Collective" Innovation Model . . .* (2003)	E. A. Hippel	61
5.	*How Open Source Software Works: "Free" User-to-User Assistance* (2003)	K. R. Lakhani	58
6.	*The Cathedral and the Bazaar* (2001, book)	E. S. Raymond	44
7.	*Community, Joining, and Specialization in [OSS] Innovation* (2003)	G. Krogh	37
8.	*Why Hackers Do What They Do: Understanding Motivation and Effort . . .* (2005)	K. R. Lakhani	33
9.	*Satisfying Heterogeneous User Needs via Innovation Toolkits* (2003)	N. Franke	33
10.	*Guarding the Commons: How Community Managed Software Projects . . .* (2003)	S. C. O'Mahony	31
11.	*Working for Free? Motivations for Participating in Open-Source Projects* (2002)	A. Hars	30
12.	*Two Case Studies of [OSS] Development: Apache and Mozilla* (2002)	A. Mockus	28
13.	*Why Open Source Software Can Succeed* (2003)	A. Bonaccorsi	25
14.	*The Sources of Innovation* (1988)	E. A. Hippel	25
15.	*A Case Study of Open Source Software Development: The Apache Serve* (2000)	A. Mockus	25
16.	*Innovation by User Communities: Learning from Open-Source Software* (2001)	E. A. Hippel	24
17.	*Essence of Distributed Work: The Case of the Linux Kernel* (2000)	J. Y. Moon	24
18.	*Democratizing Innovation* (2005)	E. A. Hippel	24
19.	*The Boston Consulting Group Hacker Survey*	K. R. Lakhani	21
20.	*How Communities Support Innovative Activities: An Exploration . . .* (2003)	N. Franke	21

publications relate to the OS phenomenon itself, rather than theory, methods, or other related phenomena: 2 out of those 20 publications (Franke and Shah 2003; Hippel 2005) focus on user innovation and user innovation communities, a closely related field. Third, 6 out of 8 papers published in the special issue of Research Policy (2003) are among the 15 most-cited OS papers overall. This illustrates the power of a special issue of a high-ranking journal, published early in the development of a new research field, to shape subsequent research.

4.4.2   Substantive Coherence of the OS Research Field

In their editorial to the special issue of *Research Policy*, Krogh and Hippel (2003) identify three central themes of open source research, as presented in that issue. Krogh and Spaeth (2007) show that research on each of these themes is undertaken from within several disciplines.

The first theme concerns the motivations of rational actors to devote private resources to the creation of a public good, the open source code, instead of free-riding on the contributions of others (Lerner and Tirole 2002; Osterloh and Rota 2007). Second, researchers have wondered about the effective governance of innovation processes carried by volunteers beyond the reach of hierarchical managerial control (O'Mahony and Ferraro 2007; Krogh and Spaeth 2007). And third, research has been conducted on competition and complementarity between open source innovation and traditional models of for-profit firm innovation (Bonaccorsi et al. 2006; Fosfuri et al. 2008).

As we include and review more recent literature, we find that these three focal themes have been surprisingly stable, while some additional topics are slowly coming to the fore. Among all core papers published in journals ranked A or B (Table 4.3), we find 29 papers (19.8%) relating to the design and justifiability of policies supporting OS software development and use, or "other" topics such as specific legal aspects of open source licenses.[5]

Research on these principal themes, although somewhat specialized, is closely connected and co-evolving. This is shown by co-citation analysis. To measure inter-theme co-citation behavior, we first calculate CoCit scores between any two publications, a measure of co-citation frequency (Gmür 2003).[6] Next, we aggregate these individual scores by computing the assortativity coefficient[7] of the co-citation network. This coefficient captures the tendency of nodes of the same type (in our case, the same theme) to be connected and is thus a measure of the extent of mixing in the network (Newman 2003). Values of r close to –1 indicate a disassortative network (i.e. publications on different themes are co-cited more frequently), values close to zero indicate random co-citation across themes, and values of r close to 1 characterize assortative networks (publications on the same topic are preferentially co-cited).

We find that research on different research themes is co-cited to a similar and substantial extent across all three phases. There is no preferential co-citation of publications on the same theme; assortativity remains close to 0

Table 4.3 Open source publications in A and B journals by year and main theme

Year	Motivation to contribute	Governance, organization, and innovation process	Competitive dynamics	Policy	Other	Total
2000		1	1			2
2001	3	1		1		5
2002	1	3			1	5
2003	6	7	2	2	1	18
2004		3	2	2	1	8
2005	2	11	2	2	1	18
2006	6	15	4	1	6	32
2007	2	11	3	1	3	20
2008	1	14	8	2	5	30
2009*	1		1			2*
Total	22	66	23	11	18	140

Motivation to contribute: addresses issues such as "individual incentives, impact of firms' participation on individual motives, impact of community participation on individual motives, relationship between incentives and technical design"**

Governance, organization, and innovation process: addresses issues such as "reconciliation of diverse and distributed contributor interests, governance of project architecture [. . .], governance of the public good, functioning and types of organizations [. . .], roles taken by contributors [. . .], coordination of innovation, processes of OSS maintenance and development"**

Competitive dynamics: addresses issues such as "impact of OSS on competition in the software industry, hybrid strategies for melding commercial and OS platforms, firms' resource allocation to OSS projects, relationship between firms and OSS projects, free revealing amongst competitors of improvements to common software platforms"**

Policy: addresses issues such as government policies to support OSS, rationales for such policies, contributions of OSS adoption towards achieving political goals***

* Data until May 2009; ** Source: Krogh and Hippel (2006, 977); *** Source: Based on Comino and Manenti (2003).

Table 4.4 Co-citation assortativity by focal research theme

Period	Theme-based assortativity
1999–2002	0.044
2003–2005	−0.007
2006–2009	0.000

for all three phases (Table 4.4). In other words, OS publications tend to draw equally on prior literature on two or more focal themes, rather than specialize on just one theme. These findings indicate a close and continual relatedness of content, i.e. strong substantive coherence of OS research as a field.

4.4.3   Interdisciplinary Co-Authorship

Substantive coherence notwithstanding, the researcher network appears to fragment over time along disciplinary divides. We can observe this both by inspecting the co-authorship network and from computing discipline assortativity of the co-authorship network.

In the co-authorship network of phase 1, interdisciplinary dyads and triples are prominent. In phases 2 and 3 larger clusters form that are mostly intra-disciplinary and often intra-institutional.[8] (A notable exception in phase 3 is a cluster of 9 co-authors around Richard Watson and Donald Wynn that comprises both management scholars and computer scientists.)

Due to space constraints, Figure 4.3 shows the co-authorship network across all three phases, rather than for each phase separately. We find five clusters of more than five authors each. They represent invisible colleges around leading scholars (Beaver and Rosen 1978; Chubin et al. 1986b). Most of the scholars within each invisible college have similar disciplinary backgrounds and often related research agendas, the cluster descriptions contain details.

While network density and centrality should be interpreted with caution due to their sensitivity to network size (which increases over time), they indicate a less dense co-author network over time. To quantify intra-disciplinary co-authoring, we again use the assortativity coefficient (Table 4.5). The phase 1 network is weakly assortative—scholars from the same discipline co-author slightly more often. In phase 2, we see a marked increase in intra-disciplinary co-authorships. This suggests that, rather early in the development of the research field, scholars return to mostly disciplinary publication strategies.

4.4.4   Interdisciplinary Publications

Publication behavior, too, becomes more intra-disciplinary over time. We study two indicators: the fraction of papers published in journals outside the authors' home disciplines[9] and the fraction of publications that the authors consider relevant for multiple disciplines.[10] Both indicators give us an idea of whom OS researchers regard as their community and the audience for their work. If they publish outside their home discipline, and/or indicate that their paper is relevant for other disciplines, they must be aware of the interdisciplinary relevance of their findings and want to disseminate them

Table 4.5   Coauthor network characteristics

Period	Discipline assortativity	Density	Degree centrality
1999–2002	0.291	0.0255	0.0241
2003–2005	0.696	0.0111	0.0248
2006–2009	0.691	0.0057	0.0152

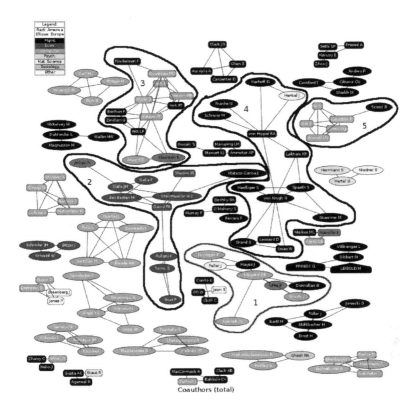

Coauthors (total)

Cluster 1	This cluster is mainly composed of scholars from computer science and information systems, with Brian Fitzgerald as the most central scholar. Their work focuses on commercial firms in OS software development, particularly their business models, value networks, and their relationship and interdependencies with the community.
Cluster 2	Economists dominate this cluster, with Paul David as the most central scholar. They investigate, e.g., developer motivation and activities, often conducting dynamic system-level analyses. The division of labor and competitive dynamics likewise constitute focal research themes.
Cluster 3	Scholars specialize in management information systems, exploring the influence of communication technology in creating new forms of community. The most central scholar is Richard Watson who is surrounded by his (former) Ph.D. students and visiting scholars at the University of Georgia.
Cluster 4	This cluster, the largest overall, comprises scholars of innovation management and strategy. They study, e.g., the workings of OS communities, the principles and limitations of free knowledge sharing, and the involvement of firms in OS projects. Eric von Hippel and Georg von Krogh are leading scholars, with Ph.D. students, post-docs and faculty colleagues surrounding them.
Cluster 5	This information science cluster is built around Kevin Crowston of Syracuse University. Research investigates new virtual forms of organizing that rely on the application of new information technology.

Figure 4.3 Co-author network across all three phases (all clusters >3 nodes are shown)

to other disciplines. The former indicator can be interpreted as involving a stronger commitment to interdisciplinary work.

As shown in Table 4.6, we find that the fraction of publications published in 'foreign' disciplines declines sharply in phase 2, and that the fraction

Table 4.6   Interdisciplinary publications

Period	Publications in 'foreign' discipline	Relevance for multiple disciplines
1999–2002	45%	42%
2003–2005	18%	35%
2006–2009	19%	30%

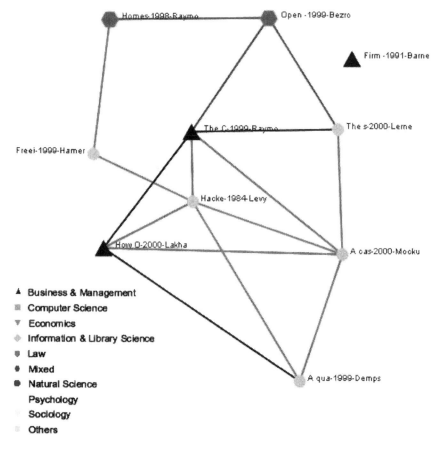

Figure 4.4   Co-citation network for Phase 1 (1999–2002) (including all publications co-cited at least three times)

of publications that the authors consider relevant for multiple disciplines declines too, albeit more slowly.

4.4.5 Interdisciplinary Co-Citations

In this final sub-section, we show that, as the research field matures, scholars tend to co-cite within a discipline, rather than across disciplines. Again, we use a dual approach of visual inspection of the co-citation networks and computation of various indicators.

The co-citation networks for the three phases are shown in Figures 4.4–4.6.

The phase 1 co-citation network is composed of only 10 nodes, 9 of which form a cluster. It is indicative of a nascent research field, characterized

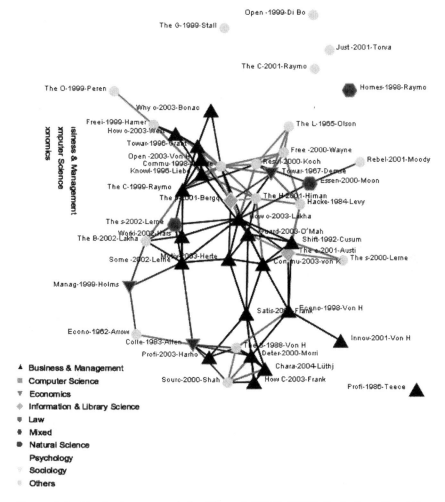

Figure 4.5 Co-citation network for Phase 2 (2003–2005) (including all publications co-cited at least five times)

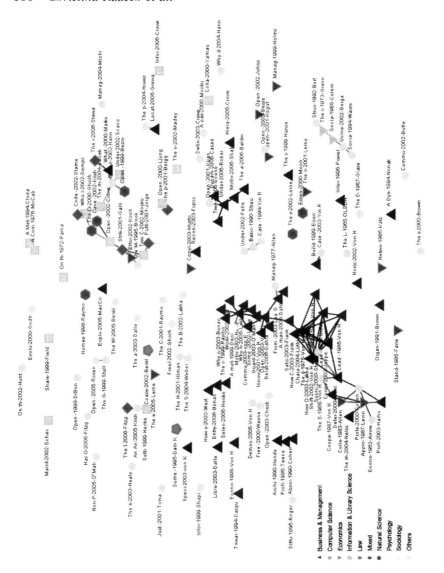

Figure 4.6   Co-citation network for Phase 3 (2006–2009) (including all publications co-cited at least five times)

by a strong standing of practice-based papers (especially Raymond's 1999 essay) as well as cohesion around a small phenomenon-based core. The paucity of prior, non-phenomenon focused works in the network indicates the diversity of the epistemic backgrounds of early OSS scholars. There is also a dearth of high-ranking, peer-reviewed journal publications, with half of the nodes being books or conference proceedings (called "other"). (Disciplinary affiliations were established for journal publications only.)

In phase 2, more documents are co-cited. The CoCit network of this phase features a single, tightly connected, interdisciplinary cluster. While management is the dominant discipline, it also contains economics, information science, and mixed-discipline papers.[11] The co-citation network indicates that many articles from this period rely on findings from multiple disciplines to build and support their claims. As the field is not yet very large, researchers tend to know and cite each other's work irrespective of disciplinary boundaries. In addition, they also discover shared foundations from several disciplines, e.g. Allen (1983), Arrow (1962), Olson (1965) and Demsetz (1967).

By phase 3, several clusters evolve which clearly follow disciplinary demarcation lines. There are several management clusters. Similarly, there is one large computer science and information science cluster, surrounded by a number of smaller ones. Another cluster is rooted in sociology and also contains papers on the theory and analysis of social networks. In addition, 12 chains, mainly consisting of two or three nodes, have formed. None of these chains combines management, economics and/or computer science.

We also note that seminal theoretical contributions from different disciplines have not (yet) become landmarks for interdisciplinary (or even intra-disciplinary) co-citation. A large number of seminal publications from different theoretical lenses are isolates in the co-citation network, even when viewed over the entire period. Among them are generalized exchange theory (Ekeh 1974) and collective action (Olson 1965); endogenous growth theory (Romer 1994); transaction cost economics (Coase 1937); evolutionary economics (Nelson and Winter 1982); property rights theory (North 1990); the resource-based theory of the firm (Barney 1991) and dynamic capabilities (Teece et al. 1997), as well as the knowledge-based view of the firm (Nonaka 1994). Most of these seminal publications are infrequently cited. Olson's book *The Logic of Collective Action* (1965) is the only one of the aforementioned contributions that is among the 50 publications most cited by OS research. The diversity of these seminal papers, and the sparsity of their citations, seems indicative of a field in search of its theoretical anchoring.

Indicators capturing interdisciplinary co-citation behavior are shown in Table 4.7. We find that density and centrality decrease, indicating increasing fragmentation. (Note, however, that the decrease in density may also be influenced by increases in network size over time.) Assortativity by

Table 4.7 Characteristics of the co-citation network

Period	Discipline assortativity	Density	Degree centrality
1999–2002	0.11	0.084	0.113
2003–2005	–0.072	0.0710	0.077
2006–2009	0.727	0.0086	0.063

discipline increases very markedly in the last phase, indicating that publications from the same discipline are co-cited considerably more often than publications from different disciplines. (Recall that a value of 1 indicates a perfectly assortative network.) These numbers support the interpretation that co-citation behavior shifts toward single-discipline citations over time.

4.5   Propositions on Interdisciplinarity in Nascent Research Fields

4.5.1   *Summary*

Researchers have many choices about how they want to conduct their research. Most fundamentally, they may (or may not) elect to contribute to a specific research field. Subsequent choices include the choice to collaborate with others, the choice to adopt knowledge from others, and the choice to share findings with others.

We conducted an in-depth longitudinal study of one research field, open source innovation, a phenomenon-based and supposedly interdisciplinary field. Specifically, we studied scholars' choices pertaining to interdisciplinary research, using bibliometric and other secondary data.

We found the open source field to have substantive coherence in the sense that different branches of research within it (focusing on different focal themes) are closely connected. To show this, we studied theme-based assortativity of co-citations across three phases of the development of the research field. We found no preponderance of within-theme citations, nor any trend in this direction. The puzzles presented by the phenomenon seem to be so inter-related that they act as a bracket, keeping the research field together as it evolves.

Despite this substantive coherence, careful analysis revealed that the field is fragmenting along disciplinary faultlines. We studied different aspects (interdisciplinary co-authorships, interdisciplinary publishing, and interdisciplinary citation behavior), and they all support this diagnosis. OS scholars study a set of closely related issues, but increasingly do so within and for their own disciplines. The shift from interdisciplinary toward multi-disciplinary research could be observed even within a relatively short time period, 10 years, in the case of our study. Interestingly, we found that "high-involvement" forms of interdisciplinary research such as co-authoring or publishing across disciplinary divides plummet only a few years after the inception of the research field. "Low-involvement forms" such as cross-disciplinary citations or publishing work that is relevant beyond the author's own discipline also decline, but later and less sharply.

4.5.2   *Limitations and Generalizability of Findings*

Our study comes with several limitations, many of which are typical of bibliometric studies (White and Griffith 1981; Ramos-Rodríguez and Ruíz-Navarro 2004). Specifically, our measures of interdisciplinary integration and exchange, while having the advantage of utilizing objective, comprehensive data, come at a cost in terms of qualitative richness of information. Bibliometric studies have inherent limitations when a research objective is to understand scholars' intentions, motivations, and reasoning. Future research should address these aspects, examining substantive as well as strategic motivations, to verify and extend our propositions.

Moreover, our study offers an in-depth analysis of one case only. We devoted great care to measuring interdisciplinarity along multiple dimensions. This required extensive data and analyses, which rendered a multi-field study impractical within the scope of this paper. We therefore cannot be certain that the findings would be the same in other fields.

However, there is some evidence that the pattern we uncovered may be a quite general one:

> P1: *The prevalence of interdisciplinary research tends to decline as research fields mature.*

Some studies of other research fields, within and outside management studies, reveal similar patterns. A related study in the field of strategic management finds increasing fragmentation over time, without going into as much detail regarding researchers' disciplines (Nerur et al. 2008). Studies of entrepreneurship research find that scholars have separated into more homogeneous, disciplinary communities, sometimes with a rather weak commitment to entrepreneurship as a field (Landstrom and Lohrke 2010). Outside management studies, research fields, particularly phenomenon-based ones, are likewise observed to fragment along disciplinary lines (e.g. terrorism research, Gordon 2010).

There is some reason to believe that this fragmentation into disciplinary clusters is particularly likely to befall phenomenon-based research fields, such as OS research. They are often fields that have no single "natural" disciplinary home base (Chubin 1976; Krogh et al. 2012b). Scholars join forces, united by a shared interest in the puzzling phenomenon, rather than shared mental frames, social networks, or epistemic base. These differences make phenomenon-based fields prone to fragmentation, particularly splitting into various disciplinary clusters that examine the phenomenon from different angles. We found this to be true even in a field where the phenomenon itself exerts a strong integrating force (cf. Section 4.2).

4.5.3 *Explanatory Propositions*

There are many reasons that lead scholars to prefer disciplinary to interdisciplinary research. Disciplinary homophily in research networks can be explained by strategic concerns of career advancement within the discipline, better-aligned research interests, and lower costs of communication and knowledge exchange, among other factors (Whitley 2000).

Emergent research fields, we argue, are more likely to present research conditions and needs that override that preference for disciplinary research.

We propose that such fields tend to be high in interdisciplinary functional dependence, i.e. interdependence among researchers from different disciplines that is created by the substance matter of the new field (Whitley 2000). Functional dependence creates the requirement for researchers to rely on each others' expertise to achieve their research objectives. It relates to the identification of good research questions as well as the finding of good answers. As interdisciplinary functional dependence declines over time, as we will argue that it tends to do, scholars return to more intra-disciplinary work. We propose:

> P2: *Interdisciplinary functional dependence tends to be higher in nascent research fields than in mature fields.*

We suggest at least three reasons that drive this tendency: search costs, task uncertainty and modularity.

First, in the very early stages of a research field, it is often unclear what other disciplines can contribute in terms of theories and related prior knowledge. Thus, there is considerable risk for any scholar of formulating questions that are either illegitimate or already solved, viewed from a different disciplinary angle. To guard against this risk, the scholar would need to find out what is known in other disciplines that might have bearing on her research problem at hand—a rather costly search, especially as her own objectives may be rather fluid in this early stage. In this situation, interdisciplinary co-authorship may be both more efficient and less in danger of missing important aspects from other disciplines. It is a way of "knowing what nobody knows". Later in the development of the field, publications from different disciplinary angles have produced an overview of relevant theories as well as areas pointed out for research that our researcher could more comfortably rely on. This may be a reason why we find co-authorship to decline earlier than co-citation. For example, a management scholar interested in OS developers' motivation and incentives to create software code for free, has access to multiple studies by, e.g., psychologists and economists, that reassure her that she is asking a legitimate research question and using an appropriate theoretical framing.

Second and more fundamentally, emergent research fields are typically characterized by high uncertainty regarding the most important problems to be studied and the most suitable methods of studying them (Edmondson and McManus 2007). Whitley (2000) refers to this situation as bearing high technical and strategic task uncertainty. The "importance of results has to be negotiated and demonstrated rather than being assured by the dominant theoretical structure" (Whitley 2000, p. 137). Assessments are likely to be subject to rapid change. In the field of OS research, we showed that scholars identified and increasingly focused on governance issues as an important area of research. While earlier work emphasized OS licenses as a key element of governance, later studies prioritized actual decision-making in the absence of formal hierarchy—a focus that required different theories as well as methods of data extraction and analysis. (While the former emphasized legal perspectives, the latter spotlighted organizational issues.)

Interdisciplinary research can be a way for researchers to address this task uncertainty. By co-authoring and citing and across disciplinary boundaries and by writing papers that are relevant to more than one discipline, researchers create options for themselves—multiple avenues to finding novelty, understanding, framing and publishing results, and earning a reputation. If and as requirements and intellectual priorities in the field change, or if their own work evolves in a somewhat unexpected direction, they are more likely to be able to accommodate these changes. Later, as research conditions become more stable and predictable, the need for this "insurance" is likely to decline.

> P3: *Task uncertainty tends to decline as research fields mature. Ceteris paribus, lower task uncertainty reduces the benefits of interdisciplinary research.*

Third, the degree of modularity typically changes as research fields evolve. Like other complex systems, scientific knowledge creation benefits from modularization (Baldwin and Clark 2004). As research fields mature, it is desirable to create modules such that scholars doing research in one area, or module, need not be deeply knowledgeable in other areas (what Parnas 1972 calls "information hiding").

It is well known that modularization follows understanding—it is very difficult to create a yet unknown system in a modular way (Simon 1969; Baldwin and Clark 2000). At the inception of a research field, it is not clear what the modules will be and how they will connect to create an understanding of the research field. Eventually, as some elements become better understood, they begin to group into more closely connected themes or clusters. Scholars can mostly work within these clusters and import and cite, e.g., stylized facts from other areas as needed, while details can remain 'hidden'.

There are strong reasons to believe that, ceteris paribus, efficient modularizations tend to be disciplinary ones: As previously explained, interdisciplinary exchange typically involves high costs. According to Birnbaum, "interdisciplinary research is a very difficult process and one which should not be undertaken lightly . . . If the problem can be decomposed before research is begun and parts of it allocated to different experts without the need for integrated effort, . . . the time, the effort, and cost of interdisciplinary research can be avoid" (Birnbaum 1981, p. 1281). If and as modularization can help to contain functional dependence within each discipline, total transaction costs are lowered (Baldwin 2008). We summarize our argument as follows:

> P4: *Increasing understanding of a research field facilitates the modularization of research efforts. Modularization will tend to follow*

disciplinary faultlines. As a consequence, interdisciplinary research tends to decline as research fields mature.

4.6　Conclusion

4.6.1　Discussion of Contribution and Future Research
The prevalence, workings and benefits of interdisciplinary research have been a focus of scholarly attention for many years. However, there are very few studies to date that measure and explain how interdisciplinary collaboration among researchers evolves over time.

In this paper, we used objective bibliometric data and other secondary data to carefully document the evolution of the field of open source research. We showed that the prevalence of interdisciplinary research in this field decreases over time and suggested some reasons behind this tendency to return to disciplinary research. We found that the unity of the phenomenon exerts cohesive power, even as disciplinary faultlines begin to cut across the research field.

Our detailed analysis of the evolution of the field will be of interest to scholars within this growing field itself and to others beyond who can use it as a reference case. The patterns we found were surprisingly clear; and they were manifest surprisingly early in the evolution of the field. It is interesting to note that OS research is commonly thought of as a strongly interdisciplinary field. This suggests that assessing the prevalence of interdisciplinary research in a field requires careful and timely analysis—it cannot be deduced from the presence of researchers from multiple disciplines within a field.

Our paper also makes a methodological contribution by proposing a tool-set of qualitative and quantitative analyses for assessing the level of interdisciplinary integration of research fields in a comprehensive way.

Also on a methodological note, this study used four different data sources. This allowed us to show that redundancy rates among these data sources was rather low—suggesting that the practice common to most bibliometric studies of using only a single data source may not be adequate.

Finally, we advanced propositions about the contingency factors driving the disciplinary fragmentation of research fields. These propositions can be operationalized and tested in future studies. If supported, they can help us make better predictions about the evolution of research fields.

4.6.2　Implications for Research Practice and Research Policy
Our findings will be relevant to individual researchers, research organizations and funding agencies.

Individual scholars and research organizations can optimize their programs by better understanding the rules by which scholarly work in their field evolves. Our findings do not imply that it is always advisable to elect interdisciplinary research in nascent fields and eschew it in mature fields.

Rather, it suggests that, in some, perhaps even in many, fields, most researchers find those approaches optimal in relation to their specific projects. This should encourage each scholar to carefully consider the costs and benefits of different forms of interdisciplinary research in relation to her project, particularly if she plans to diverge from the patterns, and possibly expectations, prevalent in her field at the time.

Our findings also have implications for research evaluation in academia and industry and for research policy. In evaluations of individual scholars' research output, corporate research, and public funding decisions, the (inter) disciplinary nature of the research (to be) undertaken often plays a role: e.g., funding schemes often demand an interdisciplinary composition of the research scheme (Huutoniemi et al. 2010). Similarly, research organizations such as university departments as well as science media often use the yardstick of a supposedly appropriate level of interdisciplinary research in assessing scholarly work (it may actually be biased against interdisciplinary approaches; cf. Fagerberg et al. 2012).

Our findings suggest that the appropriate level of interdisciplinarity against which a project proposal, a manuscript or a research record should be held, is contingent on the stage of development of the research field. For example, funding schemes and policies that favor interdisciplinary exchange among scientists may be misaligned with the situation of the field they seek to support, thus impairing research efficacy. In some fields, it may be better to support the re-export of findings into the disciplines involved in a field, e.g. disciplinary synthesis and integration of phenomenon-based findings.

ACKNOWLEDGMENTS

Our sincerest thanks go to Georg von Krogh and Eric von Hippel for their continued encouragement and their valuable comments on earlier drafts of this paper. Matthias Meyer and Michael Zaggl kindly advised us on methodological issues. We also gratefully acknowledge the financial support of the German Federal Ministry of Education and Research (BMBF, 16I1573) and the German Research Foundation (DFG, RA 1798/3–1). The authors alone are responsible for errors and omissions.

NOTES

1. Number of redundant pre-filtered publications divided by the number of total pre-filtered publications.
2. Since many rankings cover only a subset of the journals found in the preliminary database, we use an ordered list of eight ranking systems, which can be obtained from the authors.
3. The list of core papers will be shared upon request.
4. We tracked all authors who published in phase 1 (1999–2002) as well as the 30 most-cited scholars.

5. For studies on OS developers' sources of motivation, Research Policy is the most prolific outlet. Research Policy, Industrial and Corporate Change, and Organization Science are particularly strong publishers of studies relating to the organization, governance, and the process of OS development. Management Science focuses on contributions on competitive dynamics, but also organizational issues. Papers on policy and "other" issues are mostly published in law journals.
6. The CoCit score relates the absolute number of co-citations of two publications to their overall citation occurrence (Meyer et al. 2009). It ranges from 0 to 1. If we denote the number of co-citations between two references i and j by C, the CoCit score $S_{ij} = C^2_{ij} /[\min(C_{ii}, C_{jj}) \times \text{mean}(C_{ii}, C_{jj})]$ (Gmür 2003; Schäffer et al. 2006). Usually, a CoCit threshold is applied in order to suppress coincidental cocitations (Meyer et al. 2008). In line with common practice that uses threshold values between 0.2 and 0.4 (Gmür 2003; Meyer et al. 2008), we apply a threshold of 0.3.
7. $r = (\sum_i e_{ii} - \sum_i a_i^2)/(1 - \sum_i a_i^2)$, where eii is the fraction of vertices between type i and type j. a_i is the fraction of vertices that is connected to a node of type i, i.e. $a_i = \sum_j e_{ij}$.
8. Geographic proximity, too, appears to favor co-authorship—inter-continental collaborations are below 15%. US-based (49%) and European (45%) research groups prevail.
9. We compare researchers' disciplinary affiliation, as indicated by their knowledge assets, with the disciplinary affiliation of their chosen publication outlets. If economists publish in economics journals, we infer that they focus on disciplinary progress (cf., Pierce 1999).
10. We examine the subject areas to which authors indicate their work to contribute to in ISI. The disciplines that these areas are associated with are taken as a proxy for the disciplines for which the publication is relevant.
11. The predominance of management publications in the co-citation diagrams needs to be interpreted carefully. Recall that one of our conditions for including a paper in our sample was that it had some relation to business and management research. Note, however, that this does not, per se, account for the increasing paucity of interdisciplinary linkages.

REFERENCES

Aksulu, A., and Wade, M. (2010): "A comprehensive review and synthesis of open source research", *Journal of the Association for Information Systems* 11(11), Article 6.
Allen, R.C. (1983): "Collective invention", *Journal of Economic Behavior and Organization* 4, pp. 1–24.
Arrow, K.J. (1962): "Economic welfare and the allocation of resources for inventions", in *The rate and direction of economic activity*, pp. 609–625, Princeton University Press, Princeton, NJ.
Baldwin, C.Y. (2008): "Where do transactions come from? modularity, transactions, and the boundaries of firms", *Industrial and Corporate Change* 17, pp. 155–195.
Baldwin, C.Y., and Clark, K.B. (2000): *Design rules—the power of modularity*, MIT Press, Cambridge, MA.
Baldwin, C.Y., and Clark, K.B. (2004): Modularity in the design of complex engineering systems. http://www.people.hbs.edu/cbaldwin/DR2/BaldwinClarkCES.pdf.

Baldwin, C. Y., and Hippel, E. von (2011): "Modeling a paradigm shift: from producer innovation to user and open collaborative innovation", *Organization Science* 22, pp. 1399–1417.

Barney, J. (1991): "Firm resources and sustained competitive advantage", *Journal of Management* 17, pp. 99–120.

Bartunek, J. M. (2007): "Academic-practitioner collaboration need not require joint or relevant research: toward a relational scholarship of integration", *Academy of Management* 50, pp. 1323–1333.

Beaver, D. deB., and Rosen, R. (1978): "Studies in scientific collaboration", *Scientometrics* 1, pp. 65–84.

Becher, T., and Trowler, P. R. (2001): *Academic tribes and territories: intellectual enquiry and the culture of disciplines*, 2nd ed. Open University Press, Buckingham.

Birnbaum, P. H. (1981): "Contingencies for interdisciplinary research: matching research questions with research organizations", *Management Science* 27, pp. 1279–1293.

Bonaccorsi, A., Giannangeli, S., and Rossi, C. (2006): "Entry strategies under competing standards: hybrid business models in the open source software industry", *Management Science* 52, pp. 1085–1098.

Bonaccorsi, A., and Vargas, J. (2010): "Proliferation dynamics in new sciences", *Research Policy* 39, pp. 1034–1050.

Callon, M., Courtial, J., and Penan, H. (1995): *Cienciometría, el estudio cuantitativo de la actividad científica: de la bibliometría a la vigilancia tecnológica*, Gijon, Trea.

Charvet, F. F., Cooper, M. C., and Gardner, J.T. (2008): "The intellectual structure of supply chain management: a bibliometric approach", *Journal of Business Logistics* 29, p. 47.

Christensen, C. M. (2006): "The ongoing process of building a theory of disruption", *Journal of Product Innovation Management* 23, pp. 39–55.

Chubin, D. E. (1976): "State of the field: the conceptualization of scientific specialties", *Sociological Quarterly* 17(4), pp. 448–476.

Chubin, D. E., Porter, A. L., and Rossini, F. A. (1986a): "Interdisciplinary research: the why and the how", in *Interdisciplinary analysis and research*, D. E. Chubin, A. L. Porter, F. A. Rossini, and C. Terry (eds.), pp. 241–252, Lomond Publications, Mt Airy, MD.

Chubin, D. E., Porter, A. L., and Rossini, F. A. (1986b): "Interdisciplinary research: the why and the how", in *Interdisciplinary analysis and research*, D. E. Chubin, A. L. Porter, F. A. Rossini, and C. Terry (eds.), pp. 14–28, Lomond Publications, Mt Airy, MD.

Coase, R. H. (1937): "The nature of the firm", *Economica* 4, pp. 386–405.

Crowston, K., Wei, K., Howison, J., and Wiggins, A. (2012): Free/libre Open Source software development: what we know and what we do not know", *ACM Computing Surveys* 44(2), Article 7.

Dalle, J. M., David, P. A., Besten, M. den, and Steinmueller, W. E. (2008): "Empirical issues in Open Source software", *Information Economics and Policy* 20, pp. 301–304.

Darden, L., and Maull, N. (1977): "Interfield theories", *Philosophy of Science* 44, pp. 43–64.

Davis, M. S. (1971): "That's interesting!" *Philosophy of the Social Sciences* 1, pp. 309–344.

De Glas, F. (1986): "Fiction and bibliometrics: analyzing a publishing house's stocklist", *Libri* 36, pp. 40–64.

Demsetz, H. (1967): "Toward a theory of property rights", *American Economic Review* 57, pp. 347–359.

Dogan, M., and Pahre, R. (1990): "Scholarly reputation and obsolescence in the social-sciences—innovation as a team sport", *International Social Science Journal* 42, pp. 417–427.

Edmondson, A. C., and McManus, S. E. (2007): "Methodological fit in management field research", *Academy of Management Review* 32, pp. 1155–1179.

Ekeh, P. P. (1974): *Social exchange theory: the two traditions*, Harvard University Press, Cambridge, MA.

Eom, S. (2008): "All author cocitation analysis and first author cocitation analysis: a comparative empirical investigation", *Journal of Informetrics* 2, pp. 53–64.

Fagerberg, J., Landström, H., and Martin, B. R. (2012): "Exploring the emerging knowledge base of 'The Knowledge Society'", *Research Policy* 41, pp. 1121–1131.

Fagerberg, J., and Verspagen, B. (2009): "Innovation studies: the emerging structure of a new scientific field", *Research Policy* 38, pp. 218–233.

Forman, J., and Markus, M. L. (2005): "Research on collaboration, business communication, and technology", *Journal of Business Communication* 42, pp. 78–102.

Fosfuri, A., Giarratana, M. S., and Luzzi, A. (2008): "The penguin has entered the building: the commercialization of Open Source software products", *Organization Science* 19, pp. 292–305.

Franke, N., and Shah, S. (2003): "How communities support innovative activities: an exploration of assistance and sharing among end-users", *Research Policy* 32, pp. 157–178.

Ghosh, R. A. (2006): *Economic impact of Open Source software on innovation and the competitiveness of the information and communication technologies (ICT) sector in the EU*, UNU-MERIT, Maastricht.

Gibbons, M., Limoges, C., Nowotny, H., Schwartzman, S., Scott, P., and Trow, M. (1994): *The new production of knowledge: the dynamics of science and research in contemporary societies*, Sage, London.

Gmür, M. (2003): "Co-citation analysis and the search for invisible colleges: a methodological evaluation", *Scientometrics* 57, pp. 27–57.

Gordon, A. (2010): "Can terrorism become a scientific discipline? a diagnostic study", *Critical Studies on Terrorism* 3, pp. 437–458.

Hessels, L. K., and van Lente, H. (2008): "Re-thinking new knowledge production: a literature review and a research agenda", *Research Policy* 37, pp. 740–760.

Hippel, E. von (2005): *Democratizing innovation*, MIT Press, Cambridge, MA.

Hoffman, D. L., and Holbrook, M. B. (1993): "The intellectual structure of consumer research: a bibliometric study of author cocitations in the first 15 years of the Journal of Consumer Research", *Journal of Consumer Research* 19, pp. 505–517.

Huutoniemi, K., Klein, J. T., Bruun, H., and Hukkinen, J. (2010): "Analyzing interdisciplinarity: topology and indicators", *Research Policy* 39, pp. 79–88.

Klein, J. T., and Porter, A. L. (1990): "Preconditions for interdisciplinary research", in *International research management*, P. H. Birnbaum-More, F. A. Rossini and D. R. Baldwin (eds.), pp. 11–19, Oxford University Press, New York.

Knights, D., and Willmott, H. (1997): "The hype and hope of interdisciplinary management studies", *British Journal of Management* 8, pp. 9–22.

Kötter, R., and Balsiger, P. W. (1999): "Interdisciplinarity and transdisciplinarity: a constant challenge to the sciences", *Issues in Integrative Studies* 17, pp. 87–120.

Krogh, G. von, Haefliger, S., Spaeth, S., and Wallin, M. W. (2012a): "Carrots and rainbows: motivation and social practice in Open Source software development", *MIS Quarterly* 36, pp. 649–676.

Krogh, G. von, Rossi Lamastra, C., and Haefliger, S. (2012b): "Phenomena-based research in management and organization science: towards a research strategy", *Long Range Planning* 45, pp. 277–298.

Krogh, G. von, and Spaeth, S. (2007): "The open source software phenomenon: characteristics that promote research", *Journal of Strategic Information Systems* 16, pp. 236–253.

Krogh, G. F. von, and Hippel, E. von (2003): "Special issue on open source software development", *Research Policy* 32, pp. 1149–1157.

Krogh, G. von, and Hippel, E. von (2006): "The promise of research on open source software", *Management Science* 52, pp. 975–983.

Kuhn, T. S. (1962): *The structure of scientific revolutions*, University of Chicago Press, Chicago.

Landstrom, H., and Lohrke, F. (eds.) (2010): *Historical foundations of entrepreneurial research*, Edward Elgar, Cheltenham, UK.

Lerner, J., and Tirole, J. (2002): "Some simple economics of open source", *The Journal of Industrial Economics* 50, pp. 197–234.

Levy, S. (1984): *Hackers: heroes of the computer revolution*, Anchor Press/Doubleday, New York.

Lievrouw, L. A. (1990): "Reconciling structure and process in the study of scholarly communication", in *Scholarly communication and bibliometrics*, C. L. Borgman (ed.), pp. 59–69, Sage, Newbury Park, CA.

McCain, K. W. (1998): "Neural networks research in context: a longitudinal journal cocitation analysis of an emerging interdisciplinary field", *Scientometrics* 41, pp. 389–410.

Merton, R. K. (1973): *Sociology of science: theoretical and empirical investigations*, University of Chicago Press, Chicago.

Metzger, N., and Zare, R. N. (1999): "Science policy: interdisciplinary research: from belief to reality", *Science* 283, pp. 642–643.

Meyer, M., Lorscheid, I., and Troitzsch, K. G. (2009): "The development of social simulation as reflected in the first ten years of JASSS: a citation and co-citation analysis", *Journal of Artificial Societies and Social Simulation* 12.

Meyer, M., Schäffer, U., and Gmür, M. (2008): "Transfer und Austausch von Wissen in der Accounting-Forschung: Eine Zitations- und Kozitationsanalyse englischsprachiger Accounting-Journals 1990–2004", *Zeitschrift für betriebswirtschaftliche Forschung* 60, pp. 153–181.

Moody, J. (2004): "The structure of a social science collaboration network: disciplinary cohesion from 1963 to 1999", *American Sociological Review* 69, pp. 213–238.

Morillo, F., Bordons, M., and Gómez, I. (2003): "Interdisciplinarity in science: a tentative typology of disciplines and research areas", *Journal of the American Society for Information Science and Technology* 54, pp. 1237–1249.

Nelson, R. R., and Winter, S. G. (1982): *An evolutionary theory of economic change*, Harvard University Press, Cambridge, MA.

Nerur, S. P., Rasheed, A. A., and Natarajan, V. (2008): "The intellectual structure of the strategic management field: an author co-citation analysis", *Strategic Management Journal* 29, pp. 319–336.

Newman, M.E.J. (2003): "Mixing patterns in networks", *Physical Review E* 67, p. 026126.

Nissani, M. (1997): "Ten cheers for interdisciplinarity: the case for interdisciplinary knowledge and research", *The Social Science Journal* 34, pp. 201–216.

Nonaka, I. (1994): "A dynamic theory of organizational knowledge creation", *Organization Science* 5, pp. 14–37.

North, D. C. (1990): *Institutions, institutional change and economic performance*, Cambridge University Press, New York.

Olson, M. (1965): *The logic of collective action: public goods and the theory of groups*, Harvard University Press, Cambridge, MA.

O'Mahony, S., and Ferraro, F. (2007): "The emergence of governance in an open source community", *Academy of Management Journal* 50, pp. 1079–1106.

Osterloh, M., and Rota, S. (2007): "Open Source software development—just another case of collective invention?" *Research Policy* 36, pp. 157–171.

Parnas, D. L. (1972): "On the criteria to be used in decomposing systems into modules", *Communications of the ACM* 15, pp. 1053–1058.

Pierce, S. J. (1999): "Boundary crossing in research literatures as a means of interdisciplinary information transfer", *Journal of the American Society for Information Science* 50, pp. 271–279.

Pieters, R., and Baumgartner, H. (2002): "Who talks to whom? intra- and interdisciplinary communication of economics journals", *Journal of Economic Literature* 40, pp. 483–509.

Ponzi, L. J. (2002): "The intellectual structure and interdisciplinary breadth of knowledge management: a bibliometric study of its early stage of development", *Scientometrics* 55, pp. 259–272.

Qin, J., Lancaster, F. W., and Allen, B. (1997): "Levels and types of collaboration in interdisciplinary research", *Journal of the American Society for Information Science* 48, pp. 893–916.

Ramos-Rodríguez, A.-R., and Ruíz-Navarro, J. (2004): "Changes in the intellectual structure of strategic management research: a bibliometric study of the Strategic Management Journal, 1980–2000", *Strategic Management Journal* 25, pp. 981–1004.

Raymond, E. (1999): *The cathedral and the bazaar*, O'Reilly, Sebastopol, CA.

Romer, P. M. (1994): "The origins of endogenous growth", *The Journal of Economic Perspectives* 8, pp. 3–22.

Rossi, M. A. (2006): "Decoding the 'free/Open Source (F/OSS) puzzle'—a survey of theretical and empirical contributions", in *The economics of Open Source software development*, J. Bitzer and P.J.H. Schröder (eds.), pp. 15–56, Emerald Group Publishing, Amsterdam.

Schäffer, U., Binder, C., and Gmür, M. (2006): "Struktur und Entwicklung der Controllingforschung—Eine Zitations-und Kozitationsanalyse von Controllingbeiträgen in deutschsprachigen wissenschaftlichen Zeitschriften von 1970 bis 2003", *Zeitschrift für Betriebswirtschaft* 76, pp. 395–440.

Simon, H. A. (1969): *The sciences of the artificial*, MIT Press, Cambridge, MA.

Small, H. (1973): "Co-citation in the scientific literature: a new measure of the relationship between two documents", *Journal of the American Society for Information Science* 24, pp. 265–269.

Small, H., and Griffith, B. C. (1974): "The structure of scientific literatures I: identifying and graphing specialties", *Social Studies of Science* 4, pp. 17–40.

Small, H. G. (1978): "Cited documents as concept symbols", *Social Studies of Science* 8, pp. 327–340.

Smeltzer, L. R. (1994): "Confessions of a researcher: a reply to Kitty Locker", *Journal of Business Communication* 31, pp. 157–159.

Stallman, R. (1999): "The GNU operating system and the free software movement", in *Open sources: voices from the Open Source revolution*, C. DiBona, S. Ockman, and M. Stone (eds.), pp. 53–70, O'Reilly & Associates, Sebastopol, CA.

Teece, D. J., Pisano, G., and Shuen, A. (1997): "Dynamic capabilities and strategic management", *Strategic Management Journal* 18, pp. 509–533.

Tsai, W., and Wu, C. (2010): "Knowledge combination: a cocitation analysis", *The Academy of Management Journal* 53, pp. 441–450.

van Leeuwen, T., and Tijssen, R. (2000): "Interdisciplinary dynamics of modern science: analysis of cross-disciplinary citation flows", *Research Evaluation* 9, pp. 183–187.

White, H. D., and Griffith, B. C. (1981): "Author cocitation: a literature measure of intellectual structure", *Journal of the American Society for Information Science* 32, pp. 163–171.

Whitley, R. (2000): *The intellectual and social organization of the sciences*, 2nd ed., Oxford University Press, New York.

Section 2

Participant's Behavior

5 Community Joining, Progressing and Leaving
Developing an Open Source Participation Lifecycle Model

Daniel Ehls and Cornelius Herstatt

Open collaborative innovation communities, such as open source projects, established themselves as new organizational form and unite numerous people. A key challenge for these open initiatives is to attract participants and realize their subsequent community progression, termination and re-joining. Yet, membership dynamics are not well understood nor concepts put in relationship. We pursue to provide an overview of different participation phases and antecedents of progression of members. Our analysis of present research identifies four key participation phases, representing member 'landing' points, and two core concepts explaining contribution and latent activities on how, and why participants advance. Based on these findings and led by the theory of social learning we develop a participation model describing a consistent framework for community joining, contributing and leaving. This model is able to combine latest research and identify influences affecting progression. We highlight socialization and alliance building among volunteers, and provide insights into causes for membership dynamics. Moreover, we propose a yet lacking pre-participation phase highlighting community selection before joiners interact with the community. Our model solves the puzzle of an end-to-end membership perspective, and helps guiding researchers and community managers in understanding member management and participation behavior.

Keywords: community joining, volunteer advancement, membership dynamics, participation model, lifecycle perspective, member management, individual behavior

5 COMMUNITY JOINING, PROGRESSING AND LEAVING

5.1 Introduction

The Internet is filled with junk and jerks. It is commonplace for inhabitants of the Internet to complain bitterly about the lack of cooperation, decorum, and useful information. The signal-to-noise ratio, it is said, is bad and getting worse. Even a casual trip through cyberspace will turn up evidence of hostility, selfishness, and simple nonsense. Yet the wonder of the Internet is not that there is so much noise, but that there is any significant cooperation at all. Given that it is difficult or impossible to impose monetary or physical sanctions on someone, it is striking that the Internet is not literally a war of all against all. For a student of social order, what needs to be explained is not the amount of conflict but the great amount of sharing and cooperation that does occur in online communities.

(Kollock 1998, p. 220)

Online communities are "social aggregations that emerge from the Net when enough people carry on public discussions long enough, with sufficient human feeling to form webs of personal relationships in cyberspace" (Rheingold 1993, p. 5). People thereby follow a common community objective that made a online community to a collective of people connected via the Internet who interact over time around a shared purpose, interest or need (Preece 2000). Thus, communities are "voluntary association of actors, typically lacking in a priori common organizational affiliation (i.e. not working for the same firm) but united by a shared instrumental goal." (West and Lakhani 2008, p. 224). In contrast to offline communities, people collaborate within computer-mediated spaces and mostly without face-to-face meetings in reality. Despite the impersonal information exchange, online networks reduce coordination costs and facilitate social gathering (Malone and Laubacher 1998).

From a strategic and innovative point of view, a community represents a complementary asset (Dahlander and Wallin 2006), a pool of knowledge (Lesser and Prusak 2000; Swan et al. 2002), and acts as a medium for problem solving (Brown and Duguid 1991; Hargadon and Bechky 2006). Breakthrough innovations rarely happen without a community to support and diffuse inventions (Rosenkopf and Tushman 1994; Christensen and Rosenbloom 1995; Hargrave 2006; Hargadon and Douglas 2001). Especially open source communities are a source of inspiration for new ideas, product refinement and design, as well as product creation (Murray and O'Mahony 2007; O'Mahony and Bechky 2008). They exhibit a locus of collective creativity and innovation (Lee and Cole 2003) and emphasize the role of communities in the innovation process through the systematic production of goods (Hippel 2005; West and Lakhani 2008; Hippel and Krogh 2003; Verworn et al. 2004).

5.1.1 Research Gap and Objective

In order to fully benefit from the potential of a community and to interact with its members, it is essential to understand member recruitment and community participation behavior. Participation behavior research has so far concentrated on participation motives[1] and found several drivers for community participation. However, subsequent participation behavior, community interaction, and membership dynamics are unclear. Different concepts aim to describe membership dynamics from certain angels and in different participation phases. However, the relationship between these concepts is lacking. Initial reasons to join and contribute to a community differ strongly from those in subsequent stages (Fang and Neufeld 2009; Dahlander and O'Mahony 2011). Satisfaction of needs and technical contributions are central in the beginning, but sustained participation depends on community identity construction and socialization. Yet, a cohesive overview of participation behavior, and especially participation involvement is missing. This paper addresses this gap and pursues to disentangle the prevalent concepts. We review participation and joining literature for open source communities in order to uncover: (1) Which community participation stages exists? and (2) How does a member progress and particularly what causes progression? From a theory point of view, we aim to contribute with a participation lifecycle model describing in one consistent framework community joining, contributing, and leaving. This model can guide researchers and community managers in understanding member management and participation behavior.

Our analysis reveals three essential stages: Initial Participation and the Community Joining Script, Sustained Participation and Progressing Towards Center, Terminating Participation and Community Leaving. During these stages, a volunteer progresses through the phases of lurking, developing and administrating. Besides this progression, the user can leave the community and terminate participation. However, research is lacking with respect to the period before initial contribution. This study aims to fill the gap and proposes a new stage: Pre-participation. Pre-participation comprises of community identification, evaluation and selection. Based on the theory of social learning, we unite currently loosely coupled stages and provide an end-to-end participation lifecycle framework. This frameworks orders earlier research, highlights latent social influences as well as visible member contributions and leads to a coherent membership lifecycle model.

5.1.2 Participation Background: Participation Drivers and Attracting Participants

Why people engage in communities is a central question in participation research. Moreover, some people do not only participate but also contribute content, reveal their knowledge for free, and provide mundane field support. Research has revealed a wide range of participation rationales that cause engagement. These motives range from purely fun driven and ideology to process benefits like reputation, learning, and also commercial reasons like getting paid and part of a job (e.g. Hars and Ou 2001; Lakhani and Hippel 2003; Roberts et al. 2006). From the perspective of participants, contributing content to the community provides greater benefits than free riding due to aspects of reciprocity, feedback, and acknowledgement, which are only available through participation (Hippel and Krogh 2003). Sharing content with the community not only enlarges the group, but also brings greater advantages for the contributors inside, rather than outside the community (Hinds and Bailey 2003).

From a community perspective, attracting participants is a key strategic challenge (Healy and Schussman 2003; Chesbrough and Appleyard 2007). Attracting volunteers for contribution is essential for the existence of open collaborations (Butler 2001; Crowston and Scozzi 2002; Krishnamurthy 2002; Markus et al. 2000; Fang and Neufeld 2009) and project success is significantly correlated with project size (Ghosh and Prakash 2000). Projects with little active developer support are more likely to fail than projects with more active developers (Krishnamurthy 2002), and an increase in the number of peripheral developers leads to more development activity (Colazo and Fang 2009; Lee and Cole 2003).

Thus, the process of community joining and participating is central for membership dynamics, from a community perspective, in order to enlarge the community and engage new members, and individually, to choose a community to satisfy one's participation rationales.

5.1.3   Open Source Communities

Within the plethora of existing communities—including social networks (e.g. Facebook, LinkedIn), open source projects (Linux, Wikipedia, RepRap), and crowdsourcing gatherings including user uploaded content sites (YouTube, Flickr), co-creation platforms (Nike community, Spreadshirt), and open innovation mediators (InnoCentive, Hyve)—open source communities differ importantly in three criteria (O'Mahony and Ferraro 2007): Autonomy, collaboration, and ownership. Autonomy: Open source communities are independent of single employees or workplaces and are distinguished from communities of practice occurring in a firm environment. Collaboration: Participants of open source communities collaborate on a common valuable product. This implies interdependencies, coordination mechanisms and a shared understanding for integrating contributors, and distinguishes open source communities from other online communities in terms of production complexity. Ownership: The community outcome is held by the community. Individual contributors agree to reveal their product for free and relinquish ownership, even if they are paid or work for firms.

Thus, open source communities challenge traditional wisdom with respect to markets and hierarchy, representing an alternative new organizational form and market competitor (Adler 2001; Powell 2003; O'Mahony and Ferraro 2007; Fosfuri et al. 2008; Dahlander and Magnusson 2005; Levine and Prietula 2014). They are self-organized and collectively self-managed, but at the same time do not rely on formal constraints (Dahlander and O'Mahony 2011; Hardgrave et al. 2003; O'Mahony 2007). They challenge the three bases of authority (tradition, rational-legal and charisma; Weber 1956) and differ importantly from classic market models (Demil and Lecocq 2006). Vertical authority is absent (Lakhani and Hippel 2003) and governance is based on horizontal authority as well as decentralized decision making (Krogh and Hippel 2006; Demil and Lecocq 2006). Instead of 'up the career ladder', the new paradigm exhibits 'progressing to the center' (Dahlander and O'Mahony 2011). Due to this independence, and also autonomous participation and the lack of formal contracts, individuals are free to select their task and the people to work with (Dahlander and Wallin 2006; Lakhani and Hippel 2003). Volunteers' joining decisions motivate both their effort and participation (Lakhani and Tushman 2012). They are free to join a community, but also free to leave the community (Oh and Jeon 2007) and vote with their feet.

It is for these reasons we concentrate on open source joining, progressing and leaving processes as a complex social interplay, that could also be transferred to further organizational forms. For example, open source communities are compared to private firms (Bonaccorsi et al. 2006; Fosfuri et al. 2008), an external source of product development (Dahlander and Wallin 2006; Jeppesen and Frederiksen 2006), and are considered organizations that are part of a commercial-information and knowledge-based economy (Armstrong and Hagel 1996; Awazu and Desouza 2004).[2]

5.2 Participation Involvement: Stages and Steps

In order to identify present research, we follow a cross-referencing approach. Starting with the core paper "Community, joining, and specialization in open source software innovation: A case study: Open Source Software Development" (Krogh et al. 2003), we trail forward and backward citations. We repeated this approach multiple times until no more relevant papers emerged. Within this section, we describe the different community engagement activities we condensed from our study. Basically, we identify three key phases: initial participation, sustained participation and terminating participation.

5.2.1 Initial Participation and the Community Joining Script

Initial participation describes the "strategies and processes by which new people join the existing community of [software] developers, and how they initially contribute code" (Krogh et al. 2003, p. 1217). New people start by spending a significant amount of time silently observing the community, an activity referred to as 'lurking',[3] before contributing for the first time to the community. Lurking ranges from a couple of weeks to several months and is explained as gaining sufficient understanding to contribute to the technical discussion. A joiner is defined as a person who emerges from a larger group of peripheral participants and eventually earns source code database editing rights (Krogh et al. 2003). Joining interactions refer to this early contribution stage, describing the steps to reach developer status and join the group of further other developers.[4] Becoming a developer means a status change of participants from mainly community-observing to active community participation with code repository modification access (Krogh et al. 2003; Ducheneaut 2005). To gain developer status a 'joining script' behavior of peripheral community members is identified.[5]

The joining script behavior is defined as the "level and type of activity a joiner goes through to become a member of the developer community" (Krogh et al. 2003. p. 1227). The level of activity expresses "the intensity of effort until a joiner is granted developer's status" (Krogh et al. 2003. p. 1227). Contrasting emails of joiners who become developers and joiners who do not become developers, Krogh et al. reveal significantly different behaviors with respect to the level and type of activity. Future developers tend to report bugs (9.6% to 3.3%), offer bug fixes (4.8% to 1.4%), and participate in general technical discussion (43.0% to 27.6%). On the other hand, list participants give more usage feedback (9.9% to 1.4%), request more help (2.2% to 0%), and refer more often to other projects (4.3% to 0%) than upcoming developers (Krogh et al. 2003). Combining these activities to a 'joining script' construct, Krogh et al. propose that contributors who follow the script are more likely to gain developer privileges. Prospective developers start lurking silently to understand the project and learn technical details. Afterwards, they provide hands-on solutions to technical problems rather than wide-ranging feedback. As a developer interviewee confirmed: "I started working with it. I saw these problems. I fixed them. Here they are. That person gets in" (Krogh et al. 2003, p. 1229).

Ducheneaut (2005) additionally examines contributor socialization within a Python project and shows distinct steps of a developer trajectory. Firstly, a user monitors the development mailing list in order to "assimilate the norms and values of the community and analyze the activity of the experts" (p. 349). The second step represents bug reporting and simultaneously suggesting patches. While following this trajectory, the participant gains a reputation for meaningful contributions within the community, socializes, and finally becomes a patcher. The third step is obtaining code repository access and directly fixing bugs. The user has now moved from lurking the community to actively developing the community and has reached developer status. The contributor has demonstrated sufficient technical skills to move to a privileged group, progressed in socialization, and is able to "identify important controversies and enroll a network of allies to attack the problem" (Ducheneaut 2005, p. 345). While doing so, the contributor has started the next step in socialization and progresses towards the center and 'sustained participation'.

5.2.2   *Sustained Participation and Progressing Towards Center*
Motivation to join a community ranges from altruism, to one's self-satisfaction, to reputation and payment. However, altruistic and idealistic motives hardly correlate with participation efforts (Hars and Ou 2001; Bagozzi

and Dholakia 2006; Nov and Kuk 2008; Schroer and Hertel 2009). Furthermore, initial conditions for participation do not predict long-term participation (Fang and Neufeld 2009), and 80% of open source software projects fade away (Colazo and Fang 2009). Communities rely on trustworthy key persons, but as everyone can join, even under different avatars, the participants' potential is hard to evaluate. Communities therefore give full access and key roles only after an evaluation period and assimilate joiners gradually into the project (O'Mahony and Ferrarao 2007; Preece and Shneiderman 2009). A two-tier developer structure is observed: peripheral developers and core developers (Lee and Cole 2003; Fang and Neufeld 2009; Ducheneaut 2005; Dahlander and O'Mahony 2011). Peripheral developers report bugs, suggest changes, participate in technical discussions and provide pieces of content. They accomplished the joining script and now have first code repository access to fix bugs.[6] Core developers have full code repository access, oversee modules, moderate the community, and craft the project. They contribute a substantial share technically as well as additionally holding administrative roles and lateral authority. Core developers' driving motivations to participate turn out to be different. Long-term participants are driven by enjoyment of programming and community interaction; in contrast, short-term participants are driven by need and use value (Shah 2006). Bagozzi and Dholakia (2006) support these findings; novice participants are typically driven by extrinsic motivation, whereas experienced participants are self-motivated by their enjoyment and by being part of the community.

While a peripheral developer has already gained some reputation for meaningful suggestions and parallel technical contributions, to become a core developer a common developer has to "demonstrate a higher level of mastery by taking charge of a sub-module" (Ducheneaut 2005, p. 351). After gaining first repository access, subsequent steps for successfully progressing towards the center are taking charge of a module-size project, and developing this project. These steps include a much greater interaction with the community, gathering support for the project, and defending it publicly. Obtaining the approval of the core members for module integration represents the next step. At this stage, the developer is very likely to gain full code repository access and has connected intensively with the core developers and the entire community. Connecting within the community is essential to gaining lateral authority and progressing to a core developer position (Dahlander and O'Mahony 2011). Technical contribution explains the progression of individuals at an early stage, but not at a later stage after gaining developer status. To acquire authority roles beyond the developer status, coordination work and the spanning of subproject communication boundaries are significant predictors to further progress (Dahlander and O'Mahony 2011).

Summarizing the community integration process, the participant progresses from observing experts and assimilating community norms (lurking), to providing significant technical contribution and ongoing community interaction (developing), to emerge as a go-to identity and being respon-sible for modules (administrating). This socialization process of building an identity and learning from peers is found in software (Fang and Neufeld 2009; Qureshi and Fang 2011) and content (Bryant et al. 2005) communi-ties. Nevertheless, a participant can also terminate participation and leave the community.

5.2.3   *Terminating Participation and Community Leaving*

Membership retention represents an important component for open source communities, which can explain community failure or prosperity (Butler 2001; Oh and Jeon 2007). Half of the registered open source community members stop contributing after their initial posting (Ducheneaut 2005), and most developers, even core members, leave the project within one year (Shah 2006). Community participants, in contrast to traditional firms' employees, do not have a formal contract with the community. They are free to leave and can easily vote with their feet.

From a social capital perspective,[7] it is argued that the more members present within a network, the more potential and assets can be mobilized, and the more valuable it is. Social capital and the naturally evolving ties represent an essential aspect in open source projects. Singh et al. (2007) find that the stronger the cohesive member ties, the more productive the group is. If members leave a community, the network becomes smaller, and social capital, including contributing resources and cohesive ties, is reduced. Mem-bers depending on each other notice the lack of a connection as soon as a partnering role is no longer occupied. Participation rationales indicate that community involvement is due to existing community members and a sense of belonging to the community. Departure of (core) members may signal dissatisfaction, reduced commitment to the community project and proj-ect failure, triggering other members to rethink their participation (Jones 1986). Oh and Jeon (2007) prove these rationales within an open source software community. Supported by herding theory, they discover a snowball effect, that the decisions of members to leave the community are heavily influenced by neighboring members. Besides the members and their ties, leavers additionally take away the gained knowledge and experience. Even when explicit knowledge is documented, tacit knowledge vanishes. Depar-ture of members hence reduces the benefits and contribution motivation of the remaining participants (Butler 2001).

However, positive support for membership turnover exists, too. Member-ship fluidity facilitates a dynamic exchange of resources, including cognitive verve in terms of creativity, passion and social identity (Faraj et al. 2011). Turnover allows new members to join and experienced developers can prog-ress to core developer roles. Even though virtual communities are not lim-ited in size, core developer roles are rare, and prospective joiners avoid high communication levels and communities that are too full (Butler 2001; Kuk 2006). Ransbotham and Kane (2011)[8] offer two empirical findings for the distinct phases of knowledge creation and knowledge retention. Firstly, they provide evidence that moderate levels of turnover correlate positively with project success. While some retention stability is required to keep the community knowledge, turnover facilitates the gaining of new knowledge for the community, because members appear to concentrate on content creation but put less effort into preserving that content. Secondly, their longitudinal study of featured Wikipedia articles reveals a curvilinear relationship of effective collaboration, in particular between the turnover of Wikipedia editors and the quality of an article. More experienced editors increase the likelihood of raising an article in quality up to a specific point but, after that, editors with average experience decrease the quality of the article.

Concluding the discussion, membership turnover is an essential element in the community joining process and the individual membership lifecycle. Detailed knowledge of why participants leave a community provides direct insights into areas of improvement in order to control member retention, understand member behavior, and derive implications for successful community management. Terminating participation and community leaving is thus included in the membership contribution framework.

This section has described certain participation involvement stages and steps. However, the stages and steps are isolated, a (theoretical) connection is missing. We aim to combine the stages and steps and propose a participation lifecycle model.

5.3   Developing a Participation Lifecycle Model

Up to now, research in community participation has focused on describing how participants move from periphery to center, and on membership turnover. Within this study, we pursue to combine earlier research and propose an integrative contribution framework supported by theoretical thoughts.

5.3.1   Developing a Contribution Framework

Currently, the literature is silent with respect to proposing a contribution framework. Research on community joining is fragmented and progressing is discussed in isolated research stages. Only single phases or steps— for example how to progress from one phase to another—are described. We order research and address that gap with a contribution model. The model not only describes single phases, but untangles and connects previous research. The model shows the joining process including how a member progresses towards the center. It also serves as a guide to framing joining decisions and other relevant activities to consider.

A notable example proposing a joining framework is the 'Reader-to-Leader Framework' (Preece and Shneiderman 2009). The framework provides four distinct phases (Reader, Contributor, Collaborator, Leader) describing how a user becomes a leader. While steps back and forth between the phases are possible and the phase descriptions highlight participant activities and key motivations within the phase, the model shows that only a fraction of users progresses to the next phase. It fails to describe how and why a user progresses to the next step. It implies that motivations change and accordingly a user progresses due to altered usability and sociability factors that influence a certain phase. Moreover, it lacks a leaving phase, and thus an important phase for explaining membership turnover and retention.

Reviewing the above discussion about initial participation and sustained participation, a participant passes certain phases. Participants commence by lurking a community, followed by active contribution (developing), and finally progress to administrator status and governing the community. These phases are connected by steps, enabling progress to the next phase. Progressing from lurking to contributing is explained by the 'joining script' construct (initial contribution), and advancing to administrator status by enrollment of key allies with respect to coordinating work and gaining lateral authority (sustained participation). Thus, while technical contributions are important to receiving developer status, coordination work and spanning subproject communication boundaries are key elements to progressing to central roles and administrator status. Clearly, initial reasons to join and contribute to a community differ strongly from those in subsequent stages (Fang and Neufeld 2009; Dahlander and O'Mahony 2011). Satisfaction of needs and technical contributions are central in the beginning, but sustained participation depends on community identity construction and socialization. In other words, initial (peripheral) participation is open to everybody, but sustained (central) participation is limited to selected core members. Moving from periphery to center is understood as a socialization process. A new joiner learns community behavior (rules, norms) while working together with other members (Hinds and Bailey 2003). Consequently, socialization starts as soon as a user decides to follow a community by (unconsciously) learning norms and values expressed in community behavior.

From a theory point of view, we base our model, and in particular to progress to the center of the community and identity construction, on 'situated learning theory' (Lave and Wenger 1991). Situated learning theory explains socialization and increasing community interactions, including learning from each other and building up an identity. Identity construction is "the process of being identified within the community", and 'situated learning' is the "process of acting knowledgeably and purposefully in the world" (Fang and Neufeld 2009, p. 9). Especially by learning from higher ranked developers, joiners gain valuable community insights. For example, socializing with core developers strengthens their skills and joiners can get social support up to receiving patronage for subprojects (Qureshi and Fang 2011; Brown and Duguid 1991). As Lee and Cole report, "the learning process uses the cultural artifacts as an educational tool. On the one hand, the publicly archived criticisms help individuals to learn from their peers how to improve their next submission. On the other hand, they serve as documented texts to train other developers observing the peer review process.

As developers learn from their own and others' prior successes and failures, they can sort themselves into tasks appropriate to their skills, move up to more challenging tasks, and/or generate better variations of the source code" (Lee and Cole 2003, p. 644).

Lead by social learning theory and ordering accordingly above steps and phases leads to the contribution model. The model is illustrated in Figure 5.1. The steps between the phases are represented by pentagons and represent the connections between phases. Two types of steps exist: promotion step and exit step. The exit step includes leaving. Leaving can occur during all phases, thus every phase is connected to the leaving step. The promotion steps include the joining script and lateral authority progression. The phases are lurking, developing, and administrating. Socialization takes place during all phases and increases with progression toward the center.

The model covers the process from lurking to leading to leaving, and combines essential elements discussed within open source research with respect to the time users are associated with the community. However, anecdotal evidence and wider literature points to a phase even before a user is affiliated with the community: a pre-participation phase.

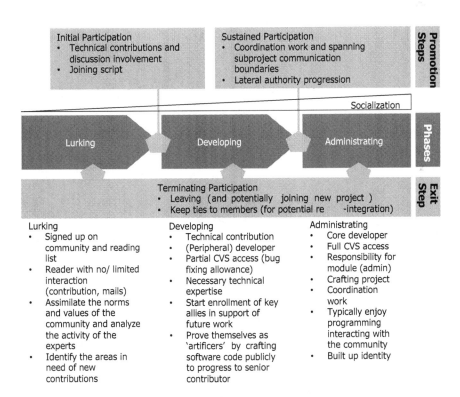

Figure 5.1 Contribution framework of open source projects

5.3.2   Extending the Contribution Framework
with Pre-Participation

Reflecting upon open source from a broader perspective and beyond contribution activities, there exist certain indications of activities even before being affiliated with the community. Trusov et al. show that word of mouth has a positive effect on member acquisition. Word of mouth "referrals have substantially longer carryover effects than traditional marketing actions and produce substantially higher response elasticities" (Trusov et al. 2009, p. 90). Hahn et al. (2008) reveal the relationship of prior collaborative ties as an explanation for project selection. The project selection likelihood grows if the prospective joiner is already familiar with the new project founder, being a past collaborator. Similarly, Kuk (2006) reports highly strategic project selection by users in order to succeed. Users enter a reciprocal interdependent relationship in order to connect to further developers. Shah (2006) supports community evaluation, describing that strangers familiarize themselves with the specific project context and make conscious decisions to join and use a community. Various externally observable community characteristics (project tenure, size, intended audience, types of software, and programming language) are instrumental to project success (Crowston and Scozzi 2002).

The inclusion of the above activities into the contribution framework calls for a further step. We propose the integration of an 'awareness' concept before the lurking phase: a pre-participation step. A pre-participation step by users takes place before the user joins a community or starts lurking. The step includes community identification and evaluation. The awareness step thus catches actions by users in choosing a community. Choosing then includes gathering information about a community, exploration initiatives (e.g. search engine usage, friend referral), and initial community evaluation. As soon as a user comes back regularly to the community and intensifies community observation, the user progresses to the lurking phase and is following the community.

Moreover, the potential of a prospective joiner to select a community exists before lurking; a personal 'scratching' exists. As Raymond reports, "every good work of software starts by scratching a developer's personal itch" (Raymond 1999, section: 'The Mail Must Get Through'). Individual motivations to participate in a community trigger a community project selection and spark a fire for community joining activities. Consequently, we term the phase before lurking the 'scratching' phase. The scratching phase describes the situation where a user is not following, and has not chosen a community yet, but already carries the intention and motives to participate, triggering subsequent actions. The phase hence incorporates the unmatched need recognized by the user as well as the problem awareness. The phase takes into account the intention of users to do an activity independent of the subsequent actually conducted behavior. The phase represents the actions of the user while outside the community, in terms of not following and not being registered. Thus, the scratching phase precedes the lurking phase. Both phases are connected by actions to select the community—the awareness step—and extend the contribution model to a participation lifecycle model.

5.3.3   Introducing the Participation Lifecycle Model

The previously introduced contribution model describes the activities of a member while within the community, or at least connected by observing the community. The above rationales suggest an extension of the contribution model to before the user is connecting with the community. Merging the awareness steps and scratching phase with the contribution model results in an end-to-end participation lifecycle model. Thus, a model starting with the inherent motivation and actions of users outside the community to leaving. The entire participation lifecycle model is illustrated in Figure 5.2. The contribution model is extended by the awareness step and the scratching phase.

The model shows an unidirectional flow indicating the member progression; however, leaving may take place during all phases. Also, stops and steps backwards can occur. Leaving ranges from stepping back from more advanced roles to more initial roles (e.g. from developer to lurker), to losing affiliations or a complete exit out of the community. The phases do not symbolize a one-way road, but represent essential stages through which a user moves gradually back and forth. Moreover, there may be certain key steps where a user is likely to be recognized as being promoted (e.g. having received initial code repository access or module responsibility). However there exists no formal process or credential to reach a certain phase. Progressing to a certain phase depends on individual skills, in particular technical and socialization skills, invested effort driven by participation rationales and previous member experience. Shah (2006), who draws on research on motivation by Roberts et al. (2006) and user background by Hertel et al. (2003), supports the heterogeneous progressing of members. Due to considerable variations in user characteristics, the socialization process varies for different users. New joiners with less experience may need more time to grasp community norms and to socialize with other members (Shah 2006). Beginners may lurk silently for a longer time. Herraiz et al. (2006) as well as Shibuya and Tamai (2009) provide empirical evidence. Herraiz et al. discover two different joining patterns: one exhibits a "sudden integration", while the second follows a "step-by-step" pattern. Step-by-step integration is observed for volunteer participants. Sudden integration is observed for firm participants and only in the coder project. Shibuya and Tamai identify the same patterns and reveal an even more determining aspect than being hired. Hired participants are already familiar with the project and are known within the community. They have previously worked together in other (sub) projects. These findings point to the relevance of a pre-project contribution phase and leaving. Former collaborators quit one project (leaving phase), but still carry motives to participate (being paid, scratching phase). Former project ties of users and community experience enable them to progress differently compared to strangers, and significantly shorten, or even skip, the lurking phase. Leaving does not necessarily mean losing connection with selected developers, but rather stepping back from stronger contribution while keeping future opportunities and developer networks open. Consequently, leaving and scratching do not represent opposite phases, but can

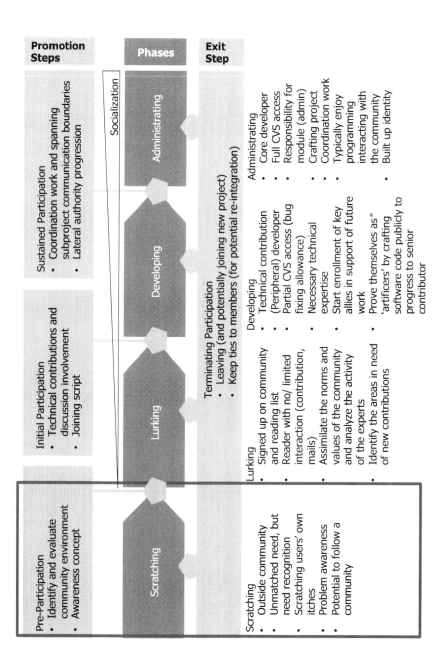

Promotion Steps

Pre-Participation
- Identify and evaluate community environment
- Awareness concept

Initial Participation
- Technical contributions and discussion involvement
- Joining script

Sustained Participation
- Coordination work and spanning subproject communication boundaries
- Lateral authority progression

Phases

Socialization

Scratching

Lurking

Developing

Administrating

Exit Step

Terminating Participation
- Leaving (and potentially joining new project)
- Keep ties to members (for potential re-integration)

Scratching
- Outside community
- Unmatched need, but need recognition
- Scratching users' own itches
- Problem awareness
- Potential to follow a community

Lurking
- Signed up on community and reading list
- Reader with no/ limited interaction (contribution, mails)
- Assimilate the norms and values of the community and analyze the activity of the experts
- Identify the areas in need of new contributions

Developing
- Technical contribution (Peripheral) developer
- Partial CVS access (bug fixing allowance)
- Necessary technical expertise
- Start enrollment of key allies in support of future work
- Prove themselves as "artificers' by crafting software code publicly to progress to senior contributor

Administrating
- Core developer
- Full CVS access
- Responsibility for module (admin)
- Crafting project
- Coordination work
- Typically enjoy programming interacting with the community
- Built up identity

Figure 5.2 Participation lifecycle model

be neighbors connected by activities out of the community (e.g. word of mouth) and can close the loop within the entire participation lifecycle.

5.4   Discussion

5.4.1   Contributions

This study provides three main contributions. First, we offer an overview of participation behavior, particularly community joining, progressing and leaving. Second, we propose a new pre-participation phase, so far lacking in research. Third, we order existing research and suggest a participation lifecycle model.

To the best of our knowledge, this is the first review providing an overview of open source joining, progressing and leaving. We highlight specific phases, representing 'landing points' and roles of members. We also provide steps between the phases and reveal why and how members progress. Specifically we identify three phases and condense research accordingly. Community contribution starts with lurking and learning cultural artifacts of the community. A joiner provides first content and follows a 'joining script' to become a developer. From being a developer, a member can further socialize and take greater responsibilities. He spans boundaries and gains lateral authority to become an administrator. Based on the review, we provide a contribution framework that concentrates on the contribution of participants to the community. Going beyond the contribution framework, we stimulate the introduction of a phase before contributing.

We propose a pre-joining phase with conscious decision processes. While the joining script (Krogh et al. 2003) describes the progress from lurking to coding, and the lateral authority concept (Dahlander and O'Mahony 2011) describes the steps towards administrating, the pre-joining actions represent the actions from scratching to lurking, a joiner awareness concept. Support for a strategic decision to join a community is provided by Kuk (2006), Shah (2006) and Ehls (2013). Their findings of strategic and conscious actions before joining underscore the behavior before being affiliated or observing the community. Moreover, within this phase, members are not influenced by the socialization and thus take decisions independent of community members and may concentrate to satisfy their needs.

From a conceptual position, we develop a participation lifecycle framework. Up to now, certain unconnected concepts of joining, socialization, and lateral authority exist within the literature. We sort these concepts and develop a coherent participation lifecycle model. This model illustrates the joining behavior from the early considerations of joining and activities outside the community, to contact with the community and joining, as well as subsequent activities like progressing within and leaving the community. It also describes steps how and why members progress and are able to link the participation phases. Thus, the model structures earlier 'joining scripts', combines certain participation perspectives, introduces a new phase and creates coherence in so far scattered research. It solves the puzzle of an end-to-end membership perspective and describes participation behavior. Also, the lifecycle model may guide researchers analyzing community participation, especially in view of mediating effects, social interaction, participation phases.

5.4.2 Limitations

Two limitations need to be kept in mind addressing the research scope and strategy.

Within the plethora of communities, we focus on the user behavior of open source communities. However, open source communities differ notably from other community types and traditional organizational forms. Nevertheless, they exhibit characteristics also found in these collaborations and spearhead open collaborative innovation. In line with latest research, we believe to transfer our results to further areas but accepting the analogy is subject to the reader.

The second area of concern targets our research strategy. In particular, we do not use a strict structured bibliometric analysis for review. As there exists no clear key words like 'participation behavior', and open source exhibits a transdisciplinary research area, we do not rely on delusive analyses and pretend rigorous but misleading results.[9] Indeed we aim to grasp a bigger picture and follow cross referencing as well as forward and backward citation to identify relevant literature but cannot guarantee to integrate all existing research.

5.4.3 Future Research Directions

This paper pursues to understand member recruitment and community participation behavior. Currently the literature has just sporadically considered member behavior. We start to ameliorate the lack of behavioral research by proposing a participation lifecycle model focusing on member behavior. The participation framework describes member behavior with special regards to community joining, progression, and leaving. While the model unites several loose research contributions and introduces a new phase, it leaves certain questions open. What exactly happens within the awareness phase and how do users decide in favor of a community? What are the preconditions for joining and what are the barriers for participation? Gaining insights into subtle mechanisms for (non-) participation provides insights into how to (un-) trigger innovation and (un-) build barriers. What are the minimum levels for participation? Do users reflect on their contribution and how carefully do joiners consider the attributes of communities in their joining decisions? Additionally, more empirical support is needed to strengthen our model and detail the transitional steps. Only a few papers (Oh and Jeon 2007; Harhoff and Mayrhofer 2010) consider why members leave a community or change to other communities. Thus, ex-post contribution decisions may help us to understand participation.

Moreover, the ongoing utilization and expansion of open source, including its communities, creates new challenges. A transformation from ideology-driven participants to a large number of commercially motivated users and the participation of firms is one example (West 2003; Bonaccorsi and Rossi 2003; Fitzgerald 2006; Rolandsson et al. 2011). Most studies treat contributors and communities as one-dimensional, ignoring the presence of differently motivated contributors, and do not break down the groups or distinguish between them. Research has concentrated on lighthouse projects like Linux or Apache. These projects often belong to established business applications and are populated with a disproportionately high percentage of paid contributors.[10] It is questionable whether these top projects are representative of the entire open source domain, or if they represent the tip of the iceberg. What about (neglected) entertainment communities? Research in open content is still nascent. Research is rare or the studies concentrate on one research object, Wikipedia. What about (neglected) entertainment communities? Are software, content, business and entertainment communities alike?

Another challenge is simply the availability of more communities (Oh and Jeon 2007; Dahlander and Magnusson 2005). Decisions under available opportunities and particularly different participation options are not yet considered. How do volunteers behave as soon as there are alternatives? What are preconditions and preferred factors for participation?

5.5 Conclusion

A community is understood as a voluntary association of actors, typically lacking in a priori common organizational affiliation but united by a shared instrumental goal. Volunteers participate and collaborate within open source due to different motives, e.g. fun, learning, reputation, need, payment. We review scattered joining and membership concepts and propose a coherent participation lifecycle model. This model illustrates the joining behavior from the first consideration of joining and activities outside the community, to contact with the community and joining, as well as subsequent activities like progressing within the community and leaving the community. The model unites several joining perspectives into a consistent approach, providing an end-to-end perspective of joining behavior, and enabling guiding of participation research.

NOTES

This contribution is based on the dissertation by Daniel Ehls, but further developed and refined.

1. For an extended review of motives for participation see e.g. von Krogh et al. (2012).
2. According to Barnard (1968), an organization represents a "system of consciously coordinated activities or forces of two or more persons". A firm

represents a collection of productive resources, where the use of these resources is determined by administrative decisions (Penrose 1959).

3. Lurkers are passive, not visible free riders, but also listening subscribers to the development mailing lists. Their level of contribution ranges from "never" (Kollock and Smith 1996) to "minimal" (Nonnecke and Preece 2000). Lurkers account for approximately 90% of all people who use online communities (Nonnecke and Preece 2000). However, while not contributing, lurkers often spread news by word of mouth and use the community product, hence increase community traffic and market share.

4. Being granted code repository access for modification represents a developer privilege.

5. Preconditions to join and barriers to participation are outside the scope of this thesis. However, preconditions exist in the form of low costs for the contributors, modular architecture in bite-size pieces, and low costs of integration (Tapscott and Williams 2008). Participation barriers exist in ease of coding, altering and integrating modules, variability of coding language, and independent working of modules (e.g. von Krogh et al. 2003; Glott et al. 2010).

6. Phases may be more nuanced. Examples and sub-phase steps are reported by Ducheneaut (2005) and include, for example, direct code repository access or contributing via admins regarding development. However, due to the flat hierarchies observable in open source communities, this thesis simplifies these steps to elemental levels and key principles.

7. Social capital is understood as "the sum of the actual and potential resources embedded within, available through, and derived from the network of relationships possessed by an individual or social unit. Social capital thus comprises both the network and the assets that may be mobilized through that network" (Nahapiet and Ghoshal 1998, p. 243). Different definitions are present within the literature; for a review see Adler and Kwon (2002).

8. Ransbotham and Kane (2011) provide a detailed overview of antecedents and consequences of community leaving and retention, also with regard to organizational theory beyond open source.

9. As of February (2013) 2014, Google Scholar provides for the research query ["open source"+"participation behavior"] only (113) 147 results, including multiple and results not hitting the intended study scope. Not mentioning browsing established databases returning only few results.

10. Considering Linux as the most business-oriented project with a high degree of commercial input and Wikipedia with close to none, as presented earlier.

REFERENCES

Adler, P. (2001): "Market, hierarchy, and trust: the knowledge economy and the future of capitalism", *Organization Science* 12(2), pp. 215–234.

Adler, P., and Kwon, S. (2002): "Social capital: prospects for a new concept", *The Academy of Management Review* 27(1), pp. 17–40.

Armstrong, A., and Hagel, J. (1996): "The real value of online communities", *Harvard Business Review* 3(May/June), pp. 134–140.

Awazu, Y., and Desouza, K. (2004): "Open knowledge management: lessons from the open source revolution", *Journal of the American Society for Information Science and Technology* 55(11), pp. 1016–1019.

Bagozzi, R.P., and Dholakia, U.M. (2006): "Open Source software user communities: a study of participation in Linux user groups", *Management Science* 52(7), pp. 1099–1115.

Barnard, C. (1968): *The functions of the executive*, Cambridge University Press, Cambridge.

Bonaccorsi, A., Giannangeli, S., and Rossi, C. (2006): "Entry strategies under competing standards: hybrid business models in the Open Source software industry", *Management Science* 52(7), pp. 1085–1098.

Bonaccorsi, A., and Rossi, C. (2003): "Why Open Source software can succeed: Open Source software development", *Research Policy* 32(7), pp. 1243–1258.

Brown, J. S., and Duguid, P. (1991): "Organizational learning and communities-of-practice: toward a unified view of working, learning, and innovation", *Organization Science* 2(1), pp. 40–57.

Bryant, S. L., Forte, A., and Bruckman, A. (2005): "Becoming Wikipedian: transformation of participation in a collaborative online encyclopedia", in *Proceedings of the 2005 international ACM SIGGROUP conference on Supporting group work*, pp. 1–10, ACM, Sanibel Island, Florida.

Butler, B. S. (2001): "Membership size, communication activity, and sustainability: a resource-based model of online social structures", *Information Systems Research* 12(4), pp. 346–362.

Chesbrough, H. W., and Appleyard, M. M. (2007): "Open innovation and strategy", *California Management Review* 50(1), pp. 57–76.

Christensen, C., and Rosenbloom, R. (1995): "Explaining the attacker's advantage: technological paradigms, organizational dynamics, and the value network", *Research Policy* 24(2), pp. 233–257.

Colazo, J., and Fang, Y. (2009): "Impact of license choice on Open Source software development activity", *Journal of the American Society for Information Science and Technology* 60(5), pp. 997–1011.

Crowston, K., and Scozzi, B. (2002): "Open source software projects as virtual organisations: competency rallying for software development", *IEE Proceedings Software* 149(1), pp. 3–17.

Dahlander, L., and Magnusson, M. (2005): "Relationships between open source software companies and communities: observations from Nordic firms", *Research Policy* 34(4), pp. 481–493.

Dahlander, L., and O'Mahony, S. (2011): "Progressing to the center: coordinating project work", *Organization Science* 22(4), pp. 961–979.

Dahlander, L., and Wallin, M. W. (2006): "A man on the inside: unlocking communities as complementary assets", *Research Policy* 35(8), pp. 1243–1259.

Demil, B., and Lecocq, X. (2006): "Neither market nor hierarchy nor network: the emergence of bazaar governance", *Organization Studies* 27(10), pp. 1447–1466.

Ducheneaut, N. (2005): "Socialization in an open source software community: a socio-technical analysis", *Computer Supported Cooperative Work (CSCW)* 14(4), pp. 323–368.

Ehls, D. (2013): *Joining decisions in open collaborative innovation communities: a discrete choice study*, Springer Gabler, Wiesbaden.

Exploring the Foundations of Cumulative Innovation: Implications for Organization Science by F. Murry and S. O' Mahony in Organization Science (78:6), pp. 2006–2021

Fang, Y., and Neufeld, D. (2009): "Understanding sustained participation in Open Source software projects", *Journal of Management Information Systems* 25(4), pp. 9–50.

Faraj, S., Jarvenpaa, S., and Majchrzak, A. (2011): "Knowledge collaboration in online communities", *Organization Science* 22(5), pp. 1224–1239.

Fitzgerald, B. (2006): "The transformation of Open Source software", *MIS Quarterly* 30(3), pp. 587–598.

Fosfuri, A., Giarratana, M. S., and Luzzi, A. (2008): "The penguin has entered the building: the commercialization of open source software products", *Organization Science* 19(2), pp. 292–305.

Ghosh, R. A., and Prakash, V. V. (2000): "The Orbiten free software survey", *First Monday* 5(7).

Glott, R., Schmidt, P., and Ghosh, R. A. (2010): *Wikipedia survey—overview of results.* http://www.wikipediasurvey.org/docs/Wikipedia_Overview_15March2010-FINAL.pdf. Accessed 30 October 2012.

Hahn, J., Moon, J. Y., and Zhang, C. (2008): "Emergence of new project teams from open source software developer networks: Impact of prior collaboration ties", *Information Systems Research* 19(3), pp. 369–391.

Hardgrave, B., Davis, F., and Riemenschneider, C. (2003): "Investigating determinants of software developers' intentions to follow methodologies", *Journal of Management Information Systems* 20(1), pp. 123–152.

Hargadon, A. B., and Bechky, B. A. (2006): "When collections of creatives become creative collectives: a field study of problem solving at work", *Organization Science* 17(4), pp. 484–500.

Hargadon, A. B., and Douglas, Y. (2001): "When innovations meet institutions: Edison and the design of the electric light", *Administrative Science Quarterly* 46(3), pp. 476–501.

Hargrave, T. (2006): "A collective action model of institutional innovation", *The Academy of Management Review* 31(4), pp. 864–888.

Harhoff, D., and Mayrhofer, P. (2010): "Managing user communities and hybrid innovation processes: concepts and design implications", *Organizational Dynamics* 39(2), pp. 137–144.

Hars, A., and Ou, S. (2001): "Working for free? motivations for participating in Open-Source projects", in *Proceedings of the 34th Annual Hawaii International Conference on System Sciences (HICSS-34)*, pp. 25–39, IEEE Computer Society, Washington, DC.

Healy, K., and Schussman, A. (2003): "The ecology of open-source software development", Department of Sociology, University of Arizona, Tucson.

Herraiz, I., Robles, G., Amor, J. J., Romera, T., and Barahona, J. M. G. (2006): "The processes of joining in global distributed software projects", in *Proceedings of the 2006 international workshop on Global software development for the practitioner*, pp. 27–33, ACM, Shanghai, China.

Hertel, G., Niedner, S., and Herrmann, S. (2003): "Motivation of software developers in Open Source projects: an Internet-based survey of contributors to the Linux kernel", *Research Policy* 32(7), pp. 1159–1177.

Hinds, P., and Bailey, D. (2003): "Out of sight, out of sync: understanding conflict in distributed teams", *Organization Science* 14(6), pp. 615–632.

Hippel, E. A. von (2005): *Democratizing innovation*, MIT Press, Cambridge.

Hippel, E. A. von, and Krogh, G. von (2003): "Open Source software and the 'private-collective' innovation model: issues for organization science", *Organization Science* 14(2), pp. 209–223.

Hippel, E. A. von, and Krogh, G. von (2006): "Free revealing and the private-collective model for innovation incentives", *R&D Management* 36(3), pp. 295–306.

Jeppesen, L. B., and Frederiksen, L. (2006): "Why do users contribute to firm-hosted user communities? the case of computer-controlled music instruments", *Organization Science* 17(1), pp. 45–63.

Jones, C. (1986): *Programming productivity*, McGraw-Hill, New York.

Kollock, P. (1998): "The economies of online cooperation: gifts and public goods in cyberspace", in *Communities in cyberspace*, M. A. Smith and P. Kollock (eds.), pp. 220–239, Routledge, London.

Kollock, P., and Smith, M. A. (1996): "Managing the virtual commons: cooperation and conflict in computer communities", in *Computer-mediated communication: linguistic, social, and cross cultural perspectives*, S. C. Herring (ed.), pp. 109–128, John Benjamins, Amsterdam.

Krishnamurthy, S. (2002): "Cave or community? an empirical examination of 100 mature open source projects", *First Monday* 7(6).

Krogh, G. von, Haefliger, S., Späth, S., and Wallin, M. W. (2012): "Carrots and rainbows: motivation and social practice in open source software development", *MIS Quarterly* 36(2), pp. 649–676.

Krogh, G. von, and Hippel, E. A. von (2006): "The promise of research on Open Source software", *Management Science* 52(7), pp. 975–983.

Krogh, G. von, Späth, S., and Lakhani, K. R. (2003): "Community, joining, and specialization in open source software innovation: a case study: Open Source software development", *Research Policy* 32(7), pp. 1217–1241.

Kuk, G. (2006): "Strategic interaction and knowledge sharing in the KDE developer mailing list", *Management Science* 52(7), pp. 1031–1042.

Lakhani, K. R., and Hippel, E. A. von (2003): "How open source software works: 'free' user-to-user assistance", *Research Policy* 32(6), pp. 923–943.

Lakhani, K. R., and Tushman, M. (2012): "Open innovation and organizational boundaries: the impact of task decomposition and knowledge distribution on the locus of innovation", *HBS Working Papers* 12–57, Harvard Business School, Cambridge, MA.

Lave, J., and Wenger, E. (1991): *Situated learning: legitimate peripheral participation*, Cambridge University Press, Cambridge.

Lee, G. K., and Cole, R. E. (2003): "From a firm-based to a community-based model of knowledge creation: the case of the Linux Kernel development", *Organization Science* 14(6), pp. 633–649.

Lesser, E., and Prusak, L. (2000): "Communities of practice, social capital and organizational knowledge", in *The knowledge management yearbook 2000–2001*, J. W. Cortada and J. A. Woods (eds.), pp. 123–131, Butterworth Heinemann, Woburn.

Levine, S., and Prietula, M. (2014): "Open collaboration for innovation: principles and performance", *Organization Science* 25(5), pp. 1414–1433.

Malone, T. W., and Laubacher, R. J. (1998): "The dawn of the e-lance economy", *Harvard Business Review* 76(5), pp. 144–152.

Markus, M., Manville, B., and Agres, C. (2000): "What makes a virtual organization work-lessons from the open source world", *Sloan Management Review* 42(1), pp. 13–26.

Nahapiet, J., and Ghoshal, S. (1998): "Social capital, intellectual capital, and the organizational advantage", *The Academy of Management Review* 23(2), pp. 242–266.

Nonnecke, B., and Preece, J. (2000): "Lurker demographics: counting the silent", in *Proceedings of the SIGCHI conference on Human factors in computing systems*, pp. 73–80, ACM, The Hague, The Netherlands.

Nov, O., and Kuk, G. (2008): "Open source content contributors' response to free-riding: the effect of personality and context", *Computers in Human Behavior* 24(6), pp. 2848–2861.

Oh, W., and Jeon, S. (2007): "Membership herding and network stability in the open source community: the Ising perspective", *Management Science* 53(7), pp. 1086–1101.

O'Mahony, S. (2007): "The governance of open source initiatives: what does it mean to be community managed?" *Journal of Management and Governance* 11(2), pp. 139–150.

O'Mahony, S., and Bechky, B. A. (2008): "Boundary organizations: enabling collaboration among unexpected allies", *Administrative Science Quarterly* 53(3), pp. 422–459.

O'Mahony, S., and Ferraro, F. (2007): "The emergence of governance in an Open Source community", *Academy of Management Journal* 50(5), pp. 1079–1106.

Penrose, E. (1959): *The theory of the growth of the firm*, Basil Blackwell, New York.

Powell, W. (2003): "Neither market nor hierarchy", *Research in Organizational Behavior* 315, pp. 295–336.

Preece, J. (2000): *Online communities: designing usability and supporting social-bilty*, Wiley, New York.

Preece, J., and Shneiderman, B. (2009): "The reader-to-leader framework: motivating technology-mediated social participation", *AIS Transactions on Human-Computer Interaction* 1(1), pp. 13–32.

Qureshi, I., and Fang, Y. (2011): "Socialization in open source software projects: a growth mixture modeling approach", *Organizational Research Methods* 14(1), pp. 208–238.

Ransbotham, S., and Kane, G. (2011): "Membership turnover and collaboration success in online communities: explaining rises and falls from grace in Wikipedia", *MIS Quarterly* 35(3), pp. 613–627.

Raymond, E.S. (1999): "Articles—The Cathedral and the Bazaar", *Knowledge, Technology and Policy* 12(3), pp. 23–49.

Rheingold, H. (1993): *The virtual community: finding connection in a computerized world*, Addison-Wesley, Boston.

Roberts, J.A., Hann, I.-H., and Slaughter, S.A. (2006): "Understanding the motivations, participation, and performance of Open Source software developers: a longitudinal study of the Apache Projects", *Management Science* 52(7), pp. 984–999.

Rolandsson, B., Bergquist, M., and Ljungberg, J. (2011): "Open source in the firm: opening up professional practices of software development", *Research Policy* 40(4), pp. 576–587.

Rosenkopf, L., and Tushman, M. (1994): "The coevolution of technology and organization", in *Dynamics of organizations*, J. A. Baum and J. V. Singh (eds.), pp. 403–424, Oxford University Press, New York.

Schroer, J., and Hertel, G. (2009): "Voluntary engagement in an open web-based encyclopedia: Wikipedians and why they do it", *Media Psychology* 12(1), pp. 96–120.

Shah, S.K. (2006): "Motivation, governance, and the viability of hybrid forms in Open Source software development", *Management Science* 52(7), pp. 1000–1014.

Shibuya, B., and Tamai, T. (2009): "Understanding the process of participating in open source communities", in *ICSE Workshop on Emerging Trends in Free/Libre/Open Source Software Research and Development, 2009. FLOSS '09.*, pp. 1–6, Vancouver, BC.

Singh, P. V., Tan, Y., and Mookerjee, V. S. (2007): "Social capital, structural holes and team composition: collaborative networks of the open source software community", in *Twenty-eighth International Conference on Information systems*.

Swan, J., Scarbrough, H., and Robertson, M. (2002): "The construction of 'communities of practice' in the management of innovation", *Management Learning* 33(4), pp. 477–496.

Tapscott, D., and Williams, A. (2008): *Wikinomics: how mass collaboration changes everything*, Portfolio Trade, New York.

Trusov, M., Bucklin, R.E., and Pauwels, K. (2009): "Effects of word-of-mouth versus traditional marketing: findings from an Internet social networking site", *Journal of Marketing* 73(5), pp. 90–102.

Verworn, B., Herstatt, C., and Sander, J. G. (2004): *Produktentwicklung mit virtuellen Communities: Kundenwünsche erfahren und Innovationen realisieren*, Gabler, Wiesbaden.

Weber, M. (1956): *Wirtschaft und Gesellschaft: Grundriss der verstehenden Soziologie*, Mohr, Tübingen.

West, J. (2003): "How open is open enough?: melding proprietary and open source platform strategies: Open Source software development", *Research Policy* 32(7), pp. 1259–1285.

West, J., and Lakhani, K. R. (2008): "Getting clear about communities in open innovation", *Industry & Innovation* 15(2), pp. 223–231.

6 Joining Open Source Communities under Alternatives
Openness Trade-Offs and User Traits Contingency

Daniel Ehls and Cornelius Herstatt

What are attractive conditions for user and distributed innovations? And, why do users join one innovation context over another? Open initiatives and communities collapse without members. Growing competition among communities and increasing user diversity including participation of firms lead to a challenge in attracting users. This study analyzes the relationship between joining decisions into open source communities and their governance aspects, specifically license constraints, access rights and sponsorship. We draw on a unique dataset of 1480 choice decisions of members of software and content, and furthermore introduce fun and business communities. Our experimental results minimize social bias and reveal openness preferences and trade-offs. We found that access is more important than usage rights and firm involvement is least important. Most crucial is the community product and user behavior. We also find that choices are contingent on participation rationales which cause highly heterogeneous tastes. Our findings solve "non-trivial managerial headaches" and contribute to organizational design, individual behavior, and open collaborative innovation.

Keywords: user innovation and communities, open innovation, contingency/configurations

6 JOINING OPEN SOURCE COMMUNITIES UNDER ALTERNATIVES

6.1 Introduction

In order to prosper and gain competitive advantages, a key strategic challenge within open-oriented organizations is to attract volunteers and understand participation (Healy and Schussman 2003; Chesbrough and Appleyard 2007). Attracting volunteers for contribution is essential for the existence of open projects (Butler 2001; Markus et al. 2000; Roberts et al. 2006; Fang and Neufeld 2009), and project success is significantly correlated with project size (Ghosh and Prakash 2000). Projects with little active developer support are more likely to fail than projects with more active developers (Krishnamurthy 2002), and an increase in the number of peripheral developers leads to more development activity (Colazo and Fang 2009; Lee and Cole 2003).

However, ongoing utilization and expansion of open initiatives, including its communities, creates new challenges like competition among initiatives and contributor diversity. A transformation from ideology-driven participants to a large number of commercially motivated users, including the participation of firms, leads to a heterogeneous member landscape, creates different ecologies and tension among participants (West 2003; Bonaccorsi and Rossi 2003; Fitzgerald 2006; Rolandsson et al. 2011). Another challenge is the increase of alternatives for participation. The continuing growth of open initiatives and the emergence of new projects lead to increased participation choices for prospective contributors. Subsequently, competition among open initiatives for talented contributors intensifies. The challenge of attracting volunteers grows (Oh and Jeon 2007; Dahlander and Magnusson 2005), and project managers are most concerned with attracting external collaborators to support production and adoption (West and O'Mahony 2008). Finally, certain degrees of openness require an organizational realignment to attract dispersed knowledge. A trade-off exists between an appropriate level of 'power and control' and capturing volunteer support. In these conflicting interests, a prospective joiner will not volunteer in an uncomfortable environment (Shah 2006). Within this realm, it is unclear, why a prospective joiner participates in one specific community, but not in another. Additionally, the influence of contextual factors on volunteering remains unclear (Boudreau 2010), especially within the field of open collaborative innovation (Fang and Neufeld 2009). Moreover, an open question exists regarding the interaction of individual user traits and social practice (Crowston et al. 2012; Krogh et al. 2012).

We address this puzzle with the basic research question: How do contextual factors influence the decisions of participants to join open communities? We analyze: How do available alternatives and the governance structure influence the decision to volunteer? Why do users join one community and not another? What are antecedents for joining behavior? In pursuing above questions, our study provides multiple insights. We (1) identify joining preferences and trade-offs of contextual factors, (2) reveal antecedents for taste heterogeneity and its contingency of motivations, (3) reduce method bias by introducing a discrete choice experiment, and (4) discover that openness is not the key factor for choosing open initiatives.

6.2   Research Scope

6.2.1   *Open Initiatives Competition*

Competitive analyses among open initiatives concentrates most often on the rivalry between 'open source' projects and commercial or 'closed' products (Casadesus-Masanell and Ghemawat 2006; Sen 2007; Cheng et al. 2011; Economides and Katsamakas 2006). Joining this conversation, surprisingly little attention has been given to the dimension of direct competition between open source communities, particularly for members.

Oh and Jean (2007) found that membership herding is highly present when external influences, for example the availability of other OSS projects, are weak, but decreases significantly when external influences increase. Also, Dahlander and Magnusson report increasing membership dynamics within open source communities as soon as the market grows and fierce competition takes off. As long as little rivalry is present, even unsatisfied members stay, but members are more likely to leave with the increasing availability of alternatives (Dahlander and Magnusson 2005). The presence of other communities creates a competitive environment among communities, increasing the challenge to attract and keep participants. How to attract innovative input if alternatives for joining exist is now an even more key strategic challenge for open initiatives. However, it is still unclear why participants select one initiative over another. Even more urgent becomes the research challenge due to the momentum of open initiatives, the opening of firms, and the ongoing emergence of communities. A "vast number of projects competes for the attention and interest of the developers and users" (Dahlander and Magnusson 2005, p. 489) and rivalry for donated labor is rising (West and O'Mahony 2008). "Competition for particularly productive or influential community members will increase, and that migration of important users will be an important phenomenon in community-driven innovation" (Harhoff and Mayrhofer 2010, p. 34). Understanding competitive dynamics of and between open initiatives is thus a major unaddressed puzzle we address in this study.

6.2.2 *Joining Decisions in Regards to Contextual Factors*

Volunteers are free to join a community, but also free to leave the community (Oh and Jeon 2007). Developers choose projects strategically (Kuk 2006) and familiarize themselves with the specific project context before consciously deciding to select a community to join (Shah 2006 Harhoff and Mayrhofer 2010). Also, firms choose open source projects intentionally and send men on the inside (Dahlander and Wallin 2006) or design their own community (West and O'Mahony 2008). Thereby the surrounding social system is likely to affect the decision of volunteers to join a community (Shah 2006; Wilson 2000). Preece and Shneiderman (2009) postulate "in a world of many choices, designers will do better if they create interesting, attractive, and relevant content". While participants will not volunteer in settings where they feel uncomfortable, the question remains open: How do differences in the governance affect a contributor's participation? (Shah 2006). Due to the distinctive characteristics of open projects, it is challenging to transfer findings from proprietary circumstances into the open source world (Fang and Neufeld 2009). Analyzing contextual factors and its contingency on volunteering thus represents a fruitful area for research (Wilson 2000). "It is not clear whether small differences in the platform owner's power or control have an appreciable effect" (Boudreau 2010, p. 1853).

6.2.3   Interrelationship Individual User Traits
and Contextual Factors

The previous discussion has concentrated on the impact of heterogeneous contextual factors, on the community surroundings (rivalry) and the community itself (governance). A third dimension of community heterogeneity is the diversity of users and their participation rationales. Participation rationales include intrinsic (e.g. fun, idealistic), extrinsic (e.g. getting paid) and externalized intrinsic (e.g. learning, reputation) factors (an overview provides e.g. Krogh et al. 2012). While these rationales in regards to participation activity, respectively the relationship of participation drivers, are analyzed (Roberts et al. 2006; Osterloh and Rota 2007), little is known how these motives cause certain behavior and are linked to community self-selection. Shah reports a fundamentally different behavior contingent on participation antecedents. Financial rewards might drive efforts towards larger market segments and innovating along customer relevant dimensions. Conversely, contributors motivated by fun tend to "explore uncharted territory" (p. 1011) and create functional novel innovations (Shah 2006). Also Grewal et al. (2006) discover "considerable heterogeneity" (p. 1043) among projects and developers with respect to project success. However, the understanding of the principal relationships between individual traits to participate and contextual factors of open source initiatives is lacking (Krogh et al. 2012). Shah (2006) calls for an analysis of whether the individual motives favor a selection mechanism in interactions with the community or not. Harhoff and Mayrhofer (2010) encourage research on heterogeneity of user motives driving decisions to join a particular community context. As Krogh et al. formulate it:

> Decades of research into other forms of collective action, ranging from lobbying and preservation of natural resources, to money collection for a good cause, have shown that institutions and individual motivations are interrelated (e.g. Morris and Mueller 1992). As a result, I believe that it is important to investigate both the individual level and the social context of development in order to understand individual behavior in a social practice.
>
> (Krogh et al. 2012, p. 14)

6.3   Research Framework

6.3.1   Firm-User-Openness Tensions

One particular contextual factor that is under the full control of the community founder from launch and independent from external factors is the governance structure. The governance of a community refers to the coordination and safeguarding of community interactions (Markus 2007). The community governance represents a 'constitution' for authority and control, for bureaucratic organization and leadership, as well as the distribution of rights and responsibilities. Harhoff and Mayrhofer (2010) highlight that communities do not exist exogenously, but that users join communities according to communities' properties, capabilities and cultures, including its openness. Accordingly, further authors (Jeppesen and Frederiksen 2006; Krogh et al. 2012) propose that the governance structure affects the joining decision of actors, as well as the specific matching of individual participants, communities and further organizational actors. Thereby the governance structure needs to solve two key challenges rooted in openness: a trade-off between appropriability and adoption as well as the tension of control and growth. The community faces a decision in regards to its openness strategy, particularly access control and usage rights.

The control versus growth tension describes the conflict of the community owner to control the community and product development in order to leverage the community in its interest. In turn, such behavior scares off contributors and limits the opportunities of communities to grow (West and O'Mahony 2008). The degree of control and influence of firms is a balancing act and a key issue. On the one hand, too much control hampers the community's energy, interest and creativity; on the other hand, too little control might jeopardize a firm's interests and even work against the objective of the community and the firm, while at the same time making the community uncontrolled and no longer manageable (Dahlander and Magnusson 2005). Within this tension, the degree of control is described with the level of the participants' influence on production. Access is understood as the possibility to participate in the product development and influence the product (West and O'Mahony 2008).

The trade-off between appropriability and adoption describes the challenge between appropriating economic benefits from innovation and providing benefits to the project users to get the project adopted (West 2003). Essential for appropriation are the usage regulations which govern the allocation of rights to commercialize the community's output. The usage regulations can be set out by the intellectual property regime applied to the product, specifically its license (West 2003; West and O'Mahony 2008; Dahlander and Magnusson 2005). The license contains essential information about modification regulations, ownership rights, and restrictions to product application. License agreements form the basis for collaboration between firms, communities, individual users and competitors (Dahlander and Magnusson 2005). They impact project success as well as participants' perceptions of the usefulness of the product (Stewart et al. 2006). For these reasons, the license choice is one of "the most important" decisions in open source projects (Bonaccorsi and Rossi 2003, p. 1248), especially because once selected they usually do not change (Fershtman and Gandal 2004).

The design of the governance and particularly the openness strategy is also essential for firms. The participation of firms in open initiatives or opening itself is based on its strategy to actively drive open innovation and capture value (West and Gallagher 2006; Garud et al. 2002). Some business models explicitly rely on active community involvement for value capture

(Chesbrough and Rosenbloom 2002). However, the nature of open source, targeted at openness and distributed development, contests the traditional mode of organization. Public product development and revealing knowledge for free represent "an unthinkable idea for traditionally minded managers" (Henkel 2006, p. 953). The tension is rooted in firms aiming for profits and exploiting products commercially, having workforces with contractual agreements, and usually excluding competitors from utilizing their developments. In contrast, the open source approach aims at publicly available source code supported by independent contributors outside hierarchical control. To mitigate the tensions, firms selectively reveal their knowledge (Henkel 2006; Bonaccorsi et al. 2006), strategically utilize openness (Fosfuri et al. 2008) and choose different interaction forms, like placing men on the community inside (Dahlander and Wallin 2006). Considering that not only firms, but also NGO or autonomous individuals establish communities, the relevance of a preferred organizational affiliation increases, yet there is little empirical evidence how users choose open initiatives that have differing affiliations and objectives.

Currently, research has considered the effect of openness and firm affiliation in regards to community activity (e.g. Colazo and Fang 2009; Subramaniam et al. 2009; Boudreau 2010). Nevertheless, higher participation efforts do not necessarily result from accessibility (Lee and Cole 2003). Initial reasons to join and contribute to a community differ strongly from those in subsequent stages as well as individual ties and community bonds impact the participation effort (Fang and Neufeld 2009; Dahlander and O'Mahony 2011). Also, before contributing volunteers need to self-select a community, but influence factors for joining decisions are unclear. So far, only Hahn et al. (2008) and Stewart et al. (2006) tangent to this area. Hahn et al. (2008) claim existence of previous ties to developers as an explanation. However, not all users have previous social bonds, what about new joiners? Social influences also limit the study of Stewart et al. (2006). They claim an overall preference for non-market organizations, despite support of commercial organizations has appealing effects, too (Dahlander and Magnusson 2005; Shah 2006; Henkel 2006; Jeppesen and Frederiksen 2006). As the downsides are prevalent for users, too (Dahlander and Magnusson 2005; Agerfalk and Fitzgerald 2008; O'Mahony and Ferraro 2007; Lerner and Tirole 2002; West and O'Mahony 2008; West 2003). The commercial affiliation is perceived "controversial and tetchy" (Harhoff and Mayrhofer 2010, p. 142). In this area of conflict, little is known about the influence of institutional sponsorship on attracting users (West and O'Mahony 2008), but a successful community-organization interaction represents an effectiveness factor for high performance (Dahlander and Magnusson 2005; Healy and Schussman 2003). Moreover, we do not know much about joining decisions in regards to openness. Going beyond isolated dimensions of access, sponsorship, and license, the question remains open, which of the dimensions is more important and which trade-offs exist. For example, Fershtman and Gandal (2004) discover a higher output per contributor in unrestricted and more commercially oriented projects. They explain their findings with stronger firm involvement and (organizational) reputation seeking participants. Thus they mix up the dimensions, a perspective, far more reflecting real world settings. We therefore address not only "vertical" comparison within one dimension, but also "horizontal" comparison between dimensions. Currently, empirical research and theoretical support for detailing differentiation is very limited; only first rough ideas and descriptions exist. Thus we use the following research proposition, instead of a hypothesis, to guide exploratory research into the preference between and within governance dimensions.

> P1: *Preference of joiners for a community is contingent on contextual factors, particularly, the specification of access, usage and sponsorship.*

6.3.2   Integrating Causes of Preference Heterogeneity

The research realm so far covers the tension of communities and firms to decide about their degree of openness, particularly their strategy in regards to access control and usage rights. However, the framework does not explain why a certain aspect is preferred over another and fails to provide reasons for different choices. Additionally, the model assumes homogeneous participant behavior. In contrast to this assumption, research reveals that users have different motives, and views access, license and sponsorship preference based on heterogeneous actors (O'Mahony and Ferraro 2007; Shah 2006). As a result, the "assumption of homogeneity can be misleading" (Qureshi and Fang 2011, p. 3) and may explain contradictions within research in regards to preference structures and activity. Detailing rationales for participation and contingent preferences address the existing lack of consensus. Introducing heterogeneity and clarifying the lines on the individual level therefore opens a way to move the conservation forward and create consensus in currently diverging results. Besides the indication of heterogeneity, the influence of participation rationales on the community choice behavior has not yet been considered and the literature lacks evidence for a relationship to contextual factors. Based on this discussion, we refrain from using an 'average open source participant' and introduce user diversity by way of individual user traits. We assume the existence of considerable taste variations. Grounded on the private-collective action model (Hippel and Kroght 2003), participation gain benefits by participation and can satisfy their needs. However, different participation rationales exist, causing different behavior. Again, empirical research and theoretical support for deriving clear hypotheses with strong reasoning is not yet present. We therefore use the following research proposition, instead of a hypothesis, to guide exploratory research into the causes of taste variations:

> P2: *Preference for contextual factors is contingent on participation motives.*

6.4   Methodological Design

6.4.1   *Experimental Design*

As open regimes differ widely in their contextual settings, care in comparative analysis and research objective selection is required (Boudreau 2010; Eisenmann et al. 2008). Strong influence factors for community joining are present, but they are not very measurable for research. Socializing effects (Hahn et al. 2008) and "we-feeling" from a social point of view (Hinds and Bailey 2003) skew joining decisions, blur real preferences, or override trade-offs. From a market analysis point of view, passionately perceived products and the availability of rival communities can impact the joining decision. In order to target these challenges and overcome local research bias, we apply a mixed method design with sample diversity.

In order to enable the identification of trade-offs and evaluation independently of distortive factors, we conduct a discrete choice field experiment. A discrete choice experiment (DCE) represents a quantitative method for estimating the relative importance of several decomposed sub-characteristics of an analyzed object which influence the choice behavior of an individual (Louviere et al. 2010a; Hensher et al. 2005). The DCE is able to predict market demand, simulate decisions and elicit individual preferences—even for prospective alternatives and unobserved trade-off decisions as in this study (Carson et al. 1995). Moreover, observed preferences and survey-based results often have low internal validity and uncontrolled measurements, impeding causal inferences (Bryman 2012). In contrast, an experiment is best suitable to identify clear cause-effect relationships and explain why these effects emerge (Colquitt 2008). The experimental set-up controls the variable exposure and allows systematic manipulation. The independence of variables and the experimental design reduce common method bias and measurement bias respectively (Podsakoff et al. 2003; Spector 2006). Finally, a discrete choice experiment answers the call for more experimental research (Colquitt 2008), particularly in innovation management (Sørensen et al. 2010) and in Open Source Innovation (Roberts et al. 2006). The field experiment "places actual employees in an environment where randomly assigned conditions have been created" and increases psychological realism (Colquitt 2008, p. 616).

6.4.2   *Measures and Operationalization of Constructs*

Describing a community as 'open' without indicating concrete mechanisms may cause confusion (Eisenmann et al. 2008). Based on the research objective, each choice alternative describes a community according to the attributes access, usage and sponsorship with its corresponding sub-levels. We consider the DCE criteria of validity, cognitive overload, degrees of freedom, behavioral choice oversimplification, and research relevance (Louviere et al. 2010a; Hanley et al. 2001; Green and Srinivasan 1990). Sponsorship is subdivided into for-profit organizational sponsorship, non-profit organizational sponsorship, and no sponsorship according to Stewart et al.

(2006). Access is broken down into accessibility, transparency and restrictiveness (West and O'Mahony 2008). Usage is split into non-profit license and for-profit license. We do not use blurred dimensions of license restrictiveness (Bonaccorsi and Rossi 2003; Lerner and Tirole 2005; Fershtman and Gandal 2004; Subramaniam et al. 2009), but explicitly isolate restrictiveness in commercialization allowance. Commercialization allowance represents a major characteristic within the free software movement, for firms, and is described in the appropriation versus adoption conflict. Thus, instead of complex license terms (Lerner and Tirole 2005; Colazo and Fang 2009) which result in slow decision making as well as uncertain proprietary claims (Rolandsson et al. 2011), or may not be entirely clear to the user, we apply an easier to understand decisive criterion to avoid confusion. This approach reduces the plethora of license options, avoids measurement bias, and allows the clear understanding of decision makers' preferences and enables unambiguous interpretation. In order to transform the DCE levels into more familiar, concrete variables and phenomenon-based indicators for decision makers, the stimuli are further described (see Table 6.1).

Reflecting the experimental design, we apply a multinomial Bayesian D-error design consisting of three choice alternatives and a fourth 'none' option. The DCE profile sets are unlabeled and checked for extreme

Table 6.1 Stimuli

	Control	Appropriability	Organizational Involvement
Dimension (Attribute)	Access • Possibility to participate in product development	Usage • Commercialization and usage constraints	Sponsorship • Publicly displayed affiliation
Construct (Levels)	• Read-Write: everybody can read everything and fully do edits • Read-Only: everybody can read everything but only registered users can do edits • Restricted: only selected users are allowed for reading and editing	• Non-Profit: you may not use this work for commercial purposes • For-Profit: you may use this work for commercial purposes. This is often compared to 'copyleft' and used in many open source products	• Commerce: a for-profit organization runs the community • NGO: a university or nongovernmental organization (NGO) runs the community • No Sponsor: neither an NGO nor a for-profit organization runs the community

combinations. Besides the statistical, theoretical and behavioral advices, we use a reviewed statistical design proposed by Kessels et al. (2009) and support the call to reveal the design principles (Scarpa and Rose 2008; Louviere 2006).

Particularly for this study, we include psychometric constructs, open feedback questions, as well as actions for survey testing. In order to endorse external validity, we adapt motivational constructs from research studying participation rationales (Roberts et al. 2006; Wu et al. 2007; Hars and Ou 2001; Wasko and Faraj 2005; Lakhani and Hippel 2003) and focus on the top five stated rationales (Crowston et al. 2012) as antecedents for choice heterogeneity. We follow the movement for short scales and brevity in constructs to reduce parsimony effects and to please respondents (Netemeyer et al. 2002; Bearden et al. 2011). Additionally, we control for further causes of preference heterogeneity. We check influences within the area demographics (user's age, sex, work experience, level of education, and topic expertise), community activity (hours reading, writing, moderating), and community type (software, content, fun, business).

To triangulate preference results, a further question requires respondents to rate the three most important community aspects when deciding between two communities. On the one hand, this question reflects the antecedents for community effectiveness; on the other hand, it contrasts the DCE aspects from a broader point of view. Finally, two open questions are asked: one for remarks regarding community differentiation and improvement, and one question to provide feedback regarding the survey.

6.4.3   Unit of Analysis and Data Collection

The units of analysis for this study are individual volunteers freely revealing their knowledge and participating in open initiatives—accordingly, we choose an Internet survey to address the distributed individuals. We echo the call to consider the "spectacularly stratified" nature of open source (Healy and Schussman 2003) and ask several members of different digital production communities to increase research variance and abstraction. In particular, the sample consists of volunteers of open source software and open source content communities. Moreover, members of entertainment and business communities are differentiated to increase the degree of generalization, reduce sampling bias of pure commercial settings or iconic projects, and to transfer findings to further open initiatives. Thus, data triangulation based on a number of individuals of several heterogeneous communities as well as utilization of actual community data is conducted to enhance research validity (Mathison 1988). Figure 6.1 shows the sampled communities. Data was collected in two waves (May 2011 to July 2011; November 2011 to December 2011). By directly contacting random community members and posting forum messages we achieved a return rate of 19.77%. The collected sample is screened for consistency, completeness and plausibility (Mooi and Sarstedt 2011; Osborne and Overbay 2008), and compared in terms of age

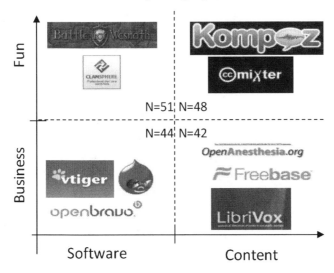

Figure 6.1 Sampled communities

and sex against earlier studies and similar distributions found. The cleared sample consists of 185 replies nearly equally spread as seen in Figure 6.1.

6.5 Data Analysis

In order to analyze the choice preferences, a prediction model needs to be specified. We employ a log-likelihood approximation approach with a correlated mixed logit panel model. Thus, we apply a continuous probabilistic distribution in combination with a model releasing the assumption of independence of irrelevant alternatives, covering random taste across individuals and considering inter-user heterogeneity, as well as accounting for repeated panel observations. The specifications are supported by qualitative factors, for example, behavioral aspects, and quantitative factors, like statistical support. We take special care for the design and estimation model to reflect real decisions and derive very similar outcomes from this stated preferences as compared to revealed tastes (Louviere and Swait 2010; Swait and Andrews 2003). Table 6.2 recapitulates the full model specifications:

Psychometric data evaluation in terms of internal consistency and construct structure checks are conducted for participation rationales and provide acceptable results. The corrected latent constructs internally correlate well above the recommendation of 0.6 (Bearden et al. 2011; Robinson et al. 1991) for a smaller number of item constructs, as well as above the general recommendation of 0.7 (Churchill Jr 1979; Nunnally 1978), and support reliability and scale unidimensionality. Additionally, mean inter-item correlation scores of above 0.4 for narrow constructs (Clark and Watson 1995),

Table 6.2   Applied discrete choice model specifications

Criteria	Specification
Type	• Mixed Logit Model
Parameters	• Choice Levels (Random parameters, effect coded) • None-Option (Fixed parameter)
Random Parameter Distribution and Drawing	• Normal distribution applied for all random parameters • 1000 Halton draws applied
Observation Correlation	• Panel data of eight repeated questions per respondent • Four stimuli per profile set, eight choice observation per individual
Parameter Cross Correlation	• Confounding effects of random parameters considered

and, besides use, above the general recommendation of 0.5 (Bearden et al. 1989) provide a second criterion for scale homogeneity. All five motivation constructs suggest validity convergence for the conceptual components and quintuple dimensionality due to directed loadings of items. In order to assess the overall validity and understanding of the survey, the survey respondents are asked to provide a brief feedback on the questionnaire via an open question at the end of the survey. Reviewing this question reveals positive statements like "survey was clear, concise and easy to follow", "looks good to me:)" and "good work!".

6.6   Empirical Results

6.6.1   *Discrete Choice Preferences and Trade-offs*
In order to analyze the DCE data set, the previously developed estimation model is applied. The model is highly significant with a "very good" model fit (Chi squared value of 1191.261 with 21 degrees of freedom results in a p-value smaller than 0.0001; and the prediction quality is measured with a McFadden pseudo-R^2 value of 0.2903) (Louviere et al. 2010a; Bateman et al. 2002). All random and fixed parameters are highly significant at a 99% confidence level, except NGO which is significant at a 90% level as shown in Table 6.3.

In order to triangulate the choice results, each survey participant is asked to indicate the three most important aspects out of a list of effectiveness, if forced to decide between two communities. The provided community

Table 6.3 Inferential statistical results

Attribute	Level	Part-worth (utility)	Level significance (p value)	Standard deviation (SD)	SD sign. (heterogeneity indicator)	Attribute utility (range)	Attribute importance
Sponsorship	Commercial	−0.73189	0.0000	1.09084	0.0000	1.306	0.2522
	NGO	+0.15770	0.0864	0.68766	0.0000		
	No Sponsor	+0.57419	Base Level	Base Level	Base Level		
Access	Read-write	+1.26631	0.0000	1.98135	0.0000	2.142	0.4136
	Restricted	−0.87587	0.0000	1.47744	0.0000		
	Read-only	−0.39044	Base Level	Base Level	Base Level		
Usage	Non-Profit	+0.86542	0.0000	1.25200	0.8528	1.731	0.3342
	For-Profit	−0.86542	Base Level	Base Level	Base Level		
Outside Alternative	Choose None	−0.38560	0.0000				

effectiveness factors include the aspects access, usage, and sponsorship, but also factors beyond the experimental set-up such as the produced product (content), member behavior (trust, activity), or technical features (stable website, data security). The results display Figure 6.2, left side. The ranking of the preferred attributes is identical to the result of the choice experiment: access, closely followed by license, and ultimately sponsorship. We furthermore apply an explorative approach for corroboration and ask participants by means of an open question, too, to find their own factors to describe unique aspects of the community. The processed, deductively derived results are revealed in Figure 6.2, right side. Access, license and community affiliation are again in the same order as previous question and as predicted by the choice experiment. Concluding, the most important factor is access, closely followed by license regimes, and then sponsorship, in all three approaches— but further important joining aspects exists.

Going further and placing the levels in relationship to each other with a share of preference prediction enables calculation of the marginal change

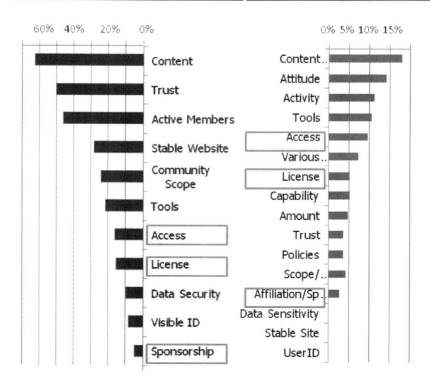

Figure 6.2   Decision factors for community joining

and selection probabilities of parameter combinations. (Parameters are uncalibrated and presented without scale factor.) This approach compares two communities and discloses the likelihood of one community being selected over the competing initiative (see equation 1).

$$P(a) = \frac{exp(U_a)}{exp(U_a) + exp(U_b)} \qquad (1)$$

Community U_b is set as the (lower) reference and constitutes of the attributes with the lowest prediction values (commercial affiliation, restricted access and for-profit license). In contrast, community (U_a) represents a competing community. The probability $P(a)$ represents the share of the preference prediction, the likelihood of choosing community (U_a). Because community (U_b) comprises the lowest preferences, calculated probabilities represent maximum values reduced if the community (U_b) does not only consist of inferior parameters. The following share predictions thus represent the increase in members if a closed proprietary community opens up. Comparing the choice predictions for the maximum value, a respondent is 99.44% likely to join the superior community and 0.56% likely to join the inferior community. Further predicted choice shares are shown in Figure 6.3. The abscissa shows the access dimension, read-write access (RW), read-only access (RO), and restricted access (RA). The ordinate represents the affiliation and license dimensions. The ordinate is subdivided into three constructs. The first construct indicates commercial affiliation (Com.Aff.), the second NGO sponsorship (NGO Aff.), and the third no affiliation (No Aff.). Each of these three constructs consists of two columns: a non-profit license and a for-profit license. Finally, the applicate marks the probability value $P(a)$ with the height of the column.

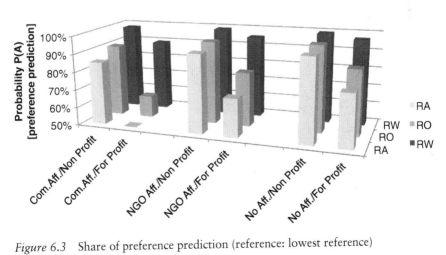

Figure 6.3   Share of preference prediction (reference: lowest reference)

Concluding, the diagram reveals why one community is preferred over another. The aspects of access-control, usage-regulations, and sponsorship-involvement including their respective levels are perceived differently by the prospective joiner and impact their joining decision significantly. Access is preferred over license over sponsorship involvement. The research proposition one is supported: Preference of joiners for a community is contingent on contextual factors, particularly, the specification of access, usage and sponsorship.

6.6.2   Sensitivity Analysis of Marginal Changes

Calculating the ratios of predicted choice-share probabilities increases the understanding of changing one particular community factor to another. It reveals the impact of marginal community modifications, enables the construction of what-if scenarios of community selection probabilities. The scenarios of marginal change (assuming highest predictions for the remaining two dimensions [Minor deviations from calculated values result from rounding; the tables provide exact values based on the calculated predictions]) are shown in Table 6.4 for affiliation, Table 6.5 for access, and Table 6.6 for modified usage regulations.

Based on these results, the impact of certain levels is exposed. Opening a community from restricted access to read-write access increases selection probability by 4.76 times, but changing an NGO affiliation to no sponsorship predicts rises in community selection by only 1.26 times. The sensitivity values are even higher if several parameters are changed. The most extreme value results from the change from a restricted access, for-profit license with

Table 6.4   Change of selection probability caused by altering community affiliation

Affiliation	To			
From	Level	No Aff.	NGO Aff.	Com. Aff.
	No Aff.	x	0.795	0.426
	NGO Aff.	1.258	x	0.536
	Com.Aff.	2.346	1.864	x

Table 6.5   Change of selection probability caused by altering community usage

Usage	To		
From	Level	Non-Profit	For-Profit
	Non-Profit	x	0.301
	For-Profit	3.323	x

Table 6.6   Change of selection probability caused by altering community access

Access	To			
From	Level	RW	RO	RA
	RW	x	0.320	0.210
	RO	3.121	x	0.656
	RA	4.759	1.525	x

commercial sponsor (0.56%) to a highest preferred community (50%), with an increase of participation likelihood by 89.29 times. Considering a scenario between an example corporate community (P(RO/For-Profit/Com. Aff.)=7.26%) competing with an NGO community with for-profit license (P(RW/For-Profit/NGO.Aff.)=92.73%) reveals a relative increase in participation probability of 12.77 times.

6.6.3   Sources of Taste Heterogeneity

The choice results represent the taste for the average population across the entire open source sample and show the preference of access over usage constraints and the minimal impact of sponsorship. However, in this study, we challenge the assumption of homogenous traits and preferences. In order to determine possible causes of preference heterogeneity and explain why certain users prefer a certain community, the interactions of choice experiment parameters with suspected sources of heterogeneity are estimated (Hensher et al. 2005; Revelt and Train 1998). However, including interaction effects increases the degrees of freedom and encourages parsimony challenges. To overcome the challenge, interactions are calculated as single variable analysis and afterwards tested in combination with adjacent[1] factors (multiple variables analysis). In order to compare results, the results from both analyses are superimposed and the result stability increased.[2] Effect directions pointing in the same direction for the single and multiple analyses are revealed and diverging effects exposed. Effect directions found diverging from each other are indicated with '+/-' and small effect magnitudes with '~0'. Table 6.7 shows the results for the control variables, and Table 6.8 for the main variables.

A positive (negative) sign within the matrix indicates a higher (lower) preference for a particular user. Thus, a user strongly motivated by a particular participation rationale, positively (negatively) connected to a community context factor, gains extra (less) value from this factor, ceteris paribus, increasing (decreasing) the likelihood of participation. At a 90% confidence level, significance is found for payment, reputation and learning, from a motivation point of view, supporting proposition two. Payment interacts with commercial affiliation, read-write access, and non-profit license. Reputation interacts with non-profit license, and read-write access with learning.

Table 6.7   Superimposed results of sources of preference heterogeneity (i)

	Com. Sponsor	NGO Sponsor	RW Access	Restricted Access	No profit license
Sex1m	+ (~0)	+ (~0)	+	–	–
Age	+	– (~0)	–	+	–
Work	+	–	–	+	–
Degree	–	+	+ (~0)	+	+
Hread	–(*)	–	–	–	+
Hwrite	–	+	–	+/-	–
Hmod	+	–	+/–	+	–
Tenure	+	–	–	+ (~0)	+/– (~0)
Expertise	–/+ (~0)	+/– (~0)	+ (*)	–	–

Table 6.8   Superimposed results of sources of preference heterogeneity (ii)

	Com. Sponsor	NGO Sponsor	RW Access	Restricted Access	No profit license
Payment	+ (**)	–	+ (*)	–	– (**)
OwnNeed	+	–	–	–	–
Learning	+	+	–(*)	+	–
Reputation	+	–	+	–	–(*)
Fun	–	+	+	–	–
Bus. to Fun	– (***)	+ (*)	– (**)	–	+
Cont. to Soft	–(*)	–	+	–	+

Concluding, the research question 'What are the causes of preference heterogeneity?' is answered with the above discussion of individual user traits. The analysis supports that varying preferences are explained by the differences in individual motivations and due to the type of open source project. Participation rationales are antecedents for joining behavior and cause the preference of certain contextual factors. We found support for our research proposition: Preference for contextual factors is contingent on participation motives.

6.7   Discussion and Implications

Our research framework includes three layers: the user, the community and the environment (particularly prospective alternatives). These layers are combined into one study for the first time and represent all three open source research areas proposed by Krogh and Hippel (2006): user motivation, community organization, and competitive dynamics. From a methodological point of view we introduce DCE into open and user innovation and propose a new measurement view for licenses.

6.7.1 Implications for Community Strategy and Competitive Dynamics

Successful community-organization and user interaction represents an effectiveness factor for high performance (Dahlander and Magnusson 2005; Healy and Schussman 2003). We apply a novel approach for determining member attraction by putting communities with different governance factors in competition to each other for being chosen. In other words, we do not ask about general success factors, but particular success antecedents if alternatives for the prospective joiner exist and the joiner can decide between these alternatives.

The insights from our study contribute multifold to the understanding of why one community is chosen over another, depending on the governance structure, and what are key decision criteria. The level of granted access to the production represents the most crucial factor, followed by usage constraints and organizational affiliation. Closer examination with trade-off examination and sensitivity analysis reveals highly different impacts with respect to the magnitude of importance. Sponsorship impact remains far less important than openness. We reveal a non-linear relationship of preferences: certain level changes in contextual attributes cause non-proportional effects and jumps in community preference. For example, the change from NGO to no sponsor has only a marginal impact compared to a change from commercial to NGO level. Moreover, instead of discussing organizational involvement, an appropriate sponsor community behavior and community content are far more important to attract joiners.

Besides these contributions, we also challenge openness as the most important aspect in community joining decisions. Member behavior and the created product of the community are more important than openness for prospective joiners. The developed product may point to the relevance of targeting (niche) markets and offering high-quality content. The community behavior points to the activity and attitude of members. These criteria strongly facilitate community joining, may even mitigate the effect of less-preferred aspects. We interpret this finding that as long as no alternatives exists or users behave appropriately, joiners are also willing to accept communities with less preferred attributes (like commercial sponsorship), but as soon as alternatives exist or their social bonds erode, they chose other communities.

6.7.2 Implications for Joining and Individual Behavior

Linking user characteristics to community context represents an area to discover (Rolandsson et al. 2011; Grewal et al. 2006; Krogh et al. 2012). So far, only two studies give (peripheral) attention to linking user traits to the community context: Oreg and Nov (2008), and Harhoff and Mayrhofer (2010). Oreg and Nov (2008) consider an interactionist perspective and compare contribution motivations in software and content communities. While they concentrate on community type differentiation, they do not link user traits to particular contextual factors as in this study, particularly do not address openness. An interrelationship between individuals' characteristics and community contextual factors is so far only touched upon by Harhoff and Mayrhofer (2010). Whereby they draw on technical sophistication as contextual community factor, we concentrate on license, access and sponsorship and the linkage to individual motives. However, within our study expert users do not differ significantly from the average user in terms of joining decisions, underscoring the need to clearly link specific user characteristics and specific contextual factors.

We deepen this conversation and provide a significant link of individual traits to institutional preferences. This link explains individual joining behavior in open collaborative institutions. Our results show that participation motives are the antecedents for joining behavior and cause self-selection of users into specific community environments. In particular, demographic diversity and heterogeneous activity levels of users exist, but do not explain community preferences. In contrast, participation rationales exhibit significant sources of preference heterogeneity and impact the user's decision to join a specific community.

Not-for-profit license terms are preferred over for-profit license terms across the entire sample, except for reputation and payment seekers. Interestingly, payment and reputation rationales exhibit the same effect direction for all interaction effects, indicating that the preference difference between the two is rather small. Considering payment and reputation as the most extrinsically driven motivations, in contrast to fun, the results reveal that extrinsically driven participants differ from the average participants in terms of preferring communities. This could indicate a silent 'crowding-out' effect, meaning communities are either chosen by intrinsic or extrinsic motivated users, at least, it creates tensions between commercial-oriented users and fun-driven participants.

In terms of production control, community members prefer a high level of control. In particular, accessibility with reading and writing rights is favored over transparency or 'closed' participation. There exists a strong preference for active involvement options and freedom for participation. Regarding organizational involvement, this study reveals heterogeneity in sponsorship preferences. In particular, a sharp contrast exists between payment-driven and fun-driven participants.

A surprising insight comes from users who are learning-driven. These users, aiming at skill advancement and information, might even accept restricted communities. The smaller preference for read-write access by learning-motivated users might at first seem contradictory. Read-write access offers users the opportunity to reciprocate, upload modifications to the central repository, and ultimately receive feedback and learn from the feedback. However, learning could also mean following the actions of the community and learning from observation. Before modifications can be provided, the user first needs to understand the community in both a technical and social manner (Krogh et al. 2003). Suggestions for modifications could be provided to the moderator and learners could receive feedback. Thus, it may be important to gain read-write access at a later stage, but the primary requirement is to follow the community, spot interesting content, and gain access to quality material, possibly without writing access. A further implication might exist within the community discussions. Users aiming to advance their knowledge may prefer not to be disrupted or feel the need to consider faulty content. They know the content and trust in known members. Thus, they prefer that not everybody has accessibility to the community and only certain members can edit the content they rely on. They probably focus on contributions from trusted and more qualified users, not learners. Real world examples include medical professional communities[3] or technically sophisticated developers.[4] Members of highly specific expert communities who benefit from not being disturbed, either by 'newbie' or external questions, or in delicate discussions, prefer to be among their peers. If a community would offer open access, their benefits diminish in terms of validated content and recognized members. As a consequence, they are sensitive to read-write access, as predicted by our model. In view of this results, the conclusions that community openness is superior to community limitation for participants (Agerfalk and Fitzgerald 2008; West and O'Mahony 2008) is challenged.

As von Krogh et al. (2012) postulate, these insights help theory building beyond isolated considerations and represent fruitful research into institutional change. These interrelationships support the design of innovation communities, organizations relying on volunteers' contributions, and the nurturing of work environments (Shah 2006). We add to the understanding of joining and institutional settings with the contribution that particular contextual factors will attract certain users. Our findings increase the understanding of joining and deepen the insight into volunteering and the free revealing of knowledge in organizations. The analyzed factors are under the control of the community and can be steered in order to remedy member dissatisfaction, facilitate collaboration and stimulate innovation participation.

This contribution also helps to clarify the lines of contextual preferences. Currently empirical support is lacking in the literature and seemingly contradictive speculations exist. We bring reconciliation to the dispute of whether certain aspects are preferred or not. We resolve the conflict and propose a new approach by grounding preferences contingent on individual level. Based on individual rationales, we explain why for some users a contextual factor is preferred, but others refrain from the same. We detail the role of individual behavior in joining decisions, bring coherence in seemingly divergent perspectives, and move the discussion forward.

6.7.3 Implications for Methodology and Measurement Approach

Most studies rely on case studies or surveys even as literature calls for more experiments. The conducted discrete choice experiment tackles the difficulty of common method bias as well as targeting the lack of experimental research in innovation management. The DCE reveals results difficult to obtain with other methods (e.g. trade-offs, exclusion of social bias) and its application provides new insights into not yet available joining behavior (traits contingency).

In avoiding clustering licenses into restrictive or non-restrictive types, we focus explicitly on commercialization as a new measure and answer the call for further research on license heterogeneity (Bonaccorsi and Rossi 2003). On the one hand, this challenges earlier findings, on the other hand, this may point to a necessary scholarly reclassification of licenses, more granular measurement requirements, and new insights. At the very least, we raise the question of whether all users are familiar with license constraints. Probably, users do not associate the allowance of for-profit use with non-restrictive licenses. They regard open source licenses as preferred, without knowing in detail about the regulations that work against their actual preference. However, a clear understanding of the underpinning license intentions is required for drawing valid implications, as ensured with the new measurement approach.

6.7.4   Recommendations for Management Practice

With this study we lessen "non-trivial managerial headaches" (Chesbrough and Appleyard 2007, p. 73) and answer the open questions: 'How can open organizations be strategically designed to foster self-selection of users?' and 'What is the impact on the attraction and contribution of users of varying the degree of openness and firm sponsorship?' We contribute to the research on the strategic challenge of gaining competitive advantages through the support of external volunteers. The selection of appropriate contextual factors enables community managers to promote and build the community in such a way as to attract the intended volunteers and develop a prospering collaboration. We show how managers can set up communities and influence the attraction of specific volunteers.

Also, the integration of volunteers represents a beneficial extension to the established firm-based model of the appropriation and revealing of knowledge (Bonaccorsi et al. 2006; Krogh and Hippel 2006; Fosfuri et al. 2008). Harnessing the creative distributed capital depends on the regulations of collaboration, whereby talented dispersed volunteers may self-select into tasks according to their preferences and the freedom to work. An appropriate form of selective openness may stimulate knowledge exchange and support employees to unfold their wider potential. This study provides the insights for managers how to design their organization to stimulate innovation due to the external support and open innovation.

6.7.5   Limitations and Future Research Directions

Despite careful consideration of theoretical and empirical challenges, as well as the application of counteractions like multifold triangulation or randomization, this study has some limitations. Discrete choice experiments represent stated preferences within an isolated environment. Certain decision attributes are not offered and interrelationships in the experimental settings are a simplification—for the sake of avoiding e.g. social influences. The underpinning sampling concentrates on a broad assortment of different online open source communities. Whereas most other studies consider members from one project type or even single cases, we intentionally broaden the scope and introduce variance by sampling software, content, entertainment and business projects. As this might lead to a potential selection bias and a limitation to digital production projects, this approach controls for the highly diverse community ecology and avoids selecting of potentially biased iconic projects. Nevertheless, first examples provide confidence that findings could be transfered to tangible products (e.g. Balka et al. 2009), and to multinational organizations (e.g. Stuermer et al. 2009), but why significant choice differences exist between community types remains an area to discover. Moreover, the question about obstacles and minimum requirements for volunteering remains largely unanswered. Probably, preferences could be structured in terms of hygiene factors (Herzberg 1968) or satisfaction levels (Kano et al. 1984). Users participate in communities even if some factors are not ideal. In particular, the community product and the community behavior are more important than access, usage and sponsorship, and compensate for less-preferred aspects. The question emerges: Are activity and trust preconditions for higher individual benefits or indications of fair behavior and social taste, and for whom? Fairness, understood as interpersonal relative payoff (Loewenstein et al. 1989), seems to impact volunteering in an open initiatives (Harhoff and Mayrhofer 2010; Nov and Kuk 2008), and organizational behavior (Colquitt et al. 2006). Yet, participation research widely ignores this aspect. As "the economic environment determines whether the fair types or the selfish types dominate equilibrium behavior" (Fehr and Schmidt 1999, p. 817), an open private-collective collaboration may represent an interesting example for studying Pareto efficiency conditions, with regard to increased individual and social welfare. Within the realm of heterogeneous actors aiming at contrary objectives, integrating behavioral aspects (Kahneman and Tversky 1979; Camerer et al. 2003), and distinguish more clearly between members, its characteristics and its behavior seems to be a fruitful field for further research.

NOTES

This contribution is based on the dissertation by Daniel Ehls, but further developed and refined.

1. Adjacent variables are the variables out of the same question group. The question groups are: Motivations (Fun, Own Need, Learning, Reputation, Payment); Open Source Type (Software, Content, Fun, Business); Demographics (Sex, Age); Aptitude (Work, Degree); Community Expertise (Expertise, Tenure); Participation Effort (HRead, HWrite, HMod).
2. Although superimposing the values may increase the validity of the effect direction, effect direction magnitudes cannot be reported as results are valid either in the single or multiple analysis model.

3. Examples include Sermo.com (US), Coliqio.de (Germany), and doctors.net. uk (UK), representing the biggest professional medical communities in their countries only accessible to approved doctors.
4. See example in Harhoff and Mayrhofer (2010).

REFERENCES

Agerfalk, P., and Fitzgerald, B. (2008): "Outsourcing to an unknown workforce: exploring opensourcing as a global sourcing strategy", *MIS Quarterly* 32(2), pp. 385–409.

Balka, K., Raasch, A.-C., and Herstatt, C. (2009): "Open source enters the world of atoms: a statistical analysis of open design", *First Monday* 14(11).

Bateman, I. J., Carson, R. T., Day, B., Hanemann, M., and Hanley, N. (2002): *Economic valuation with stated preference techniques: a manual*, Edgar Elgar, Cheltenham.

Bearden, W. O., Netemeyer, R. G., and Haws, K. L. (2011): *Handbook of marketing scales: multi-item measures for marketing and consumer behavior research*, SAGE, Los Angeles.

Bearden, W. O., Netemeyer, R. G., and Teel, J. (1989): "Measurement of consumer susceptibility to interpersonal influence", *Journal of Consumer Research* 15(4), pp. 473–481.

Bonaccorsi, A., Giannangeli, S., and Rossi, C. (2006): "Entry strategies under competing standards: hybrid business models in the Open Source software industry", *Management Science* 52(7), pp. 1085–1098.

Bonaccorsi, A., and Rossi, C. (2003): "Why Open Source software can succeed: Open Source software development", *Research Policy* 32(7), pp. 1243–1258.

Boudreau, K. (2010): "Open platform strategies and innovation: granting access vs. devolving control", *Management Science* 56(10), pp. 1849–1872.

Bryman, A. (2012): *Social research methods*, Oxford University Press, Oxford.

Butler, B. S. (2001): "Membership size, communication activity, and sustainability: a resource-based model of online social structures", *Information Systems Research* 12(4), pp. 346–362.

Camerer, C., Loewenstein, G., and Rabin, M. (eds.) (2003): *Advances in behavioral economics*, Princeton University Press, Princeton, NJ.

Carson, R. T., Wright, J., Carson, N., Aberini, A., and Flores, N. (1995): *A bibliography of contingent valuation studies and papers*, Natural Resource Damage Assessment, San Diego.

Casadesus-Masanell, R., and Ghemawat, P. (2006): "Dynamic mixed duopoly: a model motivated by Linux vs. Windows", *Management Science* 52(7), pp. 1072–1084.

Cheng, H., Liu, Y., and Tang, Q. (2011): "The impact of network externalities on the competition between Open Source and proprietary software", *Journal of Management Information Systems* 27(4), pp. 201–230.

Chesbrough, H. W., and Appleyard, M. M. (2007): "Open innovation and strategy", *California Management Review* 50(1), pp. 57–76.

Chesbrough, H. W., and Rosenbloom, R. (2002): "The role of the business model in capturing value from innovation: evidence from Xerox Corporation's technology spin-off companies", *Industrial and Corporate Change Volume* 11(3), pp. 529–555.

Churchill Jr, G. (1979): "A paradigm for developing better measures of marketing constructs", *Journal of Marketing Research* 16, pp. 64–73.

Clark, L., and Watson, D. (1995): "Constructing validity: basic issues in objective scale development", *Psychological assessment* 7(3), pp. 309–319.

Colazo, J., and Fang, Y. (2009): "Impact of license choice on Open Source software development activity", *Journal of the American Society for Information Science and Technology* 60(5), pp. 997–1011.

Colquitt, J.A. (2008): "From the editors publishing laboratory research in AMJ: a question of when, not if", *Academy of Management Journal* 51(4), pp. 616–620.

Colquitt, J.A., Scott, B., Judge, T., and Shaw, J. (2006): "Justice and personality: using integrative theories to derive moderators of justice effects", *Organizational Behavior and Human Decision Processes* 100(1), pp. 110–127.

Crowston, K., Wei, K., Howison, J., and Wiggins, A. (2012): "Free/Libre open-source software development: what we know and what we do not know", *ACM Computing Surveys* 44(2), pp. 7:1–7:35.

Dahlander, L., and Magnusson, M. (2005): "Relationships between open source software companies and communities: observations from Nordic firms", *Research Policy* 34(4), pp. 481–493.

Dahlander, L., and O'Mahony, S. (2011): "Progressing to the center: coordinating project work", *Organization Science* 22(4), pp. 961–979.

Dahlander, L., and Wallin, M.W. (2006): "A man on the inside: unlocking communities as complementary assets", *Research Policy* 35(8), pp. 1243–1259.

Economides, N., and Katsamakas, E. (2006): "Two-sided competition of proprietary vs. open source technology platforms and the implications for the software industry", *Management Science* 52(7), pp. 1057–1071.

Eisenmann, T., Parker, G., and van Alstyne, M. (2008): "Opening platforms: how, when and why?" *HBS Working Papers* 09–030, Harvard Business School, Cambridge, MA.

Fang, Y., and Neufeld, D. (2009): "Understanding sustained participation in Open Source software projects", *Journal of Management Information Systems* 25(4), pp. 9–50.

Fehr, E., and Schmidt, K. (1999): "A theory of fairness, competition, and cooperation", *The Quarterly Journal of Economics* 114(3), pp. 817–868.

Fershtman, C., and Gandal, N. (2004): "The determinants of output per contributor in Open Source projects: an empirical examination", Discussion Paper No. 4329, Centre for Economic Policy Research (CEPR), London.

Fitzgerald, B. (2006): "The transformation of Open Source software", *MIS Quarterly* 30(3), pp. 587–598.

Fosfuri, A., Giarratana, M.S., and Luzzi, A. (2008): "The penguin has entered the building: the commercialization of Open Source software products", *Organization Science* 19(2), pp. 292–305.

Garud, R., Jain, S., and Kumaraswamy, A. (2002): "Institutional entrepreneurship in the sponsorship of common technological standards: the case of Sun Microsystems and Java standards", *The Academy of Management Journal* 45(1), pp. 196–214.

Ghosh, R.A., and Prakash, V.V. (2000): "The Orbiten free software survey", *First Monday* 5(7).

Green, P., and Srinivasan, V. (1990): "Conjoint analysis in marketing: new developments with implications for research and practice", *The Journal of Marketing* 54(4), pp. 3–19.

Grewal, R., Lilien, G.L., and Mallapragada, G. (2006): "Location, location, location: how network embeddedness affects project success in Open Source systems", *Management Science* 52(7), pp. 1043–1056.

Hahn, J., Moon, J.Y., and Zhang, C. (2008): "Emergence of new project teams from open source software developer networks: Impact of prior collaboration ties", *Information Systems Research* 19(3), pp. 369–391.

Hanley, N., Mourato, S., and Wright, R.E. (2001): "Choice modelling approaches: a superior alternative for environmental valuation?" *Journal of Economic Surveys* 15(3), pp. 435–462.

Harhoff, D., and Mayrhofer, P. (2010): "Managing user communities and hybrid innovation processes: concepts and design implications", *Organizational Dynamics* 39(2), pp. 137–144.

Hars, A., and Ou, S. (2001): "Working for free? motivations for participating in Open-Source projects", in *Proceedings of the 34th Annual Hawaii International Conference on System Sciences (HICSS-34)*, pp. 25–39, IEEE Computer Society, Washington, DC.

Healy, K., and Schussman, A. (2003): "The ecology of open-source software development", Department of Sociology, University of Arizona, Tucson.

Henkel, J. (2006): "Selective revealing in open innovation processes: the case of embedded Linux", *Research Policy* 35(7), pp. 953–969.

Hensher, D. A., Rose, J. M., and Greene, W. H. (2005): *Applied choice analysis: a primer*, Cambridge University Press, Cambridge.

Herzberg, F. (1968): "One more time: how do you motivate employees?" *Harvard Business Review* 90(1), pp. 53–62.

Hinds, P., and Bailey, D. (2003): "Out of sight, out of sync: understanding conflict in distributed teams", *Organization Science* 14(6), pp. 615–632.

Hippel, E. A. von, and Krogh, G. von (2003): "Open Source software and the 'private-collective' innovation model: issues for organization science", *Organization Science* 14(2), pp. 209–223.

Jeppesen, L. B., and Frederiksen, L. (2006): "Why do users contribute to firm-hosted user communities? the case of computer-controlled music instruments", *Organization Science* 17(1), pp. 45–63.

Kahneman, D., and Tversky, A. (1979): "Prospect theory: an analysis of decision under risk", *Econometrica* 47(2), pp. 263–291.

Kano, N., Seraku, N., Takahashi, F., and Tsuji, S. (1984): "Attractive quality and must-be quality", *The Journal of the Japanese Society for Quality Control* 14(2), pp. 39–48.

Kessels, R., Jones, B., Goos, P., and Vandebroek, M. (2009): "An efficient algorithm for constructing Bayesian optimal choice designs", *Journal of Business & Economic Statistics* 27(2), pp. 279–291.

Krishnamurthy, S. (2002): "Cave or community? an empirical examination of 100 mature open source projects", *First Monday* 7(6).

Krogh, G. von, Haefliger, S., Späth, S., and Wallin, M. W. (2012): "Carrots and rainbows: motivation and social practice in open source software development", *MIS Quarterly* 36(2), pp. 649–676.

Krogh, G. von, and Hippel, E. A. von (2006): "The promise of research on Open Source software", *Management Science* 52(7), pp. 975–983.

Krogh, G. von, Späth, S., and Lakhani, K. R. (2003): "Community, joining, and specialization in open source software innovation: a case study: Open Source software development", *Research Policy* 32(7), pp. 1217–1241.

Kuk, G. (2006): "Strategic interaction and knowledge sharing in the KDE developer mailing list", *Management Science* 52(7), pp. 1031–1042.

Lakhani, K. R., and Hippel, E. A. von (2003): "How open source software works: 'free' user-to-user assistance", *Research Policy* 32(6), pp. 923–943.

Lee, G. K., and Cole, R. E. (2003): "From a firm-based to a community-based model of knowledge creation: the case of the Linux Kernel development", *Organization Science* 14(6), pp. 633–649.

Lerner, J., and Tirole, J. (2002): "Some simple economics of Open Source", *The Journal of Industrial Economics* 50(2), pp. 197–234.

Lerner, J., and Tirole, J. (2005): "The scope of Open Source licensing", *Journal of Law, Economics, and Organization* 21(1), pp. 20–56.

Loewenstein, G., Thompson, L., and Bazerman, M. (1989): "Social utility and decision making in interpersonal contexts", *Journal of Personality and Social Psychology* 57(3), p. 426.

Louviere, J. J. (2006): "What you don't know might hurt you: some unresolved issues in the design and analysis of discrete choice experiments", *Environmental and Resource Economics* 34(1), pp. 173–188.

Louviere, J. J., Flynn, T., and Carson, R. T. (2010a): "Discrete choice experiments are not conjoint analysis", *Journal of Choice Modelling* 3(3), pp. 57–72.

Louviere, J. J., and Swait, J. D. (2010): "Commentary—discussion of 'alleviating the constant stochastic variance assumption in decision research: theory, measurement, and experimental test'", *Marketing Science* 29(1), pp. 18–22.

Markus, M. (2007): "The governance of free/open source software projects: monolithic, multidimensional, or configurational?" *Journal of Management and Governance* 11(2), pp. 151–163.

Markus, M., Manville, B., and Agres, C. (2000): "What makes a virtual organization work-lessons from the open source world", *Sloan Management Review* 42(1), pp. 13–26.

Mathison, S. (1988): "Why triangulate?" *Educational Researcher* 17(2), pp. 13–17.

Mooi, E., and Sarstedt, M. (2011): *A concise guide to market research: the process, data, and methods using IBM SPSS statistics*, Springer, Heidelberg.

Morris, A., and Mueller, C. (1992): *Frontiers in social movement theory*, Yale University Press, New Haven, CT.

Netemeyer, R. G., Pullig, C., and Bearden, W. O. (2002): "Observations on some key psychometric properties of paper-and-pencil measures", *Advances in Business Marketing and Purchasing* 11, pp. 115–138.

Nov, O., and Kuk, G. (2008): "Open source content contributors' response to free-riding: the effect of personality and context", *Computers in Human Behavior* 24(6), pp. 2848–2861.

Nunnally, J. C. (1978): *Psychometric theory*, McGraw-Hill, New York.

Oh, W., and Jeon, S. (2007): "Membership herding and network stability in the open source community: the Ising perspective", *Management Science* 53(7), pp. 1086–1101.

O'Mahony, S., and Ferraro, F. (2007): "The emergence of governance in an Open Source community", *Academy of Management Journal* 50(5), pp. 1079–1106.

Oreg, S., and Nov, O. (2008): "Exploring motivations for contributing to open source initiatives: the roles of contribution context and personal values", *Computers in Human Behavior* 24(5), pp. 2055–2073.

Osborne, J. W., and Overbay, A. (2008): "Best practices in data cleaning: how outliers and 'fringeliers' can increase error rates and decrease the quality and precision of your results", in *Best practices in quantitative methods*, J. W. Osborne (ed.), SAGE, Los Angeles.

Osterloh, M., and Rota, S. (2007): "Open source software development—just another case of collective invention?" *Research Policy* 36(2), pp. 157–171.

Podsakoff, P. M., MacKenzie, S. B., Lee, J. Y., and Podsakoff, N. P. (2003): "Common method biases in behavioral research: a critical review of the literature and recommended remedies", *Journal of Applied Psychology* 88, pp. 879–903.

Preece, J., and Shneiderman, B. (2009): "The reader-to-leader framework: motivating technology-mediated social participation", *AIS Transactions on Human-Computer Interaction* 1(1), pp. 13–32.

Qureshi, I., and Fang, Y. (2011): "Socialization in open source software projects: a growth mixture modeling approach", *Organizational Research Methods* 14(1), pp. 208–238.

Revelt, D., and Train, K. (1998): "Mixed logit with repeated choices: households' choices of appliance efficiency level", *Review of Economics and Statistics* 80(4), pp. 647–657.

Roberts, J. A., Hann, I.-H., and Slaughter, S. A. (2006): "Understanding the motivations, participation, and performance of Open Source software developers: a longitudinal study of the Apache Projects", *Management Science* 52(7), pp. 984–999.

Robinson, J. P., Shaver, P., and Wrightsman, L. (1991): "Criteria for scale selection and evaluation", in *Measures of personality and social psychological attitudes*, J. P. Robinson (ed.), pp. 1–16, Academic Press, San Diego.

Rolandsson, B., Bergquist, M., and Ljungberg, J. (2011): "Open source in the firm: opening up professional practices of software development", *Research Policy* 40(4), pp. 576–587.

Scarpa, R., and Rose, J. M. (2008): "Design efficiency for non-market valuation with choice modelling: how to measure it, what to report and why", *Australian Journal of Agricultural and Resource Economics* 52(3), pp. 253–282.

Sen, R. (2007): "A strategic analysis of competition between open source and proprietary software", *Journal of Management Information Systems* 24(1), pp. 233–257.

Shah, S. K. (2006): "Motivation, governance, and the viability of hybrid forms in Open Source software development", *Management Science* 52(7), pp. 1000–1014.

Sørensen, F., Mattsson, J., and Sundbo, J. (2010): "Experimental methods in innovation research", *Research Policy* 39(3), pp. 313–322.

Spector, P. (2006): "Method variance in organizational research truth or urban legend?" *Organizational Research Methods* 9(2), pp. 221–232.

Stewart, K. J., Ammeter, A. P., and Maruping, L. M. (2006): "Impacts of license choice and organizational sponsorship on user interest and development activity in Open Source software projects", *Information Systems Research* 17(2), pp. 126–144.

Stuermer, M., Späth, S., and Krogh, G. von (2009): "Extending private-collective innovation: a case study", *R&D Management* 39(2), pp. 170–191.

Subramaniam, C., Sen, R., and Nelson, M. (2009): "Determinants of open source software project success: a longitudinal study", *Decision Support Systems* 46(2), pp. 576–585.

Swait, J. D., and Andrews, R. (2003): "Enriching scanner panel models with choice experiments", *Marketing Science* 22(4), pp. 442–460.

Wasko, M., and Faraj, S. (2005): "Why should I share? examining social capital and knowledge contribution in electronic networks of practice", *MIS Quarterly* 29(1), pp. 35–57.

West, J. (2003): "How open is open enough?: melding proprietary and open source platform strategies: Open Source software development", *Research Policy* 32(7), pp. 1259–1285.

West, J., and Gallagher, S. (2006): "Patterns of open innovation in Open Source software", in *Open innovation: researching a new paradigm*, H. W. Chesbrough, W. Vanhaverbeke, and J. West (eds.), pp. 82–106, Oxford University Press, New York.

West, J., and O'Mahony, S. (2008): "The role of participation architecture in growing sponsored open source communities", *Industry & Innovation* 15(2), pp. 145–168.

Wilson, J. (2000): "Volunteering", *Annual Review of Sociology* 26, pp. 215–240.

Wu, C.-G., Gerlach, J. H., and Young, C. E. (2007): "An empirical analysis of open source software developers' motivations and continuance intentions", *Information & Management* 44(3), pp. 253–262.

7 Exogenous vs. Endogenous Governance in Innovation Communities

Effects on Motivation, Conflict and Justice—An Experimental Investigation

Niclas Störmer and Cornelius Herstatt

In this study we examine the effects of exogenous vs. endogenous governance rules on a virtual community handling an innovative task. Specifically, we investigate the relationship between the two modes (exogenous vs. endogenous) and factors such as motivation, conflict and justice. We conducted an experiment with 70 students, divided into teams of five. We manipulated procedural legitimacy by allowing one group to choose a set of rules and giving the other group the same rules exogenously. Our study indicates that letting a team choose its own governance rules leads to increasing level of conflict negatively impacting motivation.

Keywords: governance, collaborative innovation communities

7 EXOGENOUS VS. ENDOGENOUS GOVERNANCE IN INNOVATION COMMUNITIES

7.1 Introduction

No organization, at least above a certain size, can function properly without rules and procedures. What is relevant for 'conventional' business organizations seems to also hold true for the growing number of online collaborative communities of multiple contributors such as open source software (OSS) communities or Wikipedia. Recently, a growing number of firms make use of collaborative communities by sponsoring them (O'Mahony and West 2005; Shah 2006). The emergence of firms shifts the focus from self-governance of volunteers to external, firm initiated, governance of communities.

Virtual communities of volunteers working collaboratively or developing new solutions exist in many forms. Inevitably, numerous overlapping terms ranging from *innovation communities, online communities, user communities* or *knowledge producing communities* exist (West and Lakhani 2008). However, such communities do not necessarily produce innovative outcomes. We solely focus on communities collaboratively producing innovative outcomes, which are exploited either in a private or commercial sense (Raasch et al. 2009), excluding virtual communities in the broader sense. We thus limit the scope according to the definition of West and Lakhani (2008), who define innovation communities as voluntary associations of actors who produce innovations that are brought to market. We use the term open collaborative innovation (OCI) community, which is strongly based on Baldwin and Hippel (2011), who speak of open collaborative innovation.

While the governance mechanisms to accomplish order within and between organizations have been comprehensively assessed as part of the research on economic governance (cf. Williamson 2005), the issue of governance of open collaborative innovation (OCI) communities is still an important question. Important because governance within such communities is different to the classical market or hierarchy paradigm, and may represent a new mode (Demil and Lecocq 2006). Furthermore the exchange within these communities is not that of physical goods but rather of "nonrivalrous and nonexcludable" knowledge resources (Madison et al. 2010). Some authors see the question of organization and governance as one of the key question for understanding such communities (Baldwin and Clark 2006; Lerner and Tirole 2002) and also a necessary ingredient to create an organizational climate to attract participants (Shah 2006; Markus 2007).

Especially in the field of OSS, researchers have investigated the mechanisms by which such communities govern themselves, in order to achieve direction, control and coordination among community members (Markus 2007). Numerous mechanisms have been identified, among them the division of roles and different decision rights (de Laat 2007; Shah 2006), communication rules and property rights (Bonaccorsi and Rossi 2003; Markus 2007) and modularization (de Laat 2007). Beyond identifying mechanisms of governance, the aspect of interrelations between governance and psychological states such as motivation and resulting behavior such as participation has been of interest (cf. Jeppesen and Frederiksen 2006; Shah 2006).

If firms interact with communities they can choose different modes of interaction ranging from a loose affiliation to the foundation of own communities. To a great extent, different modes of firms involvement depend on the business model of the firm (Dahlander and Magnusson 2008). A firm that regards a community as one source among many for innovation and creativity is likely to interact differently than a company that regards the value generated within the community as its major business. For that reason, one has to conclude that there is not just one firm-community interaction, but many modes and configurations.

It is evident that the goals of profit oriented firms and communities of volunteers are not inevitably the same which can result in great tension (West and O'Mahony 2008). Therefore, the question of governance is central within the relationship of firm and community since a large number of involved parties with diverse objectives, capabilities and involvement come together (Dahlander et al. 2008). The way governance is structured in sponsored communities, that is how work is organized and activities are controlled, will influence intrinsic motivation of volunteers to contribute (Jeppesen and Frederiksen 2006). Negative reactions by volunteers are reported if a firm executes too much control and unfair ownership demands (Shah 2006). Firms are aware of such challenges and try to counter it by legitimizing such decisions in letting volunteers participate by making the governance accessible (West and O'Mahony 2008; O'Mahony and West 2005). While the realization that participation in procedural processes seems indispensable, to date little is known about the precise effects of participation vs. no participation on the community. Field and experimental research from other fields provide evidence that externally imposed rules may 'crowd out' endogenous cooperative behavior (Ostrom 2000a) and preferences (Cardenas 2004), thereby possibly negatively impacting intrinsic motivation (Frey 1994). Valuable insights can be gained from these findings; however, OCI communities differ in many ways, for instance the specific nature of innovative work and contextual factors like communication over the Internet. We therefore believe it to be worthwhile to investigate the question how a community of volunteers creating innovative outcomes copes with the influence of external regulation by an authoritarian institution like a firm.

It comes down to the question whether firms should impose governance rules on a community or rather let it loose by relying on self-governance. Generally put the aim of any OCI community is to produce (innovative) beneficial outcomes. Such a goal can only be reached if certain preconditions or influential factors (e.g. motivation of participants, conflict resolution within the community) are fulfilled. Therefore the main research question that needs to be answered is how the choice between endogenous and exogenous governance rules affects such factors. In the present study we used an experimental approach to directly manipulate exogenous vs. endogenous rules.

7.2 Research Framework

Our research framework rests upon the IAD framework by Elinor Ostrom, which originally refers to the governance of common-pool resources (cf. Ostrom 2005a; Ostrom 2005b). Madison et al. (2010) have shown that with minor adaption the framework also provides a model to study the constructions of knowledge-based works. While the original framework consists of up to six components, we focus on three elements. The first component is the *action situation*, which has been described as "two or more individuals . . . faced with a set of potential actions that jointly produce outcomes" (Ostrom 2005b, p. 32). Such action situations can be found within many contexts, for example buyer-seller exchanges, legislative processes and also the creation of knowledge resources as done in OCI communities. The second component are the *participants* who interact within the given action

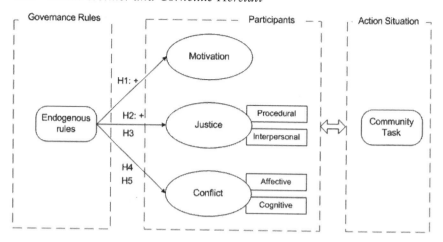

Figure 7.1 Theoretical framework and proposed relationships of variables

situation. Behavior of community members—as for any human behavior—is determined by many factors, such as psychological states of individuals and interaction between the individuals. Both components are embedded in the so called *action arena*, the central unit of analysis. As the name already suggests, the *action arena* refers to the field where the 'action' is taking place and participants interact around the given action situation. The action arena is influenced by different exogenous factors—among them *governance rules*, the third element. Governance rules can affect the behavior of participants, the way work is coordinated and exchanges of knowledge resources are secured.

Applying the proposed model to the context of collaborative innovation communities, we operationalized different elements of the model in a way to best meet the specific characteristics and also develop measures to allow the investigation of relationships between the components (see Figure 7.1). In the following section, we first lay out the characteristics of innovative work in OCI communities, second followed by the description of governance rules. In the third final section, we lay out our hypotheses regarding the effects of exogenous vs. endogenous rules on interaction behavior and psychological states of participants.

7.2.1 Action Situation—Characteristics of Innovative Work in OCI Communities

According to Baldwin and Hippel (2011), an open collaborative innovation project consists of contributors who share the work of generating a collective design. This indicates that a collective effort is an integral element of such communities. Raasch et al. (2009) highlight the collaborative aspect of several contributing actors. To allow for collaboration among many individuals, the work in OCI communities is often characterized by a modular design architecture (Baldwin and Clark 2006). Such a system distinguishes itself by elements that are partitioned into subsets and which can be processed separately (Baldwin and Hippel 2011). Furthermore, innovative work is characterized by complexity (Katz and Tushman 1979). This complexity is determined by many attributes, such as the option of multiple outcomes, multiple paths to reach the outcome, conflicting interdependence among paths and uncertainty about desired outcomes (Campbell 1988).

In the light of these findings, we define four features of tasks in OCI communities: (1) the solution must reflect a *collective effort*, (2) it calls for *collaborative work* between actors, (3) has a *modular* design and (4) shows features of *complexity*.

7.2.2 Governance Rules

As already mentioned, different categories of instruments of governance in OSS communities have been identified (Markus 2007). These mechanisms are institutionalized through rules, for example rules that describe the responsibilities and decision powers of certain roles or rules that describe how to communicate and who can join the community. In other words, all described mechanisms are embodied through a diverse set of rules. These can be either explicit or implicit. Ostrom's work on rules has led to a set of seven generic governance rules (Ostrom 2005b) which show extensive overlaps with the identified mechanisms in OSS communities (Schweik and Kitsing 2010). We are also well aware that many 'invisible' mechanisms of governance exist. Attributes like trust, solidarity and reciprocity allow for smooth interaction within communities lacking formal mechanisms. The importance of such informal mechanisms has been highlighted by different authors (e.g. Lerner and Tirole 2002; Bowles and Gintis 2002).

Governance is seen as a dynamic process that evolves over time (Heide 1994). Besides the identification of distinct mechanisms, the evolvement of governance in such communities should be considered to fully understand. It is evident that communities are not static, but grow and develop over time. For instance, the need for governance increases with the size and maturity of a community. Investigations of the emergence of governance revealed different phases, from de facto governance to a stabilized system (O'Mahony and Ferraro 2007).

While the emergence of social order is a vast field mainly reserved for sociologist and shall not be discussed in this paper (cf. Greif 1997; Streeck and Schmitter 1985), we propose a further view. If a community has to settle on explicit rules, it undergoes a process integrating possible diverse individual positions into a consensus—a process which is characterized as a group decision process. Group decision processes have been investigated comprehensively (cf. Kerr and Tindale 2004; Kaplan and Miller 1987). We consider the formation of endogenous governance by a group as a group decision process since different preferences for diverse rules have to be integrated in one set of rules which is accepted by all. Contrary exogenous governance is characterized by exclusion of community members from any decision process, giving them no participation rights for designing such rules.

7.2.3 Actors—Psychological States and Group Interaction

Participants' behavior and actions are crucial to the success of an OCI community. In fact, they are one of the key factors for successful outcomes in a community. It is known that motivation and cooperative behavior play an important role maintaining functional collaborative communities (Bonaccorsi and Rossi 2003). Therefore, we examined factors, namely motivation, justice, conflict and interaction behavior of group members. The rationale for choosing each factor and the expected interrelations between the two modes of governance are illustrated in the following section.

7.2.3.1 Motivation

One of the key questions of OCI communities is why volunteers participate. This question is especially puzzling since the contribution to a public good is counter-intuitive to the "self-interested-economic-agent paradigm" (Lerner and Tirole 2001, p. 821).[1] Consequently, different authors investigated the motivation of users in such communities. Exploring the subject of motivation includes a wide range of different aspects, for example the question why users participate (cf. Lakhani and Hippel 2003) and why do they innovate (cf. Füller et al. 2007; Jeppesen and Frederiksen 2006). Individuals vary substantially in their underlying motives (David and Shapiro 2008). Ghosh (2005) points this out by showing the mix of different motives within a heterogenic group of participants. In the attempt to organize a bundle of such diverse motives, resorting to prior work in the field of motivation seems promising. Research on the topic of motivation typically makes a distinction between intrinsic and extrinsic types of motivation (Ryan and Deci 2000). An activity is extrinsically motivated if it is carried out in order to attain a certain extrinsic return such as money or other rewards. Therefore, the source of the motivation "comes not from the activity itself but rather from the extrinsic consequences to which the activity leads" (Gagné and Deci 2005, p. 331). On the contrary, "one is said to be intrinsically motivated to perform an activity when he receives no apparent reward except the activity itself" (Deci 1971, p. 105). The relationship between extrinsic and intrinsic motivation can be conflictive as substantial experimental and field evidence suggests (Bénabou and Tirole 2003). In particular, an external reward that aims at enhancing external motivation may adversely affect intrinsic motivation. One such example of the conflictive nature is described by the motivation crowding effect where external intervention (such as monetary rewards or punishment) may undermine intrinsic motivation (cf. Frey and Jegen 2001; Frey 1994; Alexy and Leitner 2010). In a meta-analysis Deci Koestner and Ryan (1999) showed, that there are various types of external influences going beyond just monetary rewards ranging from verbal rewards to threats and deadlines, which conflict with intrinsic motivation. Frey and Jegen (2001) also formulate a general definition that all external intervention may affect intrinsic motivation, explicitly including regulations. With regards to OCI communities, both intrinsic as well as extrinsic motivations have been identified. Features of intrinsic motivation include feelings like fun and a belonging to the group (Lakhani and Hippel 2003; Füller 2006). Extrinsic motives consist of qualities such as career prospects (Lakhani and Hippel 2003) and development of skills and knowledge, personal need and to some degree of monetary rewards (Füller 2006).

While both, intrinsic and extrinsic sources of motivation are important to understand community based innovation (Jeppesen and Molin 2003), within this study we focused on intrinsic motivation. In the context of OSS communities there is evidence "that enjoyment-based intrinsic motivation . . . is the strongest and most pervasive driver" (Lakhani and Wolf 2005, p. 3). Also the question whether external intervention by any form of authority (e.g. by firms) may mislay the interest and commitment of volunteers in OCI communities is raised within the field of OCI community research (O'Mahony and Ferraro 2007). Considering adjacent research from the field of motivation crowding theory and the work of Ostrom imply that investigating the relationship between external intervention and intrinsic motivation of participants seems to be worthwhile. Ostrom (2000b) for example showed that in some settings, if individuals lose a sense of control over their own fate, external interventions crowds out intrinsic preferences. Frey and Jegen (2001) identified two psychological processes by which external interventions can affect intrinsic motivation:

a. *Impaired self-determination.* When individuals perceive an external intervention as reducing their self-determination, intrinsic motivation is substituted by extrinsic control . . .
b. *Impaired self-esteem.* When outside intervention carries the notion that the actor's motivation is not acknowledged, his or her intrinsic motivation is effectively rejected. (Frey and Jegen 2001, p. 594)

Applying those findings to the stated problem allowed for the formulation of following hypothesis:

H1: Choosing your own governance rules has a positive effect on Intrinsic Motivation.

7.2.3.2 *Procedural and Interpersonal Justice*

Governance rules can solve problems of coordination and foster cooperative behavior between participants. However, rules can be only effective if they are being followed by participants. Therefore, research has focused on the circumstances that must exist for individuals to comply with given rules.

Models that explain individual rule compliance integrate factors from economic, psychological and sociological theories (Jenny et al. 2007).

In particular crucial to the adherence of rules is whether they are perceived as legitimate (Tyler 2005). Within the context of governance system, legitimacy results in higher compliance of rules and therefore enduring stability (Walker et al. 1986). Thus, legitimacy is a prerequisite to build functional governance systems and therefore stable business institutions and OCI communities. This raises the question under what circumstances a rule normative system is perceived as legitimate. Put differently, how can one achieve legitimacy when designing governance rules and structures? One central dimension that influences the perception of legitimacy is justice (Tyler 2006). Consequently, the construct of justice, especially in organizations, has been of great interest to researchers within the last decades.[2] Within the literature, justice is viewed as multi-dimensional, differentiating between distributive justice, interpersonal justice and procedural justice. Distributive justice is fostered by outcomes and focuses on people's reaction to unfair allocation of rewards or resources (Greenberg 1987). Procedural justice centers the process by which the outcome is reached. Leventhal defines procedural justice as follows:[3] "The concept of *procedural fairness* refers to an individual's perception of the fairness of procedural components of the social system that regulate the allocative process" (Leventhal 1980, p. 35).

Leventhal (1980) states that such a process includes complex networks of events and procedures such as the appointment of decision makers and the process of reaching decisions. Regarding this definition, it is evident that procedural justice directly applies to problem stated above—whether rules are perceived as legitimate or not. Since procedural justice focuses on the rules itself and not on interpersonal relationships or the outcome of rules it proves to be a precise measure to examine the effects of exogenous vs. endogenous governance rules. In addition, the theory of procedural justice not only offers well-established constructs how to measure the perceived justice of governance rules. Furthermore, it explains why endogenous rules are expected to be perceived as legitimate, because "participation rights are essential for the legitimacy of adjudicatory procedures" (Solum 2005, p. 179).

It is known that procedural justice is not only essential for the obedience of rules but also "demonstrated to result in increased job satisfaction, organizational commitment, and organizational citizenship behaviors" (Konovsky 2000, p. 492). Moreover, procedural justice is strongly related to individual innovative behavior (Janssen 2004). One can therefore conclude that procedural justice is more than just a precondition for functional governance but moreover a lever to boost performance and innovation. Given a group the opportunity to choose their own set of governance rules should lead to higher levels of perceived procedural justice, since participation rights (according to the procedural legitimacy thesis) increases the legitimacy.

> H2: *Choosing your own governance rules has a positive effect on the perception of Procedural Justice.*

Interpersonal justice, also referred to as interactional justice,[4] is closely linked to procedural justice. Research shows that people not only focus on the fairness of the procedure but how it is enacted by a decision maker, relating to dimensions such as truthfulness and respectful treatment (Bies and Shapiro 1987). The close relationship between the procedure and the person endorsing is intuitive. Different studies show high procedural-interactional justice correlations (Colquitt 2001). It is important to distinguish whether the procedures themselves are perceived fair and the enactment of those rules on the other. This is especially important when bearing in mind that rules are usually executed by a person, for example by a project leader. The strong relationship between *Procedural* and *Interpersonal Justice* leads to the assumption that the ability to choose your own rules also relates to higher levels of interpersonal justice. However, research of group decision processes show that reaching a group decision can be a delicate issue, resulting in conflict and poor decision quality (cf. Priem and Harrison 1995). Green by investigating different social decision schemes within groups highlights the negative effects a group decision can have on negative socio-emotional behavior (Green and Taber 1980).[5] Depending on whether the group comes to an easy verdict or finds itself in a difficult discussion in the process of agreeing on rules, differential effects on the dimension of *Interpersonal Justice* are expected. Overall *Interpersonal Justice* is an important factor when it comes to endogenous vs. exogenous rules. However, we did not have a priori hypothesis of the directional effect.

> H3: *Choosing your own governance rules has an effect on the perception of Interpersonal Justice.*

7.2.3.3 Conflict

Faced with an innovative and complex task, groups experience problems of optimal coordination and communication which results in conflict, a struggle which governance mechanisms try to solve (Lattemann and Stieglitz 2005). Especially innovative behavior of individuals can provoke conflict with co-workers, if innovative ideas challenge the established framework of collaborators (Janssen 2003). Innovative tasks are therefore more likely to breed conflict for two reasons, first problems of coordination and second different intensity of innovative behavior of individuals. To some level, conflict can be beneficial by generating new ideas, however, too much conflict becomes dysfunctional (Wall and Nolan 1986). In more detail, two studies showed that innovation increases with a medium level of conflict within a team, while dropping to zero under intense conflict (de Dreu 2006).

Not only the level of conflict is decisive, but also the type of conflict. Conflict is distinguished between two forms—task oriented and interpersonal conflict (Jehn 1995). Amasons (1996) distinction between functional *Cognitive Conflict and Affective Conflict* is in line with this classification. *Affective Conflict* is characterized by personal incompatibilities or disputes and tends to be emotional, where *Cognitive Conflict* is task-oriented and encourages evaluations of alternatives. Therefore, *Cognitive Conflict* is expected to contribute to innovation, while *Affective Conflict* may demolish innovative outcomes.

In the light of the negative consequences, too much conflict can have the matter of managing conflict within communities, that needs to be solved. Hence effective and good governance must hinder the emergence of too much conflict and solve it rapidly when inevitable. Kittur and Kraut (2010) found procedures and policy likely to be the only coordination device to be effective.

Such procedures and policies are consistent with the governance rules discussed above, which affect the participants within the action arena. Since we proposed that rules selected by the community may have higher perceived legitimacy (H2), it could be expected that self-chosen rules reduce conflict better. However, the positive effect of procedures and policies can only be attained if such rules are in place. The process of agreeing on rules, as mentioned before, involves the risk of creating further conflict. Therefore, once again, hypotheses are formulated non directional, as for *Interpersonal Justice*:

> H4: *Choosing your own governance rules has an effect on Affective Conflict.*
> H5: *Choosing your own governance rules has an effect on Cognitive Conflict.*

To summarize, we propose the difference between exogenous vs. endogenous governance to affect perceived *Motivation*, *Justice* and *Conflict*. We also propose relationships between factors set out in the previous section, which can be investigated through analysis of correlation.

7.3   Method

The objective of this study is to establish clear cause and effect relationships between modes of governance and factors such as motivation. Conclusions about cause and effect relationships are best drawn by experimental studies (Aronson et al. 2010). Moreover, exogenous vs. endogenous rules represent two extreme manifestations which can be easily implemented in an experimental manipulation. To test the hypotheses, we conducted an experiment with 70 graduate students. Students were awarded with credits for participation.[6] Two treatment conditions were employed: The first allowed participants to choose their own governance rules, while teams under the second treatment were given the matching rules exogenously.

7.3.1 Basic Experimental Design

To experimentally investigate the hypotheses, we applied Bavelas (1950) 'five square puzzle', a task that reflects the four described characteristics of OCI community work. In this 15 various geometric shapes are distributed among a group of five players. Each player is required to build an individual square by exchanging shapes with the other players. Out of these shapes, many different squares can be formed, however, only one arrangement exists which allows each player to form his own square (see Figure 7.2). The initial distribution of puzzle pieces is chosen such that the probability of suboptimal solutions is increased. If those solutions are maintained, a group solution remains impractical. Notable is how the group manages the occurrence of such 'wrong' squares, since "for an individual who has completed a square, it is understandably difficult to tear it apart" (Bavelas 1950, p. 730).

Since a perfect solution can only be reached if everyone cooperates and trades pieces a *collective effort* is needed. Trading pieces demands a high degree of mutual communication and interaction between participants— therefore *collaboration* is inevitable. Furthermore it shows some signs of *modularity* since players can work on individual solutions (symbolized by individual squares). The described task clearly shows the feature of *complexity* (Ruef 1996), since different paths to the solution are possible. While the chosen task meets the four established criteria some further features— that make the task even more suitable—shall be demonstrated. In order to solve the task, participants are faced with a social dilemma situation, where individual interest may conflict with the group interest (van Dijk and Wilke 1995). A mixed motive situation may occur, if players who have already formed a square are faced with the decision to break up their solution, in order to contribute to the perfect solution. Such situation can quickly lead to free-riding behavior, when a player takes advantage of his position

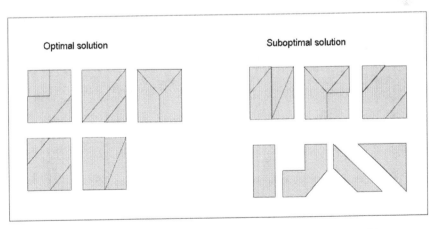

Figure 7.2 Task for the experiment to resemble work in OCI communities

and refuses to cooperate (Torre 2006), an often discussed problem in OCI communities.

Players are given 40 minutes to solve the task. To increase the already in the game characteristics inherent social dilemma—when players are faced with the decision to break up a suboptimal square—a payoff function is introduced. Players are awarded with points, whereas the point allocation is determined by the individual and group performance. After the game is finished, a count of completed squares for each group is carried out. Points for each player are calculated by following formula:

20 points for each individual square + Σ group squares x 10

Hence, a player could reach 0–70 points depending on both the individual and group performance. To provide an incentive, the 5 players with the highest number of points (across all teams) are awarded with a voucher worth €20. If there were more than 5 participants with the same number of points, the group time needed to reach the solution was taken into account as an additional criterion.

7.3.2   *Procedure and Manipulation*

Participants were randomly assigned to teams of five to solve the puzzle task. The experiment was conducted in a virtual setting where participants interacted anonymously via the Internet. Players were seated in a room and were divided by blinds. No group member knew the identity of the other players. The exchange of the different pieces was carried out via a browser-based online tool which was developed for the experiment. Communication among the participants was taking place in German via group chat. The virtual set-up was chosen to duplicate the characteristics of OCI communities where communication is conducted via chat (e.g. using IRC) and exchange of artifacts (such as source code, specification, etc.) is organized exhaustively over the Internet.

Upon arriving for the experimental session, participants were seated in the different booths in front of a computer terminal. Participants were then advised to read the instructions, which were placed next to each computer terminal on a paper sheet. After having read the instructions, a short movie explaining the use of the tool and communication via chat was shown.

The instructions for treatment A (endogenous rules) included following paragraph at the end of the instructions:

> *Before the 40 minutes are started by the administrator you have 15 minutes as a group to discuss a set of rules that might help you to come to better results as a group. The list of rules will be given to you before the discussion starts.*

The list of rules a team could choose from was presented as a print out of two set of rules to choose from. First participants could vote whether to have a project leader or not. Once they chose to have a project leader, they could choose between two options of appointing a leader, either by group vote or by fortune (appointed by the administrator).

The second block of rules was concerned with the decision right to force a participant to share a piece, a situation which is likely to occur, if a player has already completed his square and is not willing to break it up. Again a team could choose between different options. One alternative was to transfer all the decision power to the project leader. Another two choices were installing different decision schemes where the simple majority of three or an exhaustive majority of four has to agree. The last option implies installing no such rule and leaving the decision up to each individual. In total, the list of rules allowed 11 diverse configurations of governance rules.

The instructions for treatment B (exogenous rules) included following paragraph at the end of the instructions:

> *Before the 40 minutes are started by the administrator you have 15 minutes as a group to discuss any topic you like. During the 15 minutes the administrator will give you some more directions.*

Seven minutes into the group discussion the administrator announced following message via the group chat.

> *In course of the game a set of rules has to be followed. The set of rules will be passed out now.*

The administrator then handed the list of rules (again in paper form), which matched the rules chosen by the correspondent team under treatment $A_{end.}$. If the list implied the rule of voting a project leader, the group was asked at the end of the 15 minutes about their choice. The reason for introducing the rules under treatment $B_{exog.}$ after 7 minutes and not at the beginning of the 15 is as follows. The main idea is to avoid that rules are apprehended as part of the game instructions; consequently, the temporal separation is believed to assist to this objective. The reason of introducing the rules in the middle of the 15 minutes and not at the end has practical motives, since players obviously take some time to understand the meaning and implications of the rules.

The time for the group discussion was started by the administrator by announcing it over the group chat. For treatment $A_{end.}$, if the group did not announce the choice of rules by itself, the administrator asked for the group choice at the end of the 15 minutes. For both treatments time checks were announced by the administrator three minutes before the 15 minutes ended.

Upon the termination of the group discussion the puzzle game was started. After 40 minutes, or when a team accomplished the optimal solution prior to that, participants were asked to fill out a questionnaire.

7.3.3   Data Sample

Out of the 14 teams performing the task (7 under each treatment) one team had to be excluded from the sample, since the game had to be aborted due technical difficulties. Therefore, the sample consists of 13 teams (7 under treatment A, 6 for B), resulting in 65 individual responses, thereof 11 (17 %) female and 54 (83%) male respondents. Average age is 25, ranging from 22 to 30. Concerning the educational background of respondents, the sample is exceptionally homogenous, since all participants are graduate students from an engineering management program from the Hamburg University of Technology. Most respondents of the sample 57 (88%) declare German as their native language, while 8 (12%) grew up with a different language. However, it can be stated that German language skills of non-native speakers can be considered good since they attend lectures in German.

Since the sample consists of students, we want to justify why we believe it to be suitable. According to Stevens (2011), a student sample is appropriate if the underlying universalistic theory applies to all population and is not specific to one context. Since hypotheses were derived from general theories of motivation or justice, we believe them to be applicable to any population. Van Rijnsoever et al. (2012), also resorting to the work of Stevens, state a further justification for a student sample: Using a homogenous sample optimizes the internal validity. Another point is that the sample is overwhelmingly male. Since none effects of gender are expected this should not reduce the validity of the experiment. Anyhow, gender is included as a control variable, to investigate any unwanted effects. We want to conclude with one last point. OCI communities exist in many different forms, assembled of homogenous groups such as communities of doctors or very heterogeneous groups, for example contributors of Wikipedia. Therefore, any other data sample would not be inherently better or worse than the chosen student sample

7.3.4   Measures

While the rational for choosing variables and suspected hypotheses have been stated in section 7.2, the following paragraph details the exact measures. All variables were collected post the game via a questionnaire using established constructs by different authors. In addition, all chat messages were recorded, including information about sender and time sent.

In a meta-analysis Cameron and Pierce (1994) showed that intrinsic motivation has been measured with a variety of means, including free time on a task after withdrawal or reward, self-reported task interest, satisfaction and enjoyment and a subject willingness to participate in future projects. After a review of diverse measures, seven-point semantic differential scales developed by Crino and White (1982) are used to measure intrinsic *Motivation*. Since the task characteristics and set-up by Crino and White is similar to the one in this research project (also a puzzle game, same group size) it seems especially appropriate.

As for intrinsic motivation, various measurements for the dimensions of *Procedural* and *Interpersonal Justice* exist (for an overview and validation of different measures see Colquitt 2001). Drawing on the work of Colquitt, four established items for each construct are used to measure the two variables *Procedural Justice* and *Interpersonal Justice*.

Accommodating for the multidimensional aspect of conflict, we measure dysfunctional and functional conflict with two constructs. We draw on the work of Amason (1996), who distinguished between dysfunctional 'affective conflict' and functional 'cognitive conflict'. Conflict is measured using three items for *Cognitive* and four items for *Affective Conflict* previously applied by Amason.

All variables, except for *Motivation*, were measured on a 5-point Likert-type scale with anchors of 1= *not at all* and 5= *to an exceptional degree*. Additional three control variables were recorded. *Native Language* and *Gender* were included in the questionnaire. *Typing Speed* was recorded post the game by taking the time a participant needed for typing a standardized sentence.

7.4 Analysis and Results

Hypotheses were tested by statistical analysis including all self-reported measures collected via the questionnaire. To ensure robustness of findings, covariate analysis and test of sub-samples were conducted. In order to gain a deeper understanding and elevate the accuracy of the explanation of statistical results, a content analysis of chat messages was conducted post to the statistical analysis.

7.4.1 Main Effects of Manipulation

First, we ensured reliability of constructs by investigating items using Cronbach's alpha and corrected item correlation. We further conducted a confirmatory factor analysis using principal components extractions and rotating factors via varimax. Both analyses confirmed the applied constructs. Constructs were then built by calculating arithmetic means of the related items.

An inspection of variables for both treatment groups revealed differences in the mean scores. The group under treatment $A_{end.}$ had lower means concerning the constructs of *Motivation* and *Interpersonal Justice*, while the scores for both measures of *Conflict* showed higher means. Comparison of mean scores for *Procedural Justice* showed only minor differences between the groups. Table 7.1 provides a summary of group profiles for each treatment.

In order to test whether these differences proved to be significantly, a multivariate analysis of variance (MANOVA) was run for the whole sample ($N = 65$). The MANOVA revealed a significant multivariate main effect for the treatment, Wilks' $\lambda = .798$, $F_{(5; 59)} = 2.986$; $p = .018$, partial eta squared = .202. The power to detect the effect was .826. After having established significance of the overall test, univariate effects were examined. Significant

Table 7.1   Means and standard deviation of dependent variables detailed for both treatments

Means and standard deviations

	Condition	Mean	SD
Motivation	Endogenous	5.23	0.78
	Exogenous	5.68	0.54
Affective Conflict	Endogenous	2.20	1.07
	Exogenous	1.68	0.77
Cognitive Conflict	Endogenous	2.21	0.90
	Exogenous	1.89	0.78
Procedural Justice	Endogenous	3.76	0.71
	Exogenous	3.71	0.80
Interpersonal Justice	Endogenous	4.14	0.72
	Exogenous	4.53	0.54

Endogenous $N = 35$; exogenous $N = 30$.

Table 7.2   Univariate tests (between-subjects effects)

Tests of Between-Subjects Effects

	Mean Square	F^a	p	η_p^2
Motivation	3.271	7.035	.010	.100
Affective Conflict	4.312	4.822	.032	.071
Cognitive Conflict	1.661	2.315	.133	.035
Procedural Justice	.038	.068	.795	.001
Interpersonal Justice	2.359	5.645	.021	.082

a. $df = 1.63$.

univariate effects were obtained for three of the five variables: *Motivation* ($F_{(1;\,63)}= 7.035$; $p < 0.05$), *Affective Conflict* ($F_{(1;\,63)}= 4.822$; $p < 0.05$) and *Interpersonal Justice* ($F_{(1;\,63)=} 5.645$; $p < 0.05$) (see Table 7.2). The effect sizes, given partial eta squared were strongest for *Motivation*, followed by *Interpersonal Justice* and *Affective Conflict*.

Hypotheses H3 and H4 were supported by the outcome of the MANOVA. The directions of the effects indicate that exogenous rules positively influence the perception of *Interpersonal Justice* and the emergence of *Affective Conflict* (less conflict). The direction of the effect for *Motivation* is contrary to the proposed hypotheses H1, indicating exogenous rules to positively affect *Motivation*. This surprising effect was investigated in a further analysis.

7.4.2 Analysis of Mediation Effect and Correlation

The finding for *Motivation* appears to be conflictive to the stated hypotheses. Letting a group choose its own governance rules has a rather negative than positive effect on *Motivation* as indicated by the univariate effect ($F_{(1; 63)}$ = 7.035; $p < 0.05$). While at first sight the result looks atypical considering existing research discussed earlier, checking back to the theory on the association of the investigated variables, it becomes evident that a relationship between *Conflict* and *Motivation* may exist that could explain the observed effect. It is known that motivation may be influenced by different contextual factors such as organizational culture (Mitchel and Daniels 2003). Furthermore, studies show that the relationship between organizational climate and conflict has a major impact on job satisfaction (Walker et al. 1977) and negatively impacts performance (de Dreu and Weingart 2003). Since motivation is an antecedent of performance (Mitchel and Daniels 2003) and the constructs of job satisfaction and motivation show an overlap (Tietjen and Myers 1998), it is expected that the association between motivation and conflict may be analogous. Furthermore, analysis of chat interactions of participants during the game supported the theoretical implications (see content analysis 4.4). Bearing these findings in mind, a further hypothesis is formulated, investigating whether *Affective Conflict* mediates the impact of the independent variable on *Motivation*.

H6: Perceptions of Affective Conflict mediate the effects of exogenous governance rules on Motivation

To test this hypothesis, an approach by Sapienza and Korsgaard (1996) is applied. Drawing on the work of Baron and Kenny (1986) they consider three conditions that have to be met to support the mediation hypothesis. First, the independent variable must be related to the mediator. This requirement is supported by the previously reported MANOVA, showing a significant effect of treatment on *Affective Conflict*. Second, the mediator must be related to the dependent variables. Examining the reported correlations, all relationships between the mediator *Affective Conflict* and *Motivation* are significant (see Table 7.3). Third, the once significant relationship between independent and dependent variables must be either eliminated or considerably reduced if the mediator is accounted for. This condition is tested by conducting a MANCOVA introducing *Affective Conflict* as the covariate. Results show that the main effect is no longer significant ($p = .058$). These findings indicate that *Affective Conflict* may mediate the impact of the manipulated variable (exogenous vs. endogenous) on *Motivation*, supporting the formulated H6.

Relationships between dependent variables were investigated by correlations (see Table 7.3). High correlations between both measures for *Conflict* ($p < .01$) could be obtained. Measures for *Justice* showed medium correlations ($p < .05$). *Motivation* correlates highly with *Interpersonal Justice*

Table 7.3   Correlations of dependent variables

Correlation coefficients for relations between dependent variables					
Variable	1	2	3	4	5
1. Motivation		−.284*	−.220	.305*	.378**
2. Affective Conflict			.603**	−.204	−.421**
3. Cognitive Conflict				−.471**	−.473**
4. Procedural Justice					.443**
5. Interpersonal Justice					

$^*p < .05$; $^{**} p < .01$.

($p < .01$) and on a medium level with *Affective conflict* ($p < .05$) and *Procedural Justice* ($p < .05$). A further high correlation is the one between *Affective conflict* and *Interpersonal Justice* ($p < .01$).

7.4.3   Control Variables and Sub-Samples Analysis

To ascertain that the observed differences were not driven by individuals' differences in *Typing Speed*, *Native Language* and *Gender*, covariate analysis (MANCOVA) were conducted. The results for MANCOVA revealed no differences in the effects, thus we can be certain that observed differences were not explained by any covariates.

Interestingly, the chosen configurations of governance rules under treatment $A_{end.}$ were akin. For example, all teams choose to have a project leader and nearly all equipped him with extensive decision power. This fact is important to keep in mind when interpreting the statistical analysis, since no major effects of complete opposite governance configurations (no leader vs. leader) can be expected.

Out of the 13 teams 10 were able to reach a perfect solution, 5 under each treatment. Among those teams, the average time to reach the solution was 17:08 minutes, ranging from 10 to 25 minutes. Hence, differences in performance between teams exist. It is recognized that feedback may have an effect on motivation (Crino and White 1982). A form of feedback within the experimental setup is the number of points players obtain for their squares. Being aware of the payoff table of how many points they receive, players can easily asses how well they performed, which consequently may influence their self-reported *Motivation*. In order to evaluate the association of feedback with the dependent variables, a sub-sample for further analysis is selected. The sub-sample included all teams which reached a perfect solution, since they all received the same feedback through the number of points allocated and the assurance that they reached the perfect solution. The sample consisted of a total of N = 50, 25 from each treatment. Again, a MANOVA for the sub-sample, analogue to the one run for the whole sample was conducted. The MANOVA for the sub-sample revealed no significant multivariate main effect for the standard significance level of .05, however an effect for a higher significance level was revealed (Wilks' λ = .794; $F_{(5; 44)}$ = 2.284; p = .063; partial eta squared = .206; observed power = .682). Comparing means and univariate effect sizes given η_p^2, it can be stated that the results for the sub-sample point in the same direction as for the MANOVA of the whole sample. Considering the reduced power for the sub-sample suggests that in order to establish a significance p < .05 would call for a larger sample size. We therefore feel confident that the reported effects are due the manipulation and at most marginal effects of feedback on intrinsic *Motivation* are expected.

7.4.4   Content Analysis of Group Siscussions

The reported results are based on the self-reported measures of participants post to the game. While this measurement provides convincing data for inferential statistics, one disadvantage has to be acknowledged. The self-reported measures post to the game only provide a snapshot view, at best the overall perception of the game. Fluctuations of perceptions in course of the experimental sessions are not presented. Neither additional insights nor explanatory approaches for the perception can be gained. Therefore, we chose an additional content analysis of chat messages. We first focus on the group discussion since this is where the manipulation occurred and effects are expected. In order to observe interpersonal behavior of participants, an established category system originally developed by Bales in 1950 (Bales 1976) and applied by various authors (cf. Hare 1973) is used. The category system uses twelve categories to describe the process of interaction of small discussion groups. Six categories constitute social-emotional behavior: *shows solidarity, shows tension release, shows agreement* are positive reactions, while *shows disagreement, shows tension* and *shows antagonism* are negative reactions. These categories are complemented by six further ones related to the task, again divided into two groups: *gives suggestion, gives opinion* and *gives information* as problem solving attempts and *asks for information, asks for opinion* and *asks for suggestion* are subsumed as questions.

Applying the category system to the group discussion, by coding chat messages and interpreting percentage of the code categories in relation to the overall number of messages, teams showed two distinct profiles four both treatments (see Figure 7.3). Teams who choose their own rules showed distinctly more negative reactions (e.g. disagreement and antagonism), indicating more tension and conflict (on average twice the relative amount for the three categories of negative social-emotional behavior). A further finding is that they showed less solidarity and tension release, like expressions of joy or fun. Comparing task related categories, groups with external rules seemed more goal oriented, engaging more in solution proposal and less in expressing opinion.

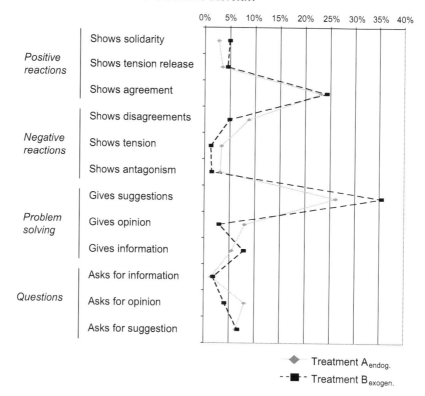

Figure 7.3   Group profiles of coded chat messages

Applying the content analysis for the course of the game showed group profiles across treatments to be much likewise. These findings support the proposition, that one major source of the measured conflict lies within the group decision process agreeing on a set of governance rules.

7.5   Discussion

This study examined the trade-offs between choosing own governance rule vs. the indoctrination of external rules on variables such as *Motivation*, *Justice* and *Conflict*. Foremost, the findings of this study reveal that indeed a relationship between the two modes of governance (endogenous vs. exogenous) and some of the identified success factors exist.

Interestingly, the rules themselves were perceived by both groups similar as shown by the means for *Procedural Justice*. This is especially notable since the manipulation between both treatments aimed directly on influencing *Procedural Justice*. Taking a pessimistic view, one could argue that the manipulation was unsuccessful, since the manipulation-check for *Procedural Justice* failed to show any effects. Another explanation (which was also supported by the statistical analysis and content analysis) is that the rules were perceived by both groups as fair, because they helped the group to perform better. In that case, it may be irrelevant if the rules are given exogenously or endogenously. A similar effect is known from motivation crowding theory, when "[e]xternal interventions *crowd in* intrinsic motivation if the individuals concerned perceive it as *supportive*" (Frey and Jegen 2001, p. 595). Whether the effect of more contradictory rules in the same setting would lead to dissimilar results is a question worthwhile revising in the future.

While the reported effects between the two treatments cannot be clarified by the rules itself, as the absence of differences for *Procedural Justice* indicate, another explanation seems very likely. As described, the manipulation itself did not aim at the rules but rather on the process of how they were implemented. However, the process of agreeing on a set of rules can be quiet strenuous. Therefore, the source for the reported differences between both treatment lies within this 'electoral process'. As the analysis of chat protocols showed, participants who had to choose rules argued intensely about the different alternatives. Such debates may result in higher levels of conflict and interpersonal friction as indicated by the reported results. This argument is also consistent with the findings of Green, who affirmed that a group decision process leads to high level of interpersonal stress (Green and Taber 1980).

The theoretical explanation by Green is also reflected in the data as findings for the other variables indicate. The first finding suggests that teams with the ability to choose their own rules experienced higher levels of conflict—especially for *Affective*, 'inter-personal' related conflicts. Further support is provided by the result for *Interpersonal Justice* which points in the same direction providing further indication that the process to agree on rules leads to interpersonal friction. An additional finding presented in the results, is the negative relationship between the ability to choose rules and motivation. A potential explanation is provided by the analysis of mediation effect of *Affective Conflict* on *Motivation*, which indicates that high levels of *Affective Conflict* may negatively impact the *Motivation*.

One shall not neglect the limitations of this study. Foremost, as for any laboratory experiment, we faced the restrictions of an artificial setting. This applied to the constructed situation of a game under time pressure, while 'real' life communities exist and evolve over a long time period. Participants in an experiment might be more willing to except appointed leadership for a short period of time than if confronted with it on an everyday basis. Another issue regarding the time aspect is recognizing the extended period it takes for informal relations and norms to develop. It is known that norms like trust and reciprocity play an important role within such communities (Lerner and Tirole 2002; Sulin 2001); however, within this study, we only focused on explicit rules. Second, the chosen sample of students was very homogenous, since they were all from the same age group and professional background. Having such homogenous sample is positive for the statistical analysis of an experimental study because parallelising of groups controls for other variables that may influence the results. However, professional background and socialization may have an effect on cooperative behavior (Frank et al. 1993).

These limitations link to promising future research by replicating similar experiments over longer periods of time and across different, less homogenous groups. Furthermore, it could be promising to counterpart findings from this study with field research. Especially the relationship between different modes of governance and conflict seems a promising field to investigate.

7.6   Conclusion

This paper offers some insights on the effects of self- versus firm-initiated governance of OCI communities, by the use of an experimental method. While questions about collaborative innovation projects have been mainly studied through case studies and surveys, we designed an experiment which we believe to represent the characteristics of collaborative project to a high degree. Applying this research method we aim to contribute to narrow the by some criticized underrepresentation of experimental methods (Colquitt 2008), especially when it comes to innovation research (Sørensen et al. 2010). The experimental task has proven to be very suitable to investigate further questions within OCI communities, for example different rule configurations.

Our study contributes to better understanding of the relationship between external intervention, for example by firms, and communities of volunteers. First, the results of our experiment have shown that external intervention through governance rules does not per se cripple motivation of volunteers, but quite the opposite positive effects could be observed. If rules are perceived as helpful and fair, they may significantly reduce conflict and increase motivation. Accordingly, the interplay of factors like justice, conflict and motivation within communities of volunteers is a further contribution of this study. Understanding this relationship provides insights for focusing on the right levers to increase motivation of volunteers.

We further showed the risks of participation processes. While they may increase legitimacy, they also inherent the risk of creating conflict and tension. Examples of endless 'vendettas' of Wikipedia volunteers deleting and reediting articles are living proof to that observation. We shall not be mistaken, democratic processes and the participation of volunteers is an important part of such communities and probably one of the key success factors. However, grass-root democratic processes can be a double-edged sword.

Several implications for the design of governance systems in communities and the interaction between firms and communities can be derived from the results. First, firms should not be afraid to execute active leadership by implementing governance structures. A promising approach for leadership beyond pure structure is found by the involvement of firm employees acting as 'men on the inside' in such communities (Dahlander and Wallin 2006; Lee et al. 2012). The next logical challenge is identifying a set of applicable fundamentals for 'good' governance rules that are perceived as tolerable and helpful by OCI communities. Again, prior work by Ostrom may provide valuable insights. Ostrom (2000a) identified a set of different design principles to create successful self-organized regimes. Several principles correspond to the context of the production of knowledge resources by communities. In particular, three principles stand out: First balancing cost and benefits by designing rules to regulate the returns one receives for his inputs. Such principle is likely to mitigate the challenge of balancing use and production of knowledge resources (Madison et al. 2010). Second, accountability and enforcement of rules should be regulated by the community, increasing the perceived fairness and identification of the community with the rules. Third, sanctions should be applied gradually, depending on the seriousness of the rule violation.

As for governance rules, firms should reconsider the concern that any external intervention may cripple motivation and reduce participation of volunteers. The opposite may be the fact, where such external rules may proof to be a lever mitigating conflict and boosting the performance of such communities. However, this finding shall not be understood as a carte blanche for authoritarian external intervention. While such influence may be beneficial for a community, external governance rules still need to be designed in a careful manner. External rules can only succeed if they are perceived as fair and helpful and serve the purpose of the community. Maybe the initial question needs to be rephrased: The key of good governance lies not between endogenous vs. exogenous, but in the design of helpful, fair and purposeful governance rules and configuration. To investigate and find such configurations and processes and to legitimize them is an avenue for further research.

NOTES

1. While the theory of a rational, self-interested individual is widely accepted, studies show that individuals may behave contrary to this paradigm, calling for a broader theory of human behavior (Ostrom 2000b).
2. For a review of literature in the field of organizational research see Konovsky (2000).
3. Leventhal uses the term of procedural fairness rather than justice. However the term justice and fairness within this context are used interchangeable (cf. Colquitt 2001).
4. Colquitt uses the term interpersonal justice however refers to the original work of other authors who apply the term of interactional justice (Colquitt 2001).
5. Socio-emotional as Green uses it refers to behaviour of others within in the process and therefore shows great overlaps with the construct of *Interpersonal Justice*.
6. Credits were given for participation only and therefore did not represent an incentive to perform better.

REFERENCES

Alexy, O., and Leitner, M. (2010): *A fistful of dollars: financial rewards, payment norms, and motivation crowding in Open Source software development*, SSRN eLibrary. http://papers.ssrn.com/sol3/papers.cfm?abstract_id=1007689

Amason, A.C. (1996): "Distinguishing the effects of functional and dysfunctional conflict on strategic decision making: resolving a paradox for top management teams", *Academy of Management Journal* 39(1), pp. 123–148.

Aronson, E., Wilson, T.D., and Akert, R.M. (2010): Sozialpsychologie (6., aktualisierte Aufl., [Nachdr.]). Pearson Studium, München.

Baldwin, C., and Hippel, E. von (2011): "Modeling a paradigm shift: from producer innovation to user and open collaborative innovation", *Organization Science* 22(6), pp. 1399–1417.

Baldwin, C.Y., and Clark, K.B. (2006): "The architecture of participation: does code architecture mitigate free riding in the Open Source development model?" *Management Science* 52(7), pp. 1116–1127.

Bales, R.F. (1976): *Interaction process analysis: a method for the study of small groups*, University of Chicago Press, Chicago.

Baron, R.M., and Kenny, D.A. (1986): "The moderator–mediator variable distinction in social psychological research: conceptual, strategic, and statistical considerations", *Journal of Personality and Social Psychology* 51(6), pp. 1173–1182.

Bavelas, A. (1950): "Communication patterns in task-oriented groups", *Journal of the Acoustical Society of America* 22(6), pp. 725–730.

Bénabou, R., and Tirole, J. (2003): "Intrinsic and extrinsic motivation", *The Review of Economic Studies* 70(3), pp. 489–520.

Bies, R.J., and Shapiro, D.L. (1987): "Interactional fairness judgments: the influence of causal accounts", *Social Justice Research* 1(2), pp. 199–218.

Bonaccorsi, A., and Rossi, C. (2003): "Why Open Source software can succeed: Open Source software development", *Research Policy* 32(7), pp. 1243–1258.

Bowles, S., and Gintis, H. (2002): "Social capital and community governance", *Economic Journal* 112(483), pp. 419–436.

Cameron, J., and Pierce, W.D. (1994): "Reinforcement, reward, and intrinsic motivation: a meta-analysis", *Review of Educational Research* 64(3), pp. 363–423.

Campbell, D.J. (1988): "Task complexity: a review and analysis", *Academy of Management Review* 13(1), pp. 40–52.

Cardenas, J.-C. (2004): "Norms from outside and from inside: an experimental analysis on the governance of local ecosystems: economics of sustainable forest management", *Forest Policy and Economics* 6(3–4), pp. 229–241.

Colquitt, J.A. (2001): "On the dimensionality of organizational justice: a construct validation of a measure", *Journal of Applied Psychology* 86(3), pp. 386–400.

Colquitt, J.A. (2008): "From the editors: publishing laboratory research in AMJ: a question of when, not if", *Academy of Management Journal* 51(4), pp. 616–620.

Crino, M.D., and White, M.C. (1982): "Feedback effects in intrinsic/extrinsic reward paradigms", *Journal of Management* 8(2), pp. 95–108.

Dahlander, L., Frederiksen, L., and Rullani, F. (2008): "Online communities and open innovation: governance and symbolic value creation", *Industry & Innovation* 15(2), pp. 115–123.

Dahlander, L., and Magnusson, M. (2008): "How do firms make use of Open Source communities?" *Long Range Planning* 41(6), pp. 629–649.

Dahlander, L., and Wallin, M.W. (2006): "A man on the inside: unlocking communities as complementary assets", special issue commemorating the 20th Anniversary of David Teece's article, "Profiting from Innovation", in Research Policy, *Research Policy* 35(8), pp. 1243–1259.

David, P. A., and Shapiro, J. S. (2008): "Community-based production of open-source software: what do we know about the developers who participate?: Empirical issues in Open Source software", *Information Economics and Policy* 20(4), pp. 364–398.

Deci, E. L. (1971): "Effects of externally mediated rewards on intrinsic motivation", *Journal of Personality and Social Psychology* 18(1), pp. 105–115.

Deci, E. L., Koestner, R., and Ryan, R. M. (1999): "A meta-analytic review of experiments examining the effects of extrinsic rewards on intrinsic motivation", *Psychological Bulletin* 125(6), pp. 627–668.

Demil, B., and Lecocq, X. (2006): "Neither market nor hierarchy nor network: the emergence of bazaar governance", *Organization Studies* 27(10), pp. 1447–1466.

Dreu, C.K.W. de (2006): "When too little or too much hurts: evidence for a curvilinear relationship between task conflict and innovation in teams", *Journal of Management* 32(1), pp. 83–107.

Dreu, C.K.W. de, and Weingart, L. R. (2003): "Task versus relationship conflict, team performance, and team member satisfaction: a meta-analysis", *Journal of Applied Psychology* 88(4), pp. 741–749.

Frank, R.H., Gilovich, T., and Regan, D. T. (1993): "Does studying economics inhibit cooperation?" *Journal of Economic Perspectives* 7(2), pp. 159–171.

Frey, B. S. (1994): "How intrinsic motivation is crowded out and in", *Rationality and Society* 6(3), pp. 334–352.

Frey, B. S., and Jegen, R. (2001): "Motivation crowding theory", *Journal of Economic Surveys* 15(5), p. 589.

Füller, J. (2006): "Why consumers engage in virtual new product developments initiated by producers", *Advances in Consumer Research* 33(1), pp. 639–646.

Füller, J., Jawecki, G., and Mühlbacher, H. (2007): "Innovation creation by online basketball communities", *Journal of Business Research* 60(1), pp. 60–71.

Gagné, M., and Deci, E. L. (2005): "Self-determination theory and work motivation", *Journal of Organizational Behavior* 26(4), pp. 331–362.

Ghosh, R. A. (2005): "Understanding free software developers: findings from the FLOSS study", in *Perspectives on free and open source software*, J. Feller (ed.), pp. 23–46, MIT Press, Cambridge, MA.

Green, S. G., and Taber, T. D. (1980): "The effects of three social decision schemes on decision group process", *Organizational Behavior and Human Performance* 25(1), pp. 97–106.

Greenberg, J. (1987): "A taxonomy of organizational justice theories", *Academy of Management Review* 12(1), pp. 9–22.

Greif, A. (1997): "On the social foundations and historical development of institutions that facilitate impersonal exchange: from the community responsibility system to individual legal responsibility in pre-modern Europe", Working paper, Department of Economics, Stanford University.

Hare, A.P. (1973): "Theories of group development and categories for interaction analysis", *Small Group Research* 4(3), pp. 259–304.

Heide, J.B. (1994): "Interorganizational governance in marketing channels", *The Journal of Marketing* 58(1), pp. 71–85.

Janssen, O. (2003): "Innovative behaviour and job involvement at the price of conflict and less satisfactory relations with co-workers", *Journal of Occupational and Organizational Psychology* 76(3), pp. 347–364.

Janssen, O. (2004): "How fairness perceptions make innovative behavior more or less stressful", *Journal of Organizational Behavior* 25(2), pp. 201–215.

Jehn, K. A. (1995): "A multimethod examination of the benefits and detriments of intragroup conflict", *Administrative Science Quarterly* 40(2), pp. 256–282.

Jenny, A., Hechavarria Fuentes, F., and Mosler, H.-J. (2007): "Psychological factors determining individual compliance with rules for common pool resource management: the case of a cuban community sharing a solar energy system", *Human Ecology* 35(2), pp. 239–250.

Jeppesen, L. B., and Frederiksen, L. (2006): "Why do users contribute to firm-hosted user communities? the case of computer-controlled music instruments", *Organization Science* 17(1), pp. 45–63.

Jeppesen, L.B.O., and Molin, M.J. (2003): "Consumers as co-developers: learning and innovation outside the firm", *Technology Analysis & Strategic Management* 15(3), p. 363.

Kaplan, M. F., and Miller, C. E. (1987): "Group decision making and normative versus informational influence: effects of type of issue and assigned decision rule", *Journal of Personality and Social Psychology* 53(2), pp. 306–313.

Katz, R., and Tushman, M. (1979): "Communication patterns, project performance, and task characteristics: an empirical evaluation and integration in an R&D setting", *Organizational Behavior and Human Performance* 23(2), pp. 139–162.

Kerr, N.L., and Tindale, R. S. (2004): "Group performance and decision making", *Annual Review of Psychology* 55(1), pp. 623–655.

Kittur, A., and Kraut, R. (eds.) (2010): "Beyond Wikipedia: coordination and conflict in online production groups", in *CSCW '10*, pp. 215–224, ACM, New York.

Konovsky, M. A. (2000): "Understanding procedural justice and its impact on business organizations", *Journal of Management* 26(3), pp. 489–511.

Laat, P. B. de (2007): "Governance of open source software: state of the art", *Journal of Management and Governance* 11(2), pp. 165–177.

Lakhani, K. R., and Hippel, E. von (2003): "How open source software works: 'free' user-to-user assistance", *Research Policy* 32(6), pp. 923–943.

Lakhani, K.R., and Wolf, R.G. (2005): "Why hackers do what they do: understanding motivation and effort in free/open source software projects", in *Perspectives on free and open source software*, J. Feller (ed.), pp. 3–22, MIT Press, Cambridge, MA.

Lattemann, C., and Stieglitz, S. (2005): "Framework for governance in Open Source communities", in *Proceedings of the 38th Hawaii International Conference on System Sciences*, p. 192b, (HICSS'05) IEEE Computer Society.

Lee, V., Herstatt, C., and Husted, K. (2012): "How firms can strategically influence open source communities: the employment of 'men on the inside'," Technische. Universität Hamburg Harburg, Institut für Technologie und Innovationsmanagement, Dissertation, Hamburg-Harburg, Gabler, Wiesbaden.

Lerner, J., and Tirole, J. (2001): "The open source movement: key research questions: 15th Annual Congress of the European Economic Association", *European Economic Review* 45(4–6), pp. 819–826.

Lerner, J., and Tirole, J. (2002): "Some simple economics of Open Source", *Journal of Industrial Economics* 50(2), p. 197.

Leventhal, G. S. (1980): "What should be done with equity theory? new approaches to the study of fairness in social relationships", in Social exchange: advances in theory and research, K.J. Gergen (ed.), pp. 27–55, Plenum Press, New York.

Madison, M.J., Frischmann, B.M., and Strandburg, K.J. (2010): "Constructing commons in the cultural environment", *Cornell Law Review* 95, pp. 657–710.

Markus, L. (2007): "The governance of free/open source software projects: monolithic, multidimensional, or configurational?" *Journal of Management and Governance* 11(2), pp. 151–163.

Mitchel, T.R., and Daniels, D. (2003): "Motivation", in *Handbook of psychology*, vol. 12, I. B. Weiner (ed.), 225–254, Wiley, Hoboken, NJ.

O'Mahony, S., and West, J. (2005): "What makes a project open source? migrating from organic to synthetic communities", in *Proceedings of the Academy of Management Conference*, Honolulu.

O'Mahony, S., and Ferraro, F. (2007): "The emergence of governance in an open source community", *Academy of Management Journal* 50(5), pp. 1079–1106.

Ostrom, E. (2000a): "Collective action and the evolution of social norms", *Journal of Economic Perspectives* 14(3), pp. 137–158.

Ostrom, E. (2000b): "Crowding out citizenship", *Scandinavian Political Studies* 23(1), pp. 3–16.

Ostrom, E. (2005a): "Doing institutional analysis digging deeper than markets and hierarchies", in *Handbook of new institutional economics*, C. Menard and M. Shirley (eds.), 819–848, Springer, New York.

Ostrom, E. (2005b): *Understanding institutional diversity*, Princeton University Press, Princeton, NJ.

Priem, R.L., and Harrison, D.A. (1995): "Structured conflict and consensus outcomes in group decision making", *Journal of Management* 21(4), pp. 691–710.

Raasch, C., Herstatt, C., and Balka, K. (2009): "On the open design of tangible goods", *R&D Management* 39(4), pp. 382–393.

Ruef, M. (1996): "The evolution of convention: conformity and innovation in task-oriented networks", *Computational & Mathematical Organization Theory* 2(1), pp. 5–28.

Ryan, R.M., and Deci, E.L. (2000): "Intrinsic and extrinsic motivations: classic definitions and new directions", *Contemporary Educational Psychology* 25(1), pp. 54–67.

Sapienza, H.J., and Korsgaard, M.A. (1996): "Procedural justice in entrepreneur-investor relations", *Academy of Management Journal* 39(3), pp. 544–574.

Schweik, C.M., and Kitsing, M. (2010): "Applying Elinor Ostrom's rule classification framework to the analysis of Open Source software commons", *Transnational Corporations Review* 2(1), pp. 13–26.

Shah, S.K. (2006): "Motivation, governance, and the viability of hybrid forms in Open Source software development", *Management Science* 52(7), pp. 1000–1014.

Solum, L.B. (2005): "Procedural justice", *University of San Diego Law and Economics Research Paper Series* 12, pp. 178–322.

Sørensen, F., Mattsson, J., and Sundbo, J. (2010): "Experimental methods in innovation research", *Research Policy* 39(3), pp. 313–322.

Stevens, C.K. (2011): "Questions to consider when selecting student samples", *Journal of Supply Chain Management* 47(3), pp. 19–21.

Streeck, W., and Schmitter, P.C. (1985): "Community, market, state and associations? the prospective contribution of interest governance to social order", *European Sociological Review* 1(2), pp. 119–138.

Sulin, B. (2001): "Establishing online trust through a community responsibility system", *Decision Support Systems* 31(3), pp. 323–336.

Tietjen, M.A., and Myers, R.M. (1998): "Motivation and job satisfaction", *Management Decision* 36(4), pp. 226–231.

Torre, A. (2006): "Collective action, governance structure and organizational trust in localized systems of production: the case of the AOC organization of small producers", *Entrepreneurship & Regional Development* 18(1), pp. 55–72.

Tyler, T.R. (2005): "Psychological perspectives on legitimacy and legitimation," *Annual Review of Psychology* 57(1), pp. 375–400.

Tyler, T.R. (2006): *Why people obey the law*, Princeton University Press, Princeton, NJ.

van Dijk, E., and Wilke, H. (1995): "Coordination rules in asymmetric social dilemmas: a comparison between public good dilemmas and resource dilemmas", *Journal of Experimental Social Psychology* 31(1), pp. 1–27.

van Rijnsoever, F.J., Meeus, M.T., and Donders, A.R.T. (2012): "The effects of economic status and recent experience on innovative behavior under environmental variablity: an experimental approach", *Research Policy* 41(5), pp. 833–847.

Walker, H.A., Thomas, G.M., and Zelditch, M., Jr. (1986): "Legitimation, endorsement, and stability", *Social Forces* 64(3), pp. 620–643.

Walker, O. C., Churchill, G. A., Jr., and Ford, N. M. (1977): "Motivation and performance in industrial selling: present knowledge and needed research", *Journal of Marketing Research* 14(2), pp. 156–168.

Wall, V. D., and Nolan, L. L. (1986): "Perceptions of inequity, satisfaction, and conflict in task-oriented groups", *Human Relations* 39(11), pp. 1033–1051.

West, J., and Lakhani, K. R. (2008): "Getting clear about communities in open innovation", *Industry & Innovation* 15(2), pp. 223–231.

West, J., and O'Mahony, S. (2008): "The role of participation architecture in growing sponsored Open Source communities", *Industry & Innovation* 15(2), pp. 145–168.

Williamson, O. E. (2005): "The economics of governance", *American Economic Review* 95(2), pp. 1–18.

8 Entrepreneurial Members in Online Innovation Communities
Blessing or Curse?

Jan Bierwald and Cornelius Herstatt

In this paper we develop initial inductive research propositions regarding the behavior of entrepreneurial members in online innovation communities (OIC). In these communities, up to thousands of volunteers collaboratively develop an innovative product. Based on a netnography analysis of 7,362 mails, we follow a micro-level-approach concentrating on individual behavior and conduct a content and co-citation analysis of community members. By explicitly distinguishing entrepreneurial from private community members, we are able to investigate differences in their contribution focus, degree of specialization and collaboration level. Entrepreneurs tend to contribute more to innovative, disruptive topics and show a lower degree of specialization compared to private members. Nevertheless, entrepreneurial members need intensive care by management as they tend to form separated cliques with their peers and thus limit collaboration within the community. Finally, we discuss implications for both research and management.

Keywords: user entrepreuner, member specialization, entrepreneurial behavior

8 ENTREPRENEURIAL MEMBERS IN ONLINE INNOVATION COMMUNITIES

8.1 Introduction

Open and user innovation has challenged established concepts of value creation and points to additional sources of innovation and entrepreneurial activity (e.g. Hippel 1976; Chesbrough 2006). This new way of innovating "rarely happens individually but rather requires interactions among like-minded" (Mahr and Lievens 2012, p. 169). Therefore, geographically widely distributed individuals participate in online innovation communities (OIC) (we subsume here open source communities, open collaborative communities, as well as distributed innovation communities). In these OIC, firms or individuals are interconnected by information transfer (Hippel 2006) that primarily takes place using the Internet (Blanchard and Horan 1998), and contribute to a jointly developed outcome that is exploited (Raasch et al. 2009). OIC are commonly used to develop software, tangible goods or content products and numerous firms use this instrument within their innovation process to benefit from external contributions (Mahr and Lievens 2012). Essential for value creation are the members of these communities

Scholars characterize members of OIC according to their motivation to participate, their community role and their background. Various intrinsic and extrinsic motivations drive members to participate in OIC. These motivations include own need for the created community product (e.g. Shah 2006; Füller et al. 2007), enjoyment (e.g. Hertel et al. 2003; Nov 2007), expertise and career enhancement (e.g. Lahkani et al. 2005; Oreg and Nov 2008) as well as reciprocity (e.g. Lakhani and Hippel 2003; Franke and Shah 2003). Furthermore, members are often classified into maintainers, developers/contributors and users (van Wendel de Joode et al. 2003), or more detailed into eight classes consisting of: passive user, reader, bug reporter, bug fixer, peripheral developer, active developer, core member and project lead (Ye et al. 2005; van Oost et al. 2008). Member's background is described with demographic data such as age (e.g. Lakhani and Wolf 2005; Ghosh et al. 2002), gender (e.g. Agerfalk and Fitzgerald 2008; Hars and Ou 2001), residence (Lakhani and Wolf 2005), education (e.g. Ghosh et al. 2002; Hars and Ou 2001), and their profession. The profession of community members is primarily classified into 'commercial' and 'private'. Commercial members comprise manufacturers of complementary goods or services as well as corporate users characterized by profit seeking (Hippel 2007). In contrast, private members are often driven by use value (Hars and Ou 2001). Of these private members, freelancers, self-employees and contract programmers seeking for business opportunities are a noticeable sub classification and represent between 5% and 14% of all members (e.g. Ghosh et al. 2002; Hars and Ou 2001).

To comprehensively understand the micro-dynamics within OIC the individual member behavior is of paramount importance. Over the last decade, several behavioral patterns have been investigated. Different community joining categories exist (Qureshi and Fang 2010) and the attraction (Butler 2001) and integration of new community members is scrutinized (e.g. Krogh et al. 2003). The contribution activity varies among different member types (e.g. Roberts et al. 2006) and in an extreme case leads to lurking[1] and free-riding[2] (e.g. Baldwin and Clark 2006). Different tasks performed by the individual community member are identified (e.g. Lakhani and Hippel 2003) including the reasoning why some members perform specific tasks and others do not (e.g. Shah 2006). Some members tend to specialize and contributing only to a small amount of OIC topics (Krogh et al. 2003). Finally, the circumstances under which members decide to leave are investigated (e.g. Oh and Jeon 2007). To explain the rationales behind member behavior the motivation of members to participate (e.g. Roberts et al. 2006; Nambisan and Baron 2010) and the role of members within the IOC are recognized (e.g. Hippel and Krogh 2003; Dahlander and Wallin 2006). The third classification criterion, member's background, is lacking in today's research, although different behavior between commercial and private members might be to some extent explainable by their different motivation. Nevertheless, the behavior of entrepreneurial community members, assumed to be found in the group of self-employees and freelancer, are not investigated so far. This is astonishing since entrepreneurship seems to foster innovation in OIC (Alexy et al. 2012) and entrepreneurial characters are clearly attributed to members of OIC (Ghosh et al. 2002; Hars and Ou 2001). We target this gap and pursue a qualitative inductive approach in order to gain initial insights into the behavior of entrepreneurial community members. We investigate one OIC in depth and derive research proposition guiding further research.

This paper is organized the following; first, we give a short overview of research about personal characteristics of entrepreneurs (section 8.2). We then review the employed research method of our study (section 8.3) before deriving our propositions based on the empirical findings (section 8.4). After discussing our findings and comparing them to existing entrepreneur theory (section 8.5), we conclude this paper by outlining implications for research and management.

8.2   Entrepreneurial Characteristics

Entrepreneurship research draws heavily on two main models for describing entrepreneurial characteristics: the internal locus of control and the need for achievement. Commonly various features characterizing entrepreneurs are allocated to one of these theories (Littunen 2000). The individual's locus of control can either be internal or external (Rotter 1996). Following the internal view, individuals see consequences of actions in relation with their own abilities or efforts whereas individuals with an external locus of control only relate outcome of actions to fate, luck or action of other individuals. The internal locus of control distinguishes entrepreneurs from others, such as owners of small business, as they strongly believe in their own ability to influence events (e.g. Cromie and Johns 1983; Begley and Boyd 1988). Typical features allocated to the internal locus of control theory are e.g. independency orientation, the need of control and a high grade of autonomy (Hornaday and Aboud 1971). Situations of high competition, independent problem solving and target setting by them inspire individuals with a high need for achievement (McClelland 1967). Personal features showing this are e.g. self-awareness and-initative, superior planning ability, goal-orientation and superb problem-solving skills (McClelland 1967).

In addition, researches frequently observe an innovative creative style and a distinctive risk-taking behavior as supplementary features (Caird 1993). Entrepreneurs show rather an innovative than adaptive style of problem solving meaning that they are driven by changing structures completely than just marginally improve existing ones (Kirton 1976). Risk-taking behavior and entrepreneurial orientation are strongly correlated (McClelland 1967) and is one explanation why entrepreneurs tend to accept high risks if they face challenges (King 1985). Nevertheless, a detailed analysis of behavior of entrepreneurs in communities is lacking, especially in contrast to other users. In order to address this gap, we follow a quantitative research strategy.

8.3   Research Strategy

This section outlines our selected case study and the reasoning behind choosing the community 'Premium'. In addition, we describe in detail the conducted content and co-citation analysis.

8.3.1   *The Case*

In order to gain a deep understanding of the unexplored phenomenon and to secure a sufficient depth of the analysis we conduct a case study (Yin 2009). Our case represents an OIC, specifically the community 'Premium', which is suitable for three main reasons: (1) The community meets the characteristics of a typical OIC defined by various scholars (e.g Blanchard and Horan 1998; Rheingold 2000; Kozinets 1999; Ridings et al. 2002; Raasch et al. 2009). All community members contribute voluntarily to a collaboratively develop product exploited to the market. The product development and coordination spans over a significant period of time and is primarily electronically; all members share a common goal; and a community culture has grown. (2) The five different member groups of the Premium community can clearly be linked to the previously described member roles (e.g. Ye et al. 2005; van Oost et al. 2008). (3) One of the five different Premium community groups group carries clear entrepreneurial tasks and differs only in this criterion from other private members. A comparison between these two groups provides a great opportunity to observe the phenomenon.

'Premium' develops and sells different tangible goods, with focus on the beverage industry. The community based company established in 2001 works closely with external service provider, such as bottlers, forwarders and bars. The main community objective is product development for beverages and improvement of corresponding business activities along the value chain, e.g. Sales and Marketing. The strongly affiliated Premium community serves as think tank and collaboratively develops new products, services or processes as well as solutions for organizational issues. All community members contribute to the same mailing list which serves as communication medium and documents all statements, including issues and solution proposals, concerning Premium. In a jointly manner, community members discuss problems statements and try to find the most appropriate solution for Premium. Over the years the OIC has helped to develop a range of new products, such as Premium beer or coffee, as well as new bottle sizes, designs or labels.

The members of the Premium community are diverse and arise e.g. from Premium representatives, customers and employees from service providers. Nevertheless, they can be classified into five groups: (1) The Central Organizer, one of the co-founders; (2) the Coordinators, Premium representatives illustrating the core members of the community; (3) the Commercials, a group consisting of employees from different commercial partners of Premium; (4) Privates, customers of the Premium products; (5) Microentrepreneurs, a sub-group of the Privates, but in addition responsible for the acquisition of shops, dealers and bars in one assigned city or region which they initially developed from scratch.

8.3.2   Content Analysis

In order to analyze the contribution behavior of entrepreneurs we apply a netnography approach and draw on the community mailing list. All mails sent to the mailing list are analyzed. As data prior March 2005 is no longer available, we downloaded all mails from March 2005 to April 2010. In this time period, 180 different members out of a total of 220 members, sent 7,362 mails to the list. Following Krippendorf (2004) and in accordance with further studies analyzing the content contributed by OIC members (e.g. Wasko and Faraj 2005; Füller et al. 2007), we applied three steps for data analyzes: sampling, unitizing and coding of the raw data. We excluded 134 mails of the 7,362 mails, as these have been sent either by non-community members or members with a total mail amount of one. After the sampling, we grouped the remaining mails into 1,371 discussion threads that represent the units for the coding procedure. The coding of the mails exhibits the central part of the content analysis since "content analysts need to transform unedited texts . . . into analyzable representations" (Krippendorff 2004, p. 84). We therefore selected a deductive approach with seven predetermined categories for coding the units. The categories emerged from several interviews with the central organizer of the Premium community are: Product Development, Operations, Sales, Marketing, Administration, Corporate Social Responsibility and Others. Before coding all units, one author of this study and two further, but not involved research scholars, coded independently form each other a sample of 276 discussion.[3] Comparing the individual coding results in an agreement of 233 of the 276 discussion, leading to a percentage agreement of 84%. This percentage rises to 98% if only agreements between two coders are considered. To sufficiently determine the intercoder reliability, we applied Fleiss Kappa, as the number of coders exceeds two. The value of 0.87 represents an almost perfect agreement and is in accordance with publications other researchers.[4] In addition, the three coders discussed the disagreements and solved the disparities. Afterwards, the same involved paper author proceeds coded the remaining

1,095 discussions as the main disagreements are solved and the intercoder reliability is very strong. To finalize the content analysis we added the number of mails sent to each of the respective discussion by the community members. Finally, we excluded one individual from the final data set as he is the only co-founder not part of the central organization and its activity outranges all other members by more than 100 percent.

8.3.3   Co-Citation Analysis

In order to observe the collaboration between the different members, we decided to adapt the co-citation analyses to community communication data. Usually, the co-citation analysis is known as a bibliometric technique "for the empirical study of the structures and developments of scientific communities and areas" (Gmür 2003, p. 27). The technique enables us to identify invisible colleges that represent a network linked without any organizational structures. An invisible college is "a set of informal communication relations among scientists or other scholars who share a specific common interest or goal" (Lievrouw 1989, p. 622). We transfer such invisible colleges to OIC as they carry on informal communication and the community members pursue a common objective. Therefore, invisible colleges should also be identifiable in OIC and the co-citation analysis seems to be appropriated to reveal the relationships. "A co-citation is taken to exist if two references or authors appear in the same bibliography. It is interpreted as the measure for similarity of content of the two references or authors" (Gmür 2003, p. 27). Adapting this understanding regarding OIC, a co-citation between two community members exists, if each of them sends at least one mail to the same discussion thread. We measure the proximity between the community members with the CoCit-Score as this index is the only one without any obvious restrictions (Gmür 2003). The CoCit-Score is defined as following:

$$CoCit_{AB} = \frac{(co-citation_{AB})^2}{min(citation_A; citation_B) \, x \, mean(citation_A; citation_B)}$$

A high CoCit-Score between two members indicates a high collaboration between these two individuals. Applying the CoCit-Score to measure collaboration between OIC members prevents misinterpretation purely based on a high activity of one member for two reasons. Firstly, multiple mails to the same thread are weighted as one mail, and secondly, the score decreases with the mean activity of both members.

In order to achieve an appropriated coverage of the science field and increase the relevance of the results, the first step in the co-citation approach exhibits in selecting the included set of authors and publications. Commonly only publications with high relevance, e.g. published in high-ranked journal, and most-cited authors are included (White and McCain 1998). Applying this approach and considering the goal of our study, to identify a high grade of collaboration between different community members, we decided to only include discussions with more than three participants (280 threats). In addition, we limited the members included by setting a lower level of at least 10% of the average activity and therefore continue with 75 members. In accordance with Schäffer et al. (2006), we followed a three-step approach. We counted the mails representing the citations sent by each included member. Secondly, we determined the co-citations between each community member pair as defined earlier in this paper. Finally, we derived the CoCit-Score matrix using the citation and co-citation data. Additionally, Schäffer et al. (2006) suggest employing a threshold value[5] for the CoCit-Score in order to identify sufficiently differentiated clusters. We decided to not use a threshold value as our goal is to identify the direct collaboration between two members and not clusters. Furthermore, we expected significant lower CoCit-Scores as firstly the number of included threads exceeds the number of publication[6] normally included; secondly, the threads contain most of the time less than ten participants compared to publications with bibliographies rarely containing below 20 authors. The next section highlights the results of the analysis.

8.4   Member Behavior

In this section, we show the results from our content and co-citation analysis and derive initial propositions for the behavior of entrepreneurial community members. We compare the member group of Privates with the Micro-entrepreneurs regarding their contribution focus, their degree of specialization and their collaboration with peers and core members of the community. We focus our results only on participants with an activity of more than 10% of the mean activity for two reasons. Firstly, we increase the robustness of our results as contortions caused by members with less than five mails are expected and secondly we perfectly match both samples, the one from the content and the one from the co-citation analysis. The following data is not normally distributed based on Kolmogorov Smirnov testing and evaluation of kurtosis and skewness. To determine the significance level α of the differences in the means between the entrepreneurial and private members we therefore use the non-parametric Mann-Whitney-U test.

8.4.1   Contribution Focus

Table 8.1 shows the contribution shares of the Micro-entrepreneurs and Privates to, Product Development, Operations, Sales and Marketing, and the product-related categories:

The results of the content analysis show a focus of the Micro-entrepreneurs on Product-related topics and particularly on Product Development on a 0.05-significance level ($\alpha = 0.02$) and Operations on a 0.1-significance level ($\alpha = 0.075$) compared to the group of Privates. Entrepreneurial members

Table 8.1   Contribution share to different categories by micro-entrepreneurs and privates

		Micro-entrepreneurs	Privates	Sign. Mann-Whitney-U
Product development	n	27	24	
	Mean	0.13	0.11	201.50
	Median	0.12	0.06	α = 0.075
	Mean Rank	30.54	20.90	
Operations	n	27	24	
	Mean	0.10	0.07	230.00
	Median	0.09	0.04	α = 0.075
	Mean rank	29.48	22.06	
Sales	n	27	24	
	Mean	0.13	0.09	253.00
	Median	0.12	0.08	α = 0.075
	Mean rank	28.63	23.04	
Marketing	n	27	24	
	Mean	0.32	0.31	305.00
	Median	0.29	0.26	α = 0.075
	Mean rank	26.70	25.21	
Prodcut-related topics	n	27	24	
	Mean	0.69	0.58	220.00
	Median	0.67	0.60	α = 0.075
	Mean rank	29.85	21.67	

seem to be more driven by developing new products and setting up organizational structures than members without entrepreneurial spirit. This leads to our first proposition:

P1: Entrepreneurial community members contribute more to product development and disruptive topics than non-entrepreneurial members.

The contribution focus of the Micro-entrepreneurs on product-related topics is significant on a 0.05-level (α = 0.05). These community members seem to be fueled by the opportunity to work on the product itself instead of contributing to the community as a whole. Therefore we derive our second proposition as following:

P2: Entrepreneurial community members tend to contribute to product-related topics rather than community-related topics.

8.4.2 Specialization

Specialization in OIC can be defined as following: "High specialization indicates that the same modules within the code base were changed over time by a developer, while generalization indicates multiple modules were changed by a developer" (Krogh et al. 2003, p. 1230). Based on our comprehensive data set, we were able to investigate the degree of specialization in two different ways. Firstly, measuring how often a member contributes to the same module (the discussion thread) and secondly, how a member allocates his or her contributions to the different categories. For the first one we measure the mail per thread ratio, meaning how many mails a member usually send to one thread. A high ratio indicates a high degree of specialization as the member tends to discuss one thread more intensively; a lower ratio vice versa indicates a lower degree of specialization. Table 8.2 shows the results for the Micro-entrepreneurs and the Privates:

The Micro-entrepreneurs reveal a lower ratio on a rather weak 0.2-significance level ($\alpha = 0.124$), still meaning they seem to be less specialized than the Privates. For determining the contribution dispersion on the different categories by each member we adapted the Gini-coefficient. The Gini-coefficient, a well-established and appropriate measurement for inequality, is commonly applied for measuring the income inhomogeneity in a specific country (Kakwani 1977) but also for other purposes, such as the geographical concentration of innovation (Audretsch and Feldmann 1996). As the coefficient can be applied for discrete probability functions, we transformed the normal Gini- coefficient:

$$G = 1 - 2 \int_{0}^{1} L(x)$$

with L(x) representing the Lorenz curve[7] to

$$G = 1 - \frac{2}{n-1}\left(\sum_{i=1}^{n-1} p_i + \sum_{i=1}^{n-2} p_i + \dots + p_1\right)$$

with $p_1, p_2, \dots, p_n$ as contribution shares for each category in ascending order and n categories.

Table 8.2 Mail per thread ratio micro-entrepreneurs and privates

		Micro-entrepreneurs	Privates	Mann Whitney-U test
Mails/threads—ratio	n	27	24	
	Mean	1.29	1.53	242.50
	Median	1.25	1.36	$\alpha = 0.124$
	Mean rank	22.98	29.40	

The transformed coefficient still takes values from zero to one. Zero represents total equality, the same contribution share to all categories, whereas one total inequality shows if a member only contributes to one out of the seven categories. Table 8.3 shows our determined Gini-coefficients for the respective member groups:

The Micro-entrepreneurs show a lower Gini-coefficient on a 0.2-significance level ($\alpha = 0.174$) and therefore probably feature a lower degree of specialization, meaning contributing more balanced to all thread categories. After indicating a lower degree of specialization, vice versa a higher degree of generalization, we conducted an initial contribution analysis to identify if entrepreneurial community members already join the community generalized. Initial contributions are commonly used in today's community research to analyze the joining process of new members (e.g. Krogh et al. 2003; Herraiz et al. 2006; Qureshi and Fang 2010). For this analysis we included only community members which made their first contribution in July 2005, four months in the observation period, to ensure that only newly joined members are taking into account (see Figure 8.1).

Table 8.3   Gini-coefficient for micro-entrepreneurs and privates

		Micro-entrepreneurs	Privates	Mann Whitney U-test
Gini coefficient	n	27	24	
	Mean	0.50	0.58	252.00
	Median	0.46	0.57	$\alpha = 0.174$
	Mean Rank	23.33	29.00	

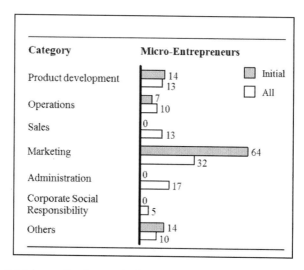

Figure 8.1   Initial contribution analysis

The analysis indicates that entrepreneurial members indeed join the community extremely specialized—two-thirds of the joining Micro-entrepreneurs choose only one category. This is a first indication that their liability to generalize seems to start after joining the community. Therefore, we derive our initial proposition regarding the specialization behavior of entrepreneurial members as following:

> P3: *After joining the community, specialized entrepreneurial members tend to generalize and contribute to a greater variety of topics than non-entrepreneurial members.*

8.4.3   Collaboration

For determining the collaboration between the different individual community members, we calculated the CoCit-Scores of all member pairings resulting in 2,775 unique CoCit-Scores. As outlined previously, this score directly measures the collaboration level between two community members. In Table 8.4 we present the mean and the median CoCit-Scores of the Micro-entrepreneurs and Privates to their peers and additionally to the core members of the Premium community, the Coordinators:

The results from the Co-citation analysis show that the Micro-entrepreneurs collaborate more intensively with their own peers than with private members on a strong significance level ($\alpha = 0.012$). Additionally, they do not show a significant higher collaboration level with the coordinators than with their peers ($\alpha = 0.692$). Contrary, the Privates feature their highest collaboration level with the core members of the community on a very strong 0.01-significance level ($\alpha = 0.002$). Nevertheless, they do not show a more intensive collaboration with their peers than with entrepreneurial members ($\alpha = 0.652$).

Table 8.4   CoCit-scores between community member groups

	10^{-3}	Micro-entrepreneurs	Privates
Coordinators	n	27	24
	Mean	11.8	11.0
	Median	7.5	6.4
Micro-entrepreneurs	n	27	24
	Mean	11.0	7.0
	Median	11.8	5.6
Privates	n	27	24
	Mean	7.0	6.5
	Median	5.6	5.7

To further analyze this phenomenon, we conducted a Social Network Analysis (SNA) using the software application ORA. SNA is widely applied in today's community research to, for example, identify knowledge brokers (Sowe et al. 2006) or highly influential members (Toral et al. 2009). We measure the total degree centrality of the Micro-entrepreneurs and the Privates. With the total degree centrality we are able to measure the amount of direct connections of a member to other network members (see Table 8.5; Wasserman and Faust 2007).

The entrepreneurial members clearly show a higher total degree centrality on a 0.05-significance level (α = 0.037), meaning they are linked to many others of the network. Referring to the high CoCit-Scores with their own peers the majority of their many connections are likely with other entrepreneurial members forming separate cliques.

To further analyze the positions of the Micro-entrepreneurs within the OIC and especially the strong collaboration with their peers, we conducted a graphical assessment. The network we sketched is an undirected but weighted network and graphically shows collaboration clusters among the community members. In the Figure 8.2, the individual members are

Table 8.5   Total degree centrality of the micro-entrepreneurs and privates

	10^{-3}	Micro-entrepreneurs	Privates	Sign.
Total degree	n	27	24	
	Mean	9.2	7.1	213.50
	Median	8.9	5.6	α = 0.037
	Mean rank	30.09	21.40	

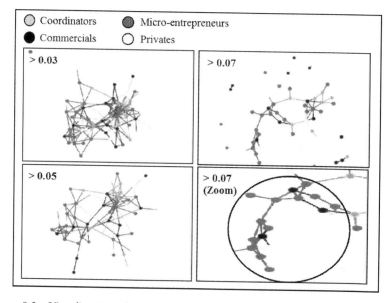

Figure 8.2   Visualization of the social network

represented by nodes, colored accordingly their group, and the CoCit-Scores between them by lines. We applied different threshold values for clarity reasons, as only connections exceeding this value between members are displayed (see Figure 8.2).

The threshold value of 0.07 enables an identification of a clear structure, a two-centered network. On the right side, we can identify a center with several Coordinators, Privates and Micro-entrepreneurs. By zooming into the left side of this network, the second center shows a strong clique of 12 Micro-entrepreneurs, representing almost half of the included 27, and 6 other non-Coordinators. This group is almost completely isolated from the Coordinators and therefore makes it less controllable for these core members of the community. Based on these insights, we aggregate the collaboration behavior of entrepreneurial members into the following proposition:

P4: *Entrepreneurial members have a high likelihood of forming separate cliques with their peers and limiting the collaboration with core members.*

8.5 Discussion

In this section, we discuss our four propositions derived from our empirical study, link them to existing research, and find further support for their validity. We integrate entrepreneurial characteristics and clarify the rationale behind the behavior of entrepreneurial community members. Their internal locus of control, need for achievement, high innovativeness and their risk propensity characterize entrepreneurs and help to explain the identified behavior.

Our first proposition, that entrepreneurial members focus more on innovative and disruptive topics, is supported by findings of Kirton (1976). The innovative creativity of entrepreneurs is a driver to rather focus on new developments than solving problems in a restricted frame, where only e.g. the type of sales channel for a product is questioned. Their need for achievement might drive their focus on product-related topics, as derived in our second proposition. Their goal-orientation and self-initiative (McClelland 1967) are presumably more satisfied by realizing and bringing products to the customer than solving problems regarding the community culture or its organization.

We identify a lower degree of specialization by entrepreneurial members, meaning that these community members tend to generalize over time and participate in a great variety of different thread categories. This finding is supported by their risk propensity (Caird 1993) as they might ignore the risk of a reputation loss when contributing to a non-familiar topic or collaborating with unknown community members. The second driver behind contributing broadly is the belief in their own ability to influence events (e.g. Boyd 1988). Entrepreneurial members might strongly believe that also contributions outside of their home turf are valuable for the environment. Lastly,

206 *Jan Bierwald and Cornelius Herstatt*

their need for achievement enables them to contribute to topics, where they not exclusively rely on their experiences or knowledge already available. Their superior problem-solving skills and self-initiative help them to actively seek and process new information and share it with other OIC members.

By conducting the co-citation and social network analysis, we are able to show the high likelihood of entrepreneurial members to form cliques and limit their collaboration with community core members, building our fourth proposition. Commonly core members of the community often with an assigned role are identified as boundary spanners or coordinators collaborating intensively with all community members (e.g. Dahlander and O'Mahony 2011). In our study, all members show their highest collaboration level with the core members of the Premium community except the Micro-entrepreneurs. Their strong internal locus of control marked by their need for control and autonomy (Hornaday and Aboud 1971) might cause this behavior. They prefer to collaborate with like-minded independently from the community management represented by the core members.

8.6 Conclusion

We studied the contribution behavior of entrepreneurial community members by using more than 7,300 mails from the community Premium. After inductively deriving four propositions regarding the contribution focus, the degree of specialization and the collaboration with other community members, we conclude that entrepreneurial members can be blessing or curse for an OIC. Firstly, they contribute more to innovative, disruptive and product-related topics, providing useful solutions and information to the OIC. Secondly, they show a lower degree of specialization, contributing to a wide range of different topics. This behavior fosters their embeddedness within the OIC and makes them a significant driving force for community discussion. Nevertheless, their tendency to form separate cliques with peers and their limited collaboration with the core members of the community can be a curse for the OIC. The controllability by the core members is restricted and in particular it can end in the decomposition into two completely separate groups by community forking. This process can lead to non-productive rivalry among groups or to duplicated efforts (Cheliotis 2009).

We compared our findings with existing theory of entrepreneurs and their determining characteristics. We increased the confidence in our inductively derived propositions by identifying rationales behind the behavior or entrepreneurial members in OIC, such as the need for achievement and the internal locus of control. Nevertheless, our study obviously has some limitations. Even though our single case was carefully selected and its fundamental characteristics are representative for a wide range of other OIC, using only one community producing a tangible good challenges the generalizability of our findings. Therefore, our initial propositions need to be verified across a wider range of cases. This also includes to analyze larger communities and a higher number of entrepreneurs. Also, we applied the co-citation analysis to investigate the micro-dynamics in OIC for the first time. Although we logically reasoned the applicability of this research method after making some appropriate adaptations, support from other research scholars is missing at this point.

In our study we distinguished entrepreneurial members from private members and could generate valuable insights for OIC research. To our knowledge, it is the first empirical study explicitly investigating the behavior of entrepreneurial community members. We are able to show how their behavioral pattern differs from private community members. Therefore, we stretched the established two-fold classification of community members, commercial and private participant, by adding this third group. We extended the current OIC research with two additional findings. Firstly, a lower degree of specialization had been identified for core members or long-term members of a community. Our research indicates that entrepreneurial characteristics are also a possible driver behind generalization. Secondly, core members usually holding central positions within the OIC network are strong collaborators with a variety of members, but seem to face challenges by collaborating with entrepreneurial members. Besides the broadening to other cases, we can identify promising further research opportunities around our investigated phenomenon. Many questions around the entrepreneurial members are yet to be answered: What attracts these individuals to join an OIC? How exactly does their entrepreneurial spirit or capability enable them to participate in topics beyond their expertise? What additional rationales for their clique building tendency can be identified? How does this clique formation jeopardize the overall success of the OIC and how can it be softened?

Providing clear recommendation for community management based on our initial inductive approach needs to be done with care as further research is necessary, but provide early food for thoughts. Entrepreneurial members are valuable contributor to the joint development within OIC. They lean towards contributing to innovative, disruptive topics and due to their generalization tendency drive forces beyond intense community activity. Therefore, community management should try to attract and retain entrepreneurial members. However, they tend to form separate cliques fueling community forking. Community management should carefully monitor their activities and assign members to actively collaborate with cliques of entrepreneurial members to foster community wide cooperation, increase control and fully benefit from entrepreneurs and the community.

NOTES

1. Lurker is a community member who does not send an mail or post at all (Nonnecke and Preece 2000).
2. "The free-rider problem, also known as social loafing, occurs when one or more members of a group do not do their fair share of the work on a group project" (Brooks and Ammons 2003, p. 268).

3. All coders have done previously research on community innovation and hold a degree in management.
4. Cf. 0.84 (Nambisan and Baron 2010) and 0.86 (Wasko and Faraj 2005).
5. Between 0.2 and 0.3 (cf. Schäffer et al. 2006).
6. Frequently approximately 100 publications analyzed (cf. e.g. Ramos-Rodríguez and Ruíz-Navarro 2004).
7. "Lorenz curve relates the cumulative proportion of income units to the cumulative proportion of income received when units are arranged in ascending order of their income" (Kakwani 1977, p. 719).

REFERENCES

Agerfalk, P. J., and Fitzgerald, B. (2008): "Outsourcing to an unknown workforce: exploring opensourcing as a global sourcing strategy", *MIS Quarterly* 32(2), pp. 385–409.

Alexy, O., Criscuolo, P., and Salter, A. (2012): "No soliciting: practice for managing unrequested innovative ideas", *California Management Review* 54(3), pp. 116–139.

Audretsch, D. B., and Feldmann M. P. (1996): "R&D spillovers and the geography of innovation and production", *The American Economic Review* 86(3), pp. 630–640.

Baldwin, Y., and Clark, K. B. (2006): "The architecture of participation: does code architecture mitigate free riding in the Open Source development model?" *Management Science* 52(7), pp. 1116–1127.

Balka, K., Raasch, C., and Herstatt, C. (2009): "Open source enters the world of atoms: a statistical analysis of open design", *First Monday* 14(11).

Begley, T. M., and Boyd, D. P. (1988): "Psychological characteristics associated with performance in entrepreneurial firms and smaller businesses", *Journal of Business Venturing* 2(1), pp. 79–93.

Blanchard, A., and Horan, T. (1998): "Virtual communities and social capital", *Social Science Computer Review* 16(3), pp. 293–307.

Boyd, R. (1988): "Is the repeated prisoner's dilemma game a good model of reciprocal altruism?" *Ethology and Sociobiology* 9, pp. 211–221.

Brooks, C. M., and Ammons, J. L. (2003): "Free riding in group projects and the effects of timing, frequency, and specificity of criteria in peer assessments", *Journal of Education for Business* 78(5), pp. 268–272.

Butler, B. (2001): "Membership size, communication activity, and sustainability: a resource-based model of online social structures", *Information Systems Research* 12(4), pp. 346–362.

Caird, S. P. (1993): "What do psychological tests suggest about entrepreneurs?" *Journal of Managerial Psychology* 8(6), pp. 11–20.

Cheliotis, G. (2009): "From open source to open content: organization, licensing and decision processes in open cultural production", *Decision Support Systems* 47(3), pp. 229–244.

Chesbrough, H. W. (2006): *Open innovation the new imperative for creating and profiting from technology*, Harvard Business Review Press, Cambridge, MA.

Cromie, S., and Johns, S. (1983): "Irish entrepreneurs: some personal characteristics", *Journal of Occupational Behaviour* 4(4), pp. 318–324.

Dahlander, L., and O'Mahony, S. (2011): "Progressing to the center: coordinating project work", *Organization Science* 22(4), pp. 961–979.

Dahlander, L., and Wallin, M. W. (2006): "A man on the inside: unlocking communities as complementary assets", *Research Policy* 35(8), pp. 1243–1259.

Franke, N., and Shah, S.K. (2003): "How communities support innovative activities: an exploration of assistance and sharing among end-users", *Research Policy* 32(1), pp. 157–178.

Füller, J., Jawecki, G., and Muhlbacher, H. (2007): "Innovation creation by online basketball communities", *Journal of Business Research* 60(1), pp. 60–71.

Ghosh, R., Glott, R., Kreiger, B., and Robles, G. (2002): The Free/libre and Open Source software: survey and study. International Institute of Infonomics, University of Maastricht and Berlecon Research GmbH, http://www.math.unipd.it/~bellio/. Accessed 5 November 2012.

Gmür, M. (2003): "Co-citation analysis and the search for invisible colleges: a methodological evaluation", *Scientometrics* 57(1), pp. 27–57.

Hars, A., and Ou, S. (eds.) (2001): "Working for free?—motivations of participating in open source projects", 34th Hawaii International Conference on System Sciences, 3–6 January.

Herraiz, I., Robles, G., Amor, J.J., Romera, T., and Barahona, J.M. (2006): "The processes of joining in global distributed software projects", Global Software Development Workshop, 23 May, Shanghai.

Hertel, G., Niedner, S., and Herrmann, S. (2003): "Motivation of software developers in Open Source projects: an Internet-based survey of contributors to the Linux kernel", *Research Policy* 32(7), pp. 1159–1177.

Hippel, E. von (1976): "The dominant role of users in the scientific instrument innovation process", *Research Policy* 5(3), pp. 212–239.

Hippel, E. von (2006): *Democratizing innovation*, MIT Press, Cambridge, MA.

Hippel, E. von (2007): "Horizontal innovation networks—by and for users", *Industrial and Corporate Change* 16(2), pp. 293–315.

Hippel, E. von, and Krogh, G. von (2003): "Open Source software and the 'private-collective' innovation model: issues for organizational science", *Organizational Science* 14, pp. 209–223.

Hornaday, J.A., and Aboud, J. (1971): "Characteristics of successful entrepreneurs", *Personnel Psychology* 24(2), pp. 141–153.

Kakwani, N.C. (1977): "Applications of Lorenz curves in economic analysis", *Econometrica* 45(3), pp. 719–728.

King, A.S. (1985): "Self-analysis and assessment of entrepreneurial potential", *Simulation & Gaming* 16(4), pp. 399–416.

Kirton, M. (1976): "Adaptors and innovators: a description and measure", *Journal of Applied Psychology* 61(5), pp. 622–629.

Kozinets, R.V. (1999): "E-tribalized marketing? the strategic implications of virtual communities of consumption", *European Management Journal* 17(3), pp. 252–264.

Krippendorff, K. (2004): *Content analysis: an introduction to its methodology*, 2nd ed., Sage Publications, Thousand Oaks, CA.

Krogh, G. von, Spaeth, S., and Lahkahni, K. (2003): "Community, joining, and specialization in open source software innovation: a case study", *Research Policy* 32(7), pp. 1217–1241.

Lakhani, K.R., and Hippel, E. von (2003): "How open source software works: 'free' user-to-user assistance", *Research Policy* 32, pp. 923–943.

Lakhani, K.R., and Wolf, R.G. (2005): "Why hackers do what they do: understanding motivation and effort in free/Open Source software projects", in *Perspectives on free and Open Source software*, J. Feller, B. Fitzgerald, S.A. Hissam, and K.R. Lakhani (eds.), pp. 3–22, MIT Press, Cambridge, MA.

Lievrouw, L.A. (1989): "The invisible college reconsidered", *Communication Research* 16(5), pp. 615–628.

Littunen, H. (2000): "Entrepreneurship and the characteristics of the entrepreneurial personality", *International Journal of Entrepreneurial Behaviour & Research* 6(6), pp. 295–310.

Mahr, D., and Lievens, A. (2012): "Virtual lead user communities: drivers of knowledge creation for innovation", *Research Policy* 41(1), pp. 167–177.

McClelland, D. C. (1967): *The achieving society*, Free Press, New York.

Nambisan, S., and Baron, R. A. (2010): "Different roles, different strokes: organizing virtual customer environments to promote two types of customer contributions", *Organization Science* 21(2), pp. 554–572.

Nonnecke, B., & Preece, J. (2000): "Lurker demographics: counting the silent", paper presented at the ACM CHI 2000 Conference on Human Factors in Computing Systems, The Hague.

Nov, O. (2007): "What motivates Wikipedians?" *Communications of the ACM* 50(11), pp. 60–64.

Oh, W., and Jeon, S. (2007): "Membership herding and network stability in the Open Source community: the Ising perspective", *Management Science* 53(7), pp. 1086–1101.

Oreg, S., and Nov, O. (2008): "Exploring motivations for contributing to open source initiatives: the roles of contribution context and personal values", *Computers in Human Behavior* 24(5), pp. 2055–2073.

Qureshi, I., and Fang, Y. (2010): "Socialization in Open Source software projects: a growth mixture modeling approach", *Organizational Research Methods* 14(1), pp. 208–238.

Ramos-Rodríguez, A.-R., and Ruíz-Navarro, J. (2004): "Changes in the intellectual structure of strategic management research: a bibliometric study of the Strategic Management Journal, 1980–2000", *Strategic Management Journal* 25(10), pp. 981–1004.

Rheingold, H. (2000): *The virtual community: homesteading on the electronic frontier*, MIT Press, Cambridge, MA..

Ridings, C. M., Gefen, D., and Arinze, B. (2002): "Some antecedents and effects of trust in virtual communities", *Journal of Strategic Information Systems* 11(3–4), pp. 271–295.

Roberts, J.A., Hann, I.-H., and Slaughter, S. A. (2006): "Understanding the motivations, participation, and performance of Open Source software developers: a longitudinal study of the Apache projects", *Management Science* 52(7), pp. 984–999.

Rotter, I. (1996): "Innovation congregations", *Technology Review* (April), pp. 47–54.

Schäffer, U., Binder, C., and Gmür, M. (2006): "Struktur und Entwicklung der Controllingforschung—Eine Zitations—und Kozitationsanalyse von Controllingbeiträgen in deutschsprachigen wissenschaftlichen Zeitschriften von 1970 bis 2003", *Zeitschrift für Betriebswirtschaft (ZfB)* 76(4), pp. 395–440.

Shah, S. K. (2006): "Motivation, governance, and the viability of hybrid forms in Open Source software development", *Management Science* 52(7), pp. 1000–1014.

Sowe, S., Stamelos, I., and Angelis, L. (2006): "Identifying knowledge brokers that yield software engineering knowledge in OSS projects", *Information and Software Technology* 48(11), pp. 1025–1033.

Toral, S.L., Martínez-Torres, M. R., Barrero, F., and Cortés, F. (2009): "An empirical study of the driving forces behind online communities", *Internet Research* 19(4), pp. 378–392.

Van Oost, E., Verhaegh, S., and Oudshoorn, N. (2008): "From innovation community to community innovation: user-initiated innovation in wireless leiden", *Science, Technology & Human Values* 34(2), pp. 182–205.

Van Wendel de Joode, R., de Bruijn, J. A., and van Eeten, M. (2003): *Protecting the virtual commons: self-organizing Open Source and free software communities and innovative intellectual property regimes*, T.M.C. Asser Press, The Hague.

Wasko, M., and Faraj, S. (2005): "Why should I share? examing social capital and knowledge contribution in electronic networks of practice", *MIS Quarterly* 29(1), pp. 35–58.

Wasserman, S., and Faust, K. (2007): *Social network analysis: methods and applications*, 16th ed. Cambridge University Press, Cambridge.

White, H.D., and McCain, K.W. (1998): "Visualizing a discipline: an author co-citation analysis of information science, 1972–1995", *Journal of the American Society of Information Science* 49(4), pp. 327–355.

Ye, Y., Nakakoji, K., Yamamoto, Y., and Kishida, K. (2005): "The co-evolution of systems and communities in free and Open Source software development", in *Free/open source software development*, S. Koch (ed.), pp. 59–82, Idea, Hershey, PA.

Yin, R.K. (2009): *Case study research: design and methods*, 4th ed., Sage Publications, Los Angeles, CA.

Section 3

Business Implications

9 How Open Is Open Source?

Software and Beyond

Kerstin Balka, Christina Raasch, and Cornelius Herstatt

Reprint: *Creativity and Innovation Management*, Volume 19, Issue 3, September 2010, Pages 248–256.

Traditionally, the protection of intellectual property is regarded as a pre-condition for value capture. The rise of open source (OS) software and OS tangible products, so-called open design, has challenged this understanding. Openness is often regarded as a dichotomous variable (open-source vs. closed-source) and it is assumed that online developer communities demand full opening of the product's source. In this paper we will explore openness as a gradual and multi-dimensional concept. We carried out an Internet survey ($N = 270$) among participants of 20 open design communities in the domain of IT hardware and consumer electronics. We find that open design projects pursue complex strategies short of complete openness and that communities value openness of software more highly than openness of hardware. Our findings suggest that open design companies can successfully implement strategies of partial openness to safeguard value capture without alienating their developer community.

Keywords: tangible open source products, gradual concept of openness, vale capture

9 HOW OPEN IS OPEN SOURCE?

9.1 Introduction

Economic theory tells us that firms generate innovations in order to reap economic rents. It also tells us that inventions require intellectual property protection in order for imitation competition to be prevented and thus for innovative firms to capture the value they created (Arrow 1962). Intellectual property rights carry this assurance and thereby serve to incentivize firms to perform their innovating function in the economy. This is the private investment model of innovation (Demsetz 1967; Krogh and Hippel 2003).

Over the last decade, researchers have directed a spotlight on open source innovation as the polar opposite of this model, which has been termed closed-source innovation accordingly. Open source innovation is understood to be 'extremely open' (cf. Gassmann 2006) since it requires information to be freely revealed to all. The innovator gives up the right to exclusive exploitation of her invention (Harhoff, Henkel and Hippel 2003)—a strategy that must seem injurious to any degree of value capture. Accordingly, researchers have been puzzled by many inconsistencies of the open source model with the private investment model of innovation (Lerner and Tirole 2001). Specifically, the motivations of supposedly rational individuals and companies to contribute to such projects and the seemingly self-contradictory notion of open-source business models have been a focus of research (Hecker 1999; Krogh et al. 2008).

In this chapter we will show that this dialectic structure is in fact an oversimplification of the concept of openness and its relation to value capture. Despite proliferating research on open source innovation, the entire construct of openness has received too little attention to date, both theoretically and empirically. Henkel (2006) and West and O'Mahony (2008) are among the very few who explore openness as a gradual and multi-dimensional concept and link intermediate levels of openness to value capture.

Within the scope of this paper we study forms of openness of software and hardware, their empirical prevalence and their relevance for members of open source communities. For this purpose, we conducted a survey ($N = 270$) among participants of 20 open design communities. We find that open design projects pursue complex strategies short of complete openness and that communities value openness of software more than openness of hardware, although both are regarded as important. Our findings suggest that well-tailored strategies of partial openness can successfully be implemented by open design companies to safeguard differentiation and value capture without alienating their developer community.

The chapter is structured as follows. The next section presents the theoretical background to our research, specifically prior findings on the concept of openness, and goes on to derive research hypotheses. After the explanation of our research methodology and data, we present empirical findings. This is followed by a discussion of our results in relation to previous findings, especially the relationship between openness and value capture, and finally we draw conclusions.

9.2   Theoretical Background

The term 'open source' (OS) originates from the software industry and denotes the free revelation of the source code. An actor grants "access [to his proprietary information] to all interested agents without imposition of any direct payment" (Harhoff, Henkel and Hippel 2003, p. 1754).

Beyond pure software development, the term 'open design' (Vallance, Kiani and Nayfeh 2001) provides a framework for sharing design information stemming from hardware as well as other physical objects. This design has different effects on aesthetics, usability, manufacturing, quality, and so forth. Manufacturers often use modular designs to organize complex products. A modular design is composed of modules that are in turn made up of components (cf. Singhal and Singhal 2002).

9.2.1 Openness as a Gradual Concept

When Harhoff, Henkel and Hippel (2003, p. 1753) discuss free revealing of proprietary information, they mean "that all existing and potential intellectual property rights to that information are voluntarily given up . . . and all interested parties are given access to it". Many researchers follow this strict definition and treat openness as a dichotomous variable—open source vs. closed source (e.g., Bitzer 2004; Dahlander 2005). Free revealing has been observed in fields as diverse as iron production (Allen 1983), pharmaceuticals (Hope 2004), and sports equipment (Franke and Shah 2003). Practitioners, however, believe that "hard-line approaches, whether open source or proprietary, don't work [that well in the world of today]" (Thomas 2008). Bonaccorsi, Rossi and Giannangeli (2006) and Henkel (2006) find that firms address this issue by revealing selectively, i.e., they carefully decide which parts to reveal and which to keep proprietary.

West (2003) moves the gradual concept of openness one step further by observing that many open source projects impose various limitations on openness. He proposes a distinction between 'open parts' and 'partly open'. The 'open parts' strategy refers to the selective free revealing of some components of a modular object. A project developing an open source embedded device could accordingly reveal its software components or hardware components or both, and within their list of software (and hardware) components they can decide which components to reveal and which to keep proprietary. The 'partly open' strategy refers to the release of a design under restrictive terms. The open source project can, for example, restrict the permitted usage to non-commercial use or limit the group of people who get access to its knowledge. Shah (2006) investigated this approach by comparing open source and 'gated source' communities. Within the scope of this study we focused on 'open parts' strategies.

9.2.2 Three Aspects of Openness

In order to analyse openness of software (SW) and hardware (HW) components in close detail, we extended a framework proposed by West and O'Mahony (2008) to account for settings beyond software. While the authors distinguish between transparency and accessibility, we added replicability as a third aspect of openness.

Transparency (T) refers to the quantity and quality of information which is freely revealed to developers. Information in that sense could, for example, be software source code or hardware schematics and design files.

Accessibility (A) denotes the possibility for community members to actively participate in product development. This participation may take place in terms of open discussions only or contributions could be directly taken up into official product releases.

Replicability (R) denotes the availability of individual components and thus the possibility for the self-assembly of the product. Objects including closed components could be copied if those components are obtainable; conversely objects which are entirely open source might not easily be copied if some components are difficult to produce and not obtainable from external suppliers.

9.2.3   The Community Perspective

Initially, the free software and open source movement described itself as a community of programmers, committed to software freedom, and working against established intellectual property owners (cf. Stallman 2007). In the scholarly domain, for example, West and O'Mahony (2008) find that by restricting access to community processes, firms limit their community's ability to attract new members and grow.

With the emergence of open source business models, the interests of the community and the commercial companies involved needed to be balanced (e.g., Mahony and Naughton 2004). Raasch, Herstatt and Balka (2009, p. 389) observe an awareness that, "by deciding to 'leave enough room to encourage private investment', the community can improve its probability of success". People in charge try to promote project success by carefully weighing community and commercial requirements. First findings suggest that this trade-off is accepted by community members, as long as the balance is perceived to be fair.

9.2.4   Research Hypotheses

In the realm of open design, the tangibility of the product may affect the form and degree of openness. For products that require heavy production cost and relatively little development cost, the open source approach could be less suitable (cf. Lee and Cole 2003). Therefore, we propose that open design products which include both hardware and software components select differing degrees of openness for tangible and non-tangible parts of their design. We suggest that across all three aspects of openness software components are more likely to be open source than hardware components. The following research hypotheses assume:

> *H1-T: In open design, software components are more transparent than hardware components, i.e., software source code is more frequently and more easily available than hardware documentation.*
> *H1-A: Software is more accessible than hardware, i.e., the community can exert more influence on software development than on hardware development.*

H1-R: Software components are more replicable than hardware components, i.e., software parts are more often available for self-assembly of the product than hardware components.

In contrast to pure software, tangible products need to be physically produced prior to being marketed. Unless community members assemble the good themselves, this production may be closed and left in the hands of a manufacturer reserving certain rights and appropriating (some portion of) the created value.

As discussed above, prior findings suggest that communities prefer openness to closedness. Still some ambiguity remains in this regard. On the one hand, openness is a basic requirement for open source activities; closed or gated approaches have hence been found to "limit cumulative development and overall value creation" (Shah 2006, p. 1010). On the other hand, openness can entail drawbacks, e.g., quality issues, lower ease of product use, less standardization, etc. (cf. Baldwin, Hienerth and Hippel 2006). This ambivalence shall be investigated in our second set of hypotheses:

H2-T: Transparency is important to open design communities.
H2-A: Accessibility is important to open design communities.
H2-R: Replicability is important to open design communities.

Taking our two sets of hypotheses together, we assume that software in general is more open than hardware in open design projects and that communities value openness. Looking at the vast number of software projects compared to the relatively small number of hardware projects (cf. Balka, Raasch and Herstatt 2009), we further assume that openness of software components is more important to communities than openness of hardware components:

H3-T: Transparency of software components is more important to open design communities than transparency of hardware components.
H3-A: Accessibility of software components is more important to open design communities than accessibility of hardware components.
H3-R: Replicability of software components is more important to open design communities than replicability of hardware components.

9.3 Empirical Research Approach

9.3.1 Methodology and Data Collection

A web-based questionnaire survey among active participants of 20 open design communities was conducted in order to systematically explore the relevance of openness.

The selection of communities was a critical task. Possibly due to the novelty of the phenomenon, there is no complete directory of open design projects. For our case selection, we followed Balka, Raasch and Herstatt (2009) and used the directory of 'Open Innovation Projects'. We carefully chose communities based on three criteria: we selected projects (1) with more than 10 active participants developing and (2) with objects which include both software and hardware components. Additionally, (3) the development must have reached a stage in which first prototypes are available. This approach ensures a sufficiently large number of potential respondents and increases the availability of secondary information about the projects. A list of the surveyed communities is given in Appendix Table 9.4.

A pre-test with 37 respondents delivering 22 full answers was conducted in August 2009 to ensure the validity of the items and to see how respondents react to the questionnaire (e.g., Garson 2002). Since overlong Internet questionnaires are often not completed (e.g., Batinic and Bosnjak 2000), we planned a completion time of about 5–7 minutes.

Data collection started on 2 September 2009 and lasted until 5 October 2009. The survey was announced on project mailing-lists and posted in forums and blogs. Moreover, a web-page was installed on which the goals of our research were explained. In order to increase the acceptability of the study, we strove to adhere to open source values by announcing that aggregated results of the study would be published on the Internet directly after completion.

The questionnaire included both multiple-choice and free-text type questions. All items relating to the degree of openness were to be answered on 5-point Likert scales from (1) 'strongly disagree' to (5) 'strongly agree'. The option 'No answer' was available for every question.

9.3.2   The Sample

During data collection we counted 688 unique visitors on the entry page, 457 of whom started the survey. A total of 270 answers are sufficiently complete to be considered for further analysis, i.e., respondents completed at least two out of five sections from the survey. This results in a response rate of 39% when taking the number of visitors as target population (cf. Batinic and Bosnjak 2000). Compared to similar studies (e.g., Roberts, Hann and Slaughter 2006; Krogh et al. 2009) this share appears satisfying. However, the number of answers per question varies between 189 and 270. The number of observations (n) therefore fluctuates. This is particularly the case for statistical analyses requiring pairs of observations to be complete.

A total of 270 participants (2% females, 98% males; mean age = 32 years, range: 14–70 years) were included in the analysis. On average the participants are involved in their projects for about 16 months (range: less than 1 month to 6 years). Their positions in the project are 3% project leaders, 9% core team members, 55% developers and 33% users. On average they spend 9 hours per week actively in the project community (range: 0–70 hours).

9.3.3   Data Analysis

Data has been analysed using the statistical software R (R Development Core Team 2005). Descriptive statistics about questionnaire items and constructs are presented by their means (μ) and variances (σ^2). One- and two-sample *t*-tests have been performed to confirm or reject our research hypotheses. All conducted tests are one-sided. We are aware that *t*-tests require normally distributed, independent samples, a requirement which is not fully met by our data set. Nevertheless, it can be assumed that *t*-tests provide reasonable results due to the large sample size. Welch approximation to the degrees of freedom is used to treat the variances as being unequal.

To support our findings we have additionally conducted one- and two-sample Wilcoxon tests (the latter is also known as the 'Mann-Whitney' test) to prove our results by non-parametric statistical methods. In every case the *p*-values from non-parametric tests are of the same magnitude as those from parametric tests. We further considered transforming the data to meet normality, but this did not significantly affect the results. Owing to better interpretability of untransformed data, we decided to present *t*-tests of the original data.

In order to assess the stability of our findings, we repeated all tests in different sub-samples. The respondents of one community, respectively, were excluded and replaced by random answers from the remaining sample to check whether our results depended on the answers from single projects. All stability tests confirmed our findings showing *p*-values below 1%; only the *p*-value for H3-T rose to up to 10% when excluding the community 'Openmoko' from the sample. Exemplary results are shown in Appendix Table 9.5; therein, we successively exclude the three projects with the greatest number of respondents from our sample and show that our findings are not driven by a specific community.

A potential self-selection bias has been investigated by comparing the demographics of the respondents of our survey to similar studies (e.g., Krogh et al. 2009). This did not result in significant differences.

9.4   Empirical Findings

9.4.1   Software Is More Open than Hardware

In our questionnaire, nine questions were included to analyse the degree of openness of software and hardware components respectively. The participants were asked to answer each question separately for software and hardware, therefore every question has been included twice. Four questions measured transparency, three evaluated accessibility, and two related to the replicability of the product or the components of the product.

Table 9.1 shows means and variances for these nine questions. Question T-3 has been put reversely; accordingly we expected its mean for software to

Table 9.1   Software–hardware difference

Question	Software		Hardware		Difference	*n*
	μ	σ²	μ	σ²		
• *Reverse question.						
T – 1a	4.4	0.8	4.2	1.2	$p < 0.001$	252
T – 1b	3.5	1.3	3.2	1.3	$p < 0.001$	221
T – 2	4.2	1.0	3.9	1.3	$p < 0.001$	249
T – 3*	2.8	1.1	3.0	1.1	$p < 0.01$	200
A – 1	4.5	0.6	4.0	1.1	$p < 0.001$	220
A – 2	4.4	0.7	3.9	1.1	$p < 0.001$	228
A – 3	4.4	0.7	3.9	1.1	$p < 0.001$	198
R – 1	4.4	0.8	3.3	2.0	$p < 0.001$	222
R – 2	3.9	0.7	3.5	1.8	$p < 0.001$	176

be lower than its mean for hardware. For the other questions we expected the opposite. *T*-tests show significant differences at 1% significance levels across all questions.

For our hypotheses H1-T, H1-A, and H1-R we are interested in differences between software and hardware components concerning the entire constructs transparency, accessibility and replicability. Those constructs must be designed as linear combinations of the respective single questionnaire items, e.g., via factor analysis. As we can see from Table 9.1, significant differences in means between software and hardware can be observed for every single questionnaire item. This ensures strong support for our three hypotheses without calculating the constructs. We hence conclude that software components in open design products are indeed more transparent, more accessible, and more replicable than hardware components.

9.4.2   *Openness Is Important to Open Design Communities*
To analyse the importance of openness we included three questions in our survey, i.e., one per construct, again measuring this variable for software and hardware respectively. As we do not distinguish between software and hardware components in H2-T, H2-A and H2-R, the respective results are merged through using their means for the analysis of this set of hypotheses.

The histograms in Figure 9.1 show a strongly right-skewed distribution of answers. For every question a clear majority of participants states that openness is indeed important to them. To evaluate our hypotheses statistically, we calculated *t*-tests, testing for item means to be significantly higher than 'Neutral' (3). As summarized in Table 9.2, we find all three hypotheses to be strongly supported at significance levels below 0.1%.

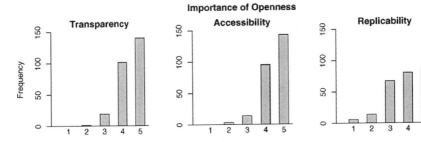

Figure 9.1 Histograms showing the frequency of answers from 'strongly disagree' (1) to 'strongly agree' (5) concerning the importance of openness across the three aspects

Table 9.2 Summary of importance of openness

Construct	μ	σ^2	*t*-test: μ > 3	*t*-test: μ > 4	*n*
Transparency	4.5	0.4	$p < 0.001$	$p < 0.001$	261
Accessibility	4.5	0.4	$p < 0.001$	$p < 0.001$	255
Replicability	3.9	1.0	$p < 0.001$	n.s.	254

To better understand the respondents' view of the importance of openness, we repeated this procedure testing for item means to be significantly higher than 'Agree' (4). For the constructs transparency and accessibility we still observe significant results, only the construct replicability does not show a mean significantly higher than 4. Therefore, we conclude that the availability of information and the opportunity to actively participate is indeed very important to open design communities. The possibility for self-assembly is also deemed important.

9.4.3 Openness of Software Components Is More Important than Openness of Hardware Components

The third set of research hypotheses—H3-T, H3-A and H3-R—is analysed by handling the questionnaire items relating to the importance of openness separately for software and hardware.

As summarized in Table 9.3, *t*-tests indicate significantly higher means for software compared to hardware at significance levels below 1%. Regarding transparency, the difference between software and hardware is small (~0.13) but still significant, because of the small variance in those variables.

Accordingly, our findings support all three hypotheses and we hence conclude that transparency, accessibility and replicability of software components

Table 9.3 Summary of differences in importance of openness between software and hardware

Construct	Software		Hardware		Difference	*n*
	μ	σ²	μ	σ²		
Transparency	4.5	0.4	4.4	0.6	$p < 0.01$	237
Accessibility	4.6	0.4	4.4	0.6	$p < 0.001$	229
Replicability	4.2	1.0	3.5	1.6	$p < 0.001$	233

are indeed more important to community members than the same aspects of openness of hardware components.

9.5   Discussion

9.5.1   Managerial Implications

Our findings suggest that open parts strategies in open design are crafted at the component level, rather than the level of the entire design. Some parts of a design can be entirely closed, whereas others are opened up. In particular, the degree of openness differs significantly between software and hardware components in the sense that software is more transparent, accessible and replicable than hardware.

We also observe that openness indeed matters to community members. For all three aspects (transparency, accessibility and replicability), respondents declared that the degree of openness is important to them, albeit to different degrees. Again, our results show significant differences between software and hardware components in this regard. Our analysis discloses that openness of software is significantly more important to community members than openness of hardware.

This suggests that companies working in open source settings can pursue differentiated strategies short of complete openness without alienating their developer communities. Every product whose design requires software and hardware development seems particularly suitable to this approach. Companies may accordingly involve communities in their software and parts of their hardware development and profit from the advantages of an open source approach, ranging from contributions from outside to increased publicity (cf. Bonaccorsi and Rossi 2004). At the same time, they can safeguard their position as manufacturers selling their product both to the community and the market. Firms in industries, such as consumer electronics, telecommunication and IT hardware in particular, may face opportunities for value capture from incorporating open source business models. Potentially, they possess even more opportunities than firms in IT software as one might suspect. The different aspects and degrees of openness yield a complex strategy space in which companies can position themselves. Thus, they retain means of value capture and differentiation from competitors.

9.5.2 Implications for Scholarly Research

In conclusion, the present study has contributed to our understanding of the perception and relevance of openness among members of open source communities. It extends the conceptional framework of West and O'Mahony (2008) to better account for non-digital innovation objects. We distinguished between three aspects of openness, i.e., transparency, accessibility and replicability. We empirically validated the existence and relevance of those aspects and highlighted significant differences in perceptions of openness of hardware and software across these three aspects. Openness is shown to be a multifaceted, gradual and context-dependent variable. Thus, our findings call for a more careful treatment of the construct of openness in future empirical work.

During the preparation of this study, we also experienced a lack of theoretical research on the concept of openness. For the purpose of this study we regarded openness as a product characteristic, albeit one that has various implications for the new product development process. An in-depth examination of the character, dimensions and implications of openness, as well as the negotiation of its configurations between communities and companies, seems strongly desirable in our view.

Four important limitations apply to the present study. First, many factors may influence perceptions of openness. In this paper, we strove to present an overview of these perceptions and an investigation of differences between software and hardware. Further research on individual perceptions would suggest questions concerning which aspect of openness is important for whom and why. Second, we focused on openness in development and production processes. It would be desirable to replicate the present study but focus on the openness in organization and governance of open design projects. Also in this regard, it would be highly interesting to investigate the individual perceptions and the reasoning behind the desire for increased openness. Third, we limited our approach on analysing open parts strategies. A close investigation of partly open strategies appears to be an interesting domain for future research. Fourth, for our survey, we chose projects in similar fields. This approach does not allow us to derive and compare findings about openness across different industries. Balka, Raasch and Herstatt (2009) study a number of different domains in which open design is already being applied; more research seems warranted, to better understand how openness can and should be handled depending on the industry environment. We hope that our work has helped to stimulate further research on openness in all these fields.

9.6   Appendix

Table 9.4   List of surveyed communities

Openmoko	Always Innovating Touch Book	Fab@home	Gp2x
OpenEEG	One laptop per child	Chumby	RepRap
Bug Labs	Neuros OSD and Link	OpenServo	Balloon
Gumstix	Beagle Board	Open WRT	SquidBee
Mikrokopter	BitsFromBytes	MakerBot	Arduino

Table 9.5   Exemplary results from stability tests for the three communities with the greatest number of respondents, conducted via excluding respondents from one community per test column

		Total		Excluded community	
		Sample	Openmoko	Gp2x	RepRap
H1	T-1a	0.26***	0.30***	0.26***	0.29***
	T-1b	0.26***	0.19**	0.26***	0.29***
	T-2	0.21***	0.23***	0.21***	0.23***
	T-3	−0.17**	−0.16**	−0.17**	−0.18**
	A-1	0.52***	0.58***	0.52***	0.57***
	A-2	0.50***	0.44***	0.49***	0.54***
	A-3	0.47***	0.40***	0.47***	0.52***
	R-1	1.12***	0.88***	1.12***	1.23***
	R-2	0.38***	0.27***	0.38***	0.39***
H2	T	1.47***	1.48***	1.47***	1.47***
	A	1.48***	1.44***	1.48***	1.48***
	R	0.69***	0.44***	0.69***	0.76***
H3	T	0.13*	0.07+	0.17***	0.16***
	A	0.24***	0.21***	0.24***	0.26***
	R	0.69***	0.44***	0.69***	0.76***

1. For H1 and H3, we present means of differences between software and hardware together with their significance rating; for H2, we present means of differences to 'Neutral' (3).
2. p value < 10%: +, <5%: *, <1%: **, <0.1%: ***

REFERENCES

Allen, R. C. (1983): "Collective invention", *Journal of Economic Behavior and Organization* 4, pp. 1–24.

Arrow, K. (1962): "Economic welfare and the allocation of resources for invention", in *The rate and direction of inventive activity: economic and social factors*, H. M. Groves (ed.), pp. 609–626, National Bureau of Economic Research.

Baldwin, C. Y., Hienerth, C., and Hippel, E. von. (2006): "How user innovations become commercial products: a theoretical investigation and case study", *Research Policy* 35, pp. 1291–313.

Balka, K., Raasch, C., and Herstatt, C. (2009): "Open Source enters the world of atoms: a statistical analysis of open design", *First Monday* 14.

Batinic, B., and Bosnjak, M. (2000): "Fragebogenuntersuchungen im Internet", in *Internet for psychologists*, B. Batinic (ed.), pp. 287–317, Hogrefe, Göttingen.

Bitzer, J. (2004): "Commercial versus Open Source software: the role of product heterogeneity in competition", *Economic Systems* 28, pp. 369–381.

Bonaccorsi, A., and Rossi, C. (2004): "Altruistic individuals, selfish firms? the structure of motivation in Open Source software", *First Monday* 9.

Bonaccorsi, A., Rossi, C., and Giannangeli, S. (2006): Adaptive entry strategies under dominant standards: hybrid business models in the Open Source software industry", *Management Science* 52, pp. 1085–1098.

Dahlander, L. (2005): "Appropriation and appropriability in Open Source software", *International Journal of Innovation Management* 9, pp. 259–285.

Demsetz, H. (1967): "Toward a theory of property rights", *American Economic Review* 57, pp. 347–359.

Franke, N., and Shah, S. (2003): "How communities support innovative activities: an exploration of assistance and sharing among end-users", *Research Policy* 32, pp. 157–178.

Garson, D. G. (2002): *Guide to writing empirical papers, thesis, and dissertations*, Marcel Dekker, New York.

Gassmann, O. (2006): "Opening up the innovation process: towards an agenda", *R&D Management* 36, pp. 223–228.

Harhoff, D., Henkel, J., and Hippel, E. von (2003): "Profiting from voluntary information spillovers: how users benefit by freely revealing their innovations", *Research Policy* 32, pp. 1753–1769.

Hecker, F. (1999): "Setting up shop: the business of open-source software", *IEEE Software* 16, pp. 45–51.

Henkel, J. (2006): "Selective revealing in open innovation processes: the case of embedded Linux", *Research Policy* 35, pp. 953–969.

Hope, J. (2004): Open Source biotechnology, PhD thesis, Australian National University, Canberra.

Krogh, G. von, and Hippel, E. von (2003): "Open Source software and the 'private-collective' innovation model: issues for organization science", *Organization Science* 14, pp. 208–223.

Krogh, G. von, Spaeth, S., Haefliger, S., and Wallin, M. (2008): "Open Source software: what we know (and do not know) about motives to contribute", Dynamics of Institutions and Markets in Europe (DIME) Working Papers on Intellectual Property Rights, http://www.dime-eu.org/files/active/0/WP38_vonKroghSpaethHaefliger WallinIPROSS.pdf. Accessed 5 October 2009.

Krogh, G. von, Spaeth, S., Stuermer, M., and Hertel, G. (2009): Results of Maemo and Openmoko community survey, http://public.smi.ethz.ch/files/MaemoOpenmoko/ PublicDescriptiveStatistics.html. Accessed 6 October 2009.

228 *Kerstin Balka et al.*

Lee, G.K., and Cole, R.E. (2003): "From a firm-based to a community-based model of knowledge creation: the case of the Linux Kernel development", *Organization Science* 14, pp. 633–649.

Lerner, J., and Tirole, J. (2001): "The Open Source movement: key research questions", *European Economic Review* 45, pp. 819–826.

Mahony, I.G., and Naughton, E.J. (2004): "Open Source software monetized: out of the bazaar and into big business", *Computer and Internet Lawyer* 21, pp. 1–17.

Raasch, C., Herstatt, C., and Balka, K. (2009): "On the open design of tangible goods", *R&D Management* 39, pp. 382–393.

R Development Core Team (2005): R: a language and environment for statistical computing [Computer Software Manual]. http://www.R-project.org. Accessed 6 February 2009.

Roberts, J.A., Hann, I.-H., and Slaughter, S.A. (2006): Understanding the motivations, participation, and performance of Open Source software developers: a longitudinal study of Apache projects", *Management Science 52*, pp. 984–999.

Shah, S.K. (2006): "Motivation, governance, and the viability of hybrid forms in Open Source software development", *Management Science 52*, pp. 1000–1014.

Singhal, J., and Singhal, K. (2002): "Supply chains and compatibility among components in product design", *Journal of Operations Management* 20, pp. 289–302.

Stallman, R. (2007): Why Open Source misses the point of free software, http://www.gnu.org/philosophy/open-source-misses-the-point.html. Accessed 5 October 2009.

Thomas, G. (2008): Microsoft and mixed source software, http://www.mylemonadestand.net/weblog/archives/12. Accessed 5 October 2009.

Vallance, R., Kiani, S., and Nayfeh, S. (2001): "Open design of manufacturing equipment", in *Proceedings of the CHIRP 1st International Conference on Agile, Reconfigurable Manufacturing*, www.opendesign.org/CHIRP_Open_Design_Mfg_Equipment.pdf. Accessed 5 December 2014.

West, J. (2003): "How open is open enough? melding proprietary and Open Source platform strategies", *Research Policy* 32, pp. 1259–1285.

West, J., and O'Mahony, S. (2008): "The role of participation architecture in growing sponsored Open Source communities", *Industry and Innovation* 15, pp. 145–68.

10 How Firms Can Strategically Influence Open Source Communities

The Employment of 'Men on the Inside'

Viktor Lee and Cornelius Herstatt

The Internet has not only revolutionized our ways of communication but has also expanded firm's potential sources of innovation. Dahlander and Wallin (2006) have shown that firms deploy their personnel, the so-called man on the inside (MOI), to participate in open source communities in order to unlock the valuable assets that are voluntarily being created in these communities. Focusing on firm-sponsored open source communities, we will detect the functions of MOI and how these individuals influence the community by applying a comparative case study of two open source software firms, which includes interviews with managers and MOI, netnographic and social network analysis of the community interactions of over 12,000 individuals. We conclude that despite the fiery situation of combining open source philosophy with a firm's profit-driven business model, firms can succeed in integrating a community into the firm's development process with the help of the MOI. These key individuals carry out five core capabilities that are crucial to become central nodes in the communication networks.

Keywords: open source innovation, knowledge-based view, dynamic capabilities, firm-sponsored communities, social network analysis

10 HOW FIRMS CAN STRATEGICALLY INFLUENCE OPEN SOURCE COMMUNITIES

10.1 Introduction

Open source software (OSS) products and services already impact on our economy massively—it is estimated (Ghosh 2006) that OSS-related products and services have impacted 4% of the European GDP (and 32% of all IT services) in 2010. Thus, it is only plausible that firms are attracted by the idea of expanding their sources of innovation beyond the firm boundaries in virtual communities of interaction (Gangi and Wasko 2009; Spaeth et al. 2010) such as in open source environments. However, the vast majority of OSS projects fail because of low frequency of communication within the OSS communities (Dahlander and Frediksen 2007) or even because of the lack of participants (Krogh 2006). The very few successful projects are mainly led or sponsored by firms deliberately employing professional developers, the so-called "man on the inside" (Dahlander and Wallin 2006), in the remainder of this document named MOI, to participate in the community. These employees are firms' key success factors to understand and interact with communities. They are bridges between the firm and community and are supposed to thrive and grow a community as well as to unlock assets from the community that the firms need in the development process of their products. Gangi and Wasko (2009) have proposed four major strategies to integrate external participants into the organizational innovation process: incorporating user toolkits, strategic positioning of personnel, engaging lead users, and implementing user innovation communities. The strategic positioning of personnel occurs when an "organization assigns and positions human resources in user innovation communities to capture the information flowing within the community and to influence the direction of the community's development efforts" (Gangi and Wasko 2009, p. 209). The metaphor of the "*man on the inside*" (Dahlander and Wallin 2006) refers to that strategic path. It is a phenomenon which can actually be observed in open source software communities. The term "man on the inside" describes a person who is part of a firm (bound by contracts, incentives or significant relations/importance to that firm) participating on behalf of a firm *inside* an open source community, as part of this professional role, in order to unlock assets that are being created within these communities. Firms *strategically assign* such persons to initiate and influence the development process of a product or service. Additional reasons why commercial firms participate in open source environments is the prospect of potential benefits that can be achieved through "external development support, setting a standard and enabling compatibility, increasing demand for complements, and signaling technical excellence or good OSS citizenship" (Henkel 2008, p. 3). Despite the seemingly colliding conceptions of open source and commercialization around open source products, communities "enable firms to sponsor peers or allow personnel to work in the community" (Dahlander and Wallin 2006, p. 1244). They are a key success factor in the process of building and growing an online community. In their work about firms trying to unlock communities as complementary assets, Dahlander and Wallin (2006) find that MOI are crucial individuals in the (GNOME) community, exhibiting significantly higher influence and connectivity in the community network compared to hobbyists. Henkel (2008) highlights a research gap regarding the roles of such employed developers.

The principle aim of this study is to obtain a more detailed knowledge about MOI who can be constituted as a firm's tool to implement its strategy by unlocking external sources of innovation. In our case, the external sources of innovation are the open source community and its members capturing enormous intangible assets for the firm. In this regard, this study particularly targets to explore three underlying objectives.

First, we aim to comprehend MOI's specific functions in building and growing a virtual community. We know that "successful OSS projects are mostly staffed . . . by professional software developers" (Healy and Schussman 2003, p. 18) and that MOI are central nodes in these community networks (Dahlander and Wallin 2006). However, only little is known on their specific functions and activities in these collaborative networks of interaction. We try to close this gap by qualitatively and quantitatively studying MOI's functions and activities.

Second, we intend to observe and measure MOI's influence regarding the integrity and cohesion of OSS community networks in various channels of communication. Thus, we intend to examine whether MOI succeed in building resources, specifically in form of social capital, in OSS communities.

An OSS community consists of a large population of members with different individual needs and also different degrees of contribution to the community. Hence, our third objective is to test whether MOI can strategically create stronger bonds with influential members of the OSS community compared to other community members.

10.2   Phenomenological and Theoretical Background

In the environment of OSS communities, *firms* try to absorb the *idea and knowledge* created in the community by *people and their capabilities*. They do so by deploying *their* MOI do take part in the community *transactions*. This chapter endeavors to bring together the theoretical pieces that have been used to rationalize and derive the research questions, propositions and hypotheses in order to address the overarching question of "*how* firms can influence open source environments". The fact that the core of this study is dealing with "people", their "knowledge and capabilities" and "transaction with others", ocularly suggest that besides of the consultation of management literature, it is worthwhile to also look at literature from outside the management discipline. In this case the investigation of networks precipitated the usage of theories from the social sciences (social network analysis).

The concepts of key individuals in the innovation management literature, such as boundary spanners and promotors, are important elements in our study as they incorporate important findings on comparable functions of individuals in the innovation process. MOI are also spanning organizational boundaries and they also execute certain functions on behalf of the firm embodying the powers of promotors.

10.2.1   *Knowledge-Based View*

The knowledge-based view of the firm can be described as an "outgrow of the resource-based view" (Grant 1996, p. 2) which characterizes knowledge as the most important resource of a firm. Knowledge-based resources are particularly "difficult to imitate and socially complex" (Alavi and Leidner

2001, p. 4). In addition, following Grant's (1996) knowledge-based view of the firm, we view a firm as a structure to integrate community members' knowledge into products (Crowston et al. 2003; Grant 1996).

A widely cited classification of the different knowledge types is that of *tacit knowledge* as "knowing how" and *explicit knowledge* as "knowing about" (Nonaka 1994; Polanyi and Sen 2009). A more detailed taxonomy on knowledge, in particular 10 different types of knowledge (tacit, explicit, individual, social, declarative, procedural, causal, conditional, relational and pragmatic), is proposed by Alavi and Leidner (2001). In the remainder of this study, we will continue using the taxonomy of tacit and explicit knowledge because it is not our target to analyze and differentiate among the different types of knowledge in an OSS community but rather to obtain a better understanding on the capabilities of MOI. The explicit knowledge is characterized by the fact that it is directly transferable and can be "articulated" (Nickols 2000). On the contrary, the tacit knowledge "cannot be articulated" and contains cognitive as well as technical elements (Nonaka 1994). The cognitive elements draw on an individual's perception of the World (Johnson-Laird 1983) whereas the technical elements derive from an individual's "concrete know-how, crafts, and skills" (Nonaka 1994, p. 16) that have been built up during a longer period of time and are therefore not directly transferable. In reviewing current perspectives on knowledge codification, we are going to employ two assumptions. The first is that information and knowledge are two different concepts. Dosi et al. (1996) considered information as well stated and codified propositions about (1) states-of-the-world (e.g. "the sun is shining"); (2) properties of nature (e.g. "A causes B"); (3) identities of other agents (e.g. "I know Mr. X and he is a taxi driver"); and (4) explicit algorithms on how to do things. These information categories, which can be directly transferred and communicated to another person, are what we summarize under explicit knowledge. Instead, (tacit) knowledge is understood as including (1) cognitive categories; (2) codes of interpretations of the information itself; (3) tacit skills; and (4) search and problem-solving heuristics irreducible to well-defined algorithms. Organizations, and particularly business organizations, are viewed here as knowledge-based rather than simple information-processing systems (Dosi and Marengo 1994; Fransman 1994; Nonaka and Takeuchi 1995).

Grant (1996, p. 112) has pointed out that it is important for firms to understand that the "primary role of the firm [is to] integrat[e] the specialist knowledge residing in individuals [and transform those] into goods and services". This view on the firm is what differentiates KBV from other organizational theories such as organizational economics. The process of integrating knowledge and in particular integrating tacit knowledge is very complex. It requires coordination skills from the firms and its employees. Opposed to the literature in knowledge creation and organizational knowledge, the KBV emphasizes the importance "upon knowledge application and the role of individuals" as it is the individuals who are the "principal repository of knowledge" (Grant 1996, p. 121).

Following Grant's conclusions, this study will focus on the roles of firm individuals, i.e. the MOI, as the main unit of analysis. We will detect their roles, resources and capabilities on individual level that is being involved in the process of producing OSS. The dynamic environment of markets and especially those of open source software require new organizational forms and trends that integrate knowledge outside the firm boundaries (Prencipe and Tell 2001). This transition of barriers broadens the opportunities of firms and the pool of knowledge to be incorporated into the production but on the flipside it demands even more complex abilities in coordination and integration.

10.2.2 Dynamic Capabilities

Following Amit's and Shoemaker's (1993) proposal to distinguish resources into resources and capabilities, the remainder of this study will understand capabilities as the ability to make "*use* of its resources" (Penrose and Pitelis 1959; Mahoney and Pandian 1992). Henderson and Cockburn (1994) have given an overview on the different terms that have been used in this context and provided a clear split between "*component competences*" which they understand as "resources" and "*architectural competences*" which they use as a synonym for "capabilities". The first category includes physical resources (Amit and Shoemaker 1993), knowledge (Conner and Prahalad 1996), skills or technical systems (Leonard-Barton 1992), whereas the latter refers to what has previously been named "integrative capabilities" (Lawrence and Lorsch 1986[1967]), "organizational architecture" (Nelson 1991), "combinative capabilities" (Kogut and Zander 1992), "absorptive capacity" (Cohen and Levinthal 1990) or "dynamic capabilities" (Teece et al. 1997).

The *dynamic* capabilities as an expanded form are defined as the "firm's ability to integrate, build and reconfigure internal and external competencies to address rapidly changing environments" (Teece et al. 1997, p. 516). The dynamic capability literature alludes that resources alone may not be enough to achieve sustained competitive advantage. Without the ability to *use* the firm's assets, the flexibility to rapidly react to changing environment, and the "management capability to effectively coordinate and redeploy internal and external competences" (Teece et al. 1997, p. 515), a firm will have difficulties to remain competitive. Firms need to make strategic decisions which determine the "trajectory or path of [its] competence development" (Teece et al. 1997, p. 515) and thus adjust the firm's capabilities to the shifts in the changing business environment. This path-dependency is a key characteristic of dynamic capabilities. Similarly to the VRIN criteria in the RBV, capabilities "must be honed to a user need, unique and difficult to replicate" (Teece et al. 1997, p. 517) in order to be strategically important. The fact that capabilities are uniquely built over a period of time and cannot be readily assembled and acquired on the market makes them hardly replicable, and thus advantageous. Teece et al. (1997) describe that three factors determine a firm's unique dynamic capabilities: processes, positions and paths. Their idea is that certain managerial and organizational processes (e.g. coordination, integration, reconfiguration, transformation) are required to shape the firm's asset position (e.g. technological assets, complementary assets, financial assets, reputational assets). Depending on its position and historical paths, a firm then needs to choose the right paths in order to optimize the usage of technological opportunities.

10.2.3   *Theories of Key Individuals in the Innovation Process*

10.2.3.1   *Boundary Spanners*

Communication impedance is a problem between organizations due to the different "idiosyncratic norms, values, time frame, and coding schemes to permit effective processing of information" (Tushman 1977, p. 590). The higher the degree of specialization among the organizations, the bigger the barriers of communication will become (Kahn et al. 1966). A key feature of organizations is that they are surrounded by boundaries, which can be either internal (within organizations, e.g. between departments) or external (across organizational boundaries) (Dahlander and Frederiksen 2007; Rosenkopf and Nerkar 2001). Innovation processes strongly depend on a firm's ability to "generate, acquire, and integrate both internal and external sources of knowledge" (Rosenkopf and Nerkar 2001, p. 287). Therefore, the barriers of communication impedance across boundaries need to be overcome- one "way to deal with the difficulties of communicating across organizational boundaries is to develop special boundary spanning roles" (Tushman 1977, p. 591). In this study we are focusing in particular on communication and boundary spanning within online communities. In alignment with Rosenkopf's and Nerkar's differentiation of boundary spanning typology, Dahlander and Frederiksen (2007) propose two general boundary categories in virtual communities which they also name internal and external boundary spanning. The former refers to boundaries within an online community, e.g. between different communication channels of a community (such as forums and bug reporting) or different sub-sections of a channel (such as forums sections). The latter refers to organizational boundaries, e.g. between the community and its sponsoring firm or between two communities. The macrocosm interface between the firm and the community on the one hand and the microcosm interfaces within a specific community on the other hand, constitute the domains of MOI demanding certain capabilities from them. Henkel (2008, p. 462) has pointed out that in OSS communities, the "importance of OSS developers . . . is particularly high when . . . they qualify as boundary spanners" within the community network. Furthermore, "future research should delve into whether and how organizations build capabilities for boundary spanning activity" (Rosenkopf and Nerkar 2001, p. 304).

10.2.3.2 Roles of Boundary Spanners

The specific roles and functions as well as the behavioral patterns of MOI in OSS communities are still unsought fields. The boundary spanning literature (e.g. Tushman 1977; Aldrich and Herker 1977; Tushman and Scanlan 1981; Friedman and Podolny 1992) provides applicable research on individuals which are situated at the border of organizations in order to interact across those boundaries. These individuals embody certain functions which Aldrich and Herker (1977) categorize as (a) *information processing* and (b) *external representation of the firm*.

INFORMATION PROCESSING

Boundary spanners are usually exposed to large amounts of information. Boundary spanners can be seen as a "defense against information overload" (Aldrich and Herker 1977, p. 218). As facilitators, boundary spanners need to consolidate, store and direct the (filtered) information to those organizational units that require the information which requires the expertise in "determining who gets what information" (219). Eventually, the information needs to be communicated to the organizational units. As often the information that has been absorbed externally is rather "domain-specific" than "common knowledge" (Carlile 2004), boundary spanners need to simplify the information in usable form (Aldrich and Herker 1977).

THE EXTERNAL REPRESENTATION OF THE FIRM

The second function of boundary spanners is opposed to the first function, more focused on inside-out activities. In this context, boundary spanners act as representatives of the organizational core. Their behavior is supposed to "reflect the policy decisions of decision makers" (Aldrich and Herker 1977, p. 220). The representation of a firm can have many different forms, such as content (e.g. an official announcement), communication style (e.g. style of speech) or behavior (e.g. politeness). It is crucial in any form of representation to maintain "the organizational image and enhancing its social legitimacy . . . and simply making the organization visible" (221) across the boundary. Careful and well-thought actions are needed to avoid conflicts. The actions of boundary spanners must mirror the organization's interest, values and legitimacy of the organization.

The boundaries in a firm-sponsored OSS environment are different from the traditional boundaries. The two organizations involved are the sponsoring firm on the one hand and the associated OSS community on the other hand. The key difference of the firm's boundary in an OSS community is that they are "semi-permeable" because the employees (i.e. MOI) acting on the organizational periphery are not only participants of the one organization (which is the firm) but are concurrently participants of the other organization (that is the community). In other words, the boundary spanners of the firms are virtually duplicated when they participate in the community.

Hence, they become members of both sides and also representatives of both sides. In our analysis we will investigate the boundary spanning activities of MOI in various communication channels of the OSS community. This will give us a broader profile of MOI behavioral patterns because we will learn about the different community activities of MOI.

10.2.3.3 Promotors

Promotors are members of an organization "who actively and intensively support innovation processes" (Witte 1977, p. 53). Opposed to the "great-man theory" of generalized champions (Schon 1973; Howell et al. 2005; Lam 2005) where one single star individual is supposedly determining the success of innovation, the promotor theory disagrees to this proposition by claiming that a group of "several different kinds of specialized promotors" (Rost et al. 2007, p. 341) can only commonly cross the barriers of decision making that hinder successful innovations. Typically, four different barriers exist within an organization, which Hauschildt (1998) describes as psychological barriers of "not-wanting", cognitive barriers of "not-knowing", organizational barriers of "not being permitted to" and financial barriers of "not being able to". These barriers have been observed within firms. On the one hand, an open source community faces similar barriers that can potentially slow down the innovation process. On the other hand, there are differences between a firm and an OSS community with regards to the barriers. Taking all these barriers of innovation within an organization into account, it is hardly imaginable that one single person can manage all the resulting problems. Thus, the promotor's literature has identified certain roles of individuals within firms that can help to specifically address the respective barriers.

The literature of promotors distinguishes among four principle types of promotors: the power-, expert-, process- and relationship-promotors (Hauschildt and Witte 1999; Walter and Gemünden 2000). The power promotors have the hierarchical power to make decisions and can be regarded as more skilful opinion leaders with focus on the implementation of concepts. Such individuals are in a position to counter psychological and/or financial barriers or blocking parties by raising sanctions or overruling them. Expert promotors are individuals that advance an innovation process by means of their "object-specific expertise" (Hauschildt and Gemünden 1998). Their omnipotent knowledge is ideal for eliminating barriers "not knowing". They can grasp problems easily and are fast in finding the right solutions. An additional key characteristic of an expert promotor is that she or he is capable of motivating others. Process promotors have an extensive and broad knowledge of the organization and manage to surmount organizational and administrative barriers. These employees are described as being socially competent and very knowledgeable regarding the processes and values of the organization. In addition, those employees are usually well-connected and frequently interacting among different parties. They are "interfacing within the organizational structures, e.g., as project leader[s] . . . [and] mediate between involved and affected parties" (Rost et al. 2007, p. 344). Relationship promotors have similar skills compared to process promotors but are focused on inter-organizational barriers, dealing primarily with partner firms or suppliers. They have an excellent network that helps them to overcome psychological and inter- and intra-organizational boundaries. They foster relationships by using their network to set up contacts and bringing together the right people in the right situation.

The scope of activity of promotors is within a company (except for the relationship promotors). Barriers are mostly created by co-workers "who either do not want the innovation or are not capable of implementing it" (Rost et al. 2007, p. 341). This is to some extent different in OSS environments given the principle philosophy of commonly developing a product and the fast pace of putting out new versions of products. This will by nature reduce the probability of community members that reject and block ideas from other members. However, that does not mean that OSS communities will not face critical situations. The challenges will be for example to organize a large number of potential developers, identify the best human resources needed to produce high quality products, balance the large number of opinions, keep the momentum going within the community or filter the right information in an appropriate time. For all these challenges it is helpful to learn from the previous findings on the roles and associated functions of promotors and to mirror these to the case of MOI.

10.2.4 Research Questions, Propositions and Hypotheses

In order to be able to conduct research on the functions and activity patterns of MOI, it is essential to create a sharp description and characterization of the term MOI as well as challenge the current definition of MOI as employees that are "strategically assigned" to participate in OSS communities (Dahlander and Wallin 2006). Thus, our first research question and proposition is:

> *RQ1a: What types of MOI exist and is their activity intentional or emergent from the company's perspective?*
> *P1: Firms strategically assign MOI to participate in communities (Dahlander/Wallin 2006)*

We have learned that MOI are important factors to establish and flourish an open source community. However, little is known about the exact functions that are being executed by MOI. They span boundaries of the organization and act as interfaces between their firm and the community facing certain barriers of innovation, which leads to the second research question and proposition.

> *RQ1b: What are the different functions/ capabilities of MOI?*
> *P2: MOI carry functions/ capabilities that are similar to those of boundary spanners (Aldrich/Herker 1977) and promotors (Witte 1973; Rost et al. 2007)*

Besides of knowing what the capabilities of MOI are, it is also important to observe how and to what extent these capabilities are being applied in the open source communities. Interviews have been applied to study which capabilities MOI obtain in open source communities, asking the management as well as the MOI themselves. In alignment with the principle that case studies should incorporate various perspectives to explore and understand a phenomenon, it is also reasonable to incorporate the community perspective. We are using a netnographic analysis of the forum posts in order to qualitatively detect MOI's actual capability patterns within the open source community. Consequently, our third research question is:

> *RQ1c: How can the capability patterns of MOI be described?*

Since, to our knowledge, the capability patterns in virtual communities (a fortiori the forum communication of firm employees in open source communities) is a novel approach in research, no propositions nor hypotheses were derived for the third research question.

All these three research questions were designed to shape a more precise definition on MOI and their specific functions as well as activity patterns in the OSS community. Moreover, it is also important to observe whether MOI are *successful* in what they are doing in these communities. As previously explained, valuable resources are being produced in an OSS community and it is the task of MOI to unlock these resources. Following Dahlander's and Wallin's approach (2006) to measure the influence of MOI by analyzing the SNA in the mailing list communication of the GNOME project, we are testing the differences between the firm's MOI and other groups within the open source community along five categories of which four (the degree-centrality, information provision, prestige and boundary spanning) have been applied in their study as well. In addition to the degree centrality, we have added the betweenness centrality as another centrality measure and the contribution in forum posts or in form of direct product enhancements (patches, projects, bug reports, etc.). We separated the analysis into two main blocks. The first block is intended to test whether the firm's MOI are able to *build resources*, in form of the five measures described above, more significantly than other groups whereas the second block aims to examine whether the firm's employees are able to *build* stronger *relations* with important community members. The relations can also be described as social capital and thus a resource. However, it is a specific form of a resource, which is why we have alienated it here from the first five hypotheses H1-H5 (building resources) and put the hypotheses H6–10 regarding the building of relations in a separate block. As a result our final research question and associated hypotheses are as follows:

> RQ2: *How do MOI succeed in building resources and relations in communities?*

10.2.4.1 Building Resources

At this point it is necessary to introduce the distinction of internal and external MOI. Internal MOI are coming from the sponsoring firm whereas external MOI are deployed by firms that do not own or sponsor the investigated community. Internal MOI have, compared to external MOI and hobbyists, higher values in terms of . . .

> H1–5: *. . . (1) total degree and betweenness centrality, (2) information provision, (3) prestige, (4) internal boundary spanning, (5) contributions*

10.2.4.2 Building Relations

Compared to external MOI and hobbyists, internal MOI are capable of building stronger ties with community members who are . . .

> H6–10: *. . . (6) most central, (7) strongest information providers, (8) most prestigious, (9) strongest boundary spanners (i.e. integrators), (10) strongest innovators/contributors*

10.3 Methodology

10.3.1 Multilevel Case Study Approach

A multilevel case study approach has been selected in which the OSS communities represent the cases or in other words the higher-level of analysis but the IMOI constitute the lower-level of analysis because the outcome of the community, ergo higher-level (which is the overall software products), is a result of a very complex accumulation of interactions and exchanges on the individual level, ergo lower-level. An OSS community is composed of many individuals that commonly shape an individual innovation culture. In order to understand which patterns and factors have contributed to the emergence and sustainability of a community, it is inevitable to understand the underlying components and patterns of its social network. Gupta et al. (2007) even refer to networks as a prototypical case for a bottom-up emerging process (specifically a compilation-emergent phenomenon) because the overall pattern of a network requires an in-depth understanding on the individual actors, in form of their network position (approximated in the centrality for instance), for instance. Additionally, we are using the *firm*'s lens which is why we focus our lower-level of analysis particularly on *firm's* MOI.

The overall goal of conducting an empirical study on multiple levels was to obtain a deeper understanding on the network cohesion. In order to be able to learn about a network's cohesion, it is necessary to understand the constructs, i.e. the network actors, underlying that network. We intended to apply the methods of SNA in order to understand these underlying patterns of the sub-components in the network. In our case these are the community members on an individual level. The cohesion of a network evolves whenever ties among actors in the network are formed (Wassermann and Faust 1994). A SNA can provide valuable insights to the quantitative patterns of the embeddedness of individual actors as well as actor groups. However, it cannot explain *how* certain ties are formed. In our study on IMOI, we are observing a contemporary phenomenon with the main goal to obtain an in-depth understanding on the functions and behavioral patterns of IMOI. In order to incorporate different perspectives in doing so, multiple methods are combined; including interviews with managers and IMOI themselves (addresses research question 1a and 1b), social network analysis on the activity patterns of IMOI (addresses research question 2), statistics (addresses research question 2) and netnographic analysis (addresses research question 1c) (Figures 10.1–10.4). Regarding the types of research questions, 1a and 1b are explorative and 1c and 2 are explanatory and thus fit to the typical application field of case studies. Finally, a control over the behavioral events is not given nor required in the respective empirical studies.

The identification process of cases included the creation of a database, definition of criteria and verification of a general fit. Using the t3n[1] ranking, the leading OSS firms have been identified. A database with information on the community size (i.e. number of members, # posts), community start date, the license type(s) chosen, firm presence, number of employees and availability of communication channels were gathered on the respective websites. We have defined seven criteria for the OSS communities that were mandatory for being a potential candidate in our empirical studies (domain of content management systems (CMS), existence of a professional organization behind the community, usage of an OS license,[2] availability of forum and contribution data, existence of community for at least three years and at least 3,000 community members). Finally, the firms were asked whether they employed MOI in the community. Only if a general fit of these seven criteria were given, the firms were asked to participate in our studies. A short-list of 14 potential OSS communities was created of which two, SilverStripe and eZ, were willing to participate in our studies and provide us with the community data and interview partners. The Norwegian company *eZ Systems* headquartered in Oslo exists since 1999 with subsidiaries in Germany, France, USA and Japan, employing around 70 employees. They

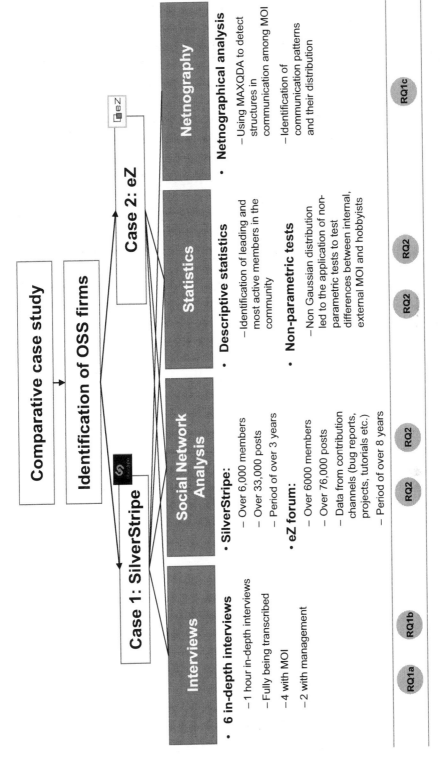

Figure 10.1 Methodological framework

provide a content management system (CMS), named "eZ Publish" with focus on enterprise solutions. SilverStripe Limited is an OSS company head-quartered in Wellington, New Zealand with subsidiaries in Auckland and Australia, employing around 50 people. SilverStripe's transformed from a closed to an open source business model. Initially, they started with propri-etary CMS products designed to run on the open source platform.

10.3.2 Semi-Structured Interviews

Altogether six semi-structured interviews (Wengraf 2001; Drever 1995) were conducted, four with SilverStripe employees and two with eZ employ-ees (management as well as from the group of IMOI). The reason for choos-ing IMOI as well as CEO as interview partners was that both perspectives were necessary to create a sharper picture on the phenomenon of IMOI. In fact, some questions could better be answered by the CEO and others by IMOI. One example for a question that could better by answered by the CEO was the interview question "*What objectives do companies pursue by placing MOI in communities?*" whereas the question "*How much do you collaborate with your colleagues (online and offline)?*" was specifically targeted at IMOI. The SilverStripe interviews took place in Wellington/ New Zealand in April 2010 and the interviews with eZ took place in Frank-furt/ Germany in September 2010. Each interview lasted 1 hour. They were conducted separately with each of the six interviewees in order to avoid bias from the responses of the interviewees. Two sets of interview questions were prepared, one for the CEOs and the other for the MOI. The prepared questions posed to eZ were identical with those of SilverStripe. In general the interview questions addressed research question 1a and 1b regarding the types of MOI and their specific functions. All interviews were audio-recorded and then fully transcribed. The interviews were then screened and analyzed according to the respective research questions. In case of the func-tions of MOI, the relevant parts of the interviews in which functions of MOI were described were coded and then allocated to the five capability patterns. Altogether, 17 codes of MOI "sub"-capabilities were found. Three scholars that were asked to independently allocate the 17 "sub"-capabilities to the five major categories. An inter-rater reliability was satisfactory achieving a rate of 94%. Differential opinions were aligned by means of a more in-depth study of the major categories from the original literature on bound-ary spanners and promotors and were then determined by a reconcilement process.

10.3.3 Netnographical Screening of Forum Posts

The firm SilverStripe has provided us with full forum communication including all post contents in electronically documented form. The Silver-Stripe forum is divided into four main topic categories, which are further segmented into a total of 20 subsections. We have conducted a system-atic screening of all forum posts coming from SilverStripe MOI since the inception of the new forum structure which covers a 9-months period (December 2008 until August 2009). During this period, 14 members of the SilverStripe team (the MOI) were actively involved in the forum. Seven of them had at least 10 posts, being responsible for the production of 1191 posts, compared to a total of 1785 members of the community who contributed 15,200 posts (310 members, given a threshold of at least 10 posts) during this 9-month period.

In order to act upon the large amounts of posts in online communities, posts should be categorized according to relevance (Kozinets 2002). The focus of this netnographic analysis is to obtain a better understanding on MOI's communication and capability patterns not only from a quantitative but also from a qualitative perspective. By qualitative we mean to delve into the contents of the forum posts in order to understand what MOI are talking about, how this adheres to their capabilities and in what frequency this occurs. Thus, all MOI posts were read and manually classified into different categories. Following the approach of Füller et al. (2007) on their research on innovation creation in online basketball communities, we chose to take a similar approach which included the compilation of a list of characteristics that account for "creative and innovative" community members and then the subsequent analysis (Amabile 1996). In similar manner, the posts were abstracted to a more general level and then allocated to the next higher level, which was the list of capabilities that have resulted from the interviews on capabilities of MOI. The process of building the netnographic database was divided into three process steps: (1) Filtering: The posts of firm MOI were identified through their identification numbers (which could be allocated to whether they are firm MOI or not) and filtered. These posts and all associated data to that post (content of post, date, ID of poster and forum levels) were then imported to the MAXQDA software program. (2) Reading and coding: The posts have been read by a student[3] who was familiar with the technical terminology used in the CMS communities. Simultaneously, each post was directly classified to an overarching topic, which we named "coding". That declaration process was iterative which means that anytime that the reader could not find a common level of abstraction for a post; a new overarching topic was created. Altogether, 42 codings or overarching topics were constructed. (3) Allocating to capabilities: The 42 codings were then allocated to the 17 sub-capabilities and hence to the associated 5 core capabilities that have resulted from the interviews. In the process of allocation, three scholars were involved. The 42 codings were independently assigned to the 17 sub-capabilities by each scholar. Overall, 41 out of 42 codings were unanimously allocated to the 17 sub-capabilities, reaching an inter-rater-reliability of 97.6%. The different opinions were aligned by means of a more in-depth discussion among the three raters. Finally, each post was labeled according to the capability categories for further analyses.

10.3.4   Social Network Analysis

Often the goal of a SNA is to identify leading individuals or groups of individuals in a network. Since terms like leading, important or prestigious are somewhat vague, many suggestions of writers have been developed to find central actors and groups within networks.

10.3.4.1   Indegree, Outdegree and Prestige

In our case of forum data, the indegree of a node is the sum of replies that node receives for all his or her initial posts from all other community members. If that individual posts to his own initial thread, this would be counted as a self-loop which would neither be counted as outdegree nor indegree. All the replies that this individual gives in the forum data to all other community members' initial threads would add up to his or her outdegree. Prestige is defined as the quotient of in- and out-degree (Wassermann and Faust 1994). Receiving more in- than outdegree in relation is regarded as prestigious in this context.

10.3.4.2   Centrality

The focus of this work is to identify individuals (or actors) in a network. Centrality can be calculated in various ways. Wassermann and Faust (1994) propose four major types of centrality measures: degree, betweenness, closeness and information. In this work, we will use the total degree centrality and the betweenness centrality. The reason for choosing two different centrality measures is that they represent two different groups of centrality measures. Centrality measures can either account for a node's direct or indirect impact in a network. The former category (degree centrality) solely considers the degrees (typically number of contacts) that are directly adjacent to a node whereas the latter (betweenness, closeness and information) includes the paths adjacent to a node which represent the reach of a node in a network. We chose the degree and betweenness centrality in our study.

10.3.4.3   Internal Boundary Spanning Value

Following the concept of knowledge brokers (Burt 2005), the transfer of ideas and experiences across boundaries is an important process. There are various realms of knowledge that can be spanned, ranging from intra- to inter-organizational interrelations. In their conference paper on "communication and boundary spanning in . . . firm-hosted communities" Dahlander and Frederiksen (2007, p. 1) have introduced the internal and external boundary spanning values. They argue that "different ways of spanning different boundaries influence the communication patterns in the focal online community" (Dahlander and Frederiksen 2007, p. 5). The internal boundary spanning refers to the conveyance of different "technological domains", or more precisely the participation "in different specialized forums within the community". In contrast, the external boundary spanning involves the crossing of "organizational boundaries". This can include the involvement in several firms and/or communities and concurrently taking bridging functions between the organizational boundaries.

IMOI are on the one hand external boundary spanners as they are the bridge between firm and community. On the other hand, they are also internal boundary spanners, moving across the boundaries within the OSS community. They participate in various discussions, reply to questions, integrate ideas and opinions and organize the product development processes. Meanwhile they are increasing their social capital and build their individual and in parallel the firm's knowledge base. Spanning the virtual boundaries is a valuable resource because it implies that the boundary spanner knows about problems that "may have been solved elsewhere" in the community and thus can save time and efforts be referring the archived discussion and avoiding redundant work (Dahlander and Frederiksen 2007). Following Dahlander's and Frederiksen's (2007) calculation method, we applied the internal boundary spanning (IBS) in this study.

10.3.4.4 *Contributions*

In an OSS community, members can contribute in different ways. The simplest form of contribution is simply the participation in a community. Typically, members would sign up in a community and then join the discussions by wither initiating conversations by posting a question (often referred to as "thread") or by answering questions or commenting on other posts. These activities would all take part in the forums of a community. Besides the forums, other channels of interaction enable more sophisticated forms of contribution. Examples would be translations, tutorials, bug reports, comments on bud reports or patches/fixes. These are all activities that usually require some more effort, expertise or level of usage compared to the forum activities. If somebody helps out on translating the product menu for instance to another language, he needs to have the cognitive social capital, which would of course be to speak the respective language and know the specific vocabulary. Another example for the prerequisite of obtaining a wider level of expertise would be the case of contributing patches/fixes. Patches or fixes are pieces of software, typically in form of programming codes, which are supposed to fix a software problem or improve the usability of software products. Not anybody is capable is providing such contributions. Hence, these contributors are very valuable and essential members of an OSS community.

10.3.5 *Statistical Testing (Non-Parametric Tests)*

In order to select appropriate statistical tests, we have analyzed the distribution of the forum and contribution data of all community members. We have plotted all dependent variables- centrality (degree and betweenness), information provision, prestige, internal boundary spanning and contributions- that were supposed to be incorporated in our statistical tests using the Q-Q plot[4] function of the program *SPSS Statistics 18* to test whether they follow a normal distribution or not, applying the graphical method to indirectly test the distribution of residue e by testing whether the distribution of the dependent variables follow a Gaussian curve (Tabachnick et al. 2001; Schmidt 2010). Overall it was found that none of the categories, neither from SilverStripe nor eZ, followed a normal distribution. The continuous line represents the expected values in case of a normal distribution of data. The dots show the actual values in the respective categories. A clear deviation of actual and expected values occur which concludes that all independent variables from SilverStripe and eZ do not follow a Gaussian distribution.

Non-parametric tests are applicable for numerical and non-numerical data independent of the data-distribution. Because of its independence of numerical data, non-parametric tests are often referred to as "ranking tests" or "order tests" (Siegel 1957). Indeed, many non-parametric tests utilize the ranking positions of data points for the analysis. Distances within observed groups will be compared to those of other groups, "following the conceptual framework of ANOVA" (Anderson 2001, p. 33).

Following the results of the data distribution, we applied non-parametric tests in this analysis because (a) the tests are independent of any distribution and thus fit our non-normal distribution of data and (b) the interpretation of transformed tests are cumbersome. As we are comparing three unrelated samples for significant differences among the three groups, IMOI, EMOI and HOB, we have applied the Kruskal-Wallis H-test, followed by the Mann-Whitney U-test.

The limitation of this test is that the distances of values are not taken into account in non-parametric tests. Also sample sizes of the respective groups should be at least 5[5] if not better 20 should be given (Anderson 2001; Field 2009).

10.3.6 *Data Collection and Processing (SNA & Statistics)*

Three major sets of data—(1) basic information, (2) forum data and (3) contribution data—have been collected from SilverStripe and eZ to analyze the activity patterns of the communities. The two firms have run data queries from their IT systems which record and archive the entire movements in the community. Each movement (e.g. a post or a contribution) can then be traced back to an individual. The vast databases comprise over 110,000 posts of over 12,000 community members since the inception of each of the communities until the date of data query in 2010.

10.3.6.1 *Basic Information*

The basic information database contains information on an individual basis on the date of joining the community, identification code of the individual (i.e. ID code number, nickname, and email address), email address domain,

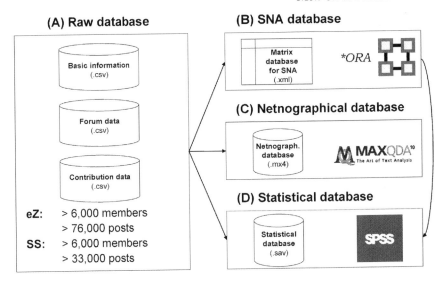

Figure 10.2   Overview of empirical databases

employment status (only if employed to the sponsoring firm) and community rank. By using the email address domains, we were able to identify MOI types. When an email address had the domain of SilverStripe or eZ, these community members were labeled IMOI. If the domain belonged to a corporate site, the community member was labeled EMOI[6] (Dahlander and Wallin 2006). The remainders were non-corporate sites, which are typically webmail providers such as Google mail or Yahoo. In this case the community member was categorized hobbyist.

10.3.6.2   Forum Data

The forum data is fundament for the social network analyses because it captures the communicative interactions among community members in the forum. The forum data contains different information per post such as the post identification number, the forum topic titles and IDs,[7] date and time of post, member ID of poster, the content of the post, the length of the post (number of characters), the number of views and the member ID of the initiator of the respective post.

10.3.6.3   Contributions

Under the term contribution, we have summarized any activity in the community that is directly related to the enhancement of a product. Typically these could be patches, bug reports, or any additional add-ons or product features that are intended to increase the quality, performance and application range of the product. For various contributions we have gathered information on topic, member ID of contributor and date of release. Also we have asked the firm to provide us with a rough ranking of the different contribution categories in order to be able to calculate a contribution score that provides an approximation for the overall contribution of an individual.

Three further databases were created with the raw data. The first database, the matrix database, was necessary for the SNA. The second database, the netnographic database, has been used for detecting the qualitative patterns of IMOI's capabilities based on the results from the interviews. The third database contains the data for the descriptive statistics as well as the statistical tests.

10.4   Results

In the introductory part of this study, we have depicted that the overarching goal of this study is to create a better understanding on the phenomenon of MOI. In particular, the three research objectives have been defined.

10.4.1   Types and Capabilities of Men on the Inside

Regarding the first objective, which was to obtain a better understanding on IMOI's specific functions in building and growing a virtual community, this study has pointed out that different types of MOI exist. More precisely, we have found that four different types of MOI exist of which not all are strategically assigned. The MOI can be classified along two dimensions—the community affiliation (internal, external) and the strategic alignment

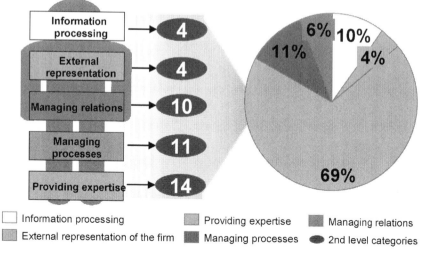

Figure 10.3   Distribution of five core capabilities (classified by forum posts of IMOI)

(emergent, intentional). Investigating *internal* MOI's capabilities, we were able to observe five major capability categories (and 42 sub-categories) that are decisive for nurturing an OSS community. These capabilities bear a significant resemblance to the extant literature on roles of boundary spanners and promotors. The most frequently occurring capability category was "providing expertise" (69% of IMOI's posts), followed by "managing processes" (11%), "information processing" (10%), "managing relations" (6%) and "external representation of the firm" (4%). However, the "information provision" is a category that typically takes place offline the forum interactions which was the source for the netnographic analysis. Around three quarters of the IMOI's posts were devoted to supporting customers in early stages of community involvement and the remaining quarter of posts were devoted to more advanced projects with focus on the product development of software.

10.4.2   Ability of Men on the Inside to Build Resources in Virtual Communities

Addressing the second research objective, which was to investigate IMOI's ability to influence the integrity and cohesion of OSS community networks in various channels of communication (by building resources in form of social capital in the community), IMOI succeeded in occupying positions in the networks that allow them to become influential participants. They manage to obtain very central (degree) positions in open source communities and to be important participants in networks of highly frequented communication. Thus, IMOI succeed in building social capital (in form of degree centrality) for the firm, even significantly more successful than EMOI and HOB.

We used the following methodology for the SNA:

SNA methodology

- Node: Community member
- Link: If A posts (subsequently) to an initial post of B
- Indegree: Sum of posts received
- Outdegree: Sum of posts sent
- Node color: Type of community member (internal, external MOI, hobbyist)
- Node size: Sum of total degree centraliy

The visualized social networks of SilverStripe and eZ (Figure 10.4) are quite similar. In the centre of the networks, the interaction among community members is high (represented by high occurrences of ties). In contrary, the ring surrounding the centre consists of isolated nodes. Those isolated nodes represent members that do not actively participate in the community. The reasons could be either that it is an inactive account or that the community member is a lurker (Preece et al. 2004; Nonnecke and Preece 2001; Nonnecke and Preece 2001). When zooming into the centre of the network, it is conspicuous that the IMOI obtain central positions in both networks.

The core difference among the two communities is that the share of EMOI (blue nodes) is higher in the eZ network (Figure 10.5). This can be explained by the fact that eZ's focus is strongly relying upon "enterprise open source" which obviously has been implemented successfully. It is indicative that those EMOI are very well represented in the core of the network.

Among the top 20 community members in terms of total degree centrality, SilverStripe employees (7 members/ 35%) as well as eZ employees (5 members/ 25%) are very present, especially given the fact that the overall share of IMOI's population is less than 1% in both communities.

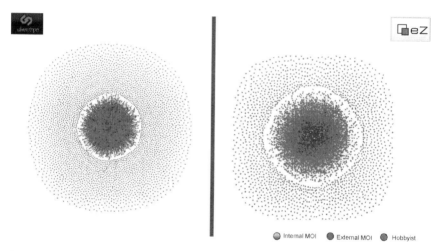

Figure 10.4 SNA of SilverStripe and eZ based on forum communication

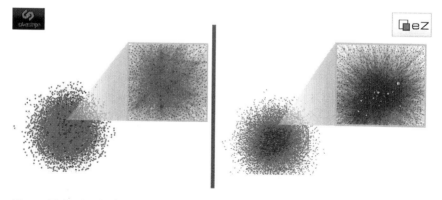

Figure 10.5 SNA of SilverStripe and eZ based on forum communication (zoomed)

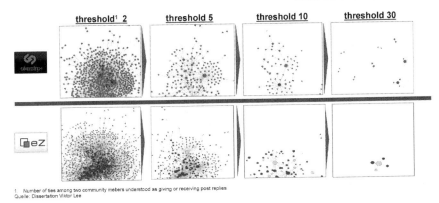

threshold¹ 2   threshold 5   threshold 10   threshold 30

1   Number of ties among two community mebers understood as giving or receiving post replies
Quelle: Dissertation Viktor Lee

Figure 10.6   SNA of SilverStripe and eZ based on forum communication (higher threshold)

With an increasing threshold[8] among two nodes (Figure 10.6), the relative share of IMOI increases even stronger. This means that in networks that have high frequencies of communication, IMOI remain important participants who are capable of establishing relations with other highly active members in the network.

The same findings result for betweenness centrality and information provision. In case of the eZ community we could confirm *significant* results also for all other the categories including prestige, internal boundary spanning[9] and contributions. In contrast, in case of SilverStripe, significantly higher tendencies of IMOI were only observed for prestige over EMOI and contributions over HOB. In all categories except for prestige, IMOI obtain the highest mean ranks.

In terms of absolute numbers, the contributions to enhance software are dominated by externals. To achieve significant contributions of external volunteers is one of the main ambitions that firms with OSS business models have. As mentioned above, the only category led by external community members is prestige. The prestige is the quotient of indegree and outdegree. It is not very surprising that externals outperform IMOI in this category given the strong dominance of IMOI regarding information provision (=outdegree). Since the inception of the communities, the overall prestige curves of IMOI are smaller than 1 and the exact contrary picture for externals (prestige above 1). This confirms the finding that IMOI heavily provide their expertise to support and service the external community members in order for them to appreciate the received value from the community and potentially become a more active member and contributor of the community.

When excluding lurkers from the statistical tests, IMOI still remain the strongest group regarding centrality (degree and betweenness), information provision, internal boundary spanning and contributions. Regarding the prestige the results again confirm that IMOI are less prestigious than the externals. In case of eZ, all results were significant while in case of SilverStripe all categories excepting IBS and contributions were significant, too.

10.4.3   Ability of Men on the Inside to Build Relations in Virtual Communities

Finally, the third research objective incorporated to examine IMOI's ability to build stronger bonds with all top performers in terms of centrality (degree and betweenness), information provision, prestige, boundary spanning and contribution in the network. We find that IMOI succeeded in creating stronger bonds, or in other higher mean tie weights, with the top performers in all categories compared to EMOI and HOB. In case of eZ, all categories even showed significant tendencies of IMOI in terms of higher tie weights with the top performers. In the SilverStripe community, the mean ranks for tie weights of IMOI was significantly higher compared to those of HOB but not compared to the EMOI only in the IBS category. The result implies that IMOI are aware of who is valuable for the community and shows that they are capable of keeping a high exchange of communication activities with the valuable community members. Being able to network with these community members is a true asset for a firm as the creativeness and innovativeness of the products often come from a few talented volunteers and keeping the talent within the community is what ascertains a firm's sustained competitive advantage.

10.5   Discussion and Conclusions

10.5.1   Contribution to the Literature

The modern management of innovation is a global challenge in dynamically changing environments. Firms face an increasing pressure on reducing costs and time-to-markets but are concurrently requested to improve the product quality. Thus, they need to look for alternative sources of innovation and leaner structures as well as processes that help them to achieve sustained competitive advantage. We have learned that open source innovation can be a proven path in this context, offering potentials to reduce costs and improve quality and customer loyalty simultaneously. However, the anti-commercial history and culture of the open source movement might exclude firms to gain full access to these sources. This study has investigated successful cases of firms running under open source business models. These firms did not only have a open source business model, but more remarkably they have managed to sponsor and flourish their *own* OSS communities with thousands of active community members that are permanently thriving the products of the firms. Hence, the first and most obvious implication on the research on innovation management is the reconcilability of open source and commercialization despite the

seemingly contradictive ethics. Not only the firm participation in externally sponsored communities (such as the GNOME project, cf. Dahlander
and Wallin [2006]) can be fruitful but the foundation of entirely owned
community, too. Certainly, the process of creating, growing and sustain-
ing an agile community is long and challenging and the vast majority of
communities fail.

It is the key individuals, mostly professionally staffed software developers in the case of OSS communities (Healy and Schussman 2003), that open
the doors to the World of OSS community for the firms. Once, the access
is given, the firms will be in a position to benefit from the knowledge and
ideas as well as the working power of volunteers who partially even help
to produce and implement the ideas (e.g. programming of software code or
creation of complementary product modules/extensions).

> *"you get more diversity and quality with the community . . . [and
> around] ninety percent of [contributions] come from the community."*
> MOI#1 of SilverStripe

Our study has shown that IMOI are viable strategic instruments that
are capable of managing and coordinating the "development and implementation of new ideas by people who over time engage in transactions
with others within an institutional context" (Van de Ven 1986)- or in
other words IMOI are able to manage the innovation processes in OSS
communities on behalf of their firms. The findings to the question on
how firms can actually influence open source environments has shown
that the capabilities on the individual level of IMOI are the conditional
enablers for creating strategically important positions in the network,
and thus on the higher organizational levels. These capabilities match
the functions of boundary spanners and promotors. The IMOI build
resources, in form of social capital and knowledge inflow, which are on
the one hand absorbed internally and on the other hand returned to the
community in order to accelerate the interaction and thus the growth of
the community network.

Following Locke and Golden-Biddle's (1997) framework on scientific
contribution opportunities for articles, the findings of this study on MOI
can be positioned to adding to the incomplete literature in various streams
by using synthesized coherence. The typology of MOI expands the term
of Dahlander and Wallin (2006) by classifying these individuals into more
granular levels incorporating their community affiliation and strategic
alignment as proposed dimensions of distinction. The chosen case studies
have deliberately been on (single) firm-sponsored communities to focus on
an under-developed area in the literature of OSI. The in-depth understanding on IMOI's functions as well as the findings on the capability patterns of
IMOI in the community are also conducive to the OSI literature by creating
a detailed view on IMOI's activity patterns. The exact functions of IMOI

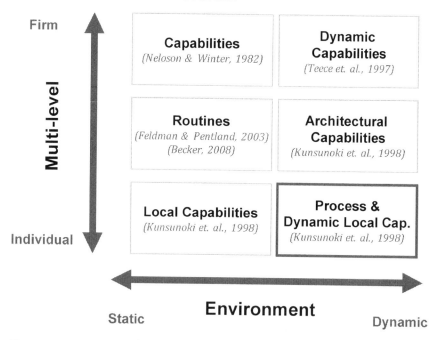

Figure 10.7 Capabilities framework

that have been observed by analyzing their daily activities over a long period of time as well as the qualitatively exploration of qualitative communication patterns, are novel. The literature on dynamic capabilities has been synthesized with concepts on key individuals in the innovation process, i.e. boundary spanning and promotors literature. The micro level research on capabilities is a neglected area and this study redounds to the micro level perspectives in the dynamic capabilities literature by combining existing conceptual frameworks (Kusunoki et al. 1998; Salvato and Rerup 2010) and allocating the under-developed areas. The capabilities of IMOI can be interpreted as the dynamic capabilities on the individual level. This study is distinct from other studies in the way that we are qualitatively identifying the exact capabilities of the individuals in their virtual domains of communication and in a second step, the actual capabilities are quantitatively measured.

The findings derived from research question 2 have shown that internal MOI can strategically increase the social capital of firms in various categories. Apart from that the examination of activity patterns in different channels of communication (forums and software contribution) is unique and harmonizes with previous findings on (external) MOI. We have incorporated not only the SNA perspective but also asked the management and internal MOI on their roles and influence on the cohesion and integrity on their OSS communities. Finally, the study proposes the measurement of community member value (CMV):

$$CMV_i(t) = \int_0^t \left(\propto_1 f_1(t) + \propto_2 f_2(t) + \propto_3 f_3(t) + \ldots + \propto_n f_n(t) \right) dt \qquad (1)$$

with
i = individual community member
t = period of time
α = weighting coefficient
f = single measurement category (e.g. degree centrality, prestige, IBS)

which brings new perspective on the interpretation of social networks because, the approach implies that:

a. an integrated dynamic perspective (t) in analyzing social networks on individual basis (i) is important
b. a customized perspective can mirror the analyzer's individual interest (α) more accurately and
c. a single measurement category (f) (e.g. degree centrality or prestige) may not be sufficient for the interpretation of a network and its participants.

A similar scoring system has actually been applied at one of the collaborating firms in this study with the aim to identify valuable community members. This helps the firm to increase the alertness of who is contributing most to the community but also as a motivation tool for community members that captures a fair approximation of the degree of contribution of an individual und thus increase her or his reputation in the community.

10.5.2 Recommendations for Managerial Practice

Statistically speaking, there is a high risk of failure (>99%) in terms of the foundation of an OSS community (Healy and Schussman 2003; Krogh 2006). It is quite difficult to attract people to participate and contribute to communities. However, the few successful projects are mostly led or sponsored by firms deploying their professional staff. The OSS communities being investigated in this work are firm-sponsored communities that employ personnel to spend parts of their working hours to participate in the firm's OSS community. Hence, the viewpoint of this research is that of a firm potentially considering to enter and adopt the open source business model. It is our purpose to extract implications from this study that practitioners can learn and potentially benefit from. Both OSS firms in this study, SilverStripe and eZ, are leading providers of OSS in their domain. Understanding their success models and learning on what has been done in order to create their prosperous communities, might be useful for practitioners that consider to create their own open source community or deploy personnel to participate in networks of social interactions. The general field of application of IMOI as firm's tools to implement their strategy in social networks (Gangi and Wasko 2009) is broad, ranging from cognate domains,[10] contiguous domains[11] to distant domains.[12] The rapid growth of virtual platforms for communication and collaboration craves for facilitators to organize and manage these unacquainted virtual rooms. The employment of IMOI is a key success factor to grow and develop an OS community. As shown in our SNA analysis, firms can strategically influence OS communities via IMOI who manage to secure central positions in the community networks. We have shown that value in social networks can have many facets. The participation of firms have different strategic facets and related expectation for the creation of value behind the participation in open source communities or even the creation of their own open source community. Here is an overview of potential targets:

1. Outsourcing labor/ cost reduction: We have observed that external community members have actually contributed significantly to the firm's products. The range of contribution varies, of course. Sometimes it is the complaint about a clumsy installation process. Another time it can be the complete translation or programming of product. In any case, people are spending their free time in the development and take over parts of the firm's working tasks. In a study on the impact of FLOSS applications, it is estimated that FLOSS impacted the software industry in such a way that potential savings in the R&D reached around 36% (Ghosh 2006).
2. Decrease time-to-market: An open source community is a global and thus twenty-four-seven working construct. Active communities are permanently working on the development of products. However, the coordination of a globally present community can also bear enormous challenges. In the case of OScar (open source car),[13] for instance, the first launch failed due to the under-estimated administrative and technical complexity of the project. Still today, the production of a car developed by the community is far from becoming reality.
3. Increase loyalty/ brand awareness: A community platform can also function as a contact point for customers. The involvement and interaction with customers can also positively affect the firm-customer relation. As shown in the netnographic study, the provision of expertise from IMOI has been the most prolific activity of IMOI in the forums. Thus, the servicing aspect of these communities becomes also obvious. Customers that receive response to their individual questions will be happy customers who might recommend the community to others.
4. Increase closeness/extraction of ideas: Collaborating with customers also means that a higher degree of closeness will be formed. This in turn creates direct access to what the customers think and demand. This is a valuable asset when firms try to better incorporate customer's

need in the implementation of a new product or adjustment of existing products. In fact, the research and development of a product cannot be any closer than integrating the customers themselves in the process.

5. Engage in dynamic environments/increase own awareness of changes: Firms are facing extreme forms of dynamism in some industries as in the case of the software industry. The speed of development often hinders a firm to be able to follow all the latest and newest trends. For example, people started to integrate Facebook functions on the websites. Just as this trend was about to spread, new forms already become trendy, such as linkages with twitter or foursquare. OS communities might also be a good platform to better understand which trends are potentially meaningful for a firm to adopt to and which are not.

6. Demonstrate presence in the open source community: The open source communities and their followers have reached a serious size. Open source applications are ranked first, second or third in market share in various markets including "web servers, server operating systems, desktop operating systems, web browsers, databases, e-mail and other ICT infrastructure systems [reaching higher] market share higher in Europe than in the US for operating systems and PCs, followed by Asia" (Ghosh 2006, p. 9). Being present and offering open source products and services in the software industry is inevitable. A proof for that is that software giants that are known for their proprietary products engage in OSS (Figure 10.8).

The right constitution of the processes involved in open source innovation projects can be divided into two principle phases.

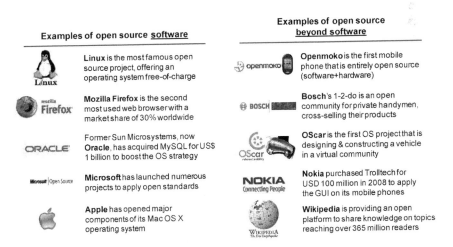

Examples of open source **software**	Examples of open source **beyond software**
Linux is the most famous open source project, offering an operating system free-of-charge	**Openmoko** is the first mobile phone that is entirely open source (software+hardware)
Mozilla Firefox is the second most used web browser with a market share of 30% worldwide	**Bosch's** 1-2-do is an open community for private handymen, cross-selling their products
Former Sun Microsystems, now **Oracle**, has acquired MySQL for US$ 1 billion to boost the OS strategy	**OScar** is the first OS project that is designing & constructing a vehicle in a virtual community
Microsoft has launched numerous projects to apply open standards	**Nokia** purchased Trolltech for USD 100 million in 2008 to apply the GUI on its mobile phones
Apple has opened major components of its Mac OS X operating system	**Wikipedia** is providing an open platform to share knowledge on topics reaching over 365 million readers

Figure 10.8 Examples of open source projects in various industries

First, it is crucial to *grow* a community. This critical phase determines whether at all a community will or can emerge. Nobody wishes to have a community of lurkers or inactivity. As we have detected in our empirical studies, the eZ community was more successful in terms of activity of community members. The share of lurkers in the eZ community was almost 20% lower than in the SilverStripe community. We have shown that EMOI in the eZ community are way more present in the high-density areas of the network. In contrast to SilverStripe, eZ is emphasizing enterprise open source solutions.

Second, the *sustainability* of a community requires alertness of the interaction patterns in that community. In order to be able to adjust the capacity of IMOI correctly, firms need to understand their community structures at any point in time in order to be able adjust accordingly.

Subsequently, we have the following seven recommendations for practitioners building on the managerial implications described above for the growth (1–3) and sustainability phases (4–7):

1. Strategically assign personnel as IMOI according to their field of expertise and ability to socialize; prior experience in OSS communities (communication skills in forums and adequate knowledge on the behavior in virtual communities) are elementary.
2. The knowledge inflow of externals must permanently be higher than the knowledge outflow in the community in order to be successful, especially in the first 1–2 years.
3. EMOI should be addressed differently than hobbyists (channel segmentation) in order to address the different needs of the two groups more precisely and efficiently and improve the orientation for customers by a more lean community structure.
4. IMOI should closely collaborate with management for a more accurate implementation and adjustment of strategy.
5. Monitoring systems to measure the community members value could help to identify key members to strategically strengthen their relation and affiliation to the firm.
6. Monitoring systems to track IMOI's influence in the community help adjusting HR resources in the community in case of under- or overcapacity.
7. Community member values (CMV) customized to the individual needs of a firm help to create precise measures for monitoring systems.

10.5.3 *Limitations and Avenues for Future Research*

We distinguished two conceptual roles that firms and their employees can play in OS communities: First, they can contribute to projects coordinated by other individual or corporate actors; and second, they themselves can act as so-called corporate sponsors (Dahlander and Frederiksen 2007).

Our research has focused on firms sponsoring their own OSS community as instruments and challenges of corporate sponsoring await investigation. Several studies have pointed out that corporate sponsorship of OS projects is a potent antecedent of project success (Dahlander and Wallin 2006; Fitzgerald 2006). Nonetheless, the majority of studies to date focus on community-managed OS projects (West and O'Mahony 2008). This study has aimed navigate towards research that leverages existing theories to advance normative and actionable recommendations for firms. It is on the one hand intended to help companies to determine their best strategy in employing their resources and capabilities requisite to design successful OSS projects and processes and on the other hand can be rewarding from a scholarly perspective.

As this object encompasses a broad scope of potential topic, this study has a number of limitations and offers some implications for future research. First of all, the unit of analysis of this study is solely limited to internal MOI. Despite the fact that other typologies are introduced and described, it does not explore the other MOI types. It would be important to understand why and how external firms deploy their personnel (EMOI) to participate in communities that are sponsored by other firms.

Apart from that, this study is limited to two firms only that are allocated in the same domain and product industry (content management systems). Future research in this area should be on observing larger-scaled cases covering several industrial domains and detecting potential variation among the different industries. It would be interesting to not only consider open source software projects but also open source projects that are beyond the software industry (Raasch et al. 2009). A closer look at whether and how controllable variables such as the governance structures, degree of openness or marketing efforts affect the community sizes is needed in order to derive best practices for practitioners. Since we have obviously only investigated two successful firms that were able to immensely grow and sustain the community over years, it would be worthwhile to also look at why other firms failed in building open source communities. It would be important to understand the main factors that influence externals to either participate or leave a community.

Thus, further research is specifically needed that illuminates the perspectives of hobbyists. How do hobbyists perceive the fact that a firm controls and influences open source communities? Do they appreciate the professionalism or do they have a critical attitude towards the idea of combining open source with commercialization? What are the benefits that they expect from a community what makes them choose to attend them and favor certain communities over others with comparable features?

In this study we have adumbrated that the role of IMOI and advanced community members changes as the community matures. We have shown that it is indicative for successfully growing a community that the prestige values of IMOI are constantly below one whereas the prestige of externals exceeds 1 at any time. Hence, further research is needed that investigates how the roles of IMOI changes and if this has impact on their network position and simultaneously on those of advanced external community members that potentially take over leading roles in the communities. Furthermore there is a gap on in-depth longitudinal studies that unveil the underlying patterns of community interaction and possible changes over time (e.g. changes in the prestige curves of IMOI and external community members). Quantitative studies that examine the correlation of community size and number of IMOI could be helpful to understand if equilibrium exists regarding the ratio of IMOI and community members.

NOTES

1. The t3n ranking (http://t3n.de/opensource/top100/) identifies leading open source providers in various categories through external factors (such as yahoo, API, Google Blog search) and user ratings.
2. Further details on the OSS licenses are available on http://www.opensource.org/licenses/alphabetical
3. Simon Riehm, a diploma student of the Hamburg University of Technology, conducted the screening of the posts as part of the netnographic analysis in his diploma thesis, having gathered experiences in virtual communities prior this study.
4. Plots the quantiles of a variable's distribution against the quantiles of any of a number of test distributions. Probability plots are generally used to determine whether the distribution of a variable matches a given distribution.
5. http://www.le.ac.uk/bl/gat/virtualfc/Stats/kruskal.html.
6. Only if at least two community members from one corporate domain existed.
7. Forums have modular structures which are supposed to help the community member to navigate to their topic of interest in a convenient way. Various levels of content describe the themes of discussion.
8. The weight of a tie. In this case this reflects the sum of in- and outdegrees shared among two nodes. If the threshold is 5, only ties with weights equal or larger than 5 are shown in the network.
9. No significant result for SilverStripe database. However same tendency and ranking order.
10. Other open source software domains, e.g. databases (MySQL, PostgreSQL, Sqlite), office and multimedia (Firefox, OpenOffice, GNOME) or commerce (osCommerce, Magento, Piwik),
11. Open hardware-, open content-, open design-, crowd sourcing-communities.
12. Inter- or intra-firm networks.
13. See article of the *Technology Review*, http://www.heise.de/tr/artikel/Das-offenste-aller-Autos-405340.html.

REFERENCES

Alavi, M., and Leidner, D.E. (2001): "Review: knowledge management and knowledge management systems: conceptual foundations and research issues", *MIS Quarterly* 25, pp. 107–136.

Aldrich, H., and Herker, D. (1977): "Boundary spanning roles and organization structure", *Academy of Management Review* 2, pp. 217–230.

Amabile, T. (1996): *Creativity in context: update to the social psychology of creativity*, Westview, Boulder, CO.

Amit, R., and Shoemaker, P.J. (1993): "Strategic assets and organization rents", *Strategic Management Journal* 14, pp. 33–46.

Anderson, M.J. (2001): "A new method for non parametric multivariate analysis of variance", *Austral Ecology* 26, pp. 32–46.

Burt, R.S. (2005): *Brokerage and closure: an introduction to social capital*, Oxford University Press, Oxford.

Carlile, P.R. (2004): "Transferring, translating, and transforming: an integrative framework for managing knowledge across boundaries", *Organization Science* 15, pp. 555–568.

Cohen, W.M., and Levinthal, D.A. (1990): "Absorptive capacity: a new perspective on learning and innovation", *Administrative Science Quarterly* 35(1), pp. 128–152.

Conner, K.R., and Prahalad, C.K. (1996): "A resource-based theory of the firm: knowledge versus opportunism", *Organization Science* 7, pp. 477–501.

Crowston, K., Annabi, H., and Howison, J. (2003): "Defining open source software project success", in *Proceedings of the International Conference on Information Systems (ICIS 2003)*, December, Seattle, WA.

Dahlander, L., and Frederiksen, L. (2007): "Communication and boundary spanning in a firm-hosted online community", *DRUID Summer Conference on Appropriability, Proximity, Routines and Innovation*, Copenhagen, 18–20 June.

Dahlander, L., and Wallin, M.W. (2006): "A man on the inside: unlocking communities as complementary assets", *Research Policy* 35, pp. 1243–1259.

Dosi, G., and Marengo, L. (1994): "Toward a Theory of organizational competencies", in *Evolutionary concepts in contemporary economics*, R.W. England (ed.), pp. 157–178, University of Michigan Press, Ann Arbor.

Dosi, G., Marengo, L., and Fagiolo, G. (1996): *Learning in evolutionary environments*, International Institute for Applied Systems Analysis, Laxenburg, Austria.

Drever, E. (1995): *Using semi-structured interviews in small-scale research*, Scottish Council for Research in Education, Edinburgh.

Field, A.P. (2009): *Discovering statistics using SPSS*, Sage Publications, London.

Fitzgerald, B. (2006): "The transformation of open source software", *MIS Quarterly* 30, pp. 587–598.

Fransman, M. (1994): 'Information, knowledge, vision and theories of the firm", *Industrial and Corporate Change* 3(3), pp. 713–757.

Friedman, R.A., and Podolny, J. (1992): "Differentiation of boundary spanning roles: labor negotiations and implications for role conflict", *Administrative Science Quarterly* 37(1), pp. 28–47.

Füller, J., Jawecki, G., and Mühlbacher, H. (2007): "Innovation creation by online basketball communities", *Journal of Business Research* 60, pp. 60–71.

Gangi, P.M., and Wasko, M. (2009): "Open innovation through online communities", *Knowledge Management and Organizational Learning* 4, pp. 199–213.

Ghosh, R.A. (2006): *Economic impact of open source software on innovation and the competitiveness of the Information and Communication Technologies (ICT) sector in the EU*, report commissioned by the Commission of the European Union NTR/04/112, http://ec.europa.eu/enterprise/ict/policy/doc/2006-11-20-flossimpact.pdf.

Grant, R.M. (1996): "Toward a knowledge-based theory of the firm", *Strategic Management Journal* 17, pp. 109–122.

Gupta, A.K., Tesluk, P.E., and Taylor, M.S. (2007): "Innovation at and across multiple levels of analysis", *Organization Science* 18, pp. 885–897.

Hauschildt, J. (1998): *Promotoren-Antriebskräfte der Innovation,* University of Klagenfurt, Inst. für Wirtschaftswiss, Klagenfurt.

Hauschildt, J., and Gemünden, H. G. (1998): *Promotoren: Champions der Innovation,* Gabler, Wiesbaden.

Hauschildt, J., and Witte, E. (1999): *Promotoren: Champions der Innovation,* Gabler, Wiesbaden.

Healy, K., and Schussman, A. (2003): "The ecology of open-source software development", Working Paper, Open Source Research Community, January, MIT, Cambridge, MA.

Henderson, R., and Cockburn, I. (1994): "Measuring competence? exploring firm effects in pharmaceutical research", *Strategic Management Journal* 15, pp. 63–84.

Henkel, J. (2008): "Champions of revealing—the role of open source developers in commercial firms", *Industrial and Corporate Change* 18, pp. 435–471.

Howell, J. M., Shea, C. M., and Higgins, C. A. (2005): "Champions of product innovations: defining, developing, and validating a measure of champion behavior", *Journal of Business Venturing* 20, pp. 641–661.

Johnson-Laird, P. N. (1983): *Mental models,* Harvard University Press, Cambridge, MA.

Kahn, R. L., Louis, R., and Katz, D. (1966): *The social psychology of organizations,* Wiley, New York.

Kogut, B., and Zander, U. (1992): "Knowledge of the firm, combinative capabilities, and the replication of technology", *Organization Science* 3(3), pp. 383–397.

Kozinets, R. V. (2002): "The field behind the screen: using netnography for marketing research in online communities", *Journal of Marketing Research* 39, pp. 61–72.

Krogh, G. von (2006): "The HBR list: breakthrough ideas for 2006", *Harvard Business Review,* pp. 35–67. http://companycommand.army.mil/aboutccl/contentFiles/HBR_Feb_2006.pdf. Accessed February 2006.

Kusunoki, K., Nonaka, I., and Nagata, A. (1998): "Organizational capabilities in product development of Japanese firms: a conceptual framework and empirical findings", *Organization Science* 9, pp. 699–718.

Lam, A. (2005): "Work roles and careers of R&D scientists in network organizations", *Industrial Relations: A Journal of Economy and Society* 44(2), pp. 242–275.

Lawrence, P. R., and Lorsch, J. W. (1986[1967]): *Organization and environment: managing differentiation and integration,* Harvard Business School Classics, Harvard Business School Press, Boston.

Leonard-Barton, D. (1992): "Core capabilities and core rigidities: a paradox in managing new product development", *Strategic Management Journal* 13(S1), pp. 111–125.

Locke, K., and Golden-Biddle, K. (1997): "Constructing opportunities for contribution: structuring intertextual coherence and 'problematizing' in organizational studies", *Academy of Management Journal* 40, pp. 1023–1062.

Mahoney, J. T., and Pandian, J. R. (1992): "The resource-based view within the conversation of strategic management", *Strategic Management Journal* 13, pp. 363–380.

Nelson, R. R. (1991): "Why do firms differ, and how does it matter?" *Strategic Management Journal* 12, pp. 61–74.

Nickols, F. (2000): "The knowledge in knowledge management", in *The knowledge management yearbook 2000–2001,* J. W. Cortada and J. A. Woods (eds.), pp. 12–21, Butterworth-Heinemann, Boston.

Nonaka, I. (1994): "A dynamic theory of organizational knowledge creation", *Organization Science* 5, pp. 14–37.

Nonaka, I., and Takeuchi, H. (1995): *The knowledge-creating company: how Japanese companies create the dynamics of innovation,* Oxford University Press, New York.

Nonnecke, B., and Preece, J. (2001): "Why lurkers lurk", Proceedings of the Americas Conference on Information Systems, August, Boston, MA.

Penrose, E., and Pitelis, C. (1959): *The theory of the growth of the firm*, Oxford University Press, Oxford.

Polanyi, M., and Sen, A. (2009): *The tacit dimension*, University of Chicago Press, Chicago.

Preece, J., Nonnecke, B., and Andrews, D. (2004): "The top five reasons for lurking: improving community experiences for everyone", *Computers in Human Behavior* 20, pp. 201–223.

Prencipe, A., and Tell, F. (2001): "Inter-project learning: processes and outcomes of knowledge codification in project-based firms", *Research Policy* 30, pp. 1373–1394.

Raasch, C., Herstatt, C., and Balka, K. (2009): "On the open design of tangible goods", *R&D Management* 39, pp. 382–393.

Rosenkopf, L., and Nerkar, A. (2001): "Beyond local search: boundary spanning, exploration, and impact in the optical disk industry", *Strategic Management Journal* 22, pp. 287–306.

Rost, K., Hölzle, K., and Gemünden, H.-G. (2007): "Promotors or champions? pros and cons of role specialisation for economic process", *Schmalenbach Business Review* 59, pp. 340–363.

Salvato, C., and Rerup, C. (2010): "Beyond collective entities: multilevel research on organizational routines and capabilities", *Journal of Management* 37, p. 468.

Schmidt, A. (2010): "Normalverteilungsannahme und Transformationen bei Regressionen", in *Methodik der empirischen Forschung* (vol. 3), A. Sönke, D. Klapper, U. Konradt, A. Walter, and J. Wolf (eds.), Wiesbaden, Gabler.

Schon, D. A. (1973): "Product champions for radical new innovations", *Harvard Business Review* 5(March/April).

Siegel, S. (1957): "Nonparametric statistics", *American Statistician* 11, pp. 13–19.

Spaeth, S., Stuermer, M., and Krogh, G. von (2010): "Enabling knowledge creation through outsiders: towards a push model of open innovation", *International Journal of Technology Management* 52, pp. 411–431.

Tabachnick, B. G., Fidell, L. S., and Osterlind, S. J. (2001): *Using multivariate statistics*, Allyn and Bacon, Boston.

Teece, D. J., Pisano, G. P., & Shuen, A. (1997): "Dynamic capabilities and strategic management", *Strategic Management Journal* 18, pp. 509–533.

Tushman, M. L. (1977): "Special boundary roles in the innovation process", *Administrative Science Quarterly* 22(4), pp. 587–605.

Tushman, M. L., and Scanlan, T. J. (1981): "Boundary spanning individuals: their role in information transfer and their antecedents", *Academy of Management Journal* 24, pp. 289–305.

Van de Ven, A. H. (1986): "Central problems in the management of innovation", *Management Science* 32, pp. 590–607.

Walter, A., and Gemünden, H. G. (2000): "Bridging the gap between suppliers and customers through relationship promoters: theoretical considerations and empirical results", *Journal of Business and Industrial Marketing* 15(2/3), pp. 86–105.

Wassermann, S., and Faust, K. (1994): *Social network analysis: methods and application*, Cambridge University Press, New York.

Wengraf, T. (2001): *Qualitative research interviewing: biographic narrative and semi-structured methods*, Sage Publications, London.

West, J., and O'Mahony, S. (2008): "The role of participation architecture in growing sponsored open source communities", *Industry and Innovation* 15, pp. 145–168.

Witte, E. (1977): "Power and innovation: a two-center theory", *International Studies of Management & Organization* 7, pp. 47–70.

11 Amplifying User and Producer Innovation
The Power of Participation Motives

Christina Raasch and Eric von Hippel

The motivation to innovate is traditionally assumed to be associated with use or sale of the innovation created—the output. In this chapter we explore benefits from *participation* in the innovation process, such as enjoyment and learning, as an additional motivator. Using data from national representative surveys in the United Kingdom, United States, and Japan, we document that a significant portion of household sector innovation is today motivated by participation benefits rather than output benefits.

We show via a formal model that purposeful and skilled harnessing of participation motives can greatly amplify the range of viable innovations for users and producers. We explain that those who find adequate reward from participation benefits only—pure 'participators'—can be recruited to amplify the total amount of paid and unpaid R&D and innovation carried out by users and producers within the household, business, and government sectors. We discuss important implications for the theory and practice of R&D and innovation.

Acknowledgements: We are always grateful to the members of our Open and User Innovation community. We work closely together, and share the joy of mutually teaching and learning. Specific to this paper, we wish to thank Joana Mendonca, Pedro Oliveira, Jeroen de Jong, Susumu Ogawa, and Kritinee Pongtanalert for sharing their survey data and thinking with us. We also want to thank Carliss Baldwin, Dietmar Harhoff and Tim Schweisfurth for sharing their ideas with us on this topic, and critically reading our paper.

Keywords: innovation efficiency, gamification, innovation process participation benefits

11 AMPLIFYING USER AND PRODUCER INNOVATION

11.1 Introduction and Overview

A fundamental question in the study of innovation is what motivates innovation. If we regard human beings as resourceful, evaluative, maximizing agents (Jensen and Meckling 1994), we must assume that they innovate because they expect some net benefit from doing so. Researchers and policymakers have long assumed that this benefit needs to be an expectation of economic profit derived from the *output* of the innovation process—the innovation itself (Schumpeter 1934; Dosi 1988). This assumption has applied whether the innovator is a producer who expects to benefit by selling the innovation he creates, or a user who expects to benefit from using the output he creates (Hippel 1988, 2005; Baldwin and Hippel 2011).

We define "participators" as individuals who expect to benefit from innovation by participating in the innovation process. We define participation as personal engagement in the innovation process, and we define the benefit this activity conveys to the innovator as participation value. It includes such things as enjoyment and learning derived from engaging in R&D and innovation processes, the feelings of personal satisfaction derived from contributing to a good cause, and building social relationships via participation. When innovators reap participation value, they are in a sense consuming the innovation process itself as a valued experience.

Innovation participants motivated solely by participation motives, "pure participators", by definition have no use for the specific innovations—the outputs—their efforts help create. As a result, they can be recruited by the promise of participation benefits to amplify the efforts of users or producers to create a wide range of innovations of use or sale value. More succinctly: users and producers seek solutions and innovation outputs; participators may choose to amplify their efforts.

Participation motivated R&D and innovation contributions (hereafter referred to as 'innovation' contributions for simplicity) come from leisure time held by individuals in the household sector. Participation motivated contributions therefore present a fundamental challenge to the underlying assumption in economics that an activity is labor (in the market or in the household) *or* leisure—but not both at the same time (Becker 1965). Scholars and practitioners have noted the potential value obtainable by turning household sector leisure time to a range of productive uses (von Ahn et al. 2008; Shirky 2010; Füller 2010).

In this paper we provide a formal framework to analyze the current and potential value of contributions to innovation drawn from leisure time. We provide empirical estimates of the prevalence of innovation contributions motivated by participation benefits, finding them quite substantial. Based on data from representative national studies of consumers innovating for their own use, we estimate an innovation amplification factor among consumer users who have both output motivations and participation motivations of 2.5. We also show that users or producers can greatly amplify effort applied to their innovation projects by inducing contributions from "the crowd" of pure participators.

The chapter is organized as follows: We start with a literature review (section 11.2). In section 11.3, we model the decision to innovate as depending on use value, profit value, and participation value. We show that participation value amplifies the range of innovation opportunities viable for users and producers. We then present empirical data on the prevalence of participation motivations to innovate in hybrid (section 11.4) and pure form (section 11.5). In section 6, we argue that purely participation-motivated innovation contributions are growing and can become quite large relative to paid R&D. In section 11.7, we discuss important implications of participation-motivated innovation for research, practice and policy.

11.2   Literature

In this section, we briefly review literature in four areas: the literature on the sources of innovation (11.2.1); the literature about time use in the household sector of the economy and its role in innovation (11.2.2); and the literature rooted in psychology on motivations for problem-solving and how to enhance them (11.2.3 and 11.2.4). We also refer to the emergent literature on crowdsourcing (11.2.5).

11.2.1   The Functional Sources of Innovation

A fundamental question in the study of innovation is what motivates innovation development. As was mentioned in the introduction, we assume human beings are resourceful, evaluative, maximizing agents (Jensen and Meckling 1994; Dosi 1988) who innovate if and as this activity gives them a net benefit.

The functional sources of innovation definition and literature follows this logic and focuses on innovation output as the motivator for innovation effort. It distinguishes two categories, both of which are output-motivated: user innovators, who are defined as those who expect to benefit from using innovation outputs they create, and producers, who are defined as those who expect to benefit from selling innovation outputs they create (Hippel 1988, 2005).

In economics and governmental statistics, too, benefits are measured in terms of innovative outputs generated only: patents obtained, numbers of new products developed, and/or sales of or profits derived from new products (National Science Board 2010). The cost of innovation is measured in terms of paid inputs only—R&D expenditures in time and money. In other words, researchers and policymakers assume that investments in innovation and innovation benefits are entirely related to expectation of economic profit. What we are calling participation benefits have not been captured by either innovation theory or measurement to this point.

11.2.2   The Household Sector as a Locus of Innovation

Traditionally, economic theory has conceived of households as microeconomic units that seek to maximize their utility, subject to a budget constraint, by *consuming* goods and services. Next to goods and services, households also consume leisure (Becker 1965)—"time spent free of obligation and necessity" or "all activities that we cannot pay somebody else to do for us and we do not really have to do at all if we do not wish to" (Burda et al. 2007, p. 1).

The notion of household *production* came into focus in the 1960s and later, when economists turned their attention to productive labor in the household sector such as childcare, DIY repair jobs, and snow shoveling (Mincer 1962; Becker 1965; Apps and Rees 1997). Household production came to be considered as value generating and costly, but not as an enjoyable form of leisure: "work in the market, work at home, or leisure" (Gronau 1977). Although the phenomenon is still only poorly measured, Berk (1987) estimates household production of products and services, such as food and child care, to be almost one third of total production—a very significant matter.

It seems a natural next step to study household sector *innovation*, but only recently have a few development economists begun to consider this. Thus, Wu (2003) and Wu and Pretty (2004) argue for the importance of household sector innovation, and document that farmers in poor, rural areas of China use informal networks to collaborate, and to develop new farming techniques.

In the marketing and innovation literatures, there is a much richer tradition of research related to household sector innovation under the terms of "consumer co-creation" and "user innovation" (Hippel 1988; Hippel et al. 2012; Payne et al. 2008). Recently, national surveys of representative samples of consumers have found that, in the United Kingdom, 2.9 million people (6.1% of the population) collectively spend $5.2 billion in opportunity cost of their time and out of pocket expenditures annually to create and modify consumer products *for their own use*. In the United States, 16 million people (5.2% of the U.S. population) collectively spend $20.2 billion, and in Japan, 4.7 million people (3.7% of the population) collectively spend $5.8 billion. Consumer-user innovators were found to be active in essentially every type of consumer product, ranging from software for personal use, to product innovations for personal medical needs, to household goods, to hobbies (Hippel et al. 2012; Ogawa and Pongtanalert 2011).

11.2.3   Participation Motives

Recall that we define participation as personal engagement in the innovation process. Specific "participation motives" include enjoyment and learning derived from engaging in R&D and innovation processes, feelings of personal satisfaction derived from contributing to a good cause, and building social relationships via participation (Franke and Schreier 2010; Franke et al. 2010; Krogh et al. 2012). In contrast, output-related motives are associated with benefits derivable from use or sale of the output of the innovation process—the innovation itself.

We may map our categorization of participation vs. output motives into the categories used in psychological literature of extrinsic or intrinsic motivation to perform tasks or engage in activities. Extrinsic motivation "refers to doing something because it leads to a separable outcome"—any effort is instrumental to achieving this outcome. Via this definition, benefits associated with the output created—the innovation that is being used or sold—are extrinsic motivators. In contrast, an action is intrinsically motivated if it is carried out for the inherent interest or joy of performing it (Deci and Ryan 1985). Intrinsic and extrinsic are endpoints on a scale, where the middle is taken by extrinsic motivations that are internalized to varying degrees (Ryan and Deci 2000). Benefits for participating in the innovation process are intrinsic or internalized extrinsic motivators. Participation motives such as enjoyment and "flow" experience (Csikszentmihalyi 1990) are intrinsic. Motives such as reputation and helping advance a good cause are internalized extrinsic.

It has been shown that intrinsic and internalized extrinsic motivation leads to better task outcomes and more positive attitudes than purely extrinsic motivation (Gagné and Deci 2005). Intrinsic motivations have been shown to lead to better performance on complex and creative tasks (Amabile 1982; Amabile et al. 1990; Grolnick and Ryan 1987). In fact, Amabile (1996) proposes that intrinsic motivation is a key determinant of creativity. Intrinsic motivation also leads to superior goal attainment (Sheldon and Elliot 1998), and to more active information seeking (Koestner and Losier 2002) and sharing (Gagné 2009).

11.2.4 *Increasing Participation Motivations and Task Participation*

Levels of participation motivation experienced for participating in an innovation project—or any other activity—can have a net positive or negative balance for an individual based both upon attributes of the task itself *and* how it is framed and carried out (e.g., "I just hate eating spinach—can't stand the taste. On the other hand, I love defeating my brother in family spinach-eating contests".)

Participation motivation can be increased or reduced by design. If we look at the issue in terms of efficiently creating outcomes, we can think of it as the practical process of developing the most economical incentives to get a particular job done.

Many examples exist of producers that engage thousands of customers in online activities related to product design (Kohler et al. 2009). Research into why consumers are willing to participate in such activities without monetary compensation explores the impacts of what we call participation benefits in some detail. Nambisan and Baron (2009) find that the extent to which interactions in online virtual customer environments offer participation benefits (cognitive, social integrative, personal integrative, and hedonic) shapes participation. Kohler et al. (2011) conducted a 20-months action research project to identify design principles for online co-creation systems involving firms and their customers. These involved design challenges, with rewards on offer being only participation value. Along with Yee (2006), these authors found that "if the experience fulfills participants' hedonic needs, the efforts involved in a co-creation system are no longer considered work" (p. 786).

A fairly recent practice, called 'gamification', involves consciously applying intrinsic motivators found within online games, such as scoring systems, to enhance participation motivation for the performance of useful tasks. "A game is a problem-solving activity, approached with a playful attitude". "[The] difference between a play activity and a work activity has nothing to do with the activity itself, but one's motivation for doing the activity" (Schell 2008, pp. 36–37). Games involve a structured, bounded system within which gamers solve problems. They create an enjoyable experience and provide rewards for achievement (Fullerton 2008).

11.2.5 Crowdsourcing

Today, both users and producers confronting innovation problems increasingly direct requests to solve problems of interest to them to the household sector via 'crowdsourcing'. Crowdsourcing is defined as "the act of outsourcing a task to a "crowd", rather than to a designated "agent", . . . in the form of an open call" (Afuah and Tucci 2012, p. 355, Howe 2006). An example of crowdsourcing by users is open source software development projects such as Linux and Apache. Examples of crowdsourcing by producers can be seen in firms such as Innocentive and in computer gaming companies (Jeppesen and Lakhani 2010; Boudreau and Jeppesen 2012). This sourcing strategy can be used for many types of development, production and service tasks (Agerfalk and Fitzgerald 2008).

Types of incentives used are not defined in crowdsourcing, nor are the motivations regarding why potential "laborers" should choose to undertake effort. Thus, contributors to crowdsourcing calls may, based upon the incentives and constraints placed by the person or organization issuing the call, be motivated by selling their solutions, and/or by creating a solution they themselves can use, and/or by participation benefits (Lakhani and Wolf 2005; Chandler and Kapelner 2012; Poetz and Schreier 2012).

Crowdsourcing has been shown to have dual advantages: the recruiting of free or lower-cost labor, and the recruiting of individuals having highly diverse information, which can contribute greatly to solving some problems in creative, 'out of the box' ways (Raymond 1999; Frey et al. 2011).

11.3 Formalizing Innovation Amplification via Participation Motives

In this section, we formalize what we mean by innovation amplification and explain why it is important. We show that participation benefits can greatly expand the range of innovation opportunities that can be viably addressed by user and producer innovators.

11.3.1 Innovation Amplification

Recall that user and producer motives for developing an innovation have been defined as purely extrinsic, dealing only with the benefits expected from the *output* of an innovation project (Hippel 1988). Therefore consider first an innovator who is motivated to innovate *only* by benefits expected from the innovative output being created (either for use or for sale). That innovator can viably develop all innovation opportunities for which his value derived from the output, v, exceeds his cost of innovating, c,

$$v > \text{with } v, c > 0. \tag{1}$$

Next, recall that we define participation value, denoted by p, as the value that can be obtained by personally engaging in the innovation process as an experience. Suppose our innovator has hybrid motivations, deriving value from the innovation process as well as its outcome. This extends the range of innovation opportunities that are viable for him to

$$v + p > c \ (p > 0), \text{ i.e. the sum of output-related value and} \\ \text{process-related value must exceed the cost of innovating.} \tag{2}$$

The extension of the range of viable product opportunities due to the addition of effort rewarded by participation benefits is what we mean by innovation amplification. In the case just given, amplification is described in terms of a single individual containing within himself both types of motives. Suppose, however, that a user or producer innovator wants to recruit more effort to his project. In that case, because participation motives can be independent of output-related motives, it is possible to find potential recruits who will enjoy participation without being at all interested in the output being created. This greatly amplifies the leisure-time 'labor pool' available.

Consider: if at least some level of output motivation is required to exist in all participants in a given innovation project, then users or producers seeking crowdsourcing contributions to such a project are restricted to the pool of potential contributors who have at least some interest in using (or selling) that specific innovation—for example whitewater kayaks or personal 3D printers. However, if some or many additional potential contributors can be adequately motivated to contribute *independently* from output created, users and producers seeking contributions to their innovation projects can seek contributors from the *entire* pool of leisure hours, in competition with other activities seeking to tap into that same resource.

We now show how recruiting contributors with participation motivation only, puts innovation opportunities within the reach of a user or producer innovator that were otherwise out of bounds. Our innovator will find it viable to recruit contributors motivated by only participation-motivated benefit into amplified innovation, if that allows him to at least break even,

$$v > a + bc, \tag{3}$$

where v is again the value of the output to the innovator, c is the cost of R&D, and b is the residual share of that cost still borne by the innovator (not crowdsourced). a denotes the amplification cost, i.e. the cost of attracting and motivating participants and of integrating their contributions.

Participants will be motivated to contribute, in the aggregate, if their share of the effort causes them costs lower than their aggregate participation value, P.

$$P > (1 - b)c \qquad (4)$$

Substituting this demand-side condition back into (3), we find, and intuitively so, that amplified innovation is viable if the value obtained by all parties involved exceed the costs they incur,

$$v + P > c + a. \qquad (5)$$

We now put all these viability conditions into a diagram in c-a space (Figure 11.1). This space represents all innovation opportunities according to their total R&D cost, c, and their amplification cost, a. a can be expected to depend on many factors, including the subject matter, its modularity and complexity (Baldwin and Clark 2000; Afuah and Tucci 2012).

Consider first the vertical line v. Innovation opportunities to the left of that line are viable for a user or producer innovator assuming he is the only innovation contributor and has only output motivations for innovating (cf. inequality (1)). If he gains process value as well as output value, his viability frontier shifts out to the right, following inequality (2), but the logic remains the same. Condition (3) is represented by the dotted downward-sloping line of slope—b. It is the break-even condition for the initiator. Condition (5) is

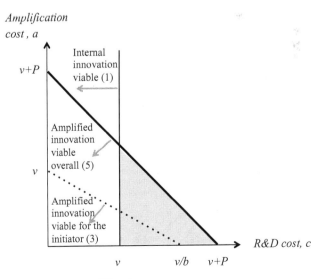

Figure 11.1   Innovation amplification

represented by the bold line of slope *(–1)* through $v + P$. That is the aggregate viability frontier for amplified innovation, taking into account both the initiator and external participants.

The diagram highlights a number of interesting points: First, due to the possibility of amplified innovation, the range of viable innovation opportunities expands by the shaded triangle. Innovation opportunities in that area newly become attainable.

Second, consider the implications of changes in "amplification technology". As amplification costs are decreasing, as is widely argued at the moment (Kohler et al. 2011; Baldwin and Hippel 2011), innovation opportunities migrate downward in our diagram. They thus become more likely to end up inside the amplified viability frontier.

Third, we assume that the value v that the initiator derives from using or selling the output is independent of how he develops it. That may not be so. If the innovator is a producer, for instance, there is evidence that consumer demand for the innovation increases as a result of perceptions of consumer empowerment and consumer involvement in innovation development (Fuchs et al. 2010; Schreier et al. 2012). If this is so, the viability frontier for amplified innovation shifts outward.

Finally, note that our model implicitly assumes that the total R&D cost will stay the same, no matter how it is split between the initiator and external participants. This need not be so. The locus of R&D will affect the total cost if parties differ in efficiency. This may be due to differential prices for inputs, differential access to tools and equipment, or differences in knowledge or experience. Even if efficiencies differ, our model still holds. The viability frontier for amplified innovation, (5), will change to

$$v + P/e > c + g, \tag{5}$$

where e is an adjustment factor for the efficiency of external participants. (When the initiator undertakes share b of the R&D effort, participants undertake $e(1 - b)$. Thus, $e < 1$ indicates that they are more efficient than he would have been, while $e > 1$ indicates that they are less efficient.)

We define the innovation amplification factor (A) of an innovation project as:

$$A = 1 + \frac{Efficiency - adjusted\ effort\ motivated\ by\ participation\ benefits}{Effort\ motivated\ by\ output\ benefits} \tag{6}$$

For the case just described, $A = 1+(1 - b)e/b$.

11.3.2 *Capturing External Participation Surplus*

Our model shows that there is a risk that project initiators will underinvest in amplification. This risk is present for all innovation opportunities lying between the dotted and the bold downward-sloping lines. It arises from the fact that the project initiator does not capture any of the surplus that he has created for participators by his investments in amplification. The initiator only benefits from the increase in the output value generated by them—surplus garnered by participators is a separate matter. Finding ways in which project initiators can capture some of this external participation surplus could solve the problem.

To explore this point, recall that the dotted line in Figure 11.1 is the break-even line for the initiator of the project if he benefits from only the output-related improvements supplied by external participators and does not share in their surplus. Any investment beyond the area closed in by that line is not justified by the value he expects to obtain from the output, v. If all participation surplus accrues to participators, while at the same time none of the amplification costs are assigned to them, then innovation opportunities beyond the dotted line, but to the inside of the bold line, are not viable for the initiator, but are viable overall, justified by P.

We thus have an inefficiency, which can be addressed by finding a way for the project initiator to internalize part of the participation surplus and/ or by assigning some of the amplification costs to participation motivated contributors themselves. If neither is the case, the initiator will not start some potentially viable projects.

Franke et al. (2010) and Franke and Schreier (2010) show how partial capture of participants' process surplus can work for producers. In essence, project initiators sell the opportunity to participate in the project instead of giving it away for free. All games that are sold and offer participation benefits only, not coupled to a useful output—for example, Solitaire—follow this model. Assignment of some of the amplification costs to participants themselves is shown whenever participants create value for each other, e.g. by improving the game, giving feedback, or conferring status (cf. Prahalad and Ramaswamy 2003).

In the next two sections, we will provide empirical evidence for innovation amplification and estimate A where presently available data permits it. Empirical data in section 11.4 shows that it is very common indeed for household-sector innovators to be motivated by use as well as participation. In section 11.5, we will then show empirical evidence for the strategy of tapping the pure participation value obtainable by others. We will show that both users and producers adopt this strategy.

11.4   Hybrid Motivations to Innovate

Hybrid motivations to innovate involve a combination of innovation process participation benefits and output benefits. Such hybrids often "happen naturally:" consumers may develop an innovation to use it or sell it and at the same time *also* gain participation value from participating in the innovation process itself. For example, a software user could decide to fix a bug in software he uses motivated in part by the improvement in use value that would result—and in part motivated by the enjoyment he will obtain by solving an interesting programming problem. (In contrast, pure participation motives would be at play if the bug were fixed "just for the fun of it" by someone with no intention to benefit from the improvement by using or selling it.)

Case studies conducted in several contexts support the view that hybrid motivations frequently exist among innovators (Lakhani and Hippel 2003; Janzik et al. 2011; Krogh et al. 2012). For example, individuals participating in open source software projects report that their motivations for contributing to the projects include both a need to use the code they are creating, *and* enjoyment and learning from participating in the development process (Lakhani and Wolf 2005).

More broadly, representative national surveys of innovation by consumers creating and modifying products *for their own use* show the same pattern; the motivation of user innovators is often a hybrid of output motives and participation motives. Representative national samples of household sector residents have been conducted in three countries—the United Kingdom, United States, and Japan (Hippel et al. 2012; Ogawa and Pongtanalert 2011). These surveys ask specifically about consumer product innovations that respondents developed or modified in order to use them. (Examples of innovations reported are: I made an automated device to feed my diabetic dog frequent small meals while I am away during the day; I improved the starter motor for my automobile.)

In addition, the surveys contain a question regarding respondents' motives for developing their innovations. (That data was not reported in the published papers and was provided to us by the authors.) Four motives were asked about across all three nations: "benefit from use of the innovation"; "benefit from enjoyment of the innovation process"; "learning and skills development"; and "helping others". In the United States and Japan, reputation benefits were added as an additional category relating to participation in the process.

Results for the motives question are shown in Table 11.1. As expected, the studies found the output-related motive of "I built it to use it" to be important for most—the studies selected *only* respondents who said at the outset that they had created or modified consumer products in order to use them.

In addition, however, the great majority of innovating users report that one or more process participation motives are *also* important to them. Enjoyment and learning are the types of participation motives that are most prevalent in all three countries.

The surveys included respondents of 18 years or over. In the representative survey of consumers in the United Kingdom (Hippel et al. 2012) respondents were asked to check all motives that applied in their cases (binary response: yes or no). In the case of the United States and Japan consumer surveys (Ogawa and Pongtanalert 2011), responses were reported on a 5-point Likert scale, ranging from 1, "I don't agree at all" to 5, "I fully

Table 11.1 Salience of participation motives among household sector innovators

	UK	US	Japan
Output-related			
Use	80%	99%	98%
Participation-related			
Enjoyment	85%	93%	99%
Learning	56%	80%	87%
Helping others	42%	73%	72%
Reputation	n.a.	62%	63%
Innovators with at least one participation-related motive	94%	96%	99%

Note: UK: $n = 104$, US: $n = 114$, Japan: $n = 83$.

Table 11.2 Household sector participation motivated innovation time vs. paid R&D time

	UK	US	Japan
Consumers innovating for own use (millions)	2.90	11.70	3.90
Days worked per innovator per year	7.10	9.92	5.51
Innovation effort by hybrid-motive innovators (millions of hours per day)	0.43	2.44	0.47
Total paid research time in public and private sector (millions of hours per day)	1.08	6.89	3.16
Innovation effort by hybrid-motive innovators as fraction of total private and government paid research time	39.3%	35.4%	14.7%

Note: Population-level estimates: Our estimates are based on the careful methodology described in the country studies (Ogawa and Pongtanalert 2011; Hippel et al. 2012). We adjust their estimates for the prevalence of participation benefits.

"Paid research": "Researchers are defined as professionals engaged in the conception and creation of new knowledge, products, processes, methods and systems as well as those who are directly involved in the management of projects. They include researchers working in both civil and military research in government, universities, research institutes as well as in the business sector". Definition and data from 2006, the latest year for which harmonized data for all three countries is available. We assume that researchers work the national average number of hours.

Source: OECD Country Statistical Profiles.

agree". To be conservative, we include only intermediate and high levels of agreement (3–5) to items related to use and participation motives (but including mild agreement would not have made a substantial difference).

In Table 11.2, we put these figures into a larger context to better understand their significance. First, drawing upon the data in Table 11.1 and data from the United Kingdom, United States, and Japanese national surveys as described in the Table 11.1 note, we find that millions of consumers in these three countries—5.7% of the British population (2.7 million consumers), 5.0% (11.2 million) of the American population, and 3.7% (3.9 million) of the Japanese population—innovate *in whole or in part* for participation motives.

The time devoted by these individuals to innovation amounts to approx. 0.4 million hours per day in the United Kingdom, 2.4 million in the United States, and 0.5 million in Japan. This equals a significant fraction of *all* paid R&D time in the private and government sectors in these countries: equaling 39.3% (UK); 35.4% (US) and 14.7 % (Japan) of paid R&D time across all industries.

A survey of all PhD recipients and medical personnel in Portugal (Mendonca et al. 2012) allows us to say a bit more about the likely *relative* weighting of output vs. participation motives. It shows that the participation motive fraction is likely to be significant among consumers innovating for their own use. Respondents in that study were asked to divide 100 points up among five motives in terms of the relative importance each had "as a reason" to develop their innovation. The results can be seen in Table 11.3.

Two clear output-related motives, to use and to sell, together accounted for 26% of the total. Two clear participation motives, to enjoy and to learn, together accounted for 46%. It is unclear how to code a fifth category, "to help other people". On the face of it, respondents may be saying something output-related, as in "I made a health innovation to help my daughter", and/or they may be reporting a participation motive, as in "I enjoy helping others with tasks important to them". Lacking a better solution, for the moment we will simply split this motive between the two categories, and we will disregard "other reasons".

If similar proportions apply in the United Kingdom, the United States and Japan, this implies that approx. 60% of the household-sector innovation

Table 11.3   "Divide up 100% to show the relative importance of the motives that lead you to develop this innovation"

Motives for innovation development	Average weightings of 201 PhD user innovators
Personal Use	22.3%
Sell / Make money	4.2%
To learn or develop skills	26.5%
To help other people	22.7%
For the pleasure of doing it	18.7%
Other reason	5.6%
TOTAL	100%

Source: Mendonca et al. (2012).

effort reported in Table 11.2 is motivated by the expectation of participation benefits. Following equation (6), and taking the motivational split as a proxy of the split in effort undertaken for output and for participation benefits respectively, this gives us an amplification factor of approximately 2.5. In other words, user innovators can justify undertaking 2.5 times more effort due to expectations of participation benefit, than would be justified by output motives alone.

11.5 Pure Participation-Motivated Innovation

As was mentioned earlier, when *only* participation motives are enough to motivate a consumer to expend time on innovation, something new and important happens. User or producer requests for problem solving efforts rewarded by *only* participation benefits potentially make household sector innovators willing to make contributions relevant to *any* R&D task: e.g., "If I am doing it entirely for the fun, I need not care whether the end result—the innovation being created—has any use or sale value to me".

Pure participators can be recruited by users or producers to "amplify" their efforts to create an innovative output for use or for sale. They use crowdsourcing to attract participants and may use gamification to enhance the participation benefits their project offers.

There are at this point no studies on national levels of participation-motives-only innovation activity. There is, however, existence proof that it is possible for both user and producer innovators to attract large numbers of individuals to make contributions to their projects by offering participation benefits only. Two illustrative case examples follow.

11.5.1 Recruiting of Pure Participators by User Innovators

Foldit is a project by scientists from the University of Washington who are studying how proteins fold in nature. They use protein folding solutions as inputs to their research. Their idea was to seek help from "the crowd" to help them generate such solutions. As there are not likely to be a lot of users or sellers of protein folding solutions in the household sector, the scientists needed to attract participants with only participation motives in mind. It was for this reason that they converted their problem into a form of game:

> To attract the widest possible audience for the game and encourage prolonged engagement, we designed the game so that the supported motivations and the reward structure are diverse, including short-term rewards (game score), long-term rewards (player status and rank), social praise (chats and forums), the ability to work individually or in a team, and the connection between the game and scientific outcomes.
>
> (Cooper et al. 2010, p. 760)

The Foldit game is difficult, and requires on-line training sessions and materials, which are provided, before actual game playing can begin. Still, the scientist-users were successful in attracting many people to help with their project—for example, there were 46,000 Fold-it gamers in 2011, all devoting leisure time to assist a handful of professional scientists in solving their problem. The crowdsourced work was very valuable to the scientists, providing specific protein folding solutions, and also methodological insights that could be used to improve computerized folding algorithms.

The scientists conducted a small and fairly informal survey asking *why* contributors chose to participate in Foldit: 48 players responded with up to 3 reasons each. Responses were categorized based on Yee's (2006) categorization of three main motivation components of achievement, social and immersion, plus an additional category related to Foldit's scientific purpose: 30% of responses reported that immersion (e.g., "it is fun and relaxing") was important; 20% mentioned achievement (e.g., "to get a higher score than the next player)"; and 10% mentioned social benefits (e.g., "great camaraderie").

Interestingly, the motivator described most often—noted in about 40% of responses—was a wish to support the purpose of the project (e.g., [I wanted to help] "to crack the protein folding code for science") (supplement to Cooper et al. 2010, p. 12). The apparent strong interest of many participants in supporting the specific purpose of the Foldit project, independent of personal use or sale interests in the output suggests that, in the competition for leisure-time participants, games with a purpose may have a competitive advantage over games without a purpose in recruiting at least a subset of potential players—those who find a specific purpose personally appealing quite apart from personal use or sale value. The situation is probably similar to that involved with charitable giving in general: one gives in part "to help others", and in part to support a *specific* cause of high personal interest (Webb et al. 2000).

11.5.2   *Recruiting of Pure Participators by Producer Innovators*

As a second example, consider Swarovski, a jewelry producer, that sought to attract consumers to participate in designing fashionable and creative new jewelry. With the help of Hyve, a company that specializes on building online amplified problem-solving sites, they created a crowdsourcing site offering volunteer participants the opportunity to develop their own jewelry designs; to showcase them; to comment on and vote on the designs of others; to upload their avatars and photos; to be included as a trendsetter in a book about trends in watch design; and so forth (Füller et al. 2006). Note that participants had no expectation of seeing their designs produced, and thus no expectation of use value. The site was successful: More than 3,000 designs were uploaded by over 1,700 participants.

Füller (2010) surveyed contributors to 10 different virtual co-creation projects hosted by Hyve for several companies, including Swarovski, ranging from the development of a baby carriage and furniture to mobile phone, backpack and jewelry design. He found that the motivators of "intrinsic innovation interest" and curiosity are given the strongest support by survey respondents. "In contrast to open source communities and user innovations, where members engage in innovation tasks because they can benefit from using their innovation, consumers engage in [Hyve] virtual new product developments mainly because they consider the engagement as a rewarding experience" (Füller 2010, p. 99).

11.6 Considering the Potential of Innovation Amplification

In this section we argue that pure-form participation-motivated innovation could be very large in both scale and scope, and provide some estimates.

11.6.1 The Labor Pool for Amplified Innovation

With respect to scale of innovation amplification potentially obtainable by tapping leisure time, note that leisure time is massive. The way time is spent by individuals in the household sector is measured in time use studies. In these studies, respondents are asked in considerable detail how they spent every hour of one or a number of days, what they did, and who else was present. Their activities are then put into one of the following categories: paid work and study, unpaid work and home production, personal care (including sleep), "leisure activities", and "not elsewhere classified". The average percentages of daily time spent by citizens of a range of nations in each category are shown in Table 11.3.

Labor that may be (or may not be) volunteered for 'innovation as consumption' comes from the pool of 'leisure time' in the household sector of the economy. In Table 11.4 we see that leisure time hours for the 18 OECD nations (last column), is 21.6% of a 24-hour day—compared with 16.5% working time—in other words, "leisure time" represents a vast pool of discretionary time (cf. von Ahn et al. 2008; Shirky 2010). With respect to our innovation focus, leisure time is larger by almost three orders of magnitude than present-day innovation by consumers as studied in section 11.4. It is also much larger than paid research time, which is in scale less than 1% of total leisure time in all three countries (UK: 0.5%, US: 0.6%, Japan: 0.9%).

11.6.2 Estimates of Total Leisure Time Accessible to Innovation Projects

With respect to scale and scope, recall that, contributions rewarded by *only* participation benefits potentially make household sector innovators willing to make contributions relevant to *any* R&D task: e.g., "If I am doing it entirely for the fun, I need not care whether the end result—the innovation being created—has any use or sale value to me". To estimate the fraction of leisure time accessible to amplified innovation projects, we need to understand the types of presently chosen leisure time activities for which innovation projects could be a substitute.

According to Jane McGonigal (2011), a researcher and gamification expert, "gamers are more likely than anyone on the planet to contribute to an online crowdsourcing project. They already have the time and the desire

Table 11.4   Share of time (% of 24 hours) given to leisure and other activities on an average day (respondents aged 15 and over)

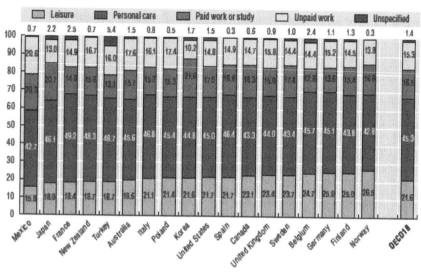

Source: OECD (2009).

Table 11.5   Recruiting gamers for innovation

	UK	US
Gamers (age 10–65) (million)	31.0	145.0
Total time spent gaming (million hours per day)	43.0	215.0
Percent of leisure time spent gaming	23.8%	27.7%
If "games with a purpose" got 10% of total video gaming time, this would equal . . . % of current paid R&D effort	397%	312%

Note: Data from the National Gamers Survey UK and US [data on Japan not available] (Newzoo 2011). "Games" considered here include "casual" online games played on a website, games on social networks, massive multiplayer online games, and other games played on mobile devices, game consoles, or computers.

to tackle voluntary obstacles. They're playing games precisely because they hunger for more and better engagement. They also have proven computer skills and an ability to learn new interactive interfaces quickly. . . . In short, gamers are already our most readily engageable citizens" (p. 233).

It is likely that non-gamers could also be engaged in amplified innovation projects, particularly if they care about the purpose (as was the case with some Fold-it players). The basic requirements are quite low—a computer and Internet access (82% of Americans have that). To be conservative, however, in Table 11.5 we focus on gamers only.

As Table 11.5 shows, the number of on-line gamers potentially attractable to games with an innovative output is very large: 31 million gamers between ages 10 and 65 in the United Kingdom spend 43 million hours per day playing video games. In the United States the numbers are 145 million people and 215 million hours per day (Newzoo 2011). Other countries show similar patterns (Newzoo 2011), and the fraction of gamers in these populations are growing at a fast pace (Lenhart et al. 2008).

It is hard to predict the success of amplified innovation projects in attracting participants. To attract gamers, one must make the game aspects better than the leisure-time games they are playing—and/or rely on the attraction of 'contributing to a good cause' or contributing to a special interest like jewelry design to offset lower gamified rewards. As will be noted in the discussion section, research will be required to get a reasonable estimate.

However, to better understand the potential importance of this free source of R&D and innovation contributions, we consider the impact if just 10% of current video gaming time can be attracted to amplified innovation (Table 11.5). We see that 10% of current gaming time—about 2.5% of the average gamer's total leisure time—if devoted to gamified innovation, would equal almost 400% of paid R&D time in the United Kingdom and more than 300% in the United States (Table 11.5, cf. Table 11.2 for paid R&D). Efficiency adjustments aside, this would imply an innovation amplification factor of 4–5.

Reliable estimates of external innovation amplification factors at the national level clearly require further research. Still, it seems reasonable to assume based on the numbers shown here that the amplification potential could be substantial.

11.7 Discussion

In this chapter, we have offered an additional basic answer to the fundamental question of "what motivates innovation?" While the literature on the sources of innovation focuses on innovation output as a motivator (for using or for selling), we explored participation in the innovation process as a source of value that can 'amplify' and pay for innovation effort, independent of output. We also formalized innovation amplification, and showed that participation benefits can greatly expand the range of innovation opportunities that can be viably addressed by user and producer innovators.

We consider three matters in more detail in the remainder of this discussion. First, we note that participation motivated effort is 'free' innovation labor not transacted via a market and not involving monetary recompense. For those reasons it is not currently measured as an innovation input. If such free labor is substantial, it affects our understandings of how the innovation process works, and the accuracy of our measurements of actual innovation efforts being applied in the economy (Gault 2011).

Second, we point out that policymakers as well as researchers should pay attention to participation motives—the effective voluntary deployment of some leisure time to 'games with a purpose' can provide a continuing and 'free' additional source of R&D and innovative effort to economies—"innovation as consumption".

Third, we point out that innovation amplification can be of great competitive value to firms, and so researchers and practitioners may wish to consider how participation motives and crowdsourcing can best be incorporated into innovation practice.

11.7.1 Towards Including Household Sector Contributions in Innovation Statistics

Today, time spent by consumers on innovation—whether on their projects to create innovations for their own use or on volunteer labor for crowdsourced user and producer-initiated innovation projects—is either entirely unmeasured or misattributed in official innovation statistics. It goes unmeasured if it is diffused peer-to-peer only and never traded via a market—as is the case, for example, with large amounts of open source software (Raasch and Hippel 2012). If and as consumer contributions are incorporated into innovations marketed by producers (or university research centers) they are misattributed to those sectors in official statistics (Gault 2011).

The results can be serious. In the field of consumer products, for example, it has been calculated that annual invisible product development investments by the household sector were 144% of paid R&D expenditures made by consumer goods producers combined in the United Kingdom, were 38% of corporate consumer goods R&D in the United States, and were 13% in Japan (Hippel et al. 2011). (In these three countries, the fraction of consumers innovating for their own use did not vary a great deal, but the size of the domestic consumer products industry did.) To the extent that consumers' innovation output spills over to producers, calculated R&D productivity of corporations in this field is inflated in official statistics. The extent of mismeasurement and hence needed correction factors will predictably differ among industries. For example, consumer contributions are likely to be much higher in consumer product development than in industrial product development.

The issue of relative efficiency will also be important to consider. Present evidence and thinking is that an hour spent by a consumer contributing to an innovation project may be more or less efficient than an hour spent by a paid researcher, depending upon the type of task, and skills required (Raymond 1999; Jeppesen and Lakhani 2010; Hienerth et al. 2012). (The single study available to date in a consumer products field [whitewater kayaking equipment] shows user consumer-innovators to be 2.4 times more efficient than producer development employees at developing important innovations [Hienerth et al. 2012].)

How can one generate the data needed to include household sector innovation effort into national innovation statistics? National representative surveys of "own use" innovations are an approach currently being developed and tested in several nations. Questions about contributions to crowdsourced R&D and innovation projects could easily be added to these. Another approach could be to use national time-use studies, described in section 11.6, to collect information on innovation efforts in the household sector. Current coding categories used in these studies render innovation development invisible—but it seems to us possible and promising to change this situation. For example, today there is a detailed listing of possible sporting activity codes—including such things as time spent playing sport X, time spent watching sport X—even waiting time associated with sport X—but no possible coding for creating or modifying a sport or sports equipment. Yet, we know from careful empirical research that all new sports studied to date are in fact created and progressively improved by consumers who play them (Franke and Shah 2003; Hienerth 2006, etc.). Similarly, there are codes for playing music and listening to music, but none for *composing* music. (In fact, the coding manual instructs interviewers to code composing music as "Listening to/playing music (not radio)" [BLS 2011].) And yet, music composition is again a major leisure-time hobby interest for many consumers (Jeppesen and Frederiksen 2006). A promising research stream would improve these coding categories to capture household sector innovation data.

It will also be important to conduct experiments capable of showing how far innovation amplification can go. (This could refine our assumption of 10% of gaming time in section 11.6.2.) Experiments to this end might involve taking average people who have not self-selected into a particular task, and see whether and how they can be motivated to participate in various types of innovation tasks. This would be crucial for projections to the entire household sector: all present calculations and estimates are based on people who have self-selected into user innovation or crowdsourcing tasks, with no understanding of how 'special' these individuals might be.

At this early stage, conscious innovation amplification by users and producers—as opposed to consumer satisfaction of own needs via partially participation motivated innovation—is still in its infancy. The potential, however, appears to be large. More research is warranted to refine the estimates presented in this chapter and develop estimates of how far this can go.

11.7.2 Why Innovation Amplification Matters for Research and Policymaking

Innovation amplification via participation benefits has major implications for both research and policymaking. At the most basic level, contributions to productive research made "for free" from household sector leisure time present a fundamental challenge to the underlying assumption in economics that an activity is labor *or* leisure—but not both at the same time. "Work in the market, work at home, or leisure" (Gronau 1977). The basic premise is that when people work less, value creation declines, GDP falls, society becomes poorer. However, if leisure can be productive, the trade-off is much softer than we thought. If innovation is often or can often be created as a side effect of consumption, this is an important "free lunch" for users, producers, and for the economy at large. It may be, for example, that current concerns about declining effective work hours may not be warranted. It may be that consumers already contribute and will increasingly contribute in other ways that are currently unmeasured, in terms of inputs and often also in terms of outputs.

It is also likely that both social welfare and economic growth increase when citizens *choose* to use leisure time in productive rather than unproductive ways because they *prefer* the productive options as a leisure-time activity. Policy research and practice should learn how to support this kind of consumer choice—such as deeper and better research into motives and motivators for participation in innovation processes (Franke et al. 2012; Hill and Monroy-Hernández 2012). It should also learn how to support improved infrastructures for crowdsourced innovation, like faster and cheaper Internet, and better processes for finding and choosing among the myriad opportunities users and producers will predictably present to the crowd in future.

11.7.3 Implications for Managerial Theory and Practice

With respect to managerial theory and practice, it may be useful to consider paid labor as a fall-back option for problems that do not attract sufficient volunteer effort and cannot be gamified effectively and efficiently (cf. Bauwens et al. 2012). The role of paid R&D, in other words, can be to solve those problems that otherwise would not get solved or would be more expensive to crowdsource and gamify than pay for. Both users and producers could choose that route. This is in line with Dahlander and Magnusson (2008) who find that it is the task of "men on the inside", paid employees in software companies, to take care of the mundane and less appealing parts of programing and documentation such that the open source community of volunteer contributors gets a rewarding, enjoyable experience. Thus a firm can have two roles: gamifier and residual solver of core problems.

Different organizational forms can be used to implement innovation amplification, e.g. contests that rely on competition, communities that rely on collaboration, and single-solver forms in which every contributor simply enjoys puzzle solving by and for himself. Hybrids are also possible and in fact common. The relationship between organizational forms and the motives and preferences of the population of potential problem solvers should be explored in more detail (Boudreau and Lakhani 2011; Hill and Monroy-Hernández 2012).

(Note also that gamification and appropriate employee selection can also enable firms to reduce the salaries that must be paid to development employees working on 'the residual' tasks. This is because of an argument proposed by Adam Smith and later formalized in the theory of compensating wage differentials [Rosen 1986] that enjoyable jobs can pay less than non-enjoyable jobs.)

Future research should also explore how the motivational dispositions prevalent in the solver population and the nature of the problem(s) to be solved can be aligned by incentive design such that no essential task is left undone. Many interesting issues arise as producers, users and gamers interact in innovation and problem solving—micro-motives need to be understood. Users and producers may differ in their ability to harness participation motives, due to differential access to resources, perceptions of fairness, and other factors. The line between tasks to which leisure time can be attracted and residual tasks is not a clear one at present, and more research is needed. Contingent answers will be required.

We conclude by noting again that participation motives can greatly amplify total investment in R&D and innovation in societies, by making it attractive for some consumers to devote some fraction of their leisure time to that purpose. We have illustrated by example that there are major implications for theory, policymaking, and practice. We suggest that further research is well justified.

REFERENCES

Afuah, A.N., and Tucci, C.L. (2012): "Crowdsourcing as a solution to distant search", *Academy of Management Review* 37(3), pp. 355–375.

Agerfalk, P.J., and Fitzgerald, B. (2008): "Opensourcing to an unknown workforce: exploring opensourcing as a global sourcing strategy", *MIS Quarterly* 32(2), pp. 385–410.

Amabile, T.M. (1982): "Social psychology of creativity: a consensual assessment technique", *Journal of Personality and Social Psychology* 43(5), pp. 997–1013.

Amabile, T.M. (1996): *Creativity in context*, Westview Press, Boulder, CO.

Amabile, T.M., Goldfarb, P., and Brackfield, S.C. (1990): "Social influences on creativity: evaluation, coaction, and surveillance", *Creativity Research Journal* 31(1), pp. 6–21.

Apps, P.F., and Rees, R. (1997): "Collective labor supply and household production", *Journal of Political Economy* 105(1), pp. 178–190.

Baldwin, C.Y., and Clark, K.B. (2000): *Design rules—the power of modularity*, MIT Press, Cambridge, MA.

Baldwin, C.Y., and Hippel, E. von (2011): "Modeling a paradigm shift: from producer innovation to user and open collaborative innovation", *Organization Science* 22(6), pp. 1399–1417.

Bauwens, M., Iacomella, F., Mendoza, N., Pinchen, C., Leonard, A., and Mootoosamy, E. (2012): Synthetic overview of the collaborative economy. P2P Foundation. http://p2p.coop/files/reports/collaborative-economy-2012.pdf. Accessed November 2013.

Becker, G.S. (1965): "A theory of the allocation of time", *Economic Journal* 75(299), pp. 493–517.

Berk, R.A. (1987): "Household production", in *The new palgrave: a dictionary of economics*, J. Eatwell, M. Milgate, and P. Newman (eds.), pp. 673–677, Stockton, New York.

BLS (2011): American time use survey activity lexicon. http://www.bls.gov/tus/lexiconwex2011.pdf. Accessed November 2013.

Boudreau, K.J., and Jeppesen, L.B. (2012): "Competing with a crowd: informally organized individuals as platform complementors", SSRN Working Paper. http://papers.ssrn.com/sol3/papers.cfm?abstract_id=1812084. Accessed November 2013.

Boudreau, K.J., and Lakhani, K. (2011): "High incentives, sorting on skills—or just a taste for competition? field experimental evidence from an algorithm design contest", Harvard Business School Technology & Operations Mgt. Unit Working Paper No. 11–107. http://papers.ssrn.com/sol3/papers.cfm?abstract_id=1815370. Accessed November 2013.

Burda, M.C., Hamermesh, D.S., and Weil, P. (2007): "Total work, gender, and social norms", Institute for the Study of Labor, IZA Discussion Paper No. 2705, Institute for the Study of Labor, IZA, Bonn.

Chandler, D., and Kapelner, A. (2012). "Breaking monotony with meaning: motivation in crowdsourcing markets", http://arxiv.org/abs/1210.0962. Accessed November 2013.

Cooper, S., Khatib, F., Treuillel, A., Barbero, J., Lee, J., Beenen, M., Leaver-Fay, A., Baker, D., Popovic, Z., and Players, F. (2010): "Predicting protein structures with a multiplayer online game", *Nature Letters* 466(5), pp. 756–760.

Csikszentmihalyi, M. (1990): *Flow—the psychology of optimal experience,* Harper Collins, New York.

Dahlander, L., and Magnusson, M.G. (2008): "How do firms make use of open source communities?" *Long Range Planning* 41(6), pp. 629–649.

Deci, E.L., and Ryan, R.M. (1985): *Intrinsic motivation and self-determination in human behaviour*, Springer, New York.

Dosi, G. (1988): "Sources, procedures, and microeconomic effects of innovation", *Journal of Economic Literature* 26, pp. 1120–1171.

Franke, N., Keinz, P., and Klausberger, K. (2012): "'Does this sound like a fair deal?' antecedents and consequences of fairness expectations in the individual's decision to participate in firm innovation", *Organization Science* 24(5), pp. 1495–1516.

Franke, N., and Schreier, M. (2010): "Why customers value self-designed products: the importance of process effort and enjoyment", *Journal of Product Innovation Management* 27, pp. 1020–1031.

Franke, N., Schreier, M., and Kaiser, U. (2010): "The 'I designed it myself' effect in mass customization", *Management Science* 56(1), pp. 125–140.

Franke, N., and Shah, S. (2003): "How communities support innovative activities: an exploration of assistance and sharing among end-users", *Research Policy* 32(1), pp. 157–178.

Frey, K., Lüthje, C., and Haag, S. (2011): "Whom should firms attract to open innovation platforms? the role of knowledge diversity and motivation", *Long Range Planning* 44, pp. 397–420.

Fuchs, C., Prandelli, E., and Schreier, M. (2010): "The psychological effects of empowerment strategies on consumers' product demand", *Journal of Marketing* 74(1), pp. 65–79.

Füller, J. (2010): "Refining virtual co-creation from a consumer perspective", *California Management Review* 52(2), pp. 98–122.

Füller, J., Hutter, K., and Faullant, R. (2006): "Why co-creation experience matters? creative experience and its impact on the quantity and quality of creative contributions", *R&D Management* 41(3), pp. 259–273.

Fullerton, T. (2008): *Game design workshop*, Morgan Kaufmann Publishers, Burlington, MA.

Gagné, M. (2009): "A model of knowledge sharing motivation", *Human Ressource Management* 48(4), pp. 571–589.

Gagné, M., and Deci, E.L. (2005): "Self-determination theory and work motivation", *Journal of Organizational Behavior* 26(4), pp. 331–363.

Gault, F. (2011): "User innovation and the market", UNU-MERIT Working Paper. http://www.merit.unu.edu/publications/wppdf/2011/wp2011–009.pdf. Accessed November 2013.

Grolnick, W.S., and Ryan, R.M. (1987): "Autonomy in children's learning: an experimental and individual difference investigation", *Journal of Personality and Social Psychology* 52(5), pp. 890–898.

Gronau, R. (1977): "Leisure, home production, and work—the theory of the allocation of time revisited", *Journal of Political Economy* 85(6), pp. 1099–1124.

Hienerth, C. (2006): "The commercialization of user innovations: the development of the rodeo kayak industry", *R&D Management* 36(3), pp. 273–294.

Hienerth, C., Hippel, E. von, and Berg Jensen, M. (2012): "Efficiency of consumer (household sector) vs. producer innovation", MIT Sloan Working Paper. http://papers.ssrn.com/sol3/papers.cfm?abstract_id=1916319. Accessed November 2013.

Hill, B.M., and Monroy-Hernández, A. (2012): "The remixing dilemma: the trade-off between generativity and originality", *American Behavioral Scientist* 57(5), pp. 643–663.

Hippel, E. von (1988): *The sources of innovation*, Oxford University Press, New York.

Hippel, E. von (2005): *Democratizing innovation*, MIT Press, Cambridge, MA.

Hippel, E. von, de Jong, J., and Flowers, S. (2012): "Comparing business and household sector innovation in consumer products: findings from a representative survey in the UK", *Management Science* 58(9), pp. 1669–1681.

Hippel, E.A. von, Ogawa, S., and de Jong, J. (2011): "The age of the consumer innovator", *MIT Sloan Management Review* 53(1), pp. 27–35.

Howe, J. (2006): "The rise of crowdsourcing", *Wired Magazine* 14(6), pp. 176–183.

Janzik, L., Raasch, C., and Herstatt, C. (2011): "Motivation in innovative online communities: why join, why innovate, why share?" *International Journal of Innovation Management* 15(4), pp. 797–836.

Jensen, M.C., and Meckling, W.H. (1994): "The nature of man", *Journal of Applied Corporate Finance* 7(2), pp. 4–19.

Jeppesen, L.B., and Frederiksen, L. (2006): "Why do users contribute to firm-hosted user communities? the case of computer-controlled music instruments", *Organization Science* 17(1), pp. 45–63.

Jeppesen, L.B., and Lakhani, K.R. (2010): "Marginality and problem solving effectiveness in broadcast search", *Organization Science* 21(5), pp. 1016–1033.

Koestner, R., and Losier, G.F. (2002): "Distinguishing three ways of being internally motivated: a closer look at introjection, identification, and intrinsic motivation", *Handbook of self-determination research*, E.L. Deci and R.M. Ryan (eds.), pp. 101–121, University of Rochester Press, Rochester, NY.

Kohler, T., Füller, J., Matzler, K., and Stieger, D. (2011): "Co-creation in virtual worlds: the design of the user experience", *MIS Quarterly* 35(3), pp. 773–788.

Kohler, T., Matzler, K., and Füller, J. (2009): "Avatar-based innovation: using virtual worlds for real-world innovation", *Technovation* 29, pp. 395–407.

Krogh, G. von, Häfliger, S., Späth, S., and Wallin, M. (2012): "Carrots and rainbows: motivation and social practice in open source software development", *MIS Quarterly* 36(2), pp. 649–676.

Lakhani, K.R., and Hippel, E. von (2003): "How open source software works: 'free' user-to-user assistance", *Research Policy* 32(6), pp. 923–943.

Lakhani, K. R., and Wolf, B. (2005): "Why hackers do what they do: understanding motivation and effort in free/open source software projects", in *Perspectives on free and Open Source software*, J. Feller, B. Fitzgerald, S. A. Hissam, and K. R. Lakhani (eds.), pp. 3–21, MIT Press, Cambridge, MA.

Lenhart, A., Jones, S., and Rankin Macgill, A. (2008): *PEW Internet and American life project*, PEW Research Center, Washington, DC.

McGonigal, J. (2011): *Reality is broken—why games make us better and how they can change the world*, Penguin Press, New York.

Mendonca, J., Oliveira, P., de Jong, J., and Hippel, E. von (2012): "Measuring user innovation: a large-scale survey in Portugal", User and Open Innovation Conference, August, Boston.

Mincer, J. (1962): "Labor force participation of married women", in *Aspects of labor economics*, H. G. Lewis (ed.), NBER, Princeton University Press, Princeton, NJ.

Nambisan, S., and Baron, R. A. (2009): "Virtual customer environments: testing a model of voluntary participation in value co-creation activities", *Journal of Product Innovation Management* 26(4), pp. 388–406.

National Science Board (2010): *Science and engineering indicators 2010*, National Science Foundation (NSB 10–01), Arlington, VA.

Newzoo (2011): National gamers survey, http://www.newzoo.com. Accessed November 2013.

OECD (2009). *Society at a Glance 2009: OECD Social Indicators*. Paris, OECD.

Ogawa, S., and Pongtanalert, K. (2011): "Visualizing the invisible innovation continent: evidence from global consumer innovation surveys", SSRN Working Paper. http://papers.ssrn.com/sol3/papers.cfm?abstract_id=1876186. Accessed November 2013.

Payne, A. F., Storbacka, K., and Frow, P. (2008): "Managing the co-creation of value", *Journal of the Academy of Marketing Science* 36(1), pp. 83–96.

Poetz, M. K., and Schreier, M. (2012): "The value of crowdsourcing: can users really compete with professionals in generating new product ideas?" *Journal of Product Innovation Management* 29(2), pp. 245–256.

Prahalad, C. K., and Ramaswamy, V. (2003): "The new frontier of experience innovation", *MIT Sloan Management Review* 44(4), pp. 12–18.

Raasch, C., and Hippel, E. von (2012): "Modeling Interactions between user and producer innovation: user-contested and user-complemented markets", MIT Sloan Working Paper. http://papers.ssrn.com/sol3/papers.cfm?abstract_id=2079763. Accessed November 2013.

Raymond, E. (1999): "The cathedral and the bazaar", *Knowledge, Technology, & Policy* 12(3), pp. 23–49.

Rosen, S. (1986): "The theory of equalizing differences", *Handbook of labor economics*, vol. 1, O. Ashenfelter and R. Layard (eds.), pp. 641–692, Elsevier Science Publishers, Amsterdam.

Ryan, R. M., and Deci, E. L. (2000): "Self-determination theory and the facilitation of intrinsic motivation, social development, and well-being", *American Psychologist* 55(1), pp. 68–78.

Schell, J. (2008): *The art of game design: a book of lenses*, Morgan Kaufmann, Burlington, MA.

Schreier, M., Fuchs, C., and Dahl, D. (2012): "The innovation effect of user design: innovation perceptions of firms selling products designed by users", *Journal of Marketing* 76(September), pp. 18–32.

Schumpeter, J. A. (1934): *The theory of economic development*, Harvard University Press, Cambridge, MA.

Sheldon, K. M., and Elliot, A. J. (1998): "Not all personal goals are 'personal': comparing autonomous and controlling goals on effort and attainment", *Personality and Social Psychology Bulletin* 24(5), pp. 546–557.

Shirky, C. (2010): *Cognitive surplus—creativity and generosity in a connected age*, Penguin Press, London.

von Ahn, L., Maurer, B., McMillen, C., Abraham, D., and Blum, M. (2008): "reCAPTCHA: human-based character recognition via web security measures", *Science* 321(12), pp. 1465–1468.

Webb, D. J., Green, C. L., and Brashear, T. G. (2000): "Development and validation of scales to measure attitudes influencing monetary donations to charitable organizations", *Journal of the Academy of Marketing Science* 28(2), pp. 299–309.

Wu, B. (2003): "Household innovative capacity in marginal areas of China: an empirical study in North Shaanxi", *Journal of Agricultural Education and Extension* 9(4), pp. 137–150.

Wu, B., and Pretty, J. (2004): "Social connectedness in marginal rural China: the case of innovation circles in Zhidan, north Shaanxi", *Agriculture and Human Values* 21, pp. 81–92.

Yee, N. (2006): "Motivations for play in online games", *CyberPsychology and Behavior* 9(6), pp. 772–775.

12 The New Normal of Innovation Management

Towards a Dual—Open and Closed—Innovation Logic

Katja Hutter and Johann Füller

To keep up with the rate of innovation in the digital era, companies must be capable of utilizing and benefiting from open and closed innovation at the same time. The article discusses major challenges and roadblocks organizations face through running open innovation and traditional innovation modes simultaneously. The study is based on the learnings and experiences companies and intermediaries made with open innovation in traditional company settings, where a systematic and structured closed innovation approach has been dominant for the last several decades. Three steps will be presented in order to merge both approaches and succeed in creating the new dual innovation logic—creating the new normal.

Keywords: open and closed innovation, challenges, dual innovation logic

12 THE NEW NORMAL OF INNOVATION MANAGEMENT

12.1 Introduction

Open innovation has become a promising approach for new and successful innovations (Chesbrough 2003). However, even open innovation pioneers such as P&G, Siemens, and Swarovski are still struggling to utilize the potential of open innovation to its full extent and to apply it on systematic and ongoing levels. Despite the gaining momentum and the dissemination of open innovation success stories, practitioners and researchers alike point out that open innovation is no panacea. Organizations should not just jump on the open innovation bandwagon due to its novelty or to keep pace with changing trends; rather, open innovation has to provide evidence that it actually leads to better innovations. Under certain conditions, traditional closed innovation approaches may even be superior to and trump open innovation. In order to succeed with innovation, companies have to be capable of applying both open and closed approaches concurrently. New effective innovation management should select between open and closed innovation approaches depending on the requirements of the respective task and innovation project (King and Lakhani 2013). This article introduces the innovation logic of open and closed innovation, and highlights why both approaches have to merge and become one integrated, dual open and closed innovation logic. It offers three steps in order to succeed in creating the new dual innovation logic. Innovation management may follow the same path as retail business, where companies for a long time distinguished between online and offline channels before they merged them into an integrated multi-channel sales and marketing approach (Dinner et al. 2014). Just as with retail business, innovation management may benefit from this merger of processes into an integrated dual innovation logic. Existing research has often compared open innovation with closed innovation and examined the benefits and drawbacks of both approaches, considering them as dissimilar and even competing options (Lakhani et al. 2013; Felin and Zenger 2014; Salter et al. 2014). Our call for a dual—open and closed—innovation logic considers open and closed as rather complementary and synergetic. It is based on the learnings and experiences companies and intermediaries made with open innovation in traditional company settings, where a systematic and structured closed innovation approach has been dominant for the last several decades. First, we show the differences between *open and closed innovation approaches*. Next, we discuss *major challenges* and roadblocks organizations face through running open innovation and traditional innovation modes simultaneously. Then, we argue why a dual innovation logic is needed and highlight what the *transformation towards a truly integrated new innovation paradigm* may look like through three steps of (1) create mind-set to open up, (2) run initial projects and gain experience, and (3) build a dual innovation logic—create the new normal.

12.2 Closed vs. Open Innovation

Traditional Closed Innovation: Companies have learned that innovation is crucial for them in order to stay competitive and differentiate their offerings from others (Drucker 1988; Hamel 2007). Thus, they installed professional innovation management, driven by either R&D or marketing departments or sometimes both grouped together in an innovation management unit (Urban et al. 1987). Most of the time, a structured stage-gate innovation process has been established, describing which tasks in each phase and decision procedures at each gate should be executed (Cooper 2008). Besides the innovation process, traditional innovation management provides organizations with methods, templates, and blueprints to manage innovation in a structured and systematic way. For ideation, for example, several brainstorming and workshop formats may be available to generate new ideas and concepts. Certain templates and business model formats may be applied to compare different concepts and evaluate their business potential (Cooper et al. 1999; Nagji and Tuff 2012). Furthermore, 3D and CAD programs have been established to build first prototypes. Project management and budget controlling tools have been installed in order to manage innovation in terms of time and budget. The established procedures and structures allow companies to effectively and efficiently manage incremental innovations. These ensure the modification of and advancements to existing products and services and aid in successfully updating the established businesses. Within such a structured innovation management system, radical and disruptive innovations are quite difficult to achieve, as radical innovations require more creative and dynamic trial and error approaches and thus do not fit into a well-defined approach (Christensen 1997).

The traditional innovation logic follows a rather static and deterministic approach in which responsibilities and tasks are assigned to employees according to their functions and positions within the organization. Once employees have been recruited and assigned to the innovation tasks, they become the ones responsible for the innovation—covering invention plus commercialization within the company. However, coming up with successful innovations is more an art than a routinized task. Standardization of innovation processes by decomposing them into standard modules may not be the best organizational form for innovation (Kogut and Metiu 2001). Glass (1995) points out that creative enterprises do not follow a fully structured approach consisting of routinized actions. Hence, one should not apply the Babbage principle of the mental division of labor to innovative ventures. He further states: "Methodologies that convert design into a disciplined activity are not suited to addressing new problems to be solved" (Glass 1995, p. 41). From an organizational design perspective, one could argue that this type of innovation management follows a sequential, step by step, weak chain approach, where the weakest part in the chain determines the overall quality of the outcome (Becker and Murphy 1992; Hansen and Birkinshaw 2007).

Open innovation, in contrast, refers to the utilization of "external as well as internal ideas as inputs to the innovation process combined with employing internal and external paths to market for the results of innovative activities" (Chesbrough 2003, p. 5) and has recently become a dominant innovation approach. Open innovation comprises three core processes: the outside-in process—integration of external knowledge; the inside-out process—external commercialization of internal innovations; and the coupled process—cooperation with complementary partners as well as competitors (Gassmann et al. 2010). Opening up the innovation process became an enticing option in order to benefit from the existing knowledge spill-overs and solutions already made within other companies and laboratories as well as by individual users and communities. However, open innovation not only implies becoming more open, it also follows a different logic. It impacts the structure, processes and distribution of innovation tasks. Beyond opening up, open innovation also means that different, even unknown players engage in the innovation process and concurrently work on various activities. Especially when bringing outside knowledge into the company or looking for problem solutions, new product and service ideas, companies often rely on crowdsourcing as a means to interact and collaborate with an anonymous external mass. The term "crowdsourcing" refers to a company's activity of outsourcing a function that was once performed by employees to an undefined (and generally large) network of people in the form of an open call on the Internet (Howe 2008). All of a sudden, it is not known who comes up with and is responsible for the innovative solution or which function, role, management level, and personal background this individual contributor may have. Existing innovation structures and processes are being challenged by such unstructured and evolutionary trial and error procedures. Well-defined roles and responsibilities and individually assigned tasks may become obsolete in this very collaborative and distributive innovation mode, while new job roles and innovation tasks may be created (Alexy and Reitzig 2013). For most companies, nowadays, it would be easy to integrate ideas and knowledge from the outside if the company would get them from established sources, such as their qualified suppliers, in a structured manner. However, within the open innovation logic, it does not matter who has been officially assigned to the task or made responsible. Open innovation instead relies on self-selection, using the philosophy that knowledgeable, skilled and highly motivated individuals who are interested in the topic will self-select the innovation task they will contribute to. Roles and responsibilities naturally emerge over time by the merits and achievements of contributors rather than established structures. Relying more on such self-organization principles means that innovation becomes more democratic and its outcomes become less predictable (Hippel 2005). Organizations attempting to establish temporary or ongoing innovation practices need to think about the right input for their innovation activities and are therefore choosing among the landscape of possibilities ranging from contest platforms, collaborative communities, complementors, and labor markets as they try to understand what kinds of problems benefit most from open innovation and why (Boudreau and Lakhani 2013). In order to tap into the knowledge of various internal and external sources so as to accelerate innovation, organizations need to understand how to attract and incentivize interested, qualified participants and garner more insights into the process of evaluating the winning ideas and contributions. While open innovation may not be necessary for incremental innovation, which has been successfully managed within the traditional innovation paradigm, it may be of critical importance for coming up with radical, game-changing innovations, especially in the digital era. Such an approach, of course, is not free of problems and raises major challenges for companies running both—often contradicting—innovation modes. Disturbance of innovation processes, lack of secrecy, intellectual property problems, and the redefinition of tasks and job roles are just a few of the potential challenges organizations face when trying to implement both approaches. R&D professionals may be apprehensive that open innovation requirements are incompatible with existing operating routines and tasks (Bartl et al. 2012; Salter et al. 2014). A comparison of the two modes of innovation (see Table 12.1) reveals fundamental differences across

Table 12.1   Open vs. closed innovation

Criteria	Closed innovation	Open innovation
Participants	– restricted to selected staff (e.g. R&D department)	– open to the external crowd or company-wide participation
Process	– step by step – sequential – structured – systematic	– collaborative – trial-and-error – iterative—loops – evolutionary
Task assignment and distribution	– by delegation – predefined job roles	– participation based on a voluntary basis – self-selection of tasks
Planning and Orientation	– input—planning of effort	– output—interested in solution
Success evaluation	– application of established evaluation criteria	– definition of objective performance criteria per project – crowd commitment through attention, time and money spent
Incentives	– part of the job-description, salary – due to career aspiration	– self-stated intrinsic interest – spurred by the offered incentives

various dimensions—participants that engage, the processes they follow, task assignment and distribution, planning and orientation, success evaluation and incentives offered. Many of the applied principles of the one approach are almost in contradiction with the other.

Questions arise as to how to successfully manage and structure open versus closed innovation. How do they fit together? Are both needed to play in different innovation leagues or should companies rely on either closed or open innovation alone?

12.3   Roadblocks Ahead: Running Traditional and Open Innovation Simultaneously

While many leading companies such as BMW, Daimler, General Electric, Intel, Lufthansa, Pfizer, P&G, and Siemens have successfully conducted various open innovation pilots, it is difficult for them to handle both open and closed innovation at the same time. In the following, we discuss possible roadblocks and major challenges for organizations as well as their managers and employees operating on the front lines of open innovation. We further provide an outlook of what may be needed to bring together and merge the application of both models. Despite an increasing trend towards a more open culture, the dominant philosophy within organizations is largely inward-facing and displays uncertainty and skepticism towards open innovation (Salter et al. 2014). The lack of willingness with regard to the propensity to innovate and take risks has been described as the greatest threat for the implementation of more open innovation practices. Established companies used to the traditional innovation logic may not have the mindset to envision the value of open innovation in their own business context and setting. While a certain interest with regard to experimentation and learning exists, the initial commitment to run open innovation pilot projects entails further challenges. Besides the selection of the right open innovation practice—ranging from ongoing innovation communities to temporary narrowed crowdsourcing contests—the recruitment of interested and qualified participant is pivotal. Communication and recruitment strategies are of great importance to get participants' attention and diminish the risk of the request for participation perishing in the daily information overload. Open innovation projects can hit a roadblock if they fail to evoke contributors' interest, which will in turn impact quantity and quality of submissions.

Reasons for lack of participation in open innovation projects can be manifold. Employees asked to participate may suppose that their contributions will not be adequately valued or considered by their colleagues, their supervisors or even the higher management level. Questions arise about whether or not participation is part of their job description and thus appreciated by senior management and tolerated by their employees. Fear of criticism due to poor or incorrect contributions keeps employees at bay and prevents them from taking an active part in open innovation projects. The lack of belief in satisfactory benefits and outcomes may hinder long-term engagement. Participants might also be confronted with insufficient clarity and transparency regarding the participation process and its outcome. In general, it is crucial to understand what motivates individuals to devote time and effort to open innovation campaigns, and then to offer the right incentive matches to foster participation (Füller 2010). Besides the overall topic of dealing with recruitment strategies and generating traffic on the platform, the evaluation of the outcome can raise another major challenge. If internal staff were selected for the idea evaluation process, they might question the quality of "external" idea submissions and may be biased in the idea evaluation process (Boudreau et al. 2012). Some employees might be demotivated when attempting to evaluate external ideas in addition to their daily workload. The identification of the right business unit or department to take on further responsibility and invest resources to evolve the idea until market launch represents another roadblock since participation in various open innovation projects is based on collaborative tasks coming from various departments. A certain business unit or work group being put in charge of the further development of the idea until market launch may cause challenges in terms of sense of ownership, the financial burden associated with the process and the division of possible future returns. In many cases the ideas perish and cannot be advanced in the classic step-by-step innovation process. Most of the time, open innovations are singular initiatives which require additional budgets or resources for implementation as their efforts are not incorporated in the annual innovation budget. Rather they are seen as pilot projects enriching innovation activities without taking a holistic approach into consideration. Furthermore, established organizations are often unable to cope with the absorption and incorporation of the obtained knowledge into their organization. Often, idea submissions are quite heterogeneous in terms of quality and level of complexity and can rarely be transferred straight into the firms' R&D efforts or processes. The measure of innovation success in connection with open innovation leads to another delicate topic. While the number of creative submissions, the engagement in the discussion and feedback can be easily measured, it is difficult to determine the actual contribution to the financial performance of a company. However, for long-term integration and future project justification, more robust measures of how open innovation contributes to a company's bottom line are needed—e.g. its contribution to turnover, earnings, or cost savings. The current detachedness from traditional innovation constitutes another major roadblock. Open innovation approaches are seen as a substitute rather than as complements. Despite the growing awareness and application of open innovation projects, organizations still struggle to align them with their innovation objective and internal procedures.

While established companies are still struggling with open and collaborative innovation, in many fields it has already become the new normal of innovation. In the IS and media content fields and for start-ups, open and collaborative innovation is rather common and well established. Consider Apple: since the opening of the App Store in 2008, users spent over $10 billion and downloaded almost three billion apps in 2013, making it one of the store's most successful years. While $7 billion went to the developers, since they keep 70% of the App Store revenue, the remaining $3 billion went to Apple.[1] It is said, that the external app developers have earned over $15 billion since the inception of the App Store. In 2012, Google Glasses started as a project in the company's Google X research lab and now many third-party developers and companies are exploring the potential and constantly releasing new apps to make the Glass more functional. Everyone can become a developer and generate applications, as also demonstrated through the Oculus Rift—an upcoming virtual reality head-mounted display. The Oculus developer kit was offered to developers to begin the integration of the device into their 3D games. Further examples of powerful community approaches of innovation are the Apache HTTP Server, which is developed and maintained by an open community of developers; Top-Coder, an online competition platform currently used by some 500,000 developers to solve programming challenges; Kickstarter, the world's largest funding platform, which has exceeded the $1 billion milestone for contributions and tallied 5.7 million people pledging on the site in March 2014. However, software development, the generation of user generated content and the pledging of money are not the only applicable examples. Hardware such as computers, cars, clothing, and real estate also get crowdsourced and innovated on in a collaborative mode. For example, Arduino—the open-source electronics prototyping platform for developers, hobbyists, students, and professionals that provides applications of interactive objects or environments; RaspberryPi, a community platform offering a credit-card-sized single-board computer that plugs into your TV and a keyboard enabling engineers to design their own embedded applications; Local Motors, an online co-creation company tapping into an online community with more than 42.000 car enthusiasts including engineers, developers, designers, and fabricators making new vehicles. Threadless is a 2.4 million strong online artist community dedicated to designing and selling t-shirts, and more recently also art prints and iPhone cases online. Quirky is an online innovation platform developing products together with the crowd that are then sold via major retail outlets such as Target; Bed, Bath & Beyond; and Amazon.com. Prodigy Network, the leader in real estate development, sales and equity syndication, uses social media to design and in addition finance commercial real estate through the use of crowdfunding. These are all further examples of crowdsourcing and open innovation.

12.4 Transformation Toward an Integrategd Dual Innovation Logic

In spite of the aforementioned examples, established companies often fail in using the crowd. So how can they benefit from the sheer creativity and power from the masses? How can they successfully apply open innovation principles? How can they integrate it into their existing innovation logic in order to make it the next new normal? We argue that at least three steps may be necessary:

1. Create a mind-set to open up
2. Run first projects and gain experience
3. Build a dual innovation logic—Create the new normal

12.4.1 Create a Mindset to Open up

First of all, organizations need to deliberate on whether open innovation will be an appropriate approach or not. They should familiarize themselves with the new methods and possible tools and then start a dialogue with open innovation experts and other organizations demonstrating open innovation experiences in order to acquaint themselves with the open innovation landscape. Market screenings, the classification of best practice examples and the identification of possible application fields will help the management team as well as the responsible business unit analyze and evaluate the potential of open innovation. Identification of the problem or field of investigation and then matching with the most appropriate open innovation mode or governance option are necessary preconditions before starting first pilots (Felin and Zenger 2014). Essential tasks within the first phase include planning a line of action, formulating recruiting strategies to create awareness—including minimizing the risk of participation recruitment communications getting lost in the daily information overload, and developing a user-friendly and appealing platform. These are necessary prerequisites for designing and developing valuable, lively open innovation pilots and for opening up the innovation mind-set within the company.

12.4.2   *Run First Projects and Gain Experience*

In the second phase, companies may initiate and realize first pilot projects. The pilot projects should involve various business units working on different tasks and assignments. Cooperation with distinct intermediaries such as Hyve, Innocentive, or Top Coder may be helpful in order to build upon their experiences and to establish a relationship with external innovation communities. In this stage, it is important that the pilot projects do not just address a single, simple task or an independent activity. Additional value is generated if the open innovation approach is applied to various tasks along the whole process. However, most of the time the open innovation projects are singular initiatives, and additional budgets or resources for ongoing application and further development are not considered. These pilot open innovation projects are often seen as initiatives to enrich single innovation activities without considering their potential as new holistic innovation logic. To justify future open innovation projects and systematic integration of open innovation, the pilot projects need to prove successful in terms of number of participants and quality of submissions, but also added value of realized open innovation projects. The challenge is for organizations to apply a rigorous assessment as to which approaches are worth further pursuing - e.g. How can organizations scale open innovation?—and which are simply lessons learned and not applicable to the company.

12.4.3   *Build a Dual Innovation Logic—Create the New Normal*

After a certain period of time and experience with open innovation, companies may adjust their innovation approach and integrate the open innovation logic into their existing innovation landscape. They may set up an Open Innovation Lab (OIL) that relies on the principles of open and collaborative innovation such as self-selection, trial and error, fast prototyping, integration of the crowd, and start-up and entrepreneurial spirit. Basically, this means that the OIL acts and operates the same as pure open innovation players such as Threadless, RaspberryPi or Local Motors do. However, the lab innovates in fields which are of strategic relevance to the entire company. In order to achieve similar innovation rates to pure open innovation players, OILs have to consist of employees who are native to open innovation or have already transformed to this new innovation logic and share this culture and aptitude. That means that the OIL itself should have all the necessary skills and capabilities to come up with commercially successful innovations. Those innovations may be similar to or even cannibalize existing business. In order to achieve this, the OIL should work in small interdisciplinary teams and engage the larger crowd whenever needed, for example for idea generation, software development or funding. In addition, the OIL may serve as an internal service provider that supports the company internal business units in their open innovation efforts either by aiding them as they conduct an open innovation project, building certain open innovation capabilities, serving as an outsourced innovation unit, or acting as an intermediary. The OIL may further think about new business models for the company that rely on open and collaborative processes and create additional value by opening up certain steps in the value chain while other business models stay closed. For instance, Apple and Google are applying these principles with their Apps through engaging external third party developers. Appiro—the cloud service consultancy—bought TopCoder to add more crowdsourcing to their business, and General Electrics (GE) announced a partnership with Local Motors to merge the inventiveness of the crowd and the advanced manufacturing competence of GE. Nivea collaborated with HYVE's innovation lab to co-create the Black and White deodorant together with the crowd (Bilgram et al. 2013). Lego engages with the crowd to build new successful Lego products such as the Lego Delorean—the car known from the movie "Back to the Future"—or Lego Minecraft, which was suggested by one of the member of the Minecraft community that plays with Lego in the virtual world. While Lego still utilizes its traditional innovation approach, it also runs this kind of OIL that is dedicated to spurring innovation at Lego through the crowd and that is fully integrated into the Lego organization. Besides harnessing the external crowd, Lego also applies open innovation principles internally. It encourages all its employees to contribute to the internal Lego ideas community, which works similarly to the external one. This integration into the existing innovation structure and landscape of Lego may offer several benefits for the OIL. The OIL may benefit from the existing infrastructure, know-how and technical expertise, operations such as production or logistics, and especially marketing and customer reach. For pure open innovation companies such as Local Motors or Quirky, market diffusion often is quite difficult as they have no established brand or customer relationships and lack the production and operation capabilities to scale in comparison to established companies like LEGO. To build up an infrastructure for vehicle manufacturing or electronic device production requires time and money as well as additional skills that pure open innovation players usually don't have. The integration of an OIL into the innovation environment of the corporate world thus may be advantageous as it generates additional value and in fact create synergies. At the same time, it may support established organizations in speeding up their innovation, coming up with more radical solutions and benefiting from the power of the crowd. Furthermore, it may support establishing the new normal of innovation management that allows for applying closed and open innovation logics concurrently. To keep up with the rate of innovation in the digital era, companies must be capable of utilizing and benefiting from open and closed innovation at the same time and able to merge those two concepts into one integrated innovation approach that can allow for the degree of openness and closeness that seems most appropriate.

NOTE

1. See http://www.apple.com/pr/library/2014/01/07App-Store-Sales-Top-10-Billion-in-2013.html?sr=hotnews.rss, accessed 7 February 2014.

REFERENCES

Alexy, O., and Reitzig, M. (2013): "Private–collective innovation, competition, and firms' counterintuitive appropriation strategies", *Research Policy* 42(4), pp. 895–891.

Bartl, M., Füller, J., Mühlbacher, H., and Ernst, H. (2012): "A manager's perspective on virtual customer integration for new product development", *Journal of Product Innovation Management* 29, pp. 1031–1046.

Becker, G. S., and Murphy, K. (1992): "The division of labor, coordination costs and knowledge", *The Quarterly Journal of Economics* 4, pp. 1137–1160.

Bilgram, V., Füller, J., Bartl, M., Biel, S., and Miertsch, H. (2013): "Eine Allianz gegen Flecken", *Harvard Business Manager* 3, pp. 63–68.

Boudreau, Kevin J., Eva Guinan, Karim R. Lakhani, and Christoph Riedl. "Looking Across and Looking Beyond the Knowledge Frontier: Intellectual Distance and Resource Allocation in Science." Management Science (forthcoming).

Boudreau, K. J., and Lakhani, K. R. (2013): "Using the crowd as an innovation partner", *Harvard Business Review* 91, pp. 60–69.

Chesbrough, H. W. (2003): *Open innovation: the new imperative for creating and profiting from technology*, Harvard Business School Press, Boston, MA.

Christensen, C. M. (1997): *The innovator's dilemma: when new technologies cause great firms to fail*, Harvard Business School Press, Cambridge, MA.

Cooper, R. G. (2008): "Perspective: the stage-gate idea-to-launch—update, what's new, and nexgen systems", *Journal of Product Innovation Management* 25, pp. 213–232.

Cooper, R. G., Edgett, S. J., and Kleinschmidt, E. J. (1999): "New product portfolio management: practices and performance", *Journal of Product Innovation Management* 16, pp. 333–351.

Dinner, I. M., van Heerde, H. J., Neslin, S. A. (2014): "Driving online and offline sales: the cross-channel effects of traditional, online display, and paid search advertising", *Journal of Marketing Research* 51(5), pp. 527–545.

Drucker, P. F. (1988): "The coming of the new organization", *Harvard Business Review* 66, pp. 45–53.

Felin, T., and Zenger, T. R. (2014): "Closed or open innovation? problem solving and the governance choice", *Research Policy* 43, pp. 914–925.

Füller, J. (2010): "Refining virtual co-creation from a consumer perspective", *California Management Review* 52, pp. 98–122.

Gassmann, O., Enkel, E., and Chesbrough, H. (2010): "The future of open innovation", *R&D Management* 40, pp. 213–221.

Glass, R. L. (1995): *Software creativity*, Prentice Hall, Englewood Cliffs, NJ.

Hamel, G. (2007): *The future of management*, Harvard Business School Press, Boston.

Hansen, M. T., and Birkinshaw, J. (2007): "The innovation value chain", *Harvard Business Review* 85, pp. 121–130.

Hippel, E. von (2005): *Democratizing innovation*, MIT Press, Cambridge, MA.

Howe, J. (2008): *Crowdsourcing: how the power of the crowd is driving the future of business*, Crown Publishing Group, New York.

King, A., and Lakhani, K. R. (2013): "Using open innovation to identify the best ideas", *MIT Sloan Management Review* 55(1), pp. 41–48.

Kogut, B., and Metiu, A. (2001): "Open Source software development and distributed innovation", *Oxford Review of Economic Policy* 17, pp. 248–264.

Lakhani, K. R., Lifshitz-Assaf, H., and Tushman, M. L. (2013): "Open innovation and organizational boundaries: task decomposition, knowledge distribution, and the locus of innovation", in *Handbook of economic organization: integrating economic and organizational theory*, A. Grandori (ed.), pp. 355–382, Elgar, Northampton, MA.

Nagji, B., and Tuff, G. (2012): "Managing your innovation portfolio", *Harvard Business Review* 90(5), pp. 67–73.

Salter, A., Criscuolo, P., and Ter Wal, A.L.J. (2014): "Coping with open innovation: responding to the challenges of external engagement in R&D", *California Management Review* 56, pp. 77–95.

Urban, G. L., Hauser, J. R., and Dholakia, N. (1987): *Essentials of new product management*, Prentice-Hall, New York.

Contributors

Kerstin Balka is a research fellow at Hamburg University of Technology and works as an Associate Principal at McKinsey & Company. Her research focuses on open source innovation and more particularly on empirical studies of open design.

Jan Bierwald studied Industrial Engineering and Management at the Hamburg University of Technology (TUHH). He joined the Institute of Technology and Innovation Management (TIM) as part of a sponsored Ph.D. program of the consultancy firm McKinsey & Company. His research concentrated on Open Source Innovation, particularly user entrepreneurship and Open Source companies. After his Ph.D. studies Mr. Bierwald returned to McKinsey and is leading several consultancy projects.

Johann Füller is a professor for innovation and entrepreneurship at the Innsbruck University School of Management. He is fellow at the NASA Tournament Lab-Research at Harvard University and chief executive officer of Hyve AG, an innovation and community company. In line with his research focus, he regularly gives guest lectures about co-creation, online branding, creative consumer behavior, online marketing, open innovation, and the utilization of online communities. From 2008 to 2010, Johann was a visiting scholar and research affiliate at MIT Sloan School of Management. Johann habilitated in business administration at the Innsbruck University–School of Management.

Katja Hutter is Assistant Professor at the Innsbruck University School of Management and a research fellow at Harvard-NASA Tournament Lab at the Institute for Quantitative Social Science. Katja holds a doctorate degree in Social and Economic Sciences from the University of Innsbruck. Her research interest is in the field of open innovation, especially idea contests and online innovation communities.

Lars Janzik has, since 2011, been Senior Director Product Management CE at Monster Worldwide, leading a cross regional product management and development team. As part of the global product organization he and his team develop the roadmap for Monster's product portfolio and roll it out in central Europe. Before Monster, Lars served 10 years as Vice President Product at Magix AG in Berlin and was responsible for the expansion of the software and cloud portfolio. Lars completed in 2011 his Ph.D. thesis in technology and innovation management at the Hamburg University of Technology.

Viktor Lee studied Industrial Engineering and Management at the Hamburg University of Technology (TUHH) and at the University of California (Berkeley). He joined the Institute of Technology and Innovation Management (TIM) as part of a sponsored Ph.D. program of The Boston Consulting Group (BCG). His research concentrated on Open Source Innovation, particularly the bibliometric structures and firms' involvement in open source communities. After his Ph.D. studies and being a guest lecturer at the University of Auckland, Mr. Lee returned to BCG continuing working as management consultant.

Christina Raasch is a professor of technology management at Technische Universität München, TUM School of Management. She conducts research on the interactions between users and producers in the development and commercialization of innovations. She studied economics and management at the Universities of St. Gallen and Oxford and received a PhD from the University of Erlangen-Nuremberg and a "habilitation" from Hamburg University of Technology. Before joining TUM in 2013, she was a Visiting Researcher at MIT Sloan School of Management.

Sebastian Spaeth studied in Germany and Sweden, receiving his Doctor in Business Administration from the University of St. Gallen, Switzerland in 2005. As senior researcher at the chair of Strategy and Innovation Management at ETH Zurich, Switzerland, he conducted research on Collaborative Open Innovation and collaborative business models. In 2013, Prof. Spaeth founded the chair of Management & Digital Markets at the University of Hamburg, Germany, which he currently holds.

Niclas Störmer was a doctoral student at the Institute of Technology and Innovation Management (TIM) at Hamburg University of Technology (TUHH). His research concentrated on Open and User Innovation and in particular on the questions how self-organized innovation communities govern themselves. Before starting his PhD he worked as a management consultant. He currently is working as a business development manager in one of Germanys leading publishing houses.

Eric von Hippel is T. Wilson Professor of Technological Innovation in the MIT Sloan School of Management. He is also a Professor in MIT's Engineering

Systems Division in the MIT School of Engineering, and is the Head of the MIT Innovation Lab. He specializes in research related to the nature and economics of distributed and open innovation, where users—rather than producers—are frequently found to be at the center of the innovation process. Dr. von Hippel also develops and teaches about practical methods that individuals, open user communities, and firms can apply to improve their product and service development processes. He holds a BA in economics from Harvard College, an SM in mechanical engineering from MIT, and a PhD in business and engineering from Carnegie-Mellon University.

Index

Note: Page numbers in *italics* followed by *f* indicate figures; by *t* indicate tables